Perspectives on Military Intelligence from the First World War to Mali

Floribert Baudet · Eleni Braat
Jeoffrey van Woensel · Aad Wever
Editors

Perspectives on Military Intelligence from the First World War to Mali

Between Learning and Law

ASSER PRESS

Springer

Editors
Floribert Baudet
Faculty of Military Sciences
Netherlands Defence Academy
Breda
The Netherlands

Eleni Braat
Department of History and Art History
Utrecht University
Utrecht
The Netherlands

Jeoffrey van Woensel
Veterans Institute
Doorn
The Netherlands

Aad Wever
Independent Scholar, Retired
Enschede
The Netherlands

ISBN 978-94-6265-182-1 ISBN 978-94-6265-183-8 (eBook)
DOI 10.1007/978-94-6265-183-8

Library of Congress Control Number: 2017939303

Published by T.M.C. ASSER PRESS, The Hague, The Netherlands www.asserpress.nl
Produced and distributed for T.M.C. ASSER PRESS by Springer-Verlag Berlin Heidelberg

Printed on acid-free paper

This T.M.C. ASSER PRESS imprint is published by Springer Nature
The registered company is Springer-Verlag GmbH Germany
The registered company address is: Heidelberger Platz 3, 14197 Berlin, Germany

Foreword

World War I had already started when in the summer of 1914 a military intelligence service was established in The Netherlands. On 15 August 1914, the Supreme Commander of the Army and Navy, Lieutenant-General C.J. Snijders, gave 1st Lieutenant H.A.C. Fabius free rein to organize a military intelligence service making decisions as he thought fit. GS III, as this department was to be named, rapidly developed from a one-man intelligence bureau to a fully fledged military intelligence and security service. After the end of the war, the department continued its activities while adding the surveillance of domestic developments as ordered by the minister of Home Affairs.

On the occasion of this centenary, the Netherlands Defence Intelligence and Security Service (DISS) and the Netherlands Intelligence Studies Association (NISA) organized a two-day conference in Amsterdam on 18 and 19 September 2014 titled: *Telling Truth to Power. The Past, Present and Future of Military Intelligence*. The present volume contains a selection of papers presented at this conference, and of contributions by authors who were approached by the editorial board.

One century after the establishment of the DISS, the world has changed considerably: Twitter has replaced the telegraph and symbolizes both the globalization and the revolution in communication. National and international security have meanwhile become fully intertwined. The web of cooperation by military intelligence services with other services, but also with domestic actors from civilian society and in deployment areas abroad, has never been so closely woven as these days. Finding replies to present-day challenges and to wicked problems will remain challenging as one century ago. But we have advanced one century and are able to draw lessons from the past and strengthen confidence in military intelligence services.

I am convinced that this volume will inspire many readers when practising and studying military intelligence activities.

I would like to thank the NISA congress organization and all speakers for their contributions to the congress. Heartfelt thanks are also extended to the DISS for their generous support and assistance. Thanks are also owed to Ms. Gerda Ransdorp of Fox-It cyber security company for her assistance in the organization. For the realization of this volume, I would like to express my thanks to NISA members Floribert Baudet, Eleni Braat, Jeoffrey van Woensel and Aad Wever; the Veterans' Institute (VI) and the Faculty of Military Sciences of the Netherlands Defence Academy (FMW/NLDA); and Martin Elands (VI), Bob de Graaff and Paul Ducheine (FMW/NLDA) in particular for their willingness to enable some members of the editorial board to spend part of their office hours on this NISA volume.

Michael Kowalski
Chairman, Netherlands Intelligence Studies Association

Contents

Editors and Contributors

About the Editors

Floribert Baudet obtained his Ph.D. from Utrecht University in 2001. He has written extensively on the history of Dutch foreign and defence policy in its broadest sense and on the former Yugoslavia. He has published in *Cold War History*, and in *Air and Space Power Journal—Africa and Francophonie.* Research topics include human rights, strategic communication, covert action, and the use and abuse of the past by (military) establishments. Since 2006, he has been working as an associate professor with the Faculty of Military Sciences of the Netherlands Defence Academy. He has been a member of the Netherlands Intelligence Studies Association since 2014.

Eleni Braat is assistant professor in International History at Utrecht University, The Netherlands. Previously, she served as the official historian of the Dutch General Intelligence and Security Service (AIVD) and lectured at the Institute for History at Leiden University. Her research interests focus on secret government activities, such as intelligence and international diplomacy, and the political tensions they led to in Europe during the twentieth century. She obtained her Ph.D. from the European University Institute in Florence, Italy, with a thesis on the disarmament negotiations in the 1920s. She holds an MA with honours in Modern Greek literature from the University of Amsterdam, and a *Diplôme d'études approfondies* (DEA) with the highest distinction in history from the *École des hautes études en sciences sociales* in Paris.

Jeoffrey van Woensel is an MA graduate and reserve first lieutenant of the Regiment Technical Troops (retired), and studied history at the Radboud University in Nijmegen. After his studies, he was conscripted as ROAG (academically trained reserve officer) in the Royal Netherlands Army. From 2001 to 2015, he worked at the Netherlands Institute for Military History, The Hague. He has published books on a number of topics including chemical warfare, the Explosive Ordnance Disposal Service of the Dutch armed forces, logistics and the Royal Netherlands Marechaussee. He currently works at the Centre of Research and Expertise of the Veterans Institute on secondment from the Ministry of Defence. Since 2012, he is the Secretary of the Netherlands Intelligence Studies Association.

Aad Wever is a graduate of Utrecht University and taught information security and intelligence at Saxion University of Applied Sciences, Enschede, The Netherlands, and at Ferris State University, Big Rapids, Michigan, USA, until his retirement in June 2016. He has contributed to several publications on the history of the Royal Netherlands Air Force during the Cold War. Since 2004, he has been engaged in educational cruises at Spitsbergen in the Norwegian Arctic. Wever is a member of the Board of the Netherlands Intelligence Studies Association.

Contributors

Floribert Baudet Netherlands Defence Academy, Breda, The Netherlands

Minne Boelens Ministry of Defence, The Hague, The Netherlands

Eleni Braat University of Utrecht, Utrecht, The Netherlands

A. Walter Dorn Defence Studies at the Royal Military College of Canada and the Canadian Forces College, Toronto, Canada

David Easter Department of War Studies, Kings College London, London, UK

Wim Klinkert Netherlands Defence Academy, Breda, University of Amsterdam, Amsterdam, The Netherlands

Chong Guan Kwa S. Rajaratnam School of International Studies, Nanyang Technological University, Singapore, Singapore

Prem Mahadevan The Global Security Team, Center for Security Studies, Eidgenössische Technische Hochschule, Zurich, Switzerland

Sebastiaan Rietjens Netherlands Defence Academy, Breda, The Netherlands

Reynaud Theunens

Aad Wever Independent scholar, retired, Enschede, The Netherlands

Cees Wiebes Institute for Security and Global Affairs (ISGA), Leiden University, The Hague, The Netherlands

Jeoffrey van Woensel Centre of Research and Expertise, Veterans Institute, Doorn, The Netherlands

Chapter 1
Military Intelligence: From *Telling Truth to Power* to Bewilderment?

Floribert Baudet, Eleni Braat, Jeffrey van Woensel and Aad Wever

Abstract This introductory chapter discusses 100 years of military intelligence and outlines the main changes that distinguish the post-Cold war period from the preceding one. This is characterised by a blurring of the boundaries between civilian and military intelligence, between investigative services and the intelligence community, and the foreign and domestic realms. The chapter also discusses the rise of oversight mechanisms. All these combined with unprecedented technological change to produce a challenging environment for intelligence services that is more unpredictable than ever before, and at the same time requires adequate, even pre-emptive responses on the part of the intelligence community. The dazzling level of adaptivity required largely obscures the fact that such adaptations were required in earlier periods as well, and intelligence professionals could profit by studying them.

Keywords Military intelligence · Globalisation · Adaptation · Learning organizations

F. Baudet (✉)
Netherlands Defence Academy, Breda, The Netherlands
e-mail: FH.Baudet@mindef.nl

E.C. Braat
University of Utrecht, Utrecht, The Netherlands
e-mail: e.c.braat@uu.nl

J. van Woensel
Centre of Research and Expertise, Veterans Institute, Doorn, The Netherlands
e-mail: jtwh.v.woensel@veteraneninstituut.nl

A. Wever
Enschede, The Netherlands
e-mail: ajmwever@hotmail.com

F. Baudet et al. (eds.), *Perspectives on Military Intelligence from the First World War to Mali*, DOI 10.1007/978-94-6265-183-8_1

Contents

1.1 Introduction

'The world is changing at an unprecedented pace. The present-day world is not necessarily more dangerous than it was during the Cold War but it has become more unstable and more unforeseeable', the former head of the French Military Intelligence Service (DRM) lt. gen. (ret.), André Ranson, summarized conventional wisdom as to the key challenge for today's intelligence community at a Conference to commemorate the 100th anniversary of the establishment of Dutch military intelligence in 2014.[1]

This book, which brings together scholars and practitioners, argues that although the intelligence community has indeed come to face new and complex challenges after the end of the Cold War, the key issue has been the intelligence community's (in)ability to adapt to changes in the environment in which it has to operate. In making this point, it does not offer a continuous narrative spanning a century's worth of intelligence successes and failures from the start of the First World War to the contemporary endeavours in Afghanistan and Mali. Instead, the book contains a collection of chapters that can be read individually, but which, implicitly or explicitly, address the issue of adaptivity. They show that changes in the operational environment are not unique to the post–1989 era. The operational context is constantly changing. It is adaptivity or the lack of it that in large part determines whether the intelligence community is able to deliver. Seen from this perspective, the end of the Cold War though of course important, is unjustly treated as a watershed between the present troubled times and the former conflict that in hindsight at least is often construed as a hallmark of stability where the profession of intelligence was an easy and simple one. In truth, the profession has never been easy and the cherished dictum of the intelligence community, 'telling truth to power', vastly simplifies reality.

To be sure, the post-Cold War period is characterised by a blurring of traditional boundaries, such as the one between civilian and military intelligence, between investigative services and the intelligence community, and the foreign and domestic

[1] Lt. gen. (ret.) André Ranson, keynote speech at the NISA/MIVD conference 'Telling truth to power', September 2014.

realms. All these combined with unprecedented technological change to produce a challenging environment for intelligence services that on the one hand is more unpredictable than ever before, and at the same time requires adequate, even pre-emptive responses on the part of the intelligence community. At the same time, a considerable part of this community feels that the legal limitations that have been put in place from the 1980s, do not suit present intelligence needs. As clear-cut dichotomies have faded, threats now seem to arise anywhere, demanding actionable and timely intelligence on a scale not seen before. Throughout the 20th century practitioners of military intelligence have had to come up with products that enabled military staffs, policy makers and officers to make sound judgments, and this has not changed. The number of policy options has multiplied though. In addition, it seems, calls for better control of the activities of the intelligence community are more vocal now than they were in earlier periods.

However, the dazzling level of adaptivity required today to a large extent obscures the fact that such adaptations were required in earlier periods as well. The intelligence community has always had to respond to change, develop new procedures and methods and reinvent itself. As today, it encountered failure when it identified the wrong lessons from earlier experiences. Leaving aside for the moment the question of whether it is possible to learn clear-cut lessons from the past at all, it is clear that today, as intelligence professionals struggle to come to grips with the challenges posed by transnational terrorism, hybrid opponents and complex stabilization missions, they, their customers, and academics, might profit from studying earlier adaptation processes. These could help identify best practices and perhaps more importantly, pitfalls. This, however, is not a recipe for success. There is at least a grain of truth in the old saying; *incidit in Scyllam qui vult evitare Garybdim.*

This introductory chapter outlines the changes in the environment in which the intelligence community operates, and then goes on to discuss how they affected this community. In the next sections, this analysis will be augmented by an analysis of learning processes, and especially the way past experiences are internalized. The case studies presented in this volume will provide insight in the complexities involved.

1.2 A Changing Environment

At first sight, the end of the Cold War is a watershed indeed. The spectacular collapse of the Soviet empire and its ideology in 1989–1991, ended a geopolitical confrontation that had lasted nearly five decades, and according to some, even longer.[2] While these momentous events initially seemed to guarantee a dominance of liberal-democratic values, the wave of neo-liberalism that swept across the globe also promoted distrust of state institutions in general, and stressed free and

---

[2] Vanden Berghe 2008.

unchecked enterprise. For some the post-1989 high-tide brought unprecedented opportunities, yet globalisation in many parts of the world eroded traditional structures and loyalties and left millions without shelter, especially in states whose leaders had until then been sponsored by one of the two sides in the Cold War. These processes resulted in the fragmentation of a significant number of states that now were labelled weak, failing or even failed states. Having lost legitimacy and relevance in the eyes of their population they became a recruiting ground for all kinds of radical groups, including ultranationalist and terrorist ones.[3]

After the end of the Cold War, international institutions and international law initially gained more prominence and many placed their hopes on an effective United Nations, but the tragic inability of this institution and the mostly western states that dominated it to prevent large-scale bloodshed in Rwanda, Somalia and the former Yugoslavia dealt a crushing blow to the initial optimism.[4] Today, the UN is often considered powerless if not outright irrelevant in the face of many of the challenges that have risen since.

The rise of new global players such as China, and to a lesser degree, India, seemed to cause, or at the very least coincide with, a relative decline of the West whose leading nations for centuries had dominated the world and in large part shaped the international system and its accompanying rules of behaviour.[5] These rules and supra-national norms came to be questioned in many western countries as well, especially in the greatly expanded EU where citizens started to 'reclaim' national sovereignty and stressed national rights, identities and particularism in a way not seen since the Second World War.[6] Meanwhile, the Pacific has become a new hotspot, whereas the Middle East, partly as a result of Western interventionism, has destabilized on a scale hardly imaginable in the mid-1990s when peace between Israel and its Arab neighbours seemed a real possibility.

At the same time technological innovations such as the invention and then stunning advance of the internet have created unprecedented opportunities. Especially when combined with the liberal democratic dogmas of freedom of speech and freedom of information, the technological advances of the last two decades have also created a powerful brew that erodes traditional sources of power. The fact that it is relatively easy to reach millions of people in one mouse click, transcending borders and circumventing controls, gave rise to the argument that the internet would spell the end for dictatorships and oppression, as ideas of democracy and human

---

[3] Scholte 2000.

[4] Cf. Fukuyama 1992. The UN critically evaluated its performance in 2000.

[5] See Ferguson 2011. On some of these contenders: Kaplan 2010; Brewster 2014; Segers 2008; Kingah and Quiliconi 2016; Stuenkel 2015. For a contrary view: Beausang 2012.

[6] Witness calls in Britain, France, The Netherlands and Switzerland to renege the European Convention on Human Rights, and such international treaties as the Convention on the Status of Refugees.

rights could now spread to the four corners of the world. The role of internet-based new media during the Arab Spring has been put forward as a case in point.[7]

Sound-bites and 140-sign messages have overtaken the slower, printed media whose formats offer more room for longer analyses and nuance, reinforcing a trend that had started with the rise of television. Real-time coverage of real-time events demands real-time responses as journalists and politicians in democratic states have discovered and every individual may become a news network if he or she so desires and finds an audience. For most young people classic media i.e., newspapers, radio and television that by their format more or less channelled access to information and selected what audiences would be exposed to, have become utterly irrelevant. Vertical relations between media and audiences have eroded while horizontal relations have multiplied beyond count.

This development could be termed democratization although it was not only democracy that benefited from it, to say the least. A key consequence of the accompanying over-supply of information is that people 'settle for 'blips' of information, which they then attempt to string together in a sensible manner to account for changes in their environment.'[8] Overarching narratives and traditional authority have lost appeal, but individuals' need for sense-making has not disappeared. Moving beyond the boundaries of the digital world, it has given weight to the *vox populi* in a way unthinkable before. As the a priori legitimacy of popular sentiment is a key element in democracy,[9] it has become a distinctly destabilizing element in many of today's democracies.

The rise of violent non-state actors has brought with it new applications. These actors use social media as a means of political communication, as with ISIL clips that show beheadings and the destruction of non-Sunni cultural heritage it considers pagan. The internet is also used for recruitment and training and ISIL for one operates a large number of Twitter accounts.[10] There are indications that at least some of these violent non-state actors have been developing offensive technical cyber capabilities as well. ISIL is suspected to have attacked the US Department of Defense which resulted in the theft of addresses of US military personnel and calls to kill those. Other examples include groups such as the Cyber Caliphate.[11] Today, intelligence services consider 'cyber terrorism' a real possibility although as yet recognized examples of terrorist cyber-attacks are absent.[12]

---

[7] Witness A Human Right 2014 and Howard 2011. For a discussion of the threats and opportunities offered by new technologies, see Kalathil and Boas 2003; Klang and Murray 2005. See further Salih 2013, pp. 185–203; Soengas 2013, pp. 147–155; Etling et al. 2010, pp. 2–10; Safranek 2012, pp. 2–10. Similar claims have been made about the end of the Suharto era: Mahdi 2002. See also Conversi 2012, pp. 1357–1379.

[8] Toffler 1980, p. 165.

[9] For an insightful discussion see Cunningham 2002.

[10] Gladstone 2015.

[11] Ingram 2015. On the rise of cyber Jihadis: Berton and Pawlak 2015; Atwan 2016.

[12] States may prefer to attribute damage to vital infrastructure and networks to bad luck, accidents and technical problems rather than admit weakness.

The so-called dark web—that part of the world-wide web that cannot easily be accessed using traditional search engines—has become a market-place of, among other things, instruction manuals and weaponry and a meeting place for people and groups whose aims and activities often are cause for serious concern.

In addition, both democratic and authoritarian states have been tempted to use the internet for their own purposes; intelligence services engage in cyber espionage, and in computer network exploitation on a daily basis. They, just like companies, make ample use of trolls to favourably influence popular sentiment through social media.[13] More worrying still, revelations such as those by Edward Snowden show that intelligence services make use of internet-based technologies to survey the movements and communications of hundreds of thousands of individuals.[14] At the same time, hacks, bots and other electronic means are used to influence the outcome of electoral processes as the 2016 US Presidential Election showed.[15]

Especially the revelations about large-scale indiscriminate surveillance caused a public outcry and reinvigorated discussions about (the lack of) control of the intelligence community. In the modern era such interest had earlier manifested itself in the aftermath of the 9/11 attacks when services were believed to have failed to 'connect the dots'; after the invasion of Iraq that was justified on the basis of what turned out to be faulty and manufactured evidence on this country's programme of weapons of mass destruction; and again as a result of a number of revelations about less than savory activities of intelligence services, such as the CIA's rendition programme that involved the abduction of suspected individuals and their transfer to facilities in states that, unlike the US, allow torture as a means to obtain information, and the role of a number of European services in this.[16] Policy makers currently face the challenge to strike a balance between the contradictory public demands for better protection against terrorist attacks and protection from infringements on their privacy. Practitioners often argue that any limitation on their work poses a risk to national security whereas human rights campaigners and numerous others feel that to grant more powers to the intelligence community undermines their constitutional rights and such legal principles as *nulla poena sine lege*.[17] It is a discussion that as yet has not reached a satisfactory outcome.

---

[13] For Russia's use of these means F-Secure Labs 2015. Cf. Bellingcat 2016; Gathmann et al. 2014.

[14] MacAskill et al. 2013.

[15] See for instance http://www.nytimes.com/interactive/2017/01/06/us/politics/document-russia-hacking-report-intelligence-agencies.html?_r=0; Glaser 2016; Markoff 2016; Mozur and Scott 2016.

[16] Committee on Legal Affairs and Human Rights of the Parliamentary Assembly of the Council of Europe 2006.

[17] Hill 2016; Eijkman and Van Ginkel 2011, p. 16; Council of Europe. Commissioner for Human Rights 2015.

1.3 Precedents

The changes outlined in the previous paragraph are indeed spectacular and adaptation to them may indeed have proven particularly difficult. Still, the 20th century has seen many more occasions of fundamental change, even though its fundamental impact nowadays seems largely forgotten as the world it shaped is taken for granted. Then, as now, adaptation to (sudden) changes in the environment was difficult, and, as now, at times it was less than adequate. And then, as now, intelligence practitioners and their customers have reacted atavistically when they had better reviewed the available information once more and be more imaginative. Intelligence communities have been outsmarted by their adversary counterparts; military establishments and policy makers have rejected analyses because they did not fit their frame of reference or policy preferences, and imminent attacks were considered unimaginable. In such cases what can be termed 'Noise Barriers' occur.[18]

The invention of the telegraph, for instance, not only stimulated interception techniques and the rise of signals intelligence, it made long-distance communication, and with it colonial rule, incomparably more effective. It gave colonial powers the upper hand and enabled direct control from the 'motherland'. During the same period advances in naval technology, in particular the advent of steam-powered warships, gave them a distinct technological edge, not to mention staying power, over indigenous opponents. Both developments, however, took time to digest, and the Dutch, to give but one example, trusted their newly acquired technological edge over their previous intelligence-based means of dominating their vast colonial holdings in present-day Indonesia. It was only after they had rediscovered the value of good intelligence, however, that they managed to gain the upper hand in the Aceh War (1873–1912).[19]

It also took time to fully grasp the potential of the aeroplane. While initially it was believed to fit for reconnaissance only, over time the aeroplane acquired additional roles, ranging from aerial bombardments to (strategic) surprise attacks using airborne troopers.[20] Aircraft thus reduced the relevance of fixed ground defences and, especially, waterways, and the possibility to freely manoeuvre ground forces. The full implications however were largely overlooked until the catastrophic events of May–June 1940 when Germany defeated France and Britain in a mere six weeks. Another consequence of the invention of the airplane was that the classic distinction between civilians and combatants became more difficult to maintain; in fact, even before the invention of aircraft, writer H.G. Wells predicted aerial bombardments on cities and industrial centres that would be decisive, as they would

---

[18] See, for instance, Metselaar 1997.

[19] Kitzen 2016.

[20] House 1993, p. 6.

result in breaking a population's will to resist.[21] While the fear of aerial bombardment was a key feature of the Inter-war years, it proved difficult to accurately assess its impact during the Second World War. It was either over-estimated or downplayed and intelligence did both—expecting German morale to break in strategic bombardments when British evidently had not.

Even the current surge in public concern over intelligence services' activities and calls for a better control of them, has its historical counterparts. Earlier decades have also witnessed a period of marked increase in interest in the intelligence community's doings. In the 1970s for instance, the CIA's operations during the preceding twenty-five years led to a Congressional inquiry that put certain limits on what the US intelligence community could and could not do.[22] As today, at the time practitioners felt that tighter controls would fatally hamper their work, yet during the 1980s and early 1990s in many Western countries steps were taken to place intelligence and security services on a statutory footing. It is fair to say that these may have indeed demanded considerable adaptation on the part of the intelligence community. Yet, a statute also provided a clear demarcation of tasks and responsibilities.[23]

1.4 A Revolution in Intelligence Affairs?

While intelligence may be dubbed the second oldest profession in the world and early literature such as the *Iliad* and the *Bible* contains examples of intelligence operations,[24] especially during the last century or so the nature and practice of intelligence has changed tremendously. Humint, which dominated most of the intelligence practice before 1900, gradually receded as aerial surveillance and telegraph intercepts gained prominence. Intelligence itself was professionalised and institutionalised and many states acquired specialized units capable of collection and analysis of foreign military data. With it came the assumption that enemy capabilities were crucial in assessing threats, if only because intentions can change overnight. During the Cold War for instance Kremlin watchers spent years trying to assess the Soviet Union's intentions, but while this spawned a whole new type of scholarship—sovietology—the main focus of military intelligence remained the Soviet Union's military capabilities if only because it proved difficult to gauge, for instance, whether the Soviets actually were guided by Lenin's teachings. 'Bean counting', assessing Soviet capabilities, therefore remained the core business of military analysts.

[21] Douhet 1921; for a discussion, see Hippler 2013. Cf. Black 2016.

[22] Hancock and Wexler 2014; Immerman 2010; Olmsted 1996.

[23] Lander 2004.

[24] See Iliad, X, 195 ff and the Bible, Numbers, 13: 1–33.

After the end of the Cold War, and especially after 9/11, as a result of the multi-faceted process of globalisation and the rise of new technologies and new threats, as outlined above, a new type of conflict arose. Intelligence requirements changed; time-tested approaches proved no longer sufficient to provide early warning or trustworthy information. As before, intelligence will have to be timely and actionable, but unlike in previous periods states face threats that to a large extent are de-territorialized and networked. And while adversaries generally do not have state-of-the-art weaponry, it is their ability to strike anywhere that is cause for concern. Often, such adversaries are millenarian in nature, and could not care less about threats of retaliation. They are also prone to hide among the population.[25] Taken together, this means that 'bean counting' is not only much more difficult than before, it is no longer sufficient. Finding the enemy has become a challenge, and he is only identified through his actions. Given the disruptive potential of terrorism, (real-time) intelligence has to be able to provide trustworthy information about intentions and it has to be pre-emptive rather than merely predictive. Yet new technologies and analytical methods, or simply a huge increase in analytical capacity did not necessarily produce the intelligence products needed to meet the new challenges.

This worrying assessment spurred a debate about the necessity of a 'revolution in intelligence affairs', a debate that revolved around the need to devise new methodologies and technologies to maintain the relevance of intelligence in this changing environment.[26] This debate was part of a wider debate on the changing character of war and the ability of (western) states to anticipate and properly react. Some, like Kaldor, identified the changes discussed above as leading to 'new wars', intimating that old ways and habits, and old responses, were rapidly becoming obsolete.[27] Intra-state war rather than interstate war was becoming the norm, and, as Smith argued, Western armed forces had to adapt better or become irrelevant. From Smith's and Kaldor's analyses it transpired that the changes at the turn of the century were fundamental and posed an existential challenge for armed forces and their intelligence apparatus alike.[28]

By contrast, in the wake of the ostensibly successful invasion of Iraq in 2003 an opposing school of thought argued that the West's military supremacy was secure for time to come as a limited hi-tech conventional force could defeat any opponent. State of the art technology in terms of aircraft, reconnaissance equipment and weapon systems would suffice. This would produce near real-time intelligence which, so the argument ran, would lead to 'network-enabled' surgical operations that guaranteed success.[29]

---

[25] Kaldor 2012 (1st edition 1999).

[26] See for example Denécé 2014.

[27] Cf. Kaldor 2012, pp. 4–5, 72–78.

[28] Smith 2005.

[29] See Cohen 2003.

In between, so to say, was Frank Hoffman's concept of 'hybrid warfare', that acknowledged the occurrence of momentous change but at the same time held that Western armed forces could in fact adapt to counter enemy forces engaged in hybrid warfare.[30] 'Conflict in the 21st century: The rise of hybrid wars', as the report was called, signalled the rise of a wide range of variety and complexity in contemporary and future conflict.[31] Hybrid threats incorporate a full range of modes of warfare including conventional capabilities, irregular tactics and formations, terrorist acts that include indiscriminate violence and coercion, and criminal disorder.[32] At the time of writing only one such enemy force could be considered as a 'hybrid' opponent: Hezbollah. Yet, since 2007 the world has seen other 'hybrid' opponents as well, which makes it a useful analytical tool.[33] ISIL, despite its ambitions to be recognized as a state actor, employs a mixture of conventional and irregular tactics, the latter comprising of untempered terror against what it considers infidels and Western agents, and a sophisticated use of modern communication techniques. Actors such as these are often labelled with different terms. Some are called terrorists, others insurgents, yet others engage in organized crime; and for a while 'violent non-state actor' served as a catch-all phrase.[34]

Taken at face value there are considerable differences between them; however, what they have in common is that these terms describe a versatile, intelligent opponent that is often network-based, highly flexible and adaptable, that is primarily non-state in scope, that is able to learn from mistakes at a higher pace than established states can, and that has an ability to exploit social and financial institutions and embed themselves in them. Lastly, they possess a distinct capacity for recovery and regeneration when they are under attack.[35]

Some states, too, have been tempted to engage in hybrid tactics such as the use of widespread disinformation campaigns. A key example here is Russia that employed 'patriotic cyber warriors' in its wars with Georgia (2008) and Ukraine (2014–present).

Against the background of this (apparent) hybridisation of warfare, intelligence requirements changed, but progress was difficult and often uneven. When the Cold War ended and new conflicts that were ostensibly different in nature erupted, public calls to employ military means to stem them were particularly strong. Although this led to a surge in UN peacekeeping operations during the 1990s, these were not

---

[30] For a discussion, see Duyvesteyn and Angstrom 2004.

[31] Hoffman 2007. Compare Malis 2012, pp. 187–190; McCulloh and Johnson 2013.

[32] Hoffman 2007, p. 36. See also Freier 2007.

[33] De Wijk 2012, p. 358.

[34] Thompson 2014; Manwaring and Corr 2008, pp. 75–77; Bunker 2012, pp. 45–53; Denécé 2014, pp. 29–30.

[35] The description is based on Kuperwasser 2007, p. 4; Hammes 2006, p. 35 and Treverton and Agrell 2009, pp. 2–3.

complemented by a rise in the number of intelligence specialists that were deployed. At the UN level traditionally there was a distinct hostility toward 'intelligence' and the organization was slow to change in this respect. It was only after such catastrophes such as in Rwanda and Srebrenica that the idea that the UN needed some sort of early-warning mechanism and some analytic capability of its own started to permeate the organisation.[36]

After 9/11, the US Government and other Western states intensified their struggle against terrorist groups. The US now proclaimed a 'war against terror'. It responded militarily in Afghanistan in 2001, and then went on to occupy Iraq, but it was not able to eradicate terrorism. In the process it found that its actions spawned new acts of terrorism as its heavy-handed approach—the use of waterboarding, the renditions programme, and its refusal to grant captive suspects a legal status—did much to erode the good will the US could command in the region. It also cost them the sympathy of traditional allies that preferred to treat terrorism not as an act of war but as a crime. Critics also pointed at the Patriot Act and similar legislation that contrasted with civil rights enshrined in the US Constitution. Proponents argue that this is necessary in view of the threats facing the US (and the Western world in general). The discussion is complicated by the fact that especially when confronted with the terrorist threat, the intelligence community faces tremendous pressure, both from policy makers and from society that wants protection. While in most countries the actual number of people killed in acts of terrorism probably does not exceed the number killed in car accidents, the social impact of such acts is such that politicians and policy makers feel compelled to prioritize the struggle against terrorism over the struggle for safer traffic. When a service is found having failed to 'connect the dots', the answer is rarely sought in smarter methodologies. Instead, services face rounds of reorganisations and ask for expanded competences and funding, which they generally receive.[37]

While the fear of terrorism propelled calls for expanded powers for the executive, the classic divide between the foreign and domestic spheres is eroding, just as the divide between investigative services and intelligence is becoming more fluid. This is understandable in that in the end a state's legitimacy is put at risk if it cannot provide security to its population. The need of governments to be seen to be effective (however defined) in the struggle against terrorism has produced a shift toward pre-emption and prevention, hence the need for intelligence.

However, to a large extent this has resulted in an amalgamation of two realms that, at least originally, have had an entirely different function; investigative services are to amass solid proof. They have to enable a prosecutor to open legal proceedings with a fair chance of success. Intelligence services, by contrast, are

[36] Cf. UN 2000.

[37] The tendency to ask for expanded competences does not only derive from the desire to become more efficient, but also from the administrative rationale to increase one's power and as such to secure its administrative 'lifeblood' (Long 1949, pp. 257–264).

about indication and warning. They are about the probability of a certain course of events taking place, not about truth per se. While accuracy is an important criterion, timeliness is even more important. To be able to tell the score of a soccer game after it was played, is nice but from an intelligence perspective it is useless: what matters is to know in advance which players will be on the pitch so that the opposing side may adjust its tactics. For an investigative service, however, accuracy is pre-eminent. The final score matters just as much as the answer to the question which players actually played the match.[38] Put differently, the prime focus of an investigative service is facts; that of intelligence services is likelihood. The blurring of these realms could well result in erosion of the rule of law, and in an increased sense of insecurity.

Since failure is not an option, and hybrid adversaries could be literally everywhere—after all, they do not care for borders—all kinds of information could be held to provide vital data. Accordingly the classic divide between military and non-military intelligence became blurred, a development that manifested itself in such concepts as 'population-centric intelligence', and 'intelligence-led operations', and in the renewed popularity of the notion of 'winning hearts and minds'. Though after 9/11 intelligence services were more lavishly funded and states engaged in wars of choice, fighting terrorists around the globe, it was found on numerous occasions that good intelligence rather than sheer numbers was the key to success, however defined.

Still, the adaptation has been markedly uneven. Today, US CENTCOM alone has some 1,500 analysts at its Headquarters, with an additional unknown but certainly larger number deployed in the wider Middle East, its area of operations. Even so, it has been forced to acknowledge that events in Iraq, Afghanistan and Syria 'surprised' them.[39] Recent examples include the Taliban offensive that resulted in the capture of Kunduz, and the direct Russian involvement in Syria. With a yearly budget of over 50 billion dollars and employing over 1.5 million personnel and contractors, apparently the US intelligence community faces enormous challenges that cannot be met by an ever-increasing budget, widening the net, outsourcing part or all of the intelligence cycle, or by expanding the authority of intelligence services.

Surprise attacks and intelligence failures will always remain hard to avoid, as the literature on intelligence history overwhelmingly shows. They are, as Perrow argues, 'normal accidents'.[40] Paradoxically, greater financial means and expanding authorities may have had counterproductive effects. In fact, long-time commentator Engelhardt has suggested that part of the explanation behind these failures in Iraq, Afghanistan and Syria is not only the inability to make sense of the enormous amount of data that US services collect, but also that collection effort itself.[41]

---

[38] As Bob de Graaff once put it eloquently.

[39] Engelhardt 2015.

[40] Perrow 1999.

[41] Engelhardt 2015.

Equally worrying is that proper collection and analysis can only be done on the basis of requirements that are to the point. Intelligence needs to be timely and accurate to be relevant but so do requirements. All too often intelligence customers still think that intelligence either has the power to predict the course of events, or can be replaced by reading the newspapers. High-quality intelligence reports need to be read to be relevant, and customers need the knowledge to establish what their requirements are. In spite of decades of close cooperation there is still a great deal of misconception about what intelligence can provide, just as there is mistrust between intelligence and other branches of the executive, not least the military.

1.5 Learning

As said, if we look at military intelligence these changes have become manifest especially after the end of the Cold War. The following description, taken from an article in the Washington Post, gives a good insight into practice as developed in Afghanistan:

> The CIA provides intelligence analysts and spycraft with sensors and cameras that can track targets, vehicles or equipment for up to 14 hours. FBI forensic experts dissect data, from cell phone information to the 'pocket litter' found on extremists. Treasury officials track funds flowing among extremists and from governments. National Security Agency staffers intercept conversations or computer data, and members of the National Geospatial-Intelligence Agency use high-tech equipment to pinpoint where suspected extremists are using phones or computers.[42]

All this is markedly different from earlier practice. Nonetheless, the rise of new technologies during the final decades of the 19th century similarly changed the nature of military intelligence and the world it had to report on. Throughout the 20th century the underlying issue has thus been the ability of the intelligence community to adapt to changes in the realms of technology, politics, economy, strategy, and law. This adaptation or the lack thereof impacted directly on the effectiveness and the quality of the intelligence community. Failure to read the signs led to military and political defeat.

While it is beyond the scope of this introduction to discuss the debate on adaptation and innovation in full, a few points need to be made here. Innovation is closely connected with the ability to learn at the organisational level. At this level, individual experiences may combine and produce a synergetic effect.[43] For this to happen, Marsick and Watkins identify a number of preconditions. These are (a) openness across boundaries, (b) resilience or the adaptivity of people and

---

[42] Warrick and Wright 2008.

[43] Merriam et al. 2012, p. 44.

systems to respond to change, (c) knowledge and expertise creation and sharing, (d) a culture, systems and structures that capture learning and reward innovation.[44] From these characteristics it transpires that military organizations and intelligence organizations are not natural-born learning organizations.

In their recent volume on military adaptation Theo Farrell, Frans Osinga and James A Russell reach a similar conclusion. They outline a number of imperatives for adaption, which they distinguish from innovation. Adaptation is doing new things with existing materiel; adaptation may lead to innovation, or it may not.[45] They hold that history clearly shows that war forces states and their militaries to adapt, as 'states and militaries that fail to adapt risk defeat'.[46] Operational challenges and technological change are the main drivers, but unfamiliarity with the terrain or the political environment may suffice to convince militaries of the need to adapt.[47] Domestic politics, strategic culture, alliance politics and civil-military relations impact on whether a perceived need will translate in actual adaptation.[48] Farrell and his co-editors argue that as conservative institutions armed forces are 'especially disinclined to change' and identify the bi- or tri-yearly rotation as a key impediment for the institutionalization of lessons learned.

Based on the Afghanistan experience, they argue that an open culture is crucial, which ties in with the findings of Marsick and Watkins discussed above. Officers of the German *Bundeswehr* were not expected to express their personal views and, accordingly, the Germans had greater difficulty in adapting to realities on the ground than other contingents. Size, by contrast, may enable adaptation as, in the absence of formal institutionalized learning, personal contacts between consecutive Dutch and Danish officers in the field helped them to identify and disseminate best practices. This informal learning, however, does not find its way into field manuals and lessons tend to be tactical only.[49]

In addition, best practices may be based on mere coincidence. While military organizations generally pride themselves in that they heed 'lessons learned', and hold that military doctrine contains the condensed valuable lessons of past experience, they generally overlook the fact that learning from the past is not a straightforward exercise. In the context of a military operation, it is difficult to make truthful claims about causality. Likewise, it is impossible to establish in advance which 'lesson' is the correct one. Furthermore, the analysis of past experience is often influenced by preferences, corporate interests and personal agendas.[50]

While intelligence services are somewhat different from military establishments they share most of their characteristics. Taking Marsick and Watkins'

[44] Marsick and Watkins 2005, p. 357.

[45] Farrell and Terriff 2002, p. 6.

[46] Farrell et al. 2013, p. 1, 4 (quote).

[47] Idem, p. 4.

[48] Idem, p. 3.

[49] Idem, pp. 305–306.

[50] Baudet 2013.

characteristics of 'healthy' learning organizations as a basis, intelligence organizations are poor learning organizations. They are not open across boundaries, as the secretive nature of their work produces a secretive internal culture. While they do create knowledge, sharing this knowledge is limited to the customer. A complicating factor is the frequent rotation of military personnel within military intelligence organizations. This precludes specialisation. Intelligence organisations perform somewhat better on the last count: they do capture learning (although mostly not in a structured way), and they generally are resilient. Their responsiveness to change is somewhat problematic, however. After all, it was concern for this matter that spurred the debate on the necessity of a revolution in intelligence affairs. Lastly, while individuals may adapt, the secretive culture of intelligence organizations may hamper innovation.

Like any bureaucracy, civilian or military, self-preservation is a primary goal. They need to be relevant in the eyes of their political bosses, who, in turn, do not want to be confronted with unpleasant surprises. This not only impacts the collection and analysis of short-term and often tactical intelligence. As to strategic intelligence this may lead to a focus upon the politician's short-term preferences rather than on mid- to long-term emerging threats.

While Farrell, Osinga and Russell hold that military adaption will most likely be the result of war, it seems that intelligence organization behave in a different way. Past experience is absorbed at a number of levels. At the individual level, as the future is inevitably obscured, past experience and the ideas it has shaped give a body of reference an analyst and a policy maker can turn to. The temptation to turn to this body of reference seems particularly strong in times of sudden change, whereas it is normal routine in periods of relative stability. This may be explained from the fact that intelligence practitioners tend to trust their instincts so to say, and apply these to analyse new information that is handed to them. This 'instinct' is informed and conditioned by past experience in a process that has been termed 'everyday learning'.[51] This need not surprise us, as Niall Ferguson, though writing in a different context, reminds us:

> The past is really our only reliable source of knowledge about the fleeting present and the multiple futures that lie before us, only one of which will actually happen.[52]

The problem of course is, that the study of the past may *suggest* a certain course of events, rather than predict.[53] Accordingly, a focus on past outcomes may well lead to misguided assumptions about the future. The past complicates both the present and future, and it limits our freedom of decision and movement.

At the institutional level, past experience may explain why intelligence organizations face the ever-present phenomenon of groupthink. This, after all is little more than a way to make sense of contradictory data by an over-appliance of a

---

[51] Illeris 2004, p. 151.

[52] Ferguson 2011, p. xx.

[53] Murray and Sennreich 2006.

common frame of reference that by its very nature is inevitably based on *past* experiences. As such it risks losing sight of the exigencies of the present, let alone the future. Groupthink is an inherent feature of intelligence, or any process in which information is analysed and processed. Scholars tend to judge the quality of new research by their own ideas on the subject. In intelligence this risk is even more present and it may well lead to the smothering of deviating views. It may therefore be tempting to disregard the past altogether and start with a clean slate, which, of course, is utterly impossible. Whether we like it or not, we are a product of our past experience.

Also at the institutional level, the past enhances the corporate identity of an agency. Specific features of intelligence as a profession, such as a penchant for secrecy and compartmentalisation, condensed as 'best practices', result from past experience and certain time-tested methodologies may still provide adequate and timely intelligence. At the same time, successful adaptation may require an overhaul of such time-tested approaches. In short, the uses of the past may engender groupthink and inflexibility.

The contributions to this book serve to illustrate the complexities of dealing with past experience in anticipation of future developments. They are based on original research and in several cases challenge conventional wisdom. Some of them, like Klinkert's and Mahadevan's chapters, highlight both professionalism at the tactical level and naïveté at the strategic. Klinkert discusses the establishment and early successes of a professional military intelligence service in The Netherlands, and outlines how at the political level, in spite of warnings by the army leadership and the intelligence community, a faulty analysis of The Netherlands' experiences in the First World War and the trends in major warfare fatally impacted on the country's preparedness to withstand the German attack of 1940.

A similar analysis is provided by Mahadevan in his discussion of the Indian intelligence community's performance in the run-up to the 1962 border war with the People's Republic of China. Its origins as a domestic security service in the British Raj, and the *savoir-faire* based on its experiences during the last decade or so of British rule, fatally impaired the Indian intelligence community's ability to adequately read Beijing's intentions. Their faulty analysis informed the decisions taken in Delhi, and the result was defeat.

Easter discusses a topic that received little attention in English-language historiography. Taking place just weeks before the better-known Cuba Crisis, the confrontation between Indonesia and The Netherlands over West New Guinea also involved secret supplies to Indonesia of Soviet manned submarines and bombers that Moscow was prepared to deploy in the event of an attack. Allied intelligence found out about their presence but failed to establish whether they would be used. Another interesting aspect is the apparent failure of the Dutch to learn from their defeat against Indonesia in the late 1940s.

Whereas the West-New-Guinea Crisis and the Cuba Crisis were classic crises in that cause and effect relations appeared rather straightforward, Kwa argues that as a result of the momentous changes that have taken place in the international system, a paradigm shift is urgently needed to handle contemporary strategic challenges, and, specifically, crises that spring from strategic surprise.

Boelens, a practitioner, is rather more optimistic about the Intelligence Community's present ability to deliver. Discussing the 2006 conflict between Israel and Hezbollah and the Israeli operation against Hamas in 2008, and experiences with interagency teams in Iraq and Afghanistan, he argues that the Israeli and US Intelligence Communities have in fact adapted to changing circumstances. These cases provide a model that others should follow.

Moving on to the realm of intelligence in peacekeeping operations, this book contains three chapters that, especially when read together, identify the major developments and ongoing challenges in peacekeeping intelligence. Discussing UNPROFOR, Wiebes, Van Woensel and Wever conclude that the fall of Srebrenica in July 1995 resulted from the failure of all intelligence services concerned to timely identify the possibility that the Bosnian Serbs would launch a full-scale attack to conquer it. United Nations intelligence structures were very weak, and the Dutch peacekeepers inside the enclave failed to take measures to redress these deficiencies. In addition, at the political and military-strategic level a belief had developed that peacekeeping operations did not require intelligence.

Theunens, who has been the head of UNIFIL's Joint Mission Analysis Centre (JMAC) since 2009, argues that the UN learned from past experience such as Bosnia and the Great Lakes area, but he identifies a number of area where further development and fine-tuning is possible, notably JMAC's relations with another new type of unit, the All-Source Intelligence Fusion Unit (ASIFU).

Whereas Theunens primarily focuses on JMACs, Rietjens and Dorn, who discuss experiences in MINUSMA, critically review ASIFU. While no doubt the Mali experience provided useful lessons for future intelligence capabilities within peacekeeping operations, the ASIFU experience also shows that lessons from previous operations were not fully internalized.

The last contribution builds upon the assumption that spurred by globalisation, international intelligence cooperation and the blurring of once well-defined and separate realms are here to stay. Braat and Baudet discuss the rise of intelligence oversight and the subsequent development of an accountability gap which resulted from the acceleration of international intelligence cooperation. They present an innovative instrument to systematically assess the quality of intelligence accountability, on a national level and for the purpose of transnational comparisons. This instrument contributes to closing the intelligence accountability gap in the field of international intelligence cooperation and striking a balance between secrecy and public trust. Proper historical research occupies an important place in this assessment instrument.

1.6 Concluding Remarks

While past experience to a large extent shaped present practice, it can never be a justification in itself.[54] Ironically, as the following chapters show it is by studying the past that this becomes evident. Uncritical adherence to best practices—the condensed experiences from the past—may lead to calamities. In fact, today more so than ever, as technologies and concepts are changing fast, analysis of past examples and experiences will need to be more precise, and more critical. Clinging to outdated best practices may be a recipe for failure, but, at the same time, past examples and experiences may also offer inspiration for new best practices, new procedures and new concepts.

Several decades ago, British military commentator Basil Liddell Hart wrote a devastating comment on the way armed forces studied the past. They tended, and to a large extend still do, to embellish their exploits and to gloss over what they did not want to be remembered. This practice produces a corporate identity, but one that is flawed. Furthermore, it may lead to failure:

> Camouflaged history not only conceals faults and deficiencies that could otherwise be remedied, but engenders false confidence—and false confidence underlies most of the failures that military history records. It is the dry rot of armies.[55]

It is no different with intelligence services and governments.

References

ahumanright.org (2014) A human right: Everyone connected http://ahumanright.org Accessed 10 December 2015.

Atwan AB (2016) Das digitale Kalifat: Die geheime Macht des Islamischen Staates. Beck, Munich

Baudet FH (2013) Quelques réflexions sur l'exploitation du passé dans les forces armées. Air and Space Power Journal – Africa and Francophonie 4(4):4–14

Beausang F (2012) Globalization and the BRICs: Why the BRICs Will Not Rule the World For Long. Palgrave McMillan, London

Bellingcat (2016) Behind the Dutch terror threat video: the St. Petersburg "Troll Factory" connection. Bellingcat 3 April 2016. https://www.bellingcat.com/news/uk-and-europe/2016/04/03/azov-video/

Berton B, Pawlak P (2015) Cyber jihadists and their web. European Union Institute for Security Studies Brief Issue 2, Brussels

Black J (2016) Air Power: A Global History. Rowman & Littlefield, London

Brewster D (2014) India's Ocean: The Story of India's Bid for Regional Leadership. Routledge, London

Bunker R (2012) Changing Forms of Insurgency: Pirates, Narco Gangs and Failed States. In: Rich PB, Duyvesteyn I (eds) The Routledge Handbook of Insurgency and Counterinsurgency. Routledge, London, pp. 45–53

---

[54] Idem.

[55] Liddell Hart 1971, p. 27.

Cohen E (2003) Supreme command. Soldiers, statesmen and leadership in wartime. Free Press, New York

Committee on Legal Affairs and Human Rights of the Parliamentary Assembly of the Council of Europe (2006) Alleged secret detentions in Council of Europe member states. Information Memorandum II, AS/Jur (2006) 03 rev http://assembly.coe.int/committeedocs/2006/20060124_jdoc032006_e.pdf Accessed 8 February 2016

Conversi D (2012) Irresponsible Radicalisation: Diasporas, Globalisation and Long-Distance Nationalism in the Digital Age. Journal of Ethnic and Migration Studies 38(9):1357–1379

Council of Europe. Commissioner for Human Rights (2015) Intelligence: "French Draft law seriously infringes human rights".

Cunningham F (2002) Theories of democracy: A critical introduction. Routledge, London

de Wijk R (2012) Hybrid Conflict and the Changing Nature of Actors. In: Lindley-French J, Boyer Y (eds) The Oxford Handbook of War. Oxford University Press, Oxford, pp 358–372

Denécé E (2014) The Revolution in Intelligence Affairs: 1989–2003. International Journal of Intelligence and Counter Intelligence 27(1):27-41

Douhet G (1921) Il dominio dell'aria. C. De Alberti, Roma

Duyvesteyn I, Angstrom J (2004) Rethinking the Nature of War. Routledge, London

Eijkman Q, Van Ginkel B (2011) Compatible or incompatible? Intelligence and human rights in terrorist trials. Amsterdam Law Forum 3(4):3–16

Engelhardt T (2015) The fog of intelligence. http://lobelog.com/the-fog-of-intelligence/ Accessed 23 October 2015

Etling B, Faris R, Palfrey J (2010) Political Change in the Digital Age: The Fragility and Promise of Online Organizing. SAIS Review of International Affairs 30(2):2–10

Farrell Th, Osinga F, Russell JA (2013) (eds) Military adaptation in Afghanistan. Stanford University Press, Stanford

Farrell Th, Terriff T (2002) The sources of military change: culture, politics, technology. Lynne Rienner, Boulder, CO

Ferguson N (2011) Civilization: The West and the Rest. Penguin, New York

Freier N (2007) Strategic Competition and Resistance in the 21st Century: Irregular, Catastrophic, Traditional, and Hybrid Challenges in Context. Strategic Studies Institute, Carlisle Barracks

F-Secure Labs (2015) The Dukes. 7 years of Russian cyberespionage. F-Secure Labs Threat Intelligence Whitepaper

Fukuyama F (1992) The End of History and the Last Man. Free Press, Glencoe, ILL

Gartmann M, Neef C, Schepp M, Stark H (2014) The Opinion-Makers: How Russia Is Winning the Propaganda War. Der Spiegel 30 May 2014

Gladstone R (2015) Activist links more than 26,000 twitter accounts to ISIS. New York Times, 31 March 2015. http://nytimes.com/2015/04/01/world/middleeast/activist-links-more-than-26000-twitter-accounts-to-isis.html Accessed 27 October 2016

Glaser A (2016) here's what we know about Russia and the DNC hack. Wired 27 July 2016. https://www.wired.com/2016/07/heres-know-russia-dnc-hack, Accessed 31 August 2016

Hammes TX (2006) The Sling and the Stone: On War in the 21st Century. Zenith, Minneapolis

Hancock L, Wexler S (2014) Shadow Warfare: The History of America's Undeclared Wars. Counterpoint Press, Berkeley

Hill R (2016) Bulk data collection by intelligence agencies breached human rights law. Public Technology.net 19 October 2016. https://www.publictechnology.net/articles/news/bulk-data-collection-intelligence-agencies-breached-human-rights-law Accessed 23 November 2016

Hippler Th (2013) Bombing the People: Giulio Douhet and the Foundations of Air-Power Strategy, 1884–1939. Cambridge University Press, Cambridge

Hoffman FG (2007) Conflict in the 21st Century: the rise of hybrid wars. The Potomac Institute for Policy Studies, Arlington

House JM (1993) Military Intelligence, 1870–1991. A Research Guide. Greenwood Press, Westport, CN

Howard Ph (2011) opening closed regimes: what was the role of social media during the Arab Spring? http://philhoward.org/opening-closed-regimes-regimes-what-was-the-role-of-social-media-during-the-arab-spring/ Accessed 29 November 2016

Illeris K (2004) Adult education and adult learning. Krieger, Malabar FL
Immerman R (2010) The CIA in Guatemala: the foreign policy of intervention. University of Texas Press, Austin
Ingram Ph (2015) US DoD website hacked by IS. Security News Desk 21 March 2015 http://www.securitynewsdesk.com/us-dod-website-hacked-by-is Accessed 24 September 2015
Kalathil S, Boas TC (2003) Open networks, closed regimes: the impact of the internet on authoritarian rule. Carnegie Endowment, New York
Kaldor M (2012) New & Old Wars: Organized Violence in a Global Era. Stanford University Press, Stanford
Kaplan R (2010) Monsoon: The Indian Ocean and the Future of American Power. Random House, New York
Kingah S, Quiliconi C (eds) (2016) Global and Regional Leadership of BRICS Countries. Springer, New York
Kitzen MWM (2016) The Course of Co-option. Dissertation, University of Amsterdam
Klang M, Murray A (2005) Human rights in the digital age. Glasshouse, London
Kuperwasser Y (2007) Lessons From Israel's Intelligence Reforms. The Brookings Institution, Washington DC
Lander S (2004) International intelligence co-operation: an inside perspective. Cambridge review of international affairs 17(3):481–493
Liddell Hart BH (1971) Why don't we learn from history? Allen Unwin, London
Long NE (1949) Power and Administration. Public Administration Review 9(4):257–264
MacAskill E, Dance G, Cage F, Chen G, Popovich N (2013) NSA files decoded: Edward Snowden's surveillance revelations explained. https://www.theguardian.com/us-news/the-nsa-files Accessed 13 October 2016
Mahdi W (2002) The Internet Factor in Indonesia: Was that All? Paper presented at the 54th Annual Meeting of the Association for Asian Studies, Washington D.C. 4–7 April 2002
Malis C (2012) Unconventional Forms of War. In: Lindley-French J, Boyer Y (eds) The Oxford Handbook of War. Oxford University Press, Oxford, pp 185–198
Manwaring MG, Corr EG (eds) (2008) Insurgency, Terrorism, and Crime: Shadows From the Past and Portents for the Future. University of Oklahoma Press, Oklahoma City
Markoff J (2016) Automated pro-Trump bots overwhelmed pro-Clinton messages, researchers say. New York Times 17 November 2016. http://www.nytimes.com/2016/11/18/technology/automated-pro-trump-bots-overwhelmed-pro-clinton-messages-researchers-say.html?smprod=nytcore-ipad&smid=nytcore-ipad-share&_r=0 Accessed 23 November 2016
Marsick VJ, Watkins KE (2005) Learning organization. In: English LM (ed) International Encyclopedia of Adult Education. Palgrave, London pp 355–360
McCulloh T, Johnson R (2013) Hybrid Warfare, JSOU Report 13-4. Joint Special Operations University, MacDill Air Force Base
Merriam SB, Caffarella RS, Baumgartner LS (2012) Learning in Adulthood. Jossey-Bass, San Francisco
Metselaar MV (1997) Understanding failures in intelligence estimates – UPROFOR, the Dutch, and the Bosnian-Serb attack on Srebrenica. In: Soeters J, Rovers JH (eds) (1997) The Bosnian Experience. Royal Netherlands Military Academy, Breda, pp. 23–50
Mozur P, Scott M (2016) Fake news in U.S. Election? Elsewhere, that's nothing new. New York Times 17 November 2016. http://www.nytimes.com/2016/11/18/technology/fake-news-on-facebook-in-foreign-elections-thats-not-new.html?smprod=nytcore-ipad&smid=nytcore-ipad-share Accessed 23 November 2016
Murray W, Sennreich R (eds) (2006) The past as prologue. The importance of history to the military profession. Cambridge University Press, Cambridge
Olmsted KS (1996) Challenging the Secret Government: The Post-Watergate Investigations of the CIA and the FBI. University of North Carolina Press, Chapel Hill. New York Times, Intelligence Report on Russian hacking. 6 January 2017. http://www.nytimes.com/interactive/2017/01/06/us/politics/document-russia-hacking-report-intelligence-agencies.html?_r=0 Accessed 9 January 2017

Perrow Ch (1999) Normal Accidents. Living with High-Risk Technologies. Basic Books, New York
Safranek R (2012) The Emerging Role of Social Media in Political and Regime Change. ProQuest Discovery Guide: 2–10
Salih KEO (2013) The Roots and causes of the 2011 Arab Uprisings. Arab Studies Quarterly:185–203. http://www.pinxit.com/page101/page115/downloads-23/files/Arab_Spring_Causes.pdf
Scholte AJ (2000) Globalization: a critical introduction. St. Martin's, New York
Segers RT (2008) (ed) A New Japan for the Twenty-First Century. Taylor & Francis, London
Smith R (2005) The Utility of Force: The Art of War in the Modern World. Allen Lane, London
Soengas X (2013) The Role of the Internet and Social Networks in the Arab Uprisings – An Alternative to Official Press Censorship. Comunicar, 21(41):147–155
Stuenkel O (2015) The BRICs and the Future of Global Order. Lexington Books, Lanham
Thompson PG (2014) Armed Groups: The 21st Century Threat. Rowman and Littlefield, London
Toffler A (1980) The Third Wave. Bantam Books, New York
Treverton GF, Agrell W (2009) National Intelligence Systems: Current Research and Future Prospects. Cambridge University Press, New York
United Nations (2000) Report of the Panel on United Nations Peace Operations
Vanden Berghe Y (2008) De Koude Oorlog. Een nieuwe geschiedenis (1917–1991). ACCO, Leuven and Voorburg
Warrick J and Wright R (2008) U.S. Teams weaken insurgency in Iraq. Washington Post 6 September 2008. http://washingtonpost.com/wp-dyn/content/article/2008/09/05/AR2008090503933.html Accessed 1 October 2016

Author Biographies

Floribert Baudet obtained his Ph.D. from Utrecht University in 2001. He has written extensively on the history of Dutch foreign and defence policy in its broadest sense and on the former Yugoslavia. He has published in *Cold War History,* and in *Air and Space Power Journal—Africa and Francophonie*. Research topics include human rights, strategic communication, covert action, and the use and abuse of the past by (military) establishments. Since 2006 he has been working as an associate professor with the Faculty of Military Sciences of the Netherlands Defence Academy. He has been a member of the Netherlands Intelligence Studies Association since 2014.

Eleni Braat is assistant professor in International History at Utrecht University, The Netherlands. Previously, she served as the official historian of the Dutch General Intelligence and Security Service (AIVD) and lectured at the Institute for History at Leiden University. Her research interests focus on secret government activities, such as intelligence and international diplomacy, and the political tensions they led to in Europe during the 20th century. She obtained her Ph.D. from the European University Institute in Florence, Italy, with a thesis on the disarmament negotiations in the 1920s. She holds an MA with honours in Modern Greek literature from the University of Amsterdam, and a *Diplôme d'études approfondies* (DEA) with the highest distinction in history from the *École des hautes études en sciences sociales* in Paris.

Jeoffrey van Woensel is an MA graduate and reserve first lieutenant of the Regiment Technical Troops (retired), studied history at the Radboud University in Nijmegen. After his studies he was conscripted as ROAG (academically trained reserve officer) in the Royal Netherlands Army. From 2001 to 2015 he worked at the Netherlands Institute for Military History, The Hague. He has published books on a number of topics including chemical warfare, the Explosive Ordnance Disposal Service of the Dutch armed forces, logistics, and the Royal Netherlands Marechaussee. He currently works at the Centre of Research and Expertise of the Veterans Institute on secondment from the Ministry of Defence. Since 2012 he is the Secretary of the Netherlands Intelligence Studies Association.

Aad Wever, a graduate of Utrecht University, taught information security and intelligence at Saxion University of Applied Sciences, Enschede, The Netherlands, and at Ferris State University, Big Rapids, Michigan, USA, until his retirement in June 2016. He has contributed to several publications on the history of the Royal Netherlands Air Force during the Cold War. Since 2004 he has been engaged in educational cruises at Spitsbergen in the Norwegian Arctic. Wever is a member of the Board of the Netherlands Intelligence Studies Association.

Chapter 2
'Espionage Is Practised Here on a Vast Scale'. The Neutral Netherlands, 1914–1940

Wim Klinkert

Abstract Its neutral stance and its geographical position, wedged in between three rivalling European major powers, made The Netherlands in the period 1914–1940 a fertile ground for espionage. Its territory was used as a springboard and a place for information exchange. Also, The Netherlands itself were the subject of military information gathering, as it was a potential area for military operations by each of the surrounding great powers. The Dutch were well aware of these activities on their soil and tried to profit from contacts with foreign agents in order to strengthen Dutch neutrality. This extensive counter espionage was successful in 1914–1918 but failed in 1939–1940. During the inter war years the Dutch service, modest in size, focused on curtailing 'bolshevism', a danger that came from abroad but formed an internal threat to state security. This led to a rudimentary internal security apparatus.

Keywords Netherlands · Neutrality · Interagency cooperation · Military planning

Contents

The title of this chapter is taken from a GS memo to the Minister of War, 13 October 1914. NA, archive GS, inventory 93.

W. Klinkert (✉)
Netherlands Defence Academy, Breda, University of Amsterdam, Amsterdam
The Netherlands
e-mail: w.klinkert.01@mindef.nl

F. Baudet et al. (eds.), *Perspectives on Military Intelligence from the First World War to Mali*, DOI 10.1007/978-94-6265-183-8_2

2.1 Introduction

The National Archives in The Hague hold a fragment of the only known diary by a Dutch First World War intelligence agent.[1] It only covers October 1915, but even so, it gives us a rare insight into the daily activities of an employee of Third Section of the General Staff (GS III). Within a period of just a few weeks, this unnamed Dutchman is in contact with German and British agents, with Dutch police officials, with the German *Nachrichtendienst* in Antwerp and he has plans to visit London. Also, he refers to information in the possession of the Dutch General Staff that is based on cracked 'secret codes' of the belligerents. This small source of just over ten pages shows us how diverse and intense Dutch counter espionage was during WW I. It brings us right into the complex and important relationship between neutrality and intelligence.

Academic interest in Dutch neutrality, especially during WW I, seems to be on the rise. Frey wrote his Ph.D. on the economic aspects of Dutch neutrality,[2] while Van Tuyll analysed both strategic, diplomatic and intelligence aspects.[3] The New Zealand historian Abbenhuis wrote the first overview of the years 1914–1918 in English.[4] Both Van Tuyll and Klinkert[5] have pointed out that intelligence was of major importance in upholding the Dutch neutral position and gave it a more solid foundation. My hypothesis is that counter-espionage and intelligence gathering done by GS III in 1914–1918 was in fact crucial in strengthening the Dutch neutral position, whereas on the eve of WW II, to put it a bit strongly for argument's sake, neutrality was not backed up by an appropriate intelligence strategy and was therefore significantly weaker and contributed significantly less to government policy.

This chapter will focus on Dutch intelligence gathering and counter-espionage related to military matters. Reliable information on one's neighbours is a valuable

1 National Archives, The Hague (NA), archive 2.22.06, inventory 172.

2 Frey 1998.

3 van Tuyll 2001.

4 Abbenhuis 2006.

5 Klinkert 2013a.

asset for a small neutral state surrounded by great powers, each of which can become either friend or foe. And it works two ways. Being in the close proximity of those major powers, and being strategically important to their military planning and operations, makes the continuity and the reliability of that neutrality an important issue for these surrounding powers as well. As a consequence, on the one hand the small neutral country is subject to pressures of all kinds, among them propaganda and espionage and on the other, needs to gather information as quickly and efficiently as possible to compensate for its military weakness and to gain time to decide its strategic course of action.

In all this, geography plays a major role as Holland lies on possible invasion routes between Germany and France on the one hand, and Germany and Britain on the other. Holland was the British gateway to the continent as well as the German springboard to England. Hence, espionage from 1914 onwards centred both on using Dutch territory—and using Dutchmen—for entering enemy territory and on getting information on the character and reliability of the Dutch neutral stance. Besides these, two other important activities can be discerned: collecting military information on Holland in case of an invasion and, from the Dutch perspective, sending signals to warring states that upholding neutrality was all the country wanted. Simultaneously the Dutch were keen to acquire information about the military planning of all their neighbours.

This contribution will show, by analysing the ways in which the Dutch military gathered information if and how their activities strengthened the neutral political stance. A substantial part of the Dutch effort was devoted to dealing with the extensive foreign intelligence activities on Dutch soil. This made counter espionage the main Dutch activity after intelligence gathering. Although one can discern much continuity between 1914–1918 and 1939–1940, the results could not have been more different. The second part of the article will therefore analyse why intelligence failed to repeat results as in 1914–1918.

Dutch neutrality was not based on any formal international treaty stipulating how Holland had to act in wartime nor was any country obliged to come to its support, but only on the rules of international law, codified at the Second Hague Peace Conference of 1907. Moreover, The Netherlands had no territorial ambitions; it had nothing to gain by war, but everything to lose. Also, it was very much aware of the fact that it could never successfully defend the mother country in Europe nor the extensive colonial possessions in East Asia against an attack by a major power. This meant that should the worst come to the worst the Dutch were free to align themselves with any power that would help them to save or regain their independence. This contrasted fundamentally with the Belgian neutrality that was based on guarantees of the great powers.

Dutch neutrality did not change during the period we are discussing here, but political and military circumstances did. While it was still conceivable (though not likely) during the First World War that the Dutch would choose the side of Germany – Dutch war planners had worked out such options – and it proved possible to stay neutral for the entire duration of the European war; 25 years later both options had become highly unlikely. Politically, ideologically and militarily an alliance with Nazi Germany was unthinkable, which meant that an important pillar supporting neutrality—complete freedom in choosing possible allies—had in fact been abolished and furthermore the scale of modern warfare excluded the option that the major powers would respect neutral Dutch territory. These changes on the one hand and the political choice to stick to neutrality in 1939 the same way as in 1914 on the other hand in fact meant that a rift between political ideals and military reality had emerged. Politically the country remained strictly neutral, but after 1918, even before Hitler came to power, especially the military leadership became more and more convinced that a repetition of 1914—remaining neutral while surrounded by fighting great powers—was highly unlikely. The General Staff was convinced that a new Franco-German war would somehow involve Dutch territory, as both their strategic map exercises and their defensive preparations indicate, but this opinion did not lead to a different approach to neutrality in Dutch politics because there were no viable alternatives that would ensure strategic security for both the colonies and the mother country. Also, the success of 1914–1918, as a result of deterrence by the army, was a narrative that governmental parties dared not question. This meant a strict policy of neutrality had to be reconciled with the option that a possible war could only be fought on the side of the Allies. That was squaring the circle. What role was there for GS III to play, especially after 1935 when the German threat became more and more obvious while politically the country clung to the idea of a repetition of 1914?

In the 1914–1918 time frame, the challenge had been a different one. How did the Dutch authorities manage foreign interest and presence in their country? Did they remain strictly neutral themselves? In what way was information gathering and counter espionage part of the policy of neutrality? And was spying done by GS III itself? Finally, the fundamental question is how neutrality was actually strengthened by the activities of GS III. As mentioned before, this contribution will focus on the point of view of the small neutral country and it will concentrate on military and security questions such as the military intentions and capabilities of the surrounding powers and the protection of Dutch military preparations. Economic issues, important as they were, especially in relation to exports to Germany, are not dealt with here.

2.2 The First World War

2.2.1 The Origins of Dutch Military Intelligence

For the Dutch military, three events brought the importance of information gathering to the fore. Firstly, the Russo–Japanese war of 1904–1905, which started with a surprise attack, so without a formal declaration of war, on Port Arthur, the Russian port in China. Combined with modern technology to improve speed in military operations, this meant a dangerous warning about the importance for timely identification of enemy intentions. It is no coincidence that the first formal warning systems were introduced in The Netherlands shortly after this conflict: a coast guard and an information service at the land border consisting of military police, border officials and reliable civilians.

Secondly, the formal codification of the rights and duties of neutral states, timely at the second Hague Peace Conference of 1907. Among other things, international law now laid more emphasis on the fact that a declaration of neutrality had to be backed up by the military means to effectively protect the neutral territory.

Thirdly, from the early 20th century Dutch military and politicians were rudely awakened by unprecedented foreign interest in the way they defended their neutrality with military means. Detailed books on possible future European war scenarios were published in Germany, France and Britain, and they no longer excluded Holland.[6] That this was not far-fetched was proven in 1910–1911 when Holland was, for the first time, the focus not of a fictional but of a real European military and diplomatic discussion on a possible future war in Western Europe: the Dutch published their plan to fortify the mouth of the Scheldt River, which controlled the route over Dutch territory to the Belgian fortress of Antwerp. As Belgian neutrality was internationally codified, and the Scheldt was seen as the route the British army and navy would take to assist Belgium, the plan became the subject of heated international political and military debate. Never before had a purely Dutch defence initiative, considered by the Dutch solely as a strengthening of their neutrality, led to such an international controversy.[7] Consequently, the Dutch General Staff in 1910 pleaded for military attachés, which all surrounding great powers had already stationed in The Hague shortly before. The Dutch government thought it too expensive and did not appoint them, Tokyo being the only exception. When shortly after the Scheldt-crisis the Second Moroccan crisis (1911) rocked Europe even more, the modest Dutch defensive war preparations of September 1911 were duly noted by the surrounding great powers. The Dutch intelligence effort remained meagre: all the Dutch army did was to send officers abroad, in civilian clothes, to act as their ears and eyes. This did not result in any relevant information. As the government did not act, the General Staff itself in 1912 appointed one officer to analyse foreign military developments, using open sources.[8]

2.2.2 *The Beginning: 1914*

Such was the situation in 1914 when troop captain Han Fabius (1878–1957) was assigned to this post. So, when the crisis of July 1914 broke out, the Dutch General

---

[6] For instance the works of Friedrich von Bernhardi 1849–1930; Demetrius Boulger 1853–1928 and Arthur Boucher 1847–1933.

[7] Klinkert 1992, pp. 451–460.

[8] Klinkert 2013a, b; and Abbenhuis 2014.

Staff did not have the intelligence apparatus it wanted. It knew foreign powers would be interested in using neutral Dutch territory in their military plans and it knew neutrality had to be protected effectively with military means to stand the test of any crisis. Foremost, it feared a German passage through Limburg towards France or a British use of the Scheldt towards Belgium.

How did the Dutch General Staff act during the crisis from an intelligence point of view? First, the Staff aimed to have the Dutch army (200,000 men) in position before the surrounding great powers mobilized, and in this they succeeded. On the basis of rudimentary information on the early preparations for mobilisation of the German army from a Dutch retired officer living in Germany, the Dutch mobilisation process was started before any other western European country.[9] On 1 August 1914, the Dutch Army was put in its prepared positions to protect the land borders and the coast. Second, it did what it had done in 1911 and before: sending plain-clothes officers across the border, Fabius himself among them; in addition it used the information service created in 1906 and had airplanes patrol the border areas. But all these efforts did not lead to very much. It must have been a relief that, even before the fighting started, both Germany and Britain formally declared they would respect Dutch neutral territory. The Germans wanted to concentrate all their military effort on the massive offensive against the French army and Britain declared it protected the rights of small neutral states. The war situation created new possibilities and Fabius quickly appeared to be the right man on the right place. In close cooperation with the Commander-in-chief, general Cornelis Jacobus Snijders (1852–1939), Fabius expanded GS III from a one-man bureau to a department of about 25 officers and conscripts, partly with an academic background.[10]

2.2.3 *Information Gathering*

The main task of GS III[11] was analysing foreign open sources as newspapers and military publications, which was an on-going process. It gave the Dutch valuable insight in the developments within the belligerent armies. But many more new sources were tapped during the war years. Just to give some examples: foreign radio transmissions were monitored. Because most archival sources have been lost, we know very little about this, but as the Dutch both in the First and the Second World War used the exceptionally gifted cryptologist Henri Koot (1883–1959) they could

[9] van Tuyll 2001, pp. 49–70.

[10] van Gent 2005, pp. 21–32; Klinkert 2013a, p. 170 and NA, GS, inventory 190.

[11] Censorship, cryptology and monitoring of telephone and telegraph messages was the work of GS IV, which acted in close cooperation with GS III. Staff officer Christoffel van Tuinen (1865–1947), who before the war was responsible for relations of the General Staff with the press, led GS IV.

certainly monitor and decode messages from foreign legations and messages to and from German U-Boats.[12] As German radio stations contacting U-Boats were placed close to the Dutch border, interception was made relatively easy.

In 1915, the Belgian and French army erected a rather extensive broadcasting and listening station in the small Belgian enclave of Baarle-Hertog, which is surrounded by Dutch territory.[13] Dutch railroads and waterways were used to transport the building material and radio equipment, without letting the Dutch authorities know what was being built. When it was finished, the Dutch authorities became aware of this impressive construction, which could be the target of German demolition attempts and thus endanger neutrality. The Allies thought the opposite was true: the Germans would never risk violating Dutch neutrality, with possibly grave consequences, to demolish only a radio tower. The tower remained functional and it is conceivable the Dutch were eavesdropping.

Also, based on the legislation that gave the Dutch military extra powers in wartime, GS III monitored telegraph and telephone cables.[14] We can assume that GS III read a great deal of the messages sent to and by foreign representatives. Censorship gave the military the power to open mail and telegrams, but only when a reason for suspicion existed and only in areas under military control. Furthermore, postal censors were used systematically to send information on belligerent countries and armies that they read in the mail, to the army headquarters in The Hague.[15]

Also, GS III interviewed Dutchmen who had travelled abroad, to Germany in particular, for private, commercial or military reasons. Many leading Dutch entrepreneurs had important and extensive networks in neighbouring countries and the same applied to the army. For many decades the Dutch military had bought weaponry in Germany and in times of crisis those ties continued to exist. So, during the war the Dutch army tried to buy weaponry, machinery, optics and radio equipment in Germany as it did in other belligerent countries and in other neutral countries like the United States and Scandinavia. GS III, however, was especially interested in information from Germany.

During the First World War previously unimaginable numbers of foreigners swarmed over Holland: refugees, wounded soldiers, deserters, airplane and submarine crews who were interned or Belgians fleeing their occupied country to join an Allied army. Many of them carried information that could be important to Dutch

---

[12] Koot worked under GS IV and was assigned to the telegraph office in Amsterdam (1914–1915 and 1918) and Rotterdam (1915–1918). After the war he compiled a manual on secret message exchange.

[13] The tower was the work of the Belgian engineer Paul Goldschmidt-Clermont (1890–1969), who was connected to the British secret service.

[14] van Gent 2005, p. 50.

[15] Article 38, Law of 1899 regulating Military Authority in Wartime. NA, GS, inventory 540. During the mobilisation, the area under military rule progressively increased to 75% of the territory. The main reasons to declare military rule were prevention of smuggling and espionage. Dehé 2014, pp. 31–34.

security. So the police questioned them or, when technical military knowledge was involved, the military did. The Dutch authorities also permitted German and English officers to question their interned comrades. In 1914–1918 the number of foreigners far exceeded 200,000, with a short-term peak of one million at the end of 1914. A small number of the refugees were political opponents of the German Imperial government who had fled to Holland to avoid German conscription or German police persecution.

The border police collected important information as well. Some officers of the army and the military police were even actively gathering information on any relevant military activity close to the border. Following the example of some police commissioners, officers of the army and the military police built up small information networks themselves. This, in fact, may have been the most active spying done by Dutchmen in government service during the mobilisation. Their information was sent to GS III in The Hague but it remains unclear if GS III decided exactly how extensive these spying activities had to be.

The Hague itself was full of representatives of belligerent states. Informal contacts of Dutch military and civil servants with representatives of those states took place on a daily basis. At their legations and consulates, but also in clubs and at all kinds of social occasions, Dutch officials met high-placed foreign officials, some of whom were known for their sympathy for the Dutch. These contacts were important sources to whom the Dutch military could give a certain degree of insight into Dutch military preparations, thereby stressing the seriousness of these preparations against possible invaders.

To manage information from foreign military attachés based in The Hague, Fabius used three handpicked Dutch officers as liaisons to the representatives of the German, British and French army. They were chosen for their well-known pre-war sympathies for and their contacts with those armies. By using these liaisons, Fabius avoided direct personal contact between GS III and foreign representatives, but received information based on the trust that existed between the liaison officers and the foreign officials. Around 1930 we see, on a small scale, a return of Fabius' idea to 'attach' Dutch General Staff officers to certain representatives of foreign armies. The Belgian attaché in The Hague, general Max Schmit, was used as a source in that way.[16]

2.2.4 *Journalists and Attachés*

Two other sources of information were of great importance and very actively used by GS III: newspaper correspondents and military attachés. Neutrality offered the opportunity to collect news from all sides, and to travel to all countries relatively

---

[16] Commander of the Field Army to minister of War 16 January 1930, NA, GS, inventory 29.

freely. Neutrality also more or less required the Dutch press to report on international developments even-handedly, and that added to the authority of Dutch reporters. The governments of the warring states actively maintained contacts with Dutch newspapers in order to influence their reports and to influence Dutch public opinion. Both the British consul in Rotterdam and the German legation established extensive networks to achieve those aims as part of their general propaganda effort.[17] One can conclude that the British propaganda service was closely connected to a number of Dutch newspapers. Dutch journalists, who could travel into Germany relatively easily, were used to gather information. The Germans in their turn often gave their spies the public appearance of a newspaper correspondent and they financed *De Toekomst* (*The Future*), a Dutch periodical that promoted German war aims.[18] Dutch GS III in fact used journalists the same way: after travelling abroad they could be debriefed in The Hague and thus form an important source of information.

Several Dutch journalists also had close personal contacts with colleagues and politicians in the belligerent countries. The best example is Marcus van Blankenstein (1880–1964) the Berlin correspondent of the Rotterdam-based liberal newspaper *NRC,* who not only on a regular basis informed GS III on both military innovations and the political situation in Germany, but did the same for British newspapers such as the *Daily Mail* and *Daily Telegraph.* Van Blankenstein's German contacts were Philipp Alfons Mumm von Schwarzenstein (1859–1924), who worked at the German Foreign Office, and Matthias Erzberger (1875–1921) a well-known German publicist and politician. In *NRC* Blankenstein regularly published articles in which he gave vivid impressions of visits to almost all European war fronts.[19]

After years of pleading by the General Staff, the Dutch government in 1916 finally agreed to send military attachés to Berlin, Paris, London and Berne. These officers quickly became important sources for detailed military information, not only based on their networks in the capital cities, but also on many journeys to the front line and to military installations and factories. Extensive reports on weapon technology, military organisations but also on the morale of the soldiers and the civilians were sent to The Hague. Occasionally they even talked to the belligerent commanders-in-chief or heads of state. It is interesting to note that the government and Parliament stressed explicitly that the attachés were to refrain from spying.[20] Perhaps the government feared foreign accusations against its attachés or it thought of spying by its representatives as an illegal activity. The officers nevertheless proved their worth.

---

[17] Eversdijk 2010, pp. 267–271 and Sanders 1982, p. 118.

[18] Eversdijk 2010, pp. 292–296.

[19] Van Blankenstein 1999, pp. 41–86.

[20] Parliamentary Proceedings 1916–1917, War Budget 1917, Annex A, Preliminary Report November 1916, part 8, p. 2.

2.2.5 Foreign Services on Dutch Soil

In 1914 Naval officer George Mansfield Cumming (1859–1923) of the Secret Intelligence Service (SIS) led the British service for espionage abroad. He had set his sights on The Netherlands at the outbreak of the war. His main agent in Holland was Richard Tinsley (1875–1942), a former merchant marine officer who had lived in Rotterdam since 1909 and was managing director of the Uranium Steamboat Company. He had been involved in sending emigrants to the United States since 1910. As soon as the war broke out, Tinsley established a close relationship with the British consul-general in Rotterdam, Ernest Maxse (1863–1943), and the British military attaché in The Hague, Laurence Oppenheim (1871–1923). In his hometown Tinsley was constantly in close contact with the Rotterdam police. He saw the head of the river police, François van 't Sant (1883–1966) on a daily basis. Van 't Sant was one of the most important sources of GS III as a result of his close contacts with both British and German agents.

Tinsley's organisation, covering Holland, Belgium and Germany, grew exceedingly rapidly in size and effectiveness. It became the largest and most important network controlled by Cumming in London. 21% of all British agents abroad were posted in Holland and half of Cumming's budget, 5000 British pounds per month, was going to Rotterdam. Tinsley sent military information to London as well as information on Dutch smugglers who illegally transported goods to Germany. He also contacted left-wing German exiles in Holland and financed their publications as *Der Kampf*.[21]

How did the Dutch authorities learn of Tinsley's activities? The first British espionage on Dutch soil took place in the northern Dutch provinces and was related to the observation of German shipping towards Britain. British consuls in the small ports close to the Frisian Isles as well as paid Dutch citizens were used to observe German activity. This information was sent either via go-betweens to Tinsley or through employees of the Dutch State Telegraph who were also paid to copy telegrams from the Dutch coast guard. All Dutch telegrams from the north were sent via Amsterdam. By using state detectives and receiving information from German sources, Dutch police discovered the activities of the consuls and the enlisted Dutch citizens in early 1915. It was the main reason to declare the north of the country under a state of siege, which in fact meant that in these areas military rule was introduced. Suspected spies could easily be evicted from this area or put on trial if it was obvious that activities had endangered Dutch neutrality.

Unravelling the British networks led the Dutch authorities to Tinsley in Rotterdam. But probably because his close relationship with Van 't Sant, with whom he traded important information, he was not arrested. The Dutch restricted themselves to prosecuting only some of Tinsley's agents, especially those who were involved in recruiting Dutchmen.[22]

---

[21] Andrew 2009, pp. 71–73; Boghardt 2004, pp. 84–107.

[22] Klinkert 2013a, pp. 189–192.

1916 was a bad year for Tinsley's organisation. The Germans intercepted the ferry between Rotterdam and England and brought it to Zeebrugge in occupied Belgium. When they searched it, they found postbags with correspondence from Tinsley and the military attaché Oppenheim to Cumming in London. This was disastrous for the British organisation that observed German military transports in Belgium, Tinsley's most important activity. Now the Germans could easily arrest some of Tinsley's main agents in Belgium and along the Dutch-Belgian border, and they wasted no time in doing so. Moreover, *De Telegraaf*, one of the leading Dutch newspapers, published an article on Tinsley as head of British intelligence in Holland. Again, the Dutch authorities held back. Tinsley could stay and carry on, but his main activity, sending information on German military train transports in Belgium to London, was taken over by one of his agents, Henry Landau (1892–1968). Also, less use was made of ferries and more of the telegraph to send information to London. The Dutch monitored this closely.

Landau built up one of the most successful information networks of the First World War. From Rotterdam he led a large number of *passeurs* ('professional' well-paid crossers of the Dutch-Belgian border which was heavily guarded by electric wire) and controlled hundreds of Belgian train watchers. From 1917 onward this gave London a good insight into German troop movements to the front. Landau also interrogated German deserters, who fled to The Netherlands in their thousands, and Landau observed German activities in Belgium from the Dutch border. He exchanged information with the Dutch authorities regularly.

Unfortunately we have only Landau's side of the story, which he published in 1934 under the title *All's fair*. Dutch police archives on him are rather silent but the detailed information the Dutch military intelligence produced on German military activity in Belgium could, at least partly, have come from Landau's network. The size of Landau's network, fed by information collected by Belgian civilians of the *Dame Blanche* organisation, is also proven by the fact that he paid £10,000 monthly to Belgian train watchers. Recent archival research on the *Dame Blanche* organisation confirms its scale, importance and also the use of Dutch territory for information transfer to Britain.[23]

The British activities in The Netherlands were, however, much more extensive than those of Tinsley's network alone. Several British secret services were active in The Netherlands: the War Office, the General Headquarters of the British Expeditionary Force and the Royal Navy all used Dutch territory to get information to and from Britain, either by ferry or by telegraph. They were interested in the German army and in Belgian men trying to make their way to Britain or France in order to join the Entente armies, and of course in information gathered by the Belgian resistance. Already in 1914–1915, for instance, GHQ had sent its agents to Maastricht and Liege.[24] Later during the war GHQ sent Sigismund Payne Best

---

[23] Decock 2011 and Verbeet 2014.

[24] This was done under the direction of Cecil Cameron (1883–1924). NRC reported on a spying network in Landau 1934, in Maastricht, working for the British on 14 June 1915. Verbeet 2014, pp. 88–105.

(1885–1978), who would gain fame in the 1939 Venlo Incident. In World War I he ran a highly successful network getting information from Belgium.

Finally, the British military authorities were interested in possible cooperation with the Dutch army in case of a German attack on Holland. In 1916 the British Admiralty developed *Scheme S* (Scheldt), the landing of a British brigade in Zeeland and the use of Dutch airfields. This was done without the Dutch military authorities knowing about it, as this was incompatible with Dutch neutrality. Only once The Netherlands was at war with Germany, Dutch-British military cooperation was foreseen. A British hostile attack on The Netherlands was not contemplated. From 1915 onwards, the British military authorities stressed the importance of Dutch neutrality repeatedly, as it kept the Germans away from the North Sea coast. When the Dutch government sent a military attaché to London in 1917, informal contacts intensified, as the British planners were well aware that without assistance, both in weaponry and men, the Dutch would be unable to withstand a serious German attack. This led to exchanges of military information and, in 1918, even a guideline, drawn up by the Dutch General Staff for British-Dutch military cooperation in case of a German attack on Holland. Although detailed information was shared between the Dutch attaché and British naval and army planners, it is unclear whether the Dutch government was informed. The Dutch military authorities probably never formally raised the question how these contacts corresponded with the Dutch neutral stance. The government stuck stubbornly to a legalistic point of view that neutrality excluded any cooperation with a belligerent power as long as The Netherlands was not at war.

The Dutch commander-in-chief frequently declared to the government that he needed time to prepare both the defence of the territory and a possible alliance in case of war. So he repeatedly pleaded to know in advance what course the government would follow. This question was never answered, as the government's concept of neutrality precluded any statement on this subject prior to an actual attack. This had annoyed the commander-in-chief already from 1915, as it would leave him with too little time to implement effective military measures in times of crisis.[25] This state of affairs might have persuaded him to agree with the British request for preliminary talks. But it was stretching the meaning of neutrality way too far. In the late 1930s we will see a similar course of events in the sense that Britain wanted to prepare the cooperation with the Dutch military anew when war loomed, but that the Dutch government forbade any preparations because of its neutrality. In 1918, the Dutch General Staff did make some preparations anyway, while in 1940 it was only GS III that kept the lines open while preparations remained a one-sided British affair.

Naturally, foreign intelligence in The Netherlands was not limited to the British. Both the German army and navy directed their intelligence efforts from Wesel and Antwerp[26] whereas the *Abwehr* had its seat in Scheveningen (The

[25] Klinkert 2014, pp. 91–93.

[26] Gottschall 2003 and Klinkert 2013b.

Hague).[27] Antwerp was also known for its 'spies school' where agents of different nationalities, including approximately a dozen Dutch, were trained for assignments in The Netherlands and France. Among other skills, they were taught to write in invisible ink, to contact *Vertrauensmänner* in Holland and to recruit people who could travel to and from Britain inconspicuously. German interests focused on information on the British army, the export of strategically important goods to Germany and on The Netherlands itself as a possible future battleground. Especially for information on Britain, the Germans had to send agents to England, either via Rotterdam or Flushing, or recruit Dutch employees on ferries or commercial travellers. The execution of two Dutchmen in the Tower of London in 1915 gives a good idea of the risks for the agents involved.

The central figure in German espionage inside Holland was the German consul in Rotterdam, Carl Richard Gneist (1868–1939). His diplomatic means of communication were used abundantly to send information to Wesel and Antwerp. Tinsley could be seen as Gneist's counterpart, as the British consul in Rotterdam, Maxse, was more involved in spreading British propaganda aimed at influencing Dutch public opinion. The Germans seemed to have given that task to their consul in Amsterdam, Carl Cremer (1858–1938), and to the cultural department of their legation in The Hague.[28]

The main German activity was recruitment of informants, especially people who could travel to Allied countries. Even the Dutch public knew this. Just as the press published about Tinsley's activities, so were also Gneist's activities made public. Dutch newspapers reported on the bogus companies the Germans established as a cover for activities to get people to and from Britain. All this centred on Wijnhaven and Nieuwehaven in Rotterdam, in fact only a few hundred yards away from Tinsley's office at Boompjes 76. Rotterdam was of great importance for the Germans, as it was the main port for imports to the Ruhr area. Even before the war, the German presence in Rotterdam had been substantial; from 1914 onward some Germans who had already lived in The Netherlands for a number of years offered their services for espionage. Other Germans joined them, disguised either as merchants, shipbrokers, salesmen in tea or tobacco, or as newspaper correspondents.

An important relationship existed in 1917–1918 between the Amsterdam police detective Karel Henri Broekhoff (1886–1946) and the German spy from the German intelligence *Stelle* in Antwerp, Leonard Balet (1879–1965), who was of Dutch origin. They met very regularly and exchanged important information how the German army and the Dutch government viewed the course of the war. This way GS III knew many details on themes that were important to the Germans in Antwerp. The Dutch used channels like these to convince the Germans about their sincere wish to stay neutral.

---

[27] Villa Arcadia, Badhuisweg 106, under Trützschler von Falkenstein.

[28] The Germans also had a consul-general in Amsterdam, A. Rienäcker, succeeded in May 1915 by Hans Paul Wilhelm Alexander von Humboldt-Dachröder (1857–1940).

The German modus operandi differed from the British in at least four ways. More than the British the *Abwehr* sent police officials to Holland, for counter espionage. These officers were in contact with the Dutch police, but the Dutch refused any close cooperation the Germans suggested.

Secondly, the Germans were more interested in the Dutch defence, motivated by the German fear of a British attack on the Dutch coast. From 1916 onwards, the German Navy planned *Fall K* (*Küste*) (coastline), to be executed in case the British tried to master the Dutch coastline and Antwerp.[29] This had to be prevented at all costs. While this plan was being developed in 1916–1917, the Germans were actively accumulating military information on the Dutch defences and the notoriously difficult Dutch waterways and polders, especially the Scheldt estuary. They used their information network in The Hague and made ample use of bribed Dutchmen, among them serving military, to get detailed information on the coastal province of Zeeland.

To 'assist' the Dutch in coastal defence, the Germans in 1918 even invited Dutch officers to inspect the coastal defence works in Flanders. These were shown in detail and the blueprints were handed over, so the Dutch could extend their coastal defences along their North Sea coast, which indeed they did. The end of the war prevented any works from actually being built.

The third typically German approach was the abduction from neutral Dutch territory of opponents of the German government. The well-known Venlo Incident of November 1939 does not stand out as a unique event. In July 1916, the Germans kidnapped a French and a Belgian spy[30] from the most southern tip of The Netherlands. The Frenchman was Emile Fauquenot (1897–1966), a young Parisian student who had family connections in the Liege area in Belgium. He had been sent by the French secret service to Maastricht to gather information from Belgium before sending it via Rotterdam or Flushing to Folkstone, the hub of Allied intelligence gathering. In the summer of 1916 the Germans rounded up a Belgian network led from Maastricht, and German agents lured Fauquenot to the Dutch-Belgian border. He was dragged across the border and imprisoned in Liege. Dutch authorities protested against this abduction by German police from Dutch territory and demanded to know exactly how the Germans had operated because a violation of Dutch neutrality was suspected. Negotiations dragged on until the armistice. The question did not disappear altogether though as a Dutch soldier, who had assisted the Germans, was brought before a Dutch military court in 1921.

In December 1917 the German revolutionary and journalist Carl Minster (1873–1942) was abducted in a similar fashion at the Dutch-German frontier, 30 kilometres east of Maastricht. This case was even more controversial than Fauquenot's. German authorities suspected that Minster, who had fled to Holland to avoid

---

[29] Klinkert 2011.

[30] This was Franz Creusen who would again gain some notoriety in 1919 when he planned the abduction of the exiled German Emperor. The Dutch police caught Creusen. Files on Creusen, NA, archive Ministry of Justice (MoJ), inventory 16433.

German military service, received information from opposition circles inside Germany, which he sent to the Allies via Holland. With British and private Dutch funding Minster published his left-wing weekly *Der Kampf* (The Struggle) in Amsterdam. His kidnapping caused uproar in the Dutch press, which might have helped delaying his trial in Germany long enough for the war to end. At the end of 1918 he returned to Holland for a short stay, before resuming his revolutionary activities in Germany.

Finally, the Germans, albeit on a small scale, made use of attacks with explosives. In the night of 29–30 July 1916 a huge explosion took place in New York, the work of German agents. In Holland a German agent was instructed to prepare similar plans for the destruction of the strategically important Moerdijk railway bridge. He turned himself in. The Dutch police also discovered plans that originated in Antwerp, where naval intelligence indeed had a sabotage section, to blow up ferries between Holland and England.[31] These plans also came to nothing, but the rumours were reported in Dutch newspapers.

2.2.6 Law and Pragmatism

How did the Dutch deal with foreign intelligence activities? Fabius' position was not to interact directly with representatives of the belligerents, but only through intermediaries such as the municipal police, the military police and state detectives who shadowed the comings and goings of many foreign agents continuously. They all reported to Fabius in The Hague. In addition, two liaison officers were appointed to report on the court cases and other developments related to espionage within the ministry of Justice. Fabius' idea was to get as much information out of the foreign agents as possible, while leaving them in peace as long as they did not disturb public order, endanger Dutch neutrality or got Dutch citizens entangled in their activities. In Dutch penal law there were no provisions for a situation of long-term mobilisation in which foreign spies used Dutch territory for activities not directed against Holland but against other belligerents.

The subsection 'state security' of the Dutch penal code contained three articles relevant to espionage, articles 98, 100, and 430. The first put a maximum of six years' imprisonment on handing over state secrets to third parties by which the interest of the state or its allies could be harmed. Article 100 put a maximum of ten years' imprisonment on actions that could implicate Holland in war. Article 430 set a maximum sentence of two months on the unauthorised drawing or measuring of military installations. Article 98 demanded criminal intent and proof that information had actually been handed over to a foreign power. In court this proved difficult to establish. The same problem arose with Article 100, which demanded evidence of criminal intent to create a situation from which war might follow.

[31] Boghardt 2004, p. 16.

Article 430 did not mention photography and was vague on what could be considered of military interest. Moreover, the modest maximum penalty prevented temporary custody for suspects.[32]

When the first cases were brought to court, they resulted in acquittals because neither the intention to harm neutrality nor the actual fact that neutrality had been jeopardised could be proven.[33] Yet another course of action did prove successful, but could not be considered a real alternative: in March 1915, a Dutch employee of the State Telegraph who had sold military information of the Dutch coast guard to the British, was convicted based on Article 363 that put a four-year maximum sentence on acceptance of money or services in exchange for neglect of duty. In 1917, three other telegraphists were convicted on the basis of the same article[34] and again five in March 1919.[35] The sentences were relatively mild, not exceeding one year. The longest sentence during the war years was three years for selling Dutch military information. The perpetrator was a Dutch soldier.

Another option was forced eviction from Holland based on the 1849 Aliens Act. Article 12 of that Act gave the possibility to expel somebody who was disturbing public peace and order.[36] Finally, the military authorities could expel people from the areas under martial law. This was done many times, after suspects had been charged for smuggling or espionage. The commander-in-chief, appalled by the behaviour of the foreign consuls, regularly stressed the need both to strengthen the laws against spying and to expand military rule over the entire country, but the government was not prepared to follow his far-reaching proposals.[37]

Fabius' system of keeping in touch with British and German agents gave the Dutch a reasonably good insight in the activities of foreign spies on Dutch territory, even without strict legislation. By giving foreign agents some leeway to ply their trade, but also by questioning them and preventing clashes between spies of different countries, the system worked two ways. Foreign agents collaborated with the

---

32 This was only possible when the maximum sentence was six years or more.

33 For instance in December 1914 the case against Georg Wilhelm Tiesing (1881–?), owner of a gasworks south of Rotterdam. See De Graafschap Bode 15 January 1915 and NRC 29 April 1915 on Article 100. The only sentence based on Article 100 was the one-year imprisonment of the German spy Hilmar Dierks (1889–1940), in October 1915. He had recruited a great number of Dutchmen.

34 Behind this was the Dutchman Pieter Constant Willem Eduard Wisdom (1870–?), a spy for the Entente, see NA, MoJ, inventory 16408.

35 Algemeen Handelsblad 14 March 1919. The Dutch employees had given telegraphic message to Major Roepell of the German secret service (Groenhovenstraat, The Hague). The German officer Ewalt Robert Anton Paul Otto Heydemann (1885–1958) (The Hague) was named as organiser.

36 The eviction of the Germans Carl Alfred Hockenholz (1879–?) and Carl Armand Ritsky (1868–?) in August 1915 was based on this article. Both were well-connected to firms in Rotterdam: Wijnmalen & Haussmann (machinery) and Robert M. Sloman Mittelmeer Linie (Hamburg).

37 Commander-in-chief to Foreign Office 25 February 1915, NA, Archive MoJ, inventory 16371.

Dutch authorities, which gave them some freedom in return as long as Dutch interests were not violated. Moreover, through the agents the Dutch let the belligerent states know time and time again that maintaining neutrality was their one and only goal.

2.3 The Early Interwar Years

From the end of 1918 onwards, the world of intelligence gathering and espionage in The Netherlands changed dramatically. Suddenly a new danger raised its head: bolshevism. It was predominantly seen as an internal threat, but one that was closely linked to the international activities of revolutionaries. Illegal cross-border arms trade, large international money transfers and journeys by left-wing revolutionaries were all part of possible revolutionary acts within The Netherlands.

To report on any extreme left-wing or pacifist activity the Central Intelligence Service (CI) was established in January 1919 functioning under the responsibility of the minister of the Interior, but connected closely to GS III. The CI continuously screened leftist and pacifist organisations, movements of 'bolshevist' foreigners and infiltration of the army. It was organized via local intelligence services, led by police commissioners, sometimes with paid informants.[38] Compared to WW I the police and the juridical authorities had stronger instruments against (potential) suspects. Impressed by the threat of revolution, Parliament had passed the Aliens Act (1918), the Firearms Act (1919) and the Revolutionary Turmoil Act (1920).

Apart from following extreme left-wing persons and activities, GS III was ordered in the 1920s to follow Indonesians residing in The Netherlands, who could be suspected of promoting nationalist agitation in the Dutch East Indies, but also to monitor pro-Belgian annexationists and communist miners in Southern Limburg, as well as weapon factories in The Netherlands, suspected of ties with Germany, to do research in support of the Dutch position at the arms-reduction negotiations in Geneva and finally to perform security checks on visa applications for entering the Netherlands. When in 1927 substantial budget cuts were announced from 40,000 to 30,000 guilders per annum, GS III complained it could no longer fulfil this wide range of tasks properly. Although the minister of Defence sympathised with his service, he was unable to add anything to its budget.[39]

Of course, GS III also kept analysing foreign armies[40]—more or less a continuation of the activities of the mobilisation period, and focused on the reliability of the armed forces as left-wing agitation was also present there. It analysed open sources and information from, among others, travellers, border police, military

[38] Attorney General to minister of Justice 29 January 1919, NA, MoJ, inventory 16430.

[39] GS to Minister of War 11 May 1927, NA, GS, inventory 29.

[40] See for instance NA, archive Field Army Head Quarters (FA), inventory 442.

police, customs officials and Dutch companies who were active abroad. A separate naval intelligence service was established not until December 1935, which was remarkably late. Similar to GS III, also the naval intelligence initially consisted of only one officer, Cornelis Moolenburgh (1901–1997). During the Second World War he would become the Dutch liaison with the British Air Ministry.[41]

A remarkable merger between internal security and foreign military intelligence gathering was performed by state detective Max Cappel (1866–1948).[42] During 1919–1923 Cappel reported extensively to the Ministry of Justice on Belgian annexationism and communism in Southern Limburg, strategically a sensitive area. The assignment had kicked off with a request from the Military Police to monitor militant volunteers in Belgium, who might attack Maastricht.[43] In the following years, he not only visited Belgium, reporting on anti-Dutch sentiments, but also Aachen, meeting Belgian occupation authorities, both military and police. His close contacts with the *Sureté Belge* in the German city were not only to exchange information on cross-border bolshevist movements and networks but also on troop movements. In the spring of 1921 for instance, and again in 1922, Cappel reported frequently on Belgian reinforcements that might indicate preparations for an occupation of the Ruhr area. This military information was sent to the minister of War.[44]

Foreign intelligence activity in The Netherlands during the twenties decreased. The German intelligence structure probably fell more or less apart, but small pockets remained active. The Dutch police pointed to the activities of the former *Stelle* of the *Abwehr* in Scheveningen and also suspected that German informants of lower ranks now worked for communist organisations. However, a closer analysis of the activities of known former German spies revealed that if they were still active, it was mostly on the anti-bolshevist side. An example was the Dutchman G. J.A.J. Petersen (1885–1948), who had been an *Abwehr* agent in Holland since 1916 and who applied for a position with the Dutch police in 1919. He was hired for his ability to infiltrate organisations and his knowledge of left-wing groups, which he used to infiltrate on behalf of his former employers.[45]

The British activities moved from Tinsley's Rotterdam-based shipping company and the Rotterdam consulate to the Passport Control Office (PCO), initially in Rotterdam under Francis Charles Benjamin Wood, who had worked as a British

[41] Jensen 1997 and van Esch 2014.

[42] A Jew of German birth especially entrusted with the safety of the Royal Family.

[43] NA, MoJ, inventory 16445.

[44] NA, MoJ, inventory 16486.

[45] Law court The Hague to MoJ, 13 March 1919, NA, MoJ, inventory 16433 and Attorney General in The Hague to MoJ, 8 April 1919, NA, MoJ, inventory 16343. See also report by the French military attaché in The Hague to the French War Office 13 February 1919, Service Historique de l'Armée de Terre, Vincennes, inventory 7 N 1181.

agent in Dutch ports in 1914–1915 and would later work for MI5. The SIS had started using PCOs for intelligence purposes in different countries. After Rotterdam, The Hague was used as a British window on Germany.[46]

The international character of the 'bolshevist threat' led to a new phenomenon: the Dutch government reacted positively on British, German[47] and American[48] overtures in 1919 to exchange intelligence on revolutionaries and their transnational activities. In Rotterdam Wood[49] became the point of contact, and war correspondent lieutenant Jan Fabius (1888–1964) was attached to the military attaché in Berlin for this purpose. The contacts in The Hague between the foreign services and GS III were held as low-key as possible so the responsible ministers could always deny any knowledge.[50]

The fear of 'bolshevism' also led to a heightened interest in urban uprisings. Both the police and the military were active, using the intelligence channels. In 1919 for example, the Dutch military attaché in Berlin reported on how the German police crushed large-scale revolutionary riots.[51] From 1920 onwards, regular contacts with Basil Thomson (1861–1939) of the Metropolitan Police were aimed at following the international itineraries of suspected bolshevists.[52] A third example is the trip of three Dutch officers to Vienna in February 1934, to hear detailed explanations by Austrian police and intelligence officials on the suppression of the recent unrest. On this occasion the leading Austrian police official Johann Presser stressed the warm, long-term relationship with the Dutch intelligence service.[53]

---

[46] Villa Johanna, Nieuwe Parklaan 57 led consecutively by Hugh Reginald Dalton (1893–1936) and Montagu Reaney Chidson (1893–1957). Chidson married the Dutchwoman Marie Josephine de Bruijn in 1919; he was sent back to London after three months (1937) because he did function well and was replaced by Major Richard Henry Stevens (1893–1967). Newhouse. National Archives London, T 162/76. Other Hague spy centres: the French embassy and Nieuwe Uitleg 10, from where allegedly the French managed an organisation for recruiting spies in Germany with the aid of Dutch citizens (see: Berliner Tageblatt and Algemeen Handelsblad 5 December 1929), and Celebesstraat 32, which was an important post for Russian intelligence in Western Europe, led from 1936–1937 by Walter Kriwitsky (1899–1941), who lived as an Austrian antique dealer named Martin Lesser.

[47] MoJ to Foreign Office 10 September 1919, NA, MoJ, inventory 16443. The initiative had come from Legationsrat Roland Koester (1883–1935) married to the Dutchwoman Anthonia Maria Dyserinck (1858–1943), see also FO to MoJ, 21 November 1919, NA, MoJ, inventory 16449 also the Nachrichtenstelle in Berlin approached the Dutch legation.

[48] MoJ to FO 17 March 1920, NA, MoJ, inventory 16455.

[49] In February 1940, the Dutch newspapers reported his return to The Hague in the capacity of the British government official for economic affairs. He escaped the country in May 1940.

[50] NA, MoJ, inventory 16433.

[51] Military attaché to Commander-in-chief, 27 March 1919, NA, FO, inventory 392.

[52] Dutch legation in London to MoJ and FO, 27 March 1920, NA, MoJ, inventory 58 and KMAR to MoJ, 7 June 1920, NA, MoJ, inventory 16461 on establishing an international police force. Marius Cornelis van Houten (1879–1953) had been in contact with Thomson since October 1919, which led to the founding of Interpol (1923). See: Smeets 2011.

[53] Report on the mission to Vienna February 1934, GS, FA, inventory 1027.

What changed dramatically after 1918 was the neutral stance of GS III. Fabius' successor Jan Willem van Oorschot (1875–1952), who would lead Dutch intelligence until November 1939, was well-known for his Allied sympathies. Already during the war, Van Oorschot had been a candidate to operate as Dutch liaison officer with the British army, the moment the two armies would fight the Germans together. This never happened, but he had been appointed by Fabius as main contact with British officials in The Hague and had visited the British front sector in France and Flanders several times. In 1921 he received a British decoration (OBE) for services rendered to Britain during the war and he was a board member of The Netherlands-England Society in The Hague. In 1938 Van Oorschot became Commander of the Order of the British Empire (civil division). He had a Surinam-Scottish wife[54] and is in fact considered in some websites as a British SIS agent himself.[55] He was also in close contact with French military intelligence, as he saw France as future ally. Every year he visited Paris for two weeks. It is even known that in the 1930s scenarios of exercises of the Dutch General Staff were secretly brought under the attention of the French attaché, to give the French insight into Dutch military thinking and operational planning.[56] In 1937 both Van Oorschot and his close colleague Van der Plassche were decorated with de *Légion d'honneur* by the French military attaché in The Hague. Van Oorschot was also a board member of the *Amitiés catholiques françaises*.

Another new development during the interwar years was the growing influence of the Justice Department in the field of counter espionage. In the late 1930s a special bureau was even set up for this purpose. The feeling within that Department was that GS III was leaning too much towards the British and French and consequently endangered neutrality.[57]

2.4 1930s: German Threat Looms; Neutrality Under Pressure

2.4.1 Van Blankenstein Returns

In the 1930s we meet the journalist Van Blankenstein again in his role as informant. He still worked for the prestigious liberal *NRC* newspaper and at the same time he was active as a liaison between GS III (Van Oorschot) and the British PCO. He

---

[54] In 1902 in Paramaribo (Surinam) he married A.I. Mavor, daughter of John Mavor, plantation owner in Surinam - killed in 1902 during an uprising at his plantation – who, in 1873, had married Agnes Shaw Grant (1847–1931) in British Guyana. She was of Scottish descent.

[55] Santrouschitz 2012 in https://tegenlichters.wordpress.com/2012/04/13/vlucht-voor-volk-en-vaderland Accessed 2 July 2015.

[56] Amersfoort 2007, p. 36.

[57] van Gent 2005, p. 52.

used his villa, close to The Hague, to arrange meetings between GS III, the main British agents in The Hague and the press attaché John Buxton Pelham Lord Chichester (1912–1944). Also, Van Blankenstein arranged contacts and agents who would work for SIS. Early in 1940 Van Blankenstein even organized the cooperation between the British and Dutch services with the Czech agents who had recently fled Prague.[58]

Furthermore, as a Jew, Van Blankenstein had valuable contacts with anti-Nazi groups in Germany, especially with the anti-Nazi youth movement, and with anti-Nazi activists living in exile in Holland such as Carl Hans Arthur Ebeling (1897–1968) and Theodor Hespers (1903–1943). He arranged meetings in Holland between British intelligence agents and Germans who were active against Hitler. He also established contact between the Jewish Central Information Office, led by David Cohen (1882–1967), British intelligence and the press. In all these activities the journalist was not particularly careful. The Germans were very well aware of his relationship with SIS. This undermined the British attempts, which partly went via Van Blankenstein, to influence and support anti-Hitler groups in Germany through émigrés in Holland. In the end German infiltration led to the notorious Venlo Incident.[59]

2.4.2 *Military Attachés*

The military attachés, who had been so important during the 1914–1918 period, disappeared after the early 1920s for budgetary reasons, only to be reinstated from 1936 onwards. In the meantime, detailed information on foreign armies was gathered via Dutch officers who attended foreign staff schools[60] or other foreign military institutions—mostly in France, or who visited manoeuvres abroad. Notable was the visit by two Dutch staff officers to the *Reichswehr*-manoeuvres near Wurzburg in September 1926. This trip brought them in close contact with the Soviet military attaché in Germany, Pavel Lunev. It probably was the first lengthy encounter of Dutch officers with a representative of the Soviet military.[61] From the early 1930s contacts with the German military became more frequent. Dutch officers studied at the war college in Berlin. Furthermore, in 1937 two Dutch cavalry officers were attached to a German reconnaissance unit for some weeks, followed in

---

[58] Van Blankenstein 1999, p. 237.

[59] Van Blankenstein 1999.

[60] NA, GS, inventory 1374.

[61] Report on the German manoeuvres 21 October 1926, NA, FA, inventory 490. Lunev, attaché in Berlin 1925–1928, was reported as being a German-trained engineer, turned into a convinced communist officer. He also told the Dutch officers the Red Army was preparing military orders with Dutch firms such as Fokker and Hazemeyer.

the summer of 1938 by an attachment to both an infantry battalion and an engineer battalion of a Dutch officer-student at the *Kriegsakademie*.[62]

The Dutch attaché in Berlin, major Gijsbert Sas (1892–1948), first studied at the *Kriegsakademie* (1935) in Berlin, as one of ten non-German officers, became military attaché in 1936–1937 and returned to Germany in April 1939 again as attaché. In September 1939, when the German invasion of Poland was still in progress, Sas, accompanied by a German officer, even visited Polish anti-tank barriers. He advised the Dutch army to strengthen its anti-tank defences and predicted a German attack on Holland shortly.[63] From his days as a student Sas knew Hans Oster (1887–1945) of the *Abwehr* and this gave him the well-known first-hand information on German campaign planning towards the West. GS III in The Hague was divided on the accuracy of Sas' information. In 1940 Fabius thought it difficult to imagine that a high German officer would betray his country (Sas did not mention his name) but he nonetheless sent all information to the commander-in-chief and the government. In fact, Sas was taken more seriously than he himself had imagined. On 9 May 1940 many military precautions were taken as a direct result of Sas's information. At that time, but also earlier, the Germans were surprised by the accurate timing of Dutch measures in relation to German attack plans.[64] In Berlin Sas shared his information with the Belgian attaché George Goethals (1888–1966), accredited since November 1939.[65]

In 1936 the Dutch government sent David van Voorst Evekink (1890–1950) as military attaché to Paris and Brussels where he came in contact with the German opposition via Max Braun (1892–1945), a German social-democrat politician from Saarland, living in exile in Paris. Moreover, from the end of 1939 Van Voorst Evekink was in direct contact with colonel Joseph Martin Gallevier de Mierry (1890–1978) of the *Deuxième Bureau*. All in all he could give The Hague reasonably correct and detailed information on German troop strength, dispositions and intentions. Another important informant was the former Dutch naval officer-turned-arms-dealer, Paul Koster (1868–1941), who lived in Paris. Since the First World War he had been in close contact with Dutch GS III, so close even that he was arrested by the Dutch police as a result of the Venlo Incident and accused of espionage. No trial ever took place. In April 1940 Van Voorst Evekink informed the French high command in detail on the Dutch operational planning and war plans.

The Dutch naval attaché in London, Alfred de Booy (1901–1990), had enjoyed good connections with the War Office since May 1936 and with the Director of Naval Intelligence, John Henry Godfrey (1888–1970), who in October 1939 stressed the need to prepare for closer Dutch-British naval cooperation. This was

[62] NA, FA, inventory 1058.

[63] Van Oorschot to the commander of the Field Army 26 September 1939, NA, FA, inventory 1111.

[64] van Gent 2005.

[65] From December 1935, the Belgian attaché in The Hague was Pierre Diepenryckx; he succeeded general Schmit, who had been in The Hague and Berlin since 1919.

reminiscent of the British initiative for military cooperation of 1918, but this time no steps were taken at all. The Dutch government did not want to give the Germans any pretext for accusations that it did not strictly uphold its neutrality. Finally, in 1938 Johan Everhard Meijer Ranneft (1885–1982) was posted as naval attaché in Washington.

As in 1916–1918, the attachés were important sources of information, producing extensive reports on military developments, technical innovations and the military organisation and legislation of the country they lived in. In 1940 they were the main liaisons between the Dutch political and military leadership and their British and French counterparts. The moment Germany attacked The Netherlands the attachés informed the Allies on all details of the Dutch defence strategy and the Dutch operational plans, avoiding political complications that might arise because of the Dutch neutrality.

Compared with 1914–1918 the rules for Dutch officers to share information with foreign attachés were much stricter. The government just wanted to avoid giving the Germans any pretext to accuse the Dutch of not honouring neutrality. The British military, among them the British naval attaché Gerald Dickens (1879–1962), who were very interested to prepare future wartime cooperation, were frustrated by this Dutch stance.[66] Only Jacobus George Marie van der Plassche (1888–1961)[67] of GS III informed the British attaché W.L. Gibson personally on Dutch defence preparations.[68] Van der Plassche especially analysed events in Germany and had a good idea of German troops dispositions and intentions. This played a role on the four occasions that military precautions and other measures were taken in 1939–1940.

2.4.3 *Foreign Activities*

In 1917 the Chief of the Imperial Staff, William Robertson (1860–1933), had declared, 'the whole of our secret service would break down, as it is through her [Holland] that almost all of our best information is received.'[69] A quarter of a century later one of the most important PCOs was the one in The Hague; the geographical and political realities made Holland just as important as before. Maybe even more so, because cooperation between the Dutch and British services was closer in 1939 than it had been in 1914.

---

[66] De Jong 1969, pp. 263–266.

[67] Assisted, especially on German affairs, since 1934 by captain Cornelius Martinus Olifiers and Theo Haze (1903–1972).

[68] National Archives London, inventory FO 371/24458.

[69] Intelligence paper by Macdonogh on the situation in Holland 7 June 1917, National Archives London, WO 106/1514.

As we have seen, the PCO had close contacts with GS III and also hired Dutchmen especially those who could travel easily to and from Germany to work directly for Britain, just as during World War I.[70] Another example of the close ties between GS III and the British service was Pieter Brijnen van Houten (1907–1991), who became secretary of a Dutch organisation of anti-Nazi intellectuals and who used his position as a cover for a private intelligence service directed against Hitler-Germany. This made him an interesting contact both for the Dutch and for the British and indeed both employed him. To MI5 he was known as *The Cat*. The British also used a Dutchman who owned a radio transmitter in the north of The Netherlands to report on German shipping. The operator was active until November 1939.[71] Again, the similarity with 1914 is striking.

An even more direct link with the First World War period was Sigismund Payne Best. After his demobilisation in 1919 Best had returned to Holland, where he and his partner in business and intelligence Pieter Nicolaas van der Willik (1890–?), set up a trading company, mainly in pharmaceutical products, and a consultancy agency for British businessmen. Best's cover, however, was a very thin one. Although married to a Dutch lady,[72] Best's distinguished tall figure, his spats and his monocle made him in the eyes of many Dutchmen the prototype of a British spy. At times Best would think it safe to admit that this assumption was wholly justified.[73]

Best led the so-called Z-organisation, set up in 1936 by Claude Dansey (1876–1947) as a parallel organisation to SIS. Dansey used The Hague as the main location of transfer of intelligence from the continent to London. After the outbreak of the war in September 1939 Best's Z-organisation was placed under Stevens' PCO, that is, directly under SIS. Should Best require so, Stevens would put his means of communication and money at Best's disposal; he was warned not to interfere with Best's activities. Although no complete amalgamation was ordered, Dansey had instructed Best already weeks before that in case of war he would have to join forces with Stevens. Now Best's organisation also became known to the *Abwehr*, which had already infiltrated Stevens' PCO successfully. This infiltration culminated in one the major events in intelligence history, the Venlo Incident, the spectacular result of years of work by the German intelligence services.

After Hitler had come to power the Low Countries step by step resumed their intelligence activities similar to the period of the Great War. Simultaneously, more and more Germans who opposed the Nazis fled their country to settle in neutral Holland.[74] In 1936 the first German attempts to infiltrate the PCO were made by Adolf von Feldmann of *Abwehr III F* in Hamburg, a nephew of Wilhelm Canaris

---

[70] De Jong 1969, pp. 80–90; Brammer 1989, p. 71; Farago 1971, p. 122.

[71] Brijnen van Houten 1988; De Jong 1969, p. 91 and 108.

[72] Maria Margaretha van Rees (1892–1980).

[73] De Graaff no date; Koblank 2006.

[74] Verhoeyen 2011.

(1887–1945).[75] His work was continued in 1937 by the *Abwehr* agent and former naval officer Traugott Andreas Richard Protze (1876–?) who was ordered by Canaris to both investigate Germans in Holland working against Hitler and to find information on the workings of the British and French services in Holland. Protze, who lived in the same town near The Hague as Van Blankenstein, successfully infiltrated the British intelligence network in The Netherlands from 1938 onwards. After the breakthrough made by Protze, Hermann J. Giskes (1896–1977) of *Abwehr III F* was appointed to coordinate actions against British intelligence in Netherlands.

Another important German agent was G. Walter Schulze-Bernett (1896–?). He was born in Germany but had lived in Holland during the 1920s and early 1930s. In 1935 he was recruited by the *Abwehr* and in the autumn of 1938 attached to the German legation in The Hague, assigned to build networks for military information from The Netherlands spreading over France and Britain. From September 1939 he also worked on collecting military information on Holland specifically. Schulze-Bernett made use of pro-German Dutchmen, Dutch conscripts living in Germany and pro-Nazi Germans in Holland.[76] All in all in 1939–1940 the German legation in Holland numbered about 250 people, four times as many as the Dutch Foreign Office.

2.4.4 *The Venlo Incident*

Both the British and the Germans were very active in The Netherlands in the late 1930s, a period dominated by the successful infiltration of the *Sicherheitsdienst* of the British spy network in Holland culminating in the Venlo Incident of November 1939. At first, British agents had indeed contacted prominent anti-Nazi figures in Germany, but weeks before a meeting was to be held at the border in Venlo, the Germans 'turned the tables on the British' as Bob de Graaff has shown.[77] Unaware of this, the SIS agents accompanied by a Dutch employee of GS III, were lured to the Dutch-German border and abducted. This capture of the British and Dutch agents was a heavy blow both for SIS and for the Dutch. With the gamble the Dutch took, siding with the British so completely and believing, almost naively, that a viable opposition against Hitler did exist, GS III compromised Dutch neutrality and gave the Germans an excuse for invading the country six months later. For Van Oorschot and his organisation, the real nature of the new German regime was probably literally unimaginable. As had been obvious since 1937, and also when compared to the First World War, the Germans were now playing by a completely different set of rules. Moreover, the fact Van Oorschot did not inform the

---

[75] Brammer 1989, p. 70.

[76] These Germans were led and organized by Otto Butting (1898–?), leader of *Reichsdeutsche Gemeinschaft*, who had lived in Holland since the summer of 1937 and was expelled in April 1940 accused of spying. In the Dutch press he was called a staff member of the German legation. De Jong 1969, pp. 317–328.

[77] De Graaff 2007.

government of the activities of the British agents and the Dutch involvement probably indicated that he was aware that these actions were at odds with neutrality.

The Venlo Incident was discussed in the press everywhere, although the public at large could have had no idea how much damage had been done to the British intelligence structure in Holland. The Dutch government, for its part, was embarrassed by the whole affair. It had its Government Information Service issue a statement on 10 November, which only said that one person had been wounded and others been kidnapped near Venlo.[78] That same day the Dutch minister in Berlin explained at the German Foreign Office, that Van Oorschot, by attaching the Dutch GS III officer Dirk Klop (1906–1939) to Best and Stevens, had only tried to ease diplomatic tension. He requested the return of Klop (or his body) and asked for an enquiry into the events. This and eight other statements up to 18 March 1940 were to no avail. On 21 November 1939 the German government issued a press statement, giving voice to their amusement at the British Secret Service, which had been fooled by fake conspirators.[79] In 2006 the episode figured prominently in the spy novel *Restless* by William Boyd.

All that remained of the British in The Hague, except for the military attachés, was Rodney Dennys (1911–1993), head of counter espionage. It had been his first posting. He stayed in The Netherlands until the Germans overran the Low Countries in May 1940, escaping with one of the last available boats, which was just as well, given that his name appeared second on the Gestapo hit list for The Netherlands.

2.4.5 Dutch Military Planning in the Run-Up to World War II

In the late 1930s both Britain and Germany were very interested in the neutral Netherlands as part of their war preparations. Their activities differed widely. The British military planners hoped the neutrality of The Netherlands could stay intact, just as in 1914–1918, but by late 1938 policy makers and planners had realized this hope was forlorn. Yet Britain lacked the means to offer the Dutch any substantial military assistance as the British Expeditionary Force was positioned in France. Moreover, the Dutch refused formal negotiations to prepare future military cooperation, as that would constitute a breach of neutrality. Only informal contacts took place.[80] They showed a striking parallel with 1918 when the British military planners wanted to know what military materiel was needed by the Dutch in order to fight a German invader. That request had resulted in an extensive Dutch wish list together with informal talks. In 1939 the same questions were asked, now answered

[78] Nater 1984, p. 133.

[79] Best 1950; De Jong 1969, pp. 79–115; Nater 1984; Jeffery 2010, pp. 382–386 and De Graaff no date [1990].

[80] van Gent 2009, pp. 46–48.

not by the Dutch military leadership but at a much lower level by GS III and consequently with far fewer practical results.[81] This time the military leadership complied with government instructions.

During the autumn of 1939 British fears of a German occupation of Holland further increased. Such an occupation would represent a real threat to the security of the British Isles, as the *Luftwaffe* would probably use Dutch airfields to attack Britain.[82] What Britain had to offer in October 1939 was bomber attacks against a German invasion and small-scale naval actions on the Dutch coast. The Royal Navy actually began to plan the destruction of Dutch ports, industrial infrastructure and oil storage by demolition teams from 1939 onwards. To prepare for that, secret reconnaissance in Dutch ports took place. This was probably the only British military espionage directly related to operational planning in The Netherlands. The result was the XD Operations of May 1940.[83] British air attacks were prepared in more detail in April 1940 again without any formal contacts with the Dutch.[84] Only informal contacts on the level of military attaches existed. Meanwhile, British land forces were concentrated in France and planned to advance northward into Belgium. On 10 May 1940 the Dutch government asked for two divisions; Britain sent just one battalion, very limited air support and executed the XD operation—all in all very meagre compared with the British strategic interest claimed, but an inevitable consequence of the choice to concentrate all British land and air forces in France.

The German intelligence had been, just as in WW I, much more active in gathering military information in The Netherlands. All branches of the armed forces were engaged. Friedrich Karl Rabe von Pappenheim (1895–1977), military attaché in The Hague and Brussels since October 1937, coordinated the military intelligence effort. There he joined the naval and air attachés.[85]

More detailed operational and even tactical information for Army Group B, and especially for the 18th Army, had been gathered since February 1940 by classical HUMINT operations under the direction of Wilhelm Otzen (1896–1943), an employee of the military attaché. He focused on information about the best route of attack and the strength of Dutch defensive positions.[86] Together with information from Dutchmen in Germany, the Germans compiled a remarkably detailed and generally accurate picture of the Dutch defences. They profited from the Dutch restraint in hindering HUMINT intelligence gathering by foreign powers, again in the rather naive belief that it could be construed as a breach of neutrality. Even

---

[81] De Jong 1969, p. 90.

[82] van Gent 2009, pp. 46–48.

[83] Brazier 2004; Van Gent 2009, pp. 146–167 and National Archives London, inventory WO 106/1603 and FO 371/24458.

[84] Van Gent 2009, p. 201.

[85] Kurt Besthorn and Ralph Wenninger 1890–1945.

[86] De Jong 1969, pp. 335, 339, 385–386, and 509, and Amersfoort 2010, p. 264.

when it became public knowledge that Otzen moved freely around sensitive military objects, not much action was taken.[87]

Information gathering by aerial observation started probably already around 1936 when *Fernaufklärungsgruppe* (long-range reconnaissance groups) of the *Luftwaffe*[88] worked in close cooperation with the *Abwehr*. The number of these flights increased steadily and from the end of 1939 flights were made on a daily basis, photographing defence lines and defence works to prepare not only accurate topographical maps but also to further detailed military operational planning. Also civilian *Lufthansa* flights were used for this purpose.[89] In September 1939 German planes (*Küstenfliegergruppen*) (coastal patrol groups) started to monitor British shipping in the North Sea.[90] It is remarkable that the Germans still encountered a few surprises when the fighting actually took place.

The *Abwehr* was keen to find any evidence for British-Dutch military cooperation, to substantiate claims that the Dutch violated their neutrality. But that was not visible, although the RAF violated Dutch neutral air space on a daily basis, just as the RFC had done 25 years earlier. The Germans could interpret these countless violations as tacit Dutch support for the British, so as a serious violation of Dutch neutrality.[91] To prevent this, the Dutch protested against all violations of their air space and routinely shot at foreign planes. It is remarkable, to say the least, that the Dutch army only started to collect tactical information as part of its operational planning process at the very end of 1939.[92]

2.5 Conclusion

From being almost non-existent, intelligence gathering in The Netherlands was quickly taken to hand up from 1914 onwards and became very diverse. The General Staff used all possible sources; it realized the importance of intelligence and early warning for a small state. The main message the Dutch wanted to get across to the belligerents was that all warring states could trust its neutrality. In part this message was conveyed by means of confidential contacts with belligerent officials as well as agents, to give a certain transparency to Dutch war preparations to enhance this trust. At the same time the Dutch received some insight into belligerent military planning and were even well-informed on German military activity just across their border.

[87] De Jong 1969, p. 387.

[88] Under command of Theodor Rowehl 1894–1978.

[89] De Bruin 1988, pp. 150–163.

[90] De Bruin 1988, p. 83 ff.

[91] De Bruin 1988, pp. 191–258.

[92] van Gent 2005, p. 61.

The extensive and complex foreign intelligence activities on Dutch soil were tolerated and, to a certain degree, made use of. The information gathered by these contacts, by the intercepted telephone, telegraph and radio messages and by multiple informal contacts in The Hague, strengthened the Dutch position. But it is difficult to assess exactly how essential it was for the survival of neutrality. Lack of archival sources, because many documents were destroyed, forms a serious problem, as is the fact that continuance of Dutch neutrality was profitable to the belligerents anyway, both economically and strategically. Ironically, as Holland was important for the intelligence position of the warring states, this in turn supported Dutch neutrality itself.

We know is that both belligerent sides had accurate, and sometimes very detailed, information on Dutch defence matters, even if some facts on Dutch weapons production and military exercises remained beyond their grasp. During times of heightened tension, the many informal contacts that existed, gave essential information on how to interpret acts by the belligerents. All these pieces of the intelligence puzzle were assembled by GS III and shared with general Snijders and the government. Unfortunately, no sources survive either on how and what information was transferred to the government or how the government managed information gathering.

When we compare the First World War with the 1936–1940 period, the similarities are striking. Continuity in methods and the type of sources (journalists, Dutchmen abroad, cryptology, personal contacts, open sources and military attachés) are widespread. Sometimes even the same people were involved. Geography and the small scale of the Dutch intelligence apparatus can explain this continuity. But major differences are clearly visible, too. GS III relied more strongly than before on the British. The military leadership and the leading intelligence personnel no longer acted in the former neutral tradition, but for the political leadership neutrality remained 'sacred'. A fundamental debate on this issue was absent.

Compared to 1914–1918 the relationship between the Dutch and the Germans was very different. There was no close personal contact, no exchange of information, so a Dutch-German intelligence relationship was in fact non-existent. The Germans were unwilling to share; moreover, the Dutch were very short of money and the British were willing to pay, both for the benefit of the Dutch and for their own.

Another important difference was the active German spying against The Netherlands itself, probably underestimated by the Dutch. Not only were the Germans highly successful in penetrating the British secret service organisation in The Netherlands, they also gathered huge amounts of detailed military information on The Netherlands itself. These German activities were countered by a Dutch intelligence organisation that was no match for the ruthlessness and magnitude of the German service. Seen in this light, the successes booked by the Dutch attachés in Berlin and Paris were no small feat. But when the political leadership, the military leadership and the intelligence community are unclear about the course the country is to follow, even successes like these are not decisive.

In the case of neutral Holland intelligence meant collecting information from open sources, SIGINT, through personal contacts, and by means of counter espionage by police officials. Spies were not employed, other than paid local informants either by border officials (WW I) or police commissioners (Interwar years). Espionage was not seen as an acceptable activity by the government. Neutrality had to be protected, but that implied a defensive position. The idea of what kind of behaviour was to be expected from the state and its representatives did not include espionage. This resulted in a certain naivety, certainly in the 1930s. A coherent policy on security, which included the full possibilities a secret service could offer, was lacking. In 1914–1918 GS III had first and foremost been a military affair, and it is difficult to tell how much discussion took place between the government and the General Staff in relation to security matters because records of such a discussion lack. But we know that during moments of crises GS III informed government ministers. During the interwar years, GS III (and the CI, which was, as we have seen, closely linked to it) was almost exclusively focused on left-wing, pacifist, anarchist and—from 1932 onwards—fascist threats and undesirable aliens related to those threats. Especially in the 1920s this was seen as part of an international threat against the state, requiring international cooperation.

The fast and impressive growth of German intelligence activities within The Netherlands after 1936 could take place without serious obstruction by the Dutch: GS III was small; the government wanted to remain as neutral as possible and prevent conflicts with neighbouring states in the hope of preventing involvement in a next war. In WW I GS III actively supported the preservation of neutrality; in 1939–1940 GS III was more isolated and scarcely neutral itself.

In the two conflicts The Netherlands was both a battleground for information for Germans and British, and at the same time a geographically useful location for accessing enemy territory. This was a fact the Dutch had to deal with, making the best of it with limited means and with legality and an idea of choosing the moral high ground of avoiding power politics and rejecting might over right as leading principles underlying the neutral stance. Furthermore, besides being a battleground for a battle fought by others, The Netherlands was a place of exchange and encounter. Neutrality meant that The Hague was full of civilian and military representatives of belligerent powers. Informal contacts took place constantly. The Dutch profited from this, especially during WW I. In 1939–1940 the game had different rules by which the Dutch refused to play and, as a result, their contacts had become one-sided.

References

General

National Archives The Hague (NA)
General Staff (GS)
Headquarters of the Field Army (FA)
Ministry of Justice (MoJ)
Ministry of War (MoW)

Specific

Abbenhuis M (2006) The art of staying neutral. Amsterdam University Press, Amsterdam
Abbenhuis M (2014) An Age of Neutrals. Cambridge University Press, Cambridge
Amersfoort H (2007) Een harmonisch leger voor Nederland. Nederlandse Defensie Academie, Breda
Amersfoort H, Kamphuis PH (2010) May 1940. The Battle for the Netherlands. Brill, Leiden
Andrew C (2009) The Defence of the Realm. MacMillan, London
Best SP (1950) The Venlo Incident. Hutchinson, London
Boghardt T (2004) Spies of the Kaiser. Palgrave MacMillan, Basingstoke
Brammer U (1989) Spionageabwehr und Geheimer Meldedienst. Rombach, Freiburg
Brazier CCH (2004) XD Operations. Pen & Sword, Barnsley
Brijnen van Houten P (1988) Brandwacht in de coulissen. Een kwart eeuw geheime diensten. De Haan, Houten
de Bruin R (1988) Illusies en incidenten. De militaire luchtvaart en de neutraliteitshandhaving tot 10 mei 1940. Ministerie van Defensie, The Hague
de Graaff BGJ (no date [1990]) The Venlo Incident. http://www.mythoselser.de/texts/graaff.htm Accessed 31 March 2015
de Graaff BGJ (2007) From seduction to abduction: How the Venlo Incident occurred. In: de Graaf BGJ, de Jong B (eds) Battleground Western Europe. Intelligence Operations in Germany and the Netherlands in the Twentieth Century. Het Spinhuis, Amsterdam
de Jong L (1969) Het Koninkrijk der Nederlanden in de Tweede Wereldoorlog, Vol. 2. Staatsuitgeverij, The Hague
Decock P (2011) Dame Blanche, un réseau de renseignements de la Grande Guerre, 1916–1918. ULB, Bruxelles
Dehé J, Simons F (2014) Nederlandse postcensuur in de Eerste Wereldoorlog. Posthistorische Studie 31. http://www.po-en-po.nl/publicaties/posthistorische-studies/phs-31-nl-censuur-wo-i Accessed 3 January 2015
Engelen D (2000) De militaire inlichtingendienst. SDU, Den Haag
Eversdijk N (2010) Kultur als politisches Werbemittel. Waxman Verlag, Münster
Farago L (1971) Het spel van de vossen. Nieuwe Wieken Omega, Amsterdam
Frey M (1998) Der erste Weltkrieg und die Niederlande. Akademie Verlag, Berlin
Gottschall TD (2003) By Order of the Kaiser. Naval Institute Press, Annapolis
Jeffery K (2010) MI6. Bloomsbury, London
Jensen MW (1997) De MARID. SDU, The Hague
Klinkert W (1992) Het vaderland verdedigd. Plannen en opvattingen over de verdediging van Nederland 1874–1914. SDU, The Hague
Klinkert W (2011) Fall K: German offensive war plans against the Netherlands, 1916–1918. In: Amersfoort H, Klinkert W (eds) Small Powers in the Age of Total War. Brill Publishers, Leiden

Klinkert W (2013a) Defending neutrality. The Netherlands prepares for war, 1900–1925. Brill Publishers, Leiden
Klinkert W (2013b) A Spy's Paradise? German espionage in the Netherlands 1914–1918. Journal for Intelligence History 12(1):21–35
Klinkert W, Kruizinga S, Moeyes P (2014) Nederland neutraal. De Eerste Wereldoorlog 1914–1918. Boom, Amsterdam
Koblank P (2006) Der Venlo-Zwischenfall. Britische Geheimagenten am 9.11.1939 entführt. http://www.venlo-zwischenfall.de/ Accessed 31 March 2015
Landau H (1934) All's fair. GP Putman & Sons, New York
Nater JP (1984) Het Venlo incident. Donker, Rotterdam
Sanders ML (1982) British propaganda during the First World War. MacMillan, London
Smeets J (2011) Marius van Houten. Boom, Amsterdam
van Blankenstein E (1999) M. van Blankenstein. SDU, The Hague
van Esch J (2014) A Finger in the Pie. PhD, University of Amsterdam
van Gent T (2005) Majoor GJ Sas was geen Cassandra. In: Enthoven V, Acda G, Bon A (eds) Een saluut van 26 schoten. Liber amicorum aangeboden aan Ger Teitler. Bataafsche Leeuw, Amsterdam (ed)
van Gent T (2009) Het falen van de Nederlandse neutraliteit. Bataafsche Leeuw, Amsterdam
van Tuyll H (2001) The Netherlands and World War I. Brill Publishers, Leiden
Verbeet GJB (2014) 1914–1918. Moeilijke jaren voor de beide Limburgen. Libero, Maastricht
Verhoeyen E (2011) Spionnen aan de achterdeur. Maklu, Antwerpen

Author Biography

Wim Klinkert, Professor of Military History at the University of Amsterdam and at the Faculty of Military Sciences of The Netherlands Defence Academy. He holds a doctoral degree in Dutch History from Leiden University (1992). Klinkert has published widely about Dutch military history in the 19th and 20th century, and on the history of military education. His current research focus is the First World War and the Inter-war Years. With Herman Amersfoort he co-edited *Small States in the Age of Total War* (2011) and is the author of *Defending Neutrality. The Netherlands prepares for War, 1900–1925* (2013) and (with Samuël Kruizinga and Paul Moeyes) *Nederland Neutraal. De Eerste Wereldoorlog 1914–1918* (2014).

Chapter 3
Intelligence and the Sino-Indian War of 1962

Prem Mahadevan

Abstract The 1962 war between India and China was marked by lapses in intelligence performance on the part of the defeated country, India. These lapses originated from resource constraints and lack of analytical experience. A civilian agency with a policing culture was tasked with collecting and assessing military intelligence. The result was an inability to appreciate the profound impact that subtle differences in Chinese domestic calculations and military postures could have on Beijing's readiness to escalate hostilities.

Keywords India · China · Aksai Chin and Arunachal Pradesh · Organizational culture · Intelligence failure

Contents

P. Mahadevan (✉)
The Global Security Team, Center for Security Studies,
Eidgenössische Technische Hochschule, Zurich, Switzerland
e-mail: mahadevan@sipo.gess.ethz.ch

F. Baudet et al. (eds.), *Perspectives on Military Intelligence from the First World War to Mali*, DOI 10.1007/978-94-6265-183-8_3

3.1 Introduction

How and why did Indian Intelligence misread Chinese strategic intentions in the months preceding the Sino-Indian War of 1962? This chapter concludes that threat assessments were based on patchy information, which was interpreted according to an outdated paradigm. The result was a military defeat from whose shadow India has not yet emerged. Even while allowing for subsequent improvement in intelligence collection systems, the ease with which New Delhi sleepwalked into disaster deserves attention. The Sino-Indian War demonstrated the dangers of leaving military intelligence analysis to civilian experts who are unable to comprehend the operational implications of the information they have received.[1] It serves to mitigate any argument for fusing military and civilian intelligence agencies, even at the analytical and assessment levels, and suggests instead that military intelligence ought to remain distinct.

It is necessary to first situate the timeframe of this study within the larger Sino-Indian conflict. Relations between India and China had steadily deteriorated for three years prior to 1962, and loose concerns about war were already being articulated on both sides. Thus, no one was surprised by the outbreak of armed clashes along the disputed border between the two countries. What stunned the Indian security establishment was the alacrity with which China escalated a localized border dispute to the level of a serious military conflict. In opting for such escalation, Beijing demonstrated that contrary to the preconceived notions of the Indian political elite (at the time consisting overwhelmingly of the leftist-inclined Congress party), China was prepared to run the gauntlet with both Cold War superpowers, the United States and the Soviet Union, as well as seriously jeopardise its past cordial relations with India. Why, despite knowing that China had developed aggressive intentions by the summer of 1962, did Indian Intelligence massively underestimate the scale of the military offensive that occurred in October–November of that year? Here, we focus primarily on this question.

An alternative approach might have been to merely look at 'Intelligence' as a catchall theme regarding the 1962 War. There has long been a controversy about whether India or China initiated hostilities. A 1970 book by the Australian journalist Neville Maxwell, titled India's China War, squarely blamed New Delhi for the conflict. Citing a secret Indian military report, Maxwell asserted that gullible politicians, influenced by incompetent generals and belligerent spymasters, plunged headlong into a confrontation with a restrained (and quite reasonable) China. On the other hand, a top Indian official (considered a leading China analyst within the intelligence community) told this author in 2008 that Maxwell had been personally cultivated by Chinese premier Chou En-Lai as a political and propaganda asset. This officer insisted that Maxwell artfully used wordplay in his book to weave a contrived narrative that whitewashed Beijing's own duplicity.

---

[1] On various aspects of Indian intelligence before and during the 1962 war see: Mahadevan 2008, 2011; Hoffmann 1972 and, controversially, Maxwell 2000.

In my view, Maxwell's readiness to give China the benefit of doubt regarding its intentions and actions along the border, while simultaneously assigning the most malevolent of motives to New Delhi, casts doubts on his objectivity. He does not look into the thesis, subsequently advanced by some scholars, that it was actually Chinese misreading of Indian intentions towards Tibet which caused Beijing to launch an unnecessary war.[2] If there was a failure of Indian Intelligence in 1962, there might just as well have been a parallel failure of Chinese Intelligence. The war was not won by the better-informed side, but by the side with the stronger Army. Nevertheless, Maxwell's book remains a good example of how it is difficult to separate the question of 'intelligence failure' from larger issues of political complacency and military inexperience, when analysing the reasons for India's defeat in 1962.

Rather than wade into a political and bureaucratic quagmire, and attribute blame for the overall Indian defeat, this chapter limits the scope of its survey to a brief period just before the fighting broke out in October 1962. It does so in the hope that such a timeframe would allow its conclusions to be tested for analytical rigour, instead of being instrumentalized in a polemical debate. Undoubtedly, India misread Chinese long-term intentions as early as the 1950 Occupation of Tibet, and believed erroneously that China would not wish to claim further territories that lay within India's direct control.

It is not clear however, whether such a misreading can be attributed to an 'intelligence failure'. Nor is it clear whether the Indian civilian or military intelligence apparatus was to blame for failing to track the accretion of Chinese military power in contested areas of the Sino-Indian border. Almost four decades after the 1962 War, in 1999 a similar controversy erupted over the failure to detect Pakistani military incursions in the Kargil sector of Jammu and Kashmir. Although the Kargil Crisis was subjected to a detailed and publicized review by both governmental and non-governmental experts, the question of whether it represented a 'failure' of Indian Intelligence is still an explosive one, even accounting for the usually cordial relations between civilian intelligence agencies and the Indian military.

Specifically, this chapter examines reports by the Indian Intelligence Bureau (IB) over the period September 1961–September 1962. It tracks changes in the inferential slant of threat assessments, to illustrate that contrary to conventional belief that the 1962 Indian intelligence failure was one of analysis rather than collection as the reputed Indian defence expert K. Subrahmanyam and the Israeli scholar Yaacov Vertzberger have argued, India's warning failure occurred as much due to inadequate collection as flawed analysis.[3] Although basic reporting on Chinese troop deployments and pre-operational manoeuvres was sound, the quality of coverage weakened once consumer requirements crossed into the realm of

[2] Hoffman 2006, pp. 182–183.

[3] Subrahmanyam and Monteiro 2005, p. 72. Vertzberger 1984, p. 196. It needs to be mentioned however, that Mr. Subrahmanyam subsequently distanced himself from his earlier findings in an interview with the author on 7 September 2008. He claimed to have developed a view that the failure extended to both collection and analysis, which would fit the argument of this chapter.

current and estimative intelligence. The IB could not predict what would happen next, and it avoided answering the most important question of all: What were the Chinese war aims?

The chapter is divided into three parts. Part I outlines the controversy that has dogged the IB's perceived role in the events of 1962. It also describes the agency's handicaps while tracking political developments in China. Part II looks at the assumptions and informational content that shaped IB assessments during the 12 months preceding the War. Finally, part III examines why these assumptions were flawed, and what essential data was missing from the Indian intelligence picture.

To briefly orientate readers: the Sino-Indian conflict arose from a border dispute over two large chunks of territory (see Fig. 3.1). In the north, the remote Aksai Chin region (adjacent to the India-Pakistan-China tri-junction, Fig. 3.2) is administered by China but claimed by India. In the east, the province of Arunachal Pradesh (adjacent to the India-Burma-China tri-junction, Fig. 3.3) is formally administered by India but claimed by China. Aksai Chin is very sparsely populated, while Arunachal Pradesh has a large tribal population and a correspondingly heavier presence of civilian government officials.

3.2 An Experience of Enduring Relevance

The Indian intelligence community in 1962 consisted, for all practical purposes, of a single agency responsible for domestic, foreign and military intelligence. This was the Intelligence Bureau. Set up in 1887 by British colonial authorities to carry out political surveillance within India, it was a professional but vastly under-resourced organization. Although its strength at the time of formation remains unclear, what is known is that even three decades afterwards, it would obtain the vast bulk of its raw data from police forces across India. Its own intelligence collection capability was quite limited. Only with the partial democratization of Indian politics in 1935, did the colonial government see fit to upgrade the IB's agent recruiting infrastructure, in order to ensure that the newly elected Indian legislatures did not act against the interests of the British crown.

Previously, when British control over India had been direct and absolute, there had been little need for a strong, centralized domestic intelligence apparatus. During the first half of the 20th century it had struggled to keep track of the burgeoning Indian nationalist movement, whose success led to Indian independence in 1947. The IB was an anonymous casualty of the colonial power transfer—crippled by the departure of experienced British officers, it was taken over by Indian police officials who had no training in high-level intelligence management.

This in itself was bad enough, but an executive decision in 1951 to make the agency additionally responsible for border security and foreign intelligence stretched its already limited operational capacity beyond breaking point. The agency ended up being responsible for all domestic and foreign intelligence activities (civilian and military), plus having to take charge of border policing, a job which

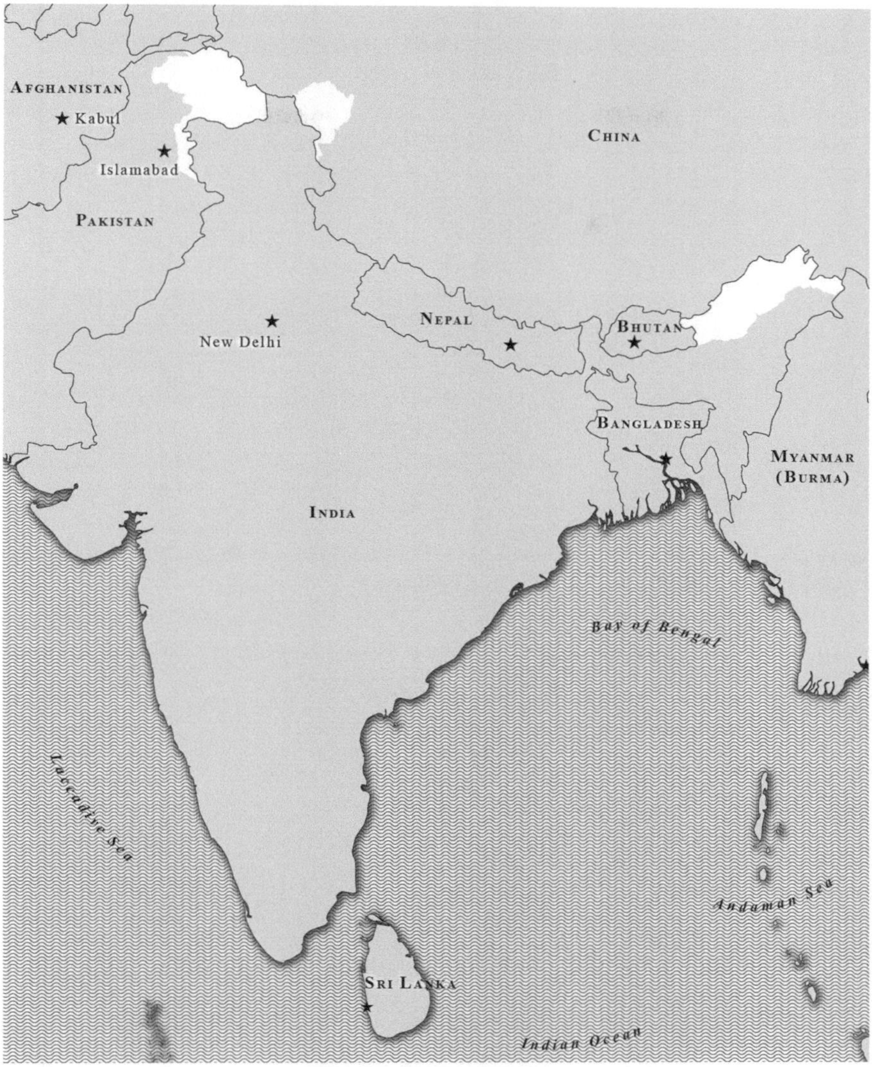

Figure 3.1 The Sino-Indian border (disputed areas are shown in detail). *Source* P. Mahadevan

required high-visibility operations and logically, would have been at odds with intelligence work. But so severe was the security deficit of the newly created Indian state that the IB had no option except to accept its expanded mandate.[4]

Part of the problem lay with the incipient intelligence culture of India, which was taking shape along the lines of the United Kingdom. According to this,

[4] Askew 2002, p. 201.

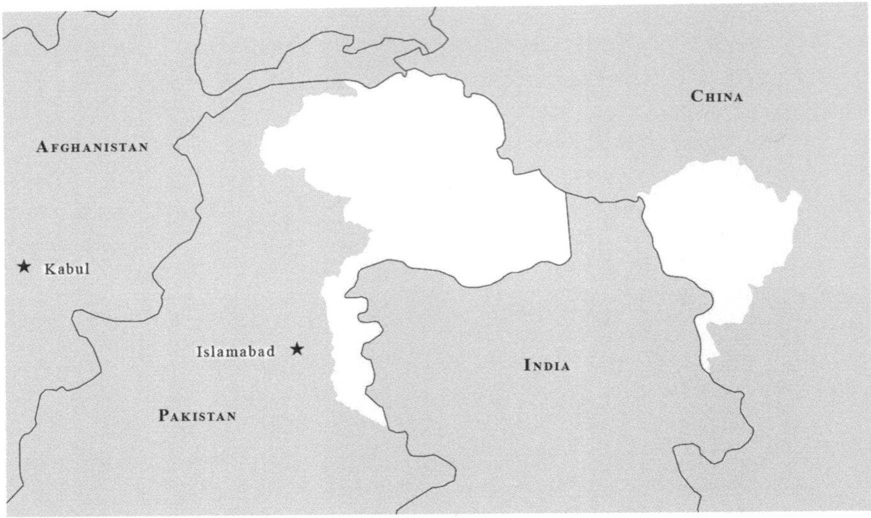

Figure 3.2 Aksai Chin (*right* administered by China and claimed by India). Also shown—areas disputed between Pakistan and India. *Source* P. Mahadevan

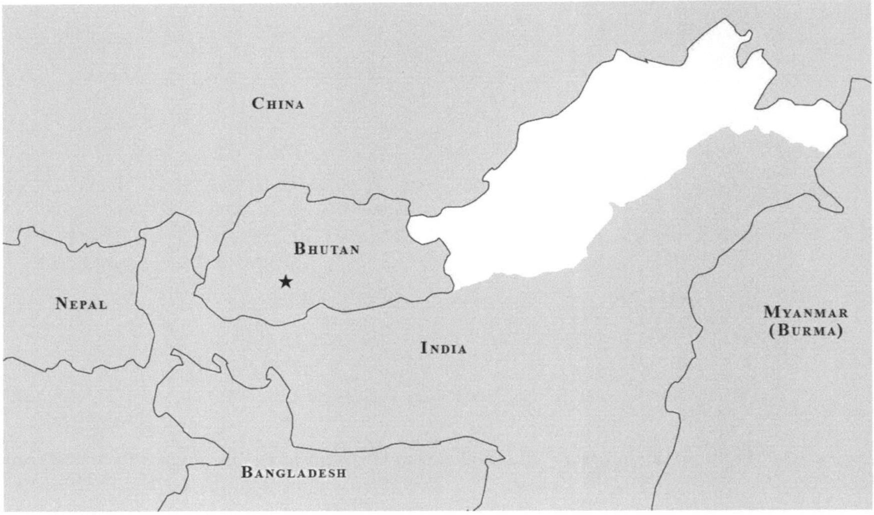

Figure 3.3 Arunachal Pradesh (administered by India and claimed by China). *Source* P. Mahadevan

'intelligence' was merely one more channel of sensitive information among others, with assessment being an extrinsic part of the production process.[5] (The US system in contrast, tended to treat intelligence as a guide for decision-making based on

[5] Davies 2004, pp. 499–500.

all-rounded assessment that was presented to policy elites in its full complexity.) The IB's operations-minded leadership thus placed much lower emphasis on rigorous analysis of data, than on agent running.

This would not have been a problem if the agency had been confined to a narrow range of tasks and targets. But its multiple responsibilities pitchforked it to the apex of the national intelligence assessment process. The agency was officially under the Indian Ministry of Home Affairs, and thus reported regularly to the Home Minister, the second-most powerful politician in India. In reality, however, the Director IB had an exclusive right of direct access to the Prime Minister at all hours—the only civilian or military official in India to enjoy such a privilege, which continues to this day. Thus, the agency (especially due to its wide range of security responsibilities) had a de facto monopoly on policy briefings. It is not surprising, then, that the IB's institutional view on national security questions became the mind-set of even the supposedly independent Joint Intelligence Committee (another institution patterned after its British counterpart).[6]

Although the JIC in theory was supposed to supervise the IB and evaluate its assessments for accuracy, in conjunction with other intelligence agencies, so weak was its authority, and so strong was the IB's, that any attempt at objective evaluation of IB reports was farcical. Such outsized dominance was only to be expected —a multi-jurisdictional intelligence monolith commanded more political and bureaucratic weight than a specialized agency focused on a narrow subject domain. However, the downside of this was that an environment of forced collegiality appeared in Indian Intelligence. The system became vulnerable to the vagaries of groupthink, with limited external willingness to question IB estimates since other agencies lacked the same political access. It had a further problem of not being able to focus on key intelligence questions like China's operational readiness for artillery and infantry combat—the kind of encounters most relevant in mountain warfare—instead adopting a broad-brush approach to security analysis which conflated topics across specializations and jurisdictions.

The problem was particularly acute with regard to military affairs. Although the IB was put in charge of this issue—the Indian Army having yet to build up an endogenous intelligence capability until the late 1960s, after the 1965 India-Pakistan War—being an exclusively civilian agency the IB had neither competence nor credibility in military intelligence.

In tracing the Indian warning failure of 1962, I find that the expertise gap between civilian and military intelligence analysis played a crucial role.[7] The Indian political establishment had burdened an under-resourced civilian agency with

---

[6] As one writer has noted, organizational mindsets 'become an Achilles heel to a professional strategist or intelligence analyst when they become out of date because of new international dynamics'. This is precisely what happened to the IB in 1962. George 2004, p. 387.

[7] Interestingly, this problem seems to have been noted right from the time civilian intelligence agencies were created in the UK prior to the First World War. Bennett 2014, p. 55.

tracking a highly fluid external threat environment. The lessons learnt from the Sino-Indian War demonstrate that military intelligence cannot be automatically subsumed within a 'grand strategic' paradigm which situates current events against the background of an analytical framework based on policymakers' hunches.

Indeed, one needs to study the military-operational dynamics of a regional power balance quite independently of its diplomatic-policy dynamics. Perhaps most tellingly of all, India's experience in 1962 provides a counter-example to the Israeli warning failure that preceded the 1973 Yom Kippur War. On the latter occasion, military intelligence had dominated threat analysis to the point of impinging on civilian decision-making prerogatives.[8] Although the Israeli example is used to illustrate the confusion that 'militarization' of civilian intelligence can engender amidst political debates, the Indian case of 1962 cautions against 'civilizing' military intelligence to the point where it is no longer in touch with operational reality.

3.3 Part I: Know Your Adversary, Know Yourself: What Really Was the 'Warning Failure'?

After the 1962 War, India accused China of 'betrayal'.[9] New Delhi felt that at a diplomatic level it had done much to rehabilitate Beijing's image in the international system, following the communist revolution of 1949, the invasion of Tibet in 1950 and the Chinese intervention in Korea. Indian diplomatic intercession had been crucial in forcing the West to recognize China as a legitimate player in the Korean War, despite the United States being furious about Beijing's intervention on behalf of North Korea. India also had championed China's case for a permanent seat in the United Nations Security Council. Against this backdrop, China's initiation of hostilities on 20 October 1962 and the stunning defeat that India suffered exactly a month later were incomprehensible to the Indian government. Indian policy makers could only make sense of this chain of events by accusing Beijing of treachery and rank ingratitude.

Yet, the flashpoints for conflict had become evident at least three years previously, in 1959. That was when the Sino-Indian border dispute, a legacy of frontiers inherited from the British Empire, produced its first fatalities. Ten Indian border guards were killed by Chinese troops, and news leaked out that China had occupied

---

[8] Pascovich 2014, pp. 236–237.

[9] The words most commonly featured in Indian discourse on the 1962 war are 'betrayal' and 'aggression'. Regimental museums in the Indian Army for instance, refer to soldiers killed during the 1962 War as 'martyrs to Chinese aggression'. Bhola Nath Mullik, a former IB chief who headed the agency between 1950 and 1964 and thus played a decisive role in the events described here, later saw fit to subtitle one volume of his memoirs as 'The Chinese Betrayal'. Mullik 1971.

roughly 38,000 km^2 of territory in Aksai Chin. Even more outrageous was the revelation that Beijing was laying claim to almost the entire state of Arunachal Pradesh on the far eastern edge of the border, amounting to another 90,000 km^2.

There was another dynamic, hidden far from public view, which contributed to the deterioration in Sino-Indian relations. Each side suspected the other of secretly collaborating with its worst enemy. In India's case, the Intelligence Bureau believed that China had made overtures to Pakistan, as far back as 1955, with the long-term intention of militarily hedging against India's rise.[10] This assessment of a latent Sino-Pakistani axis (which actually was validated after the 1962 Sino-Indian War) played a significant but underestimated role in colouring Indian threat assessments prior to hostilities. On the Chinese side, the communist party leadership believed that India was sponsoring the rebellion which had erupted in Tibet in 1959. At a Politburo meeting on 17 March 1959, less than a week after the Tibetan rebellion had begun, Chinese premier Chou En Lai speculated that the rebels were being supported by India. He advanced a hypothesis that the revolt was being directed from the Indian border town of Kalimpong, by American and British agents working in collusion with Indian authorities. This view quickly gained currency among other top leaders, including Chairman Mao Zedong.[11]

Although the Chinese suspicion was unfounded, it contributed to the decision to attack India when the border conflict escalated, with both sides jockeying for control of territory in Aksai Chin. The Sino-Indian War of 1962 was not a bolt from the blue; it was foreseen by Indian Intelligence, which nevertheless, was still surprised by its occurrence. How could this happen?

3.3.1 A Warning Ignored

As border tensions simmered during the summer of 1962, the Indian Intelligence Bureau issued a warning note, dated 8 June, that Beijing planned to initiate war during the coming fall.[12] The note was dispatched to top decision-makers in the Indian security establishment (routinely considered as the Ministry of Defence as well as Army Headquarters) including, allegedly, the Prime Minister himself.

Many years later, after India's defeat, this solitary missive was cited to disprove claims of 'intelligence failure'. Yet, for 8 months prior to issuing this warning, and even for 4 months afterward, the IB advocated forward deployment of Indian troops along the border. By doing so, it may have inadvertently placed India in a politically and militarily untenable position.

The forward deployment was cited by Beijing as a casus belli. Moreover, it dispersed Indian combat capability over a wide front, leaving the Indian Army

[10] Mullik 1971, p. 230.

[11] Chen 2006, pp. 85–86.

[12] Khanduri 2006, p. 323.

exposed to a sudden, locally concentrated attack by an enemy with a far superior logistical network and a 5:1 numerical advantage. In effect, the IB's assertive policy recommendations appear to have both triggered the war and caused the Indian defeat—a damning hypothesis which has since been accepted by most scholars on the conflict, such as Maxwell.[13]

Since 1962, the agency has been blamed for having urged the Indian political leadership onto a confrontational path vis-à-vis China; one that made military humiliation inevitable. There are two flaws with this argument. First, the IB was not alone in arguing for greater assertiveness along the border. Even senior Indian military officials had supported such a policy. Moreover, the Indian government could not afford to look weak to its electorate, who were incensed that China was occupying territory claimed by India.[14] Second, the IB kept up a steady stream of reports on Chinese military activity and noticed the force accretion that took place in the summer of 1962. So there was no failure of assessment when it came to the quantum of troops and firepower that Beijing fielded.

If specific warning of aggressive Chinese intentions was delivered in June, and followed by reports of increased war-readiness, where did the warning failure actually occur? Close examination of available evidence suggests that the IB had accurately assessed the probability of hostilities, but vastly underestimated their scale. The agency predicted armed clashes but incorrectly assumed that these would be localized. Rather than the outbreak of fighting, it was the extent to which Beijing was prepared to go in pursuit of its claims that stunned Delhi. Tactical reporting by the IB had been accurate (in that it was factually correct, if not always timely and specific), but it was analytically weak. Strategic reporting was crippled by shortcomings which cancelled out the benefits of good ground-level sources who provided detailed information that was not fused together in time to revise national-level threat assessments. Thus, such threat assessments were unable to grasp the severity of Indian military weakness, which in turn produced a poor combat performance.

3.3.2 Why Did India Underestimate the Chinese Offensive?

At the root of India's warning failure lay politico-military hubris; a belief that the Indian Army of 1962 was far more tactically sophisticated than it actually was.[15]

---

[13] Cited in Hoffmann 1972, pp. 970–971.

[14] Guruswamy 2006, pp. 224–226.

[15] Many years later, an IB official who had drafted assessments of Chinese intentions in 1962 observed that warning analysis must also extend to studying the defensive capabilities of one's own side. He noted that although this task was normally outside the mandate of intelligence agencies, it was necessary in order to prepare policymakers for dealing with the aftermath of a shock defeat. Dave 2006, p. 32.

For roughly a year prior to the war, a view had taken hold among the Indian strategic elite (including the IB leadership) that China recognized this 'reality' and was constrained from escalating the border conflict. The likely source of this delusion was the success of Indian military forces in occupying the Portuguese colonial enclave of Goa, on India's western coast, in December 1961. The operation lasted two days and was carried out with minimal casualties, largely because the vastly outnumbered Portuguese garrison mounted only a token resistance. Senior Indian generals jumped at the opportunity to grandstand before the press, little knowing that less than a year later, they would be defeated by a far more capable force than the hapless Portuguese.[16]

The Indian establishment found support for its views in the fact that the Chinese did not exploit their evidently superior military strength to seize more territory in Aksai Chin. For why else would they restrain themselves? For the past 3 years, India had viewed itself as a victim of creeping aggression in Aksai Chin, wherein Chinese troops had moved into areas that were claimed by both countries but administered by neither. Once the troops were firmly in place, the contested area became de facto Chinese territory. No similar manoeuvres had been attempted in Arunachal Pradesh, because the Indian administrative and military presence there was much more solid, and because Chinese troops had no foothold in the province.

Furthermore, according to the contemporary Indian reading of events as later explained by former IB chief Bhola Nath Mullik, by autumn 1961 the Chinese had demonstrated an intention to encroach on more vacant spaces in Aksai Chin. At stake was an additional 2000 km^2 of territory that India claimed but which remained unoccupied by either side. Whenever India had responded to Chinese advances by establishing a military outpost in this territory, Chinese troops would avoid attacking it. The unspoken (and incorrect) inference drawn by India was that China knew that it had no legitimate basis to impose territorial claims upon a region controlled by India, and therefore would not pursue a false and fabricated claim in the face of physical opposition. The difference in Chinese behaviour between the two disputed territories (Aksai Chin and Arunachal Pradesh) also seemed to suggest that China was acting out of purely opportunistic motives. Thus, on 26 September 1961, the IB recommended that the Indian Army establish more outposts in Aksai Chin.[17] The agency believed that Beijing was intent on further testing India's resolve, while stopping short of full-blown war.

It was at this point that the IB's analytical shortcomings surfaced. Its leadership, fed by optimistic human intelligence reports obtained from Tibetan itinerant agents (who wished to secure Indian assistance in liberating their homeland from Chinese rule), did not realize that the sheer magnitude of Chinese military strength gave Beijing an offensive option that reduced escalation risks to a 'tolerable' level.[18]

---

[16] Verghese 2012.

[17] Palit 1991, pp. 97–98.

[18] CIA 1963a, b, p. 32.

China could leverage its superior force posture along the border to initiate devastating local assaults, thereby goading India into mounting a counterattack that would serve as a pretext for a general offensive. This was exactly what Beijing had done in 1950, when it intervened in the Korean War. Initially sending 'volunteers' to skirmish with UN forces and lure them forward, China used the subsequent counterattack as an excuse to launch a full-scale invasion a month later that quickly routed UN troops.[19] The 1962 Sino-Indian War unfolded in an almost identical manner, down to the time gap between the two offensive phases.

An IB analyst with a sense of military history might have foreseen the possibility of China reusing its Korean stratagem against India. There were no such analysts, as is usually the case in any politically driven intelligence organization. The agency's officer cadre consisted of career policemen with no expertise in military intelligence. They were more accustomed to thinking in terms of legality (hence, the disproportionate emphasis on the supposed 'legitimacy' of India's stand in the border dispute, vis-à-vis a more pragmatic and militarily powerful China). Moreover, until 1951, the IB was not even tasked with monitoring strategic trends beyond India's borders, focusing instead on domestic security. In the years since, its capacity to collect intelligence in Tibet had been increased, as a result of fresh personnel recruitment and new border observation posts. But this did not compensate for lack of analytical expertise in military affairs, especially logistics. Reportedly, all that the IB had by way of a military analysis cell was a single mid-ranking Army officer, assisted by a warrant officer.[20]

Failure to grasp the force imbalance along the border meant that the IB worked primarily according to geopolitical rather than military logic. (Geopolitical logic meant that the IB looked at the Sino-Indian border dispute from the largest possible framework, that of bipolar super-power competition in the Cold War, and India's privileged role as leader of the Non-Aligned Movement in this competition. Military logic on the other hand, would have alerted the agency to ground realities along the border. It would have indicated that Indian Army defences were too weak to withstand any serious attack, thus allowing China to win an easy victory while running a relatively low risk.)

In the geopolitical realm, it simply did not make sense for China to attack India for the sake of Aksai Chin, a desolate area far from both countries' economic and cultural power centres.[21] But in assuming that the Chinese shared this view, New Delhi made a mistake by treating Aksai Chin as the sole area of contention. It chose to believe that the Chinese claim to Arunachal Pradesh was intended as a

---

[19] Grabo 2004, p. 114.

[20] Interview of former senior IB officer by the author. The officer later transferred to the Research and Analysis Wing (India's foreign intelligence service) upon the latter's creation in 1968. Interview date: 25 July 2008, location withheld.

[21] Bhargava 1964, pp. 64–65.

negotiating tactic and nothing more.[22] While this may have been true, it also masked the real depth of concern that Beijing felt about the border dispute—to the Chinese, the conflict with India was part of a larger strategic squeeze that was intensifying on multiple fronts. The most prominent of these were Taiwan and the Sino-Soviet border, where another territorial dispute had just erupted, leaving Beijing feeling encircled and more inclined towards using force.

India had poor strategic intelligence on the mind-set of the Chinese leadership. It depended heavily on estimates furnished by American and British agencies on this issue. These agencies in turn, drew the bulk of their data from technical collection which was geared to suit Western requirements. Since neither the US nor the UK faced a military threat from China, their assessments tended to be more generic than was sufficient for Delhi's needs (for instance, Sino-Soviet relations were a particular area of focus). But India had no means of independently monitoring Chinese strategic thinking, especially Beijing's view of the Tibetan rebellion. Starting in 1950, when the Indian consulate in Xinjiang had been closed down, New Delhi had steadily lost access to various levels of Chinese officialdom. Indian trade agents in Tibet had their movements restricted and their freedom to report to Delhi was constrained.[23] Indian diplomats in Beijing were denied appointments with top Chinese officials. They thus missed out the sense of paranoia which had gripped the Chinese leadership following the Sino-Soviet split and the disastrous failure of the 'Great Leap Forward'. And in the summer of 1962, they did not know that Mao was seeking to deflect some of the intra-elite criticism that was building up against him personally, towards an external target.

3.4 Part II: Beijing's 'Crisis of Nerves'

The IB's warning of 8 June 1962 was the clearest forecast that was ever produced about Chinese strategic intentions in the months preceding the War. It was partly based on a source report that a top Chinese diplomat had recently said that Beijing would launch a military offensive, if India did not stop its troop build-up in Aksai Chin.[24] By this time, the agency was so strongly committed to the troop build-up that it did not caution against discontinuing this. Soon thereafter, the agency received another, independent report from Pakistan. According to this second source, Pakistani leaders were considering a joint attack on India, alongside China. The attack would take the form of a conventional assault on the plains of Punjab,

---

[22] CIA (1963b) central Intelligence Agency—Freedom of Information Act Electronic Reading Room, accessed online at http://www.foia.cia.gov/sites/default/files/document_conversions/14/polo-08.pdf on 28 July 2014, p. 18 and p. 41.

[23] Arpi 2004, p. 128 and Chakravarti 1961, pp. 56, 60.

[24] Malhotra 2005, p. xxxii.

while Chinese troops used guerrilla tactics in the Himalayas to keep Indian forces pinned down.

It is unknown whether the IB sent the report from Pakistan to the Ministry of Defence and Army Headquarters, as it had done with the first report about Chinese intentions. In any case, viewed with hindsight, this second IB report may have crucially misled Indian assessments about the scale and thrust of China's autumn offensive. For it implied that the attack's focus would be primarily on Aksai Chin. Logically, if China went to war, it would want to do so in an area where it could expect assistance from a willing ally located nearby. With its desire to seize Kashmir, Pakistan could help China in the north but its meagre forces in East Pakistan (now Bangladesh) would be hard-pressed to provide comparable support to a Chinese attack on Arunachal Pradesh. In any case, there seemed to be little chance of a large-scale Chinese offensive in Arunachal Pradesh, because Indian troops were firmly entrenched in the province. So, the focus of Indian military preparations went into Aksai Chin, even as China secretly prepared for a lightning strike on both Aksai Chin and Arunachal Pradesh.

This still begs the question: after June 1962, why did India persist with its forward deployment in Aksai Chin, despite knowing that China was prepared to go to war? There are two possible explanations. First, New Delhi might have thought that if a joint attack did indeed materialize from China and Pakistan, it would need as much military manpower in the combat theatre as possible. In addition, strengthening its force posture in Aksai Chin might actually help deter a collusive attack. Put simply, the risk of provoking war might have appeared smaller than the risk of inaction. Second, although China posed a military threat, Indian policy-makers may have doubted that the threat would grow to its fullest potential.

From subsequent research, it seems that they banked heavily on the presumption that larger global forces, coupled with China's dire economic situation, would significantly constrain its ability to attack India at a level beyond minor skirmishes.[25] While Beijing enjoyed an enormous military advantage on the ground, practical sense suggested that it would be cautious about employing this. Any attack could thus be expected to be a localized one.

What the IB did not know, was that Beijing was quietly breaking free of precisely those same constraints that New Delhi was counting on. There were three such constraints:

In the first place, mention should be made of Soviet dissuasion. Indian policy-makers assumed that Moscow would exert pressure on Beijing to hold back from escalating hostilities. As a leading member of the Non-Aligned Movement, India was a key swing state in the geopolitical battle between East and West. Just as Washington wanted to avoid antagonizing New Delhi, so did Moscow. Indian strategists assumed that this would translate into indirect leverage over Beijing. They did not realise that as a result of the Sino-Soviet split, China was slowly becoming a third pole in the Cold War, distinct from the Soviet Union. By the

[25] Mullik 1971, pp. 329–333, 410.

summer of 1962, the Chinese communist leadership had even begun to view the Soviet Union as a bigger security threat than the United States. Soviet diplomats in Xinjiang were being expelled for allegedly aiding separatist rebels and Moscow had publicly committed to providing India with Mig-21 fighter aircraft. Through its ideologically-tinted lenses, Beijing viewed the latter decision in particular as betrayal of a fellow socialist state (China) in favour of a Western-leaning lackey (India). By going to war with New Delhi, it would demonstrate its contempt for Soviet 'revisionism'.[26]

Secondly, there was the Taiwanese invasion threat; throughout the first half of 1962, Beijing had been worried about an invasion by Chinese Nationalist forces based on Taiwan. Its worst fear was that of a two-front attack by Nationalists in the east and India in the west. Yet, tellingly, the official communist press made no reference to this security concern during the months when it was most intense, probably due to state censorship. Only after the invasion threat subsided in June 1962, did Chinese newspapers begin cautioning Indian policymakers not to take advantage of Beijing's preoccupation with Taiwan and push more troops into Aksai Chin.[27] The IB, which like many intelligence agencies culled its reports on Chinese official thinking from open sources, did not realise that these warnings pertained to a 'crisis of nerves' that Chinese leaders had undergone some months previously, and which the latter no longer felt paralysed by. Instead, the agency seems to have mistakenly assessed the media commentary as being indicative of on-going Chinese policy concerns in the latter half of 1962. By this time, Beijing had already resolved to freeze the status quo along the border through a swift, decisive military campaign.

Lastly, China faced serious economic difficulties. The spectacular failure of China's Great Leap Forward was known to Indian and Western intelligence analysts, even though its scale remained a secret in China itself. On 25 October 1961, Tibetan guerrillas had seized military documents totalling 1600 pages. US analysts poring over these learnt a great deal about morale problems among Chinese soldiers. Food shortages on military bases, coupled with families starving back home and a lack of combat experience among junior officers had made for a fragile disciplinary situation. It is likely that a summary of the main findings was passed to the Indian IB. This would explain why the latter remained so confident that any Chinese action in Aksai Chin would stop well short of its maximum potential, since China was in no state to precipitate an all-out war. The agency did not realise that Chinese Chairman Mao was a firm believer in the principle of externalising blame for his own policy failures, by rallying the population against a foreign adversary.[28] The same conditions that made Indian analysts believe that war was unlikely, made Chinese policymakers believe that it was necessary for their own political survival.

---

[26] Karnow 1990, pp. 438–439; Brugger 1981, pp. 240, 255.

[27] Dhar 2009, pp. 132–139.

[28] In 1958, Mao had precipitated an international crisis by ordering artillery bombardment of two small islands in the Taiwan Strait. He later explained the logic of this action: 'A tense situation helps to mobilize people, in particular those who are backward, those middle-of-the-roaders'. Quoted in Dikotter 2011, p. 45.

Despite its assessment that a major conflict with China was unlikely, as the summer wore on, the IB observed a build-up of Chinese forces across the border. It was able to do this through well-placed human sources within the Tibetan resistance forces. These sources provided the agency with updates about the issuance of assault rifles to Chinese frontline battalions, the movement of artillery and reserve brigades to forward areas, the visits of senior officers to such areas, and collective training sessions. All indicators pointed towards a Chinese attack in the autumn. Small wonder then, that the then IB chief Mullik claimed in his memoirs that there was 'no blind spot about Chinese preparations in Tibet'.[29] What he did also mention is equally important: that there was a large time-lag in agent reporting. A human source deep inside Tibet could take up to four months to cross the country safely and speak to his handler on the Sino-Indian border. Of 77 intelligence posts that existed along the border, only half were equipped with wireless sets. The remainder had to do with an inefficient courier system, which generated an additional month's delay in reporting. This meant that even if IB data was generally accurate (up to 75%, as later claimed by Mullik), it was not timely enough to satisfy the immediate needs of Indian military commanders.[30] Neither was it often specific enough to provide a focal point for intense combat preparation. There was no mention of attack time or place, in part because the Chinese only drew up a detailed campaign plan just before the first attack was due to begin. As a result, it was not until the latter half of September 1962 that a realization began to dawn upon Indian planners that China might have been preparing for a much larger offensive than they had envisaged.

3.5 Part III: A Little Knowledge Is a Dangerous Thing…

Between May and September 1962, the IB based its assessments on a paradigm that, unknown to it, was fast becoming obsolete. The agency's weakness in military intelligence information and analysis contributed significantly to this misinterpretation. Because India only had enough airlift capacity to deploy a single brigade at short notice, Indian planners assumed that China, with its weak air force infrastructure in Tibet, would be worse off.[31] They did not weigh this assumption against intelligence reports that Beijing had built a border roads system that was vastly superior to its Indian counterpart. China actually had the capacity to rush several divisions into the combat zone if necessary, but by the time this became clear to Indian analysts, the window of opportunity for making effective war preparations had closed.

---

[29] Mullik 1971, p. 195.

[30] Mullik 1971, pp. 498–499.

[31] Dalvi 1969, p. 123.

From that point onwards, New Delhi tried to convince itself that because India had not provoked China, beyond deterring further Chinese expansionism in Aksai Chin, Beijing would not jeopardise bilateral relations by initiating a war. One school of thought, put forward by the Indian Army's Operations Directorate, held that China was merely buffering its defences along the border but would wait another 18 months to launch an offensive. This timeframe was based on an estimate that it would take China until at least 1964 to build a rail link between Tibet and the Han heartland and thus consolidate control over the troubled province.[32]

The war of October–November 1962 proved that China did not need a quiescent Tibet in order to inflict a localized but severe defeat on India. Much later, scholars would discover that Beijing had in fact acted partly out of its paranoid belief that India was secretly aiding Tibetan rebels.[33] The war had been intended as much as punishment to India for supporting the Tibetans, as to settle the border dispute. The Chinese leadership envisaged a short, sharp campaign that would achieve both results simultaneously. The actual planning for this campaign was only completed by 16 October 1962, 4 days before the first wave of Chinese attacks began on 20 October. In the following weeks, the biggest shock to New Delhi came not from the Chinese attack, but from the collapse of Indian defences.

3.5.1 Know Yourself, if You Cannot Know the Enemy

To understand why the war of 1962 remains a traumatic event for the Indian security establishment, it is necessary to look at how India had prepared to fight this war. Knowing that the Chinese army was far larger and led by battle-hardened generals, the Indian high command had planned to stage a rapid retreat within Arunachal Pradesh at the onset of hostilities. It expected the Chinese to over-stretch their supply lines while occupying the province, thereby opening themselves to a massive Indian counterattack. All this was based on a premise that a Sino-Indian War would last many months.

What actually happened was that the war began and ended in 31 days, with only 10 days of actual combat bracketing between the onset and closure of hostilities. For roughly 3 weeks in between, neither side made a move.[34] This hiatus led the Indian leadership to grow restive and abandon their original plan. They instead fell into the trap of launching an early and ill-prepared counterattack—exactly what the Chinese wanted. Having got an excuse to unleash its devastating second wave of

---

[32] Official 1962 War History, Ministry of Defence, Government of India, accessed at http://www.bharat-rakshak.com/LAND-FORCES/Army/History/1962War/PDF/1962Chapter10.pdf, on 28 July 2014, p. 430.

[33] Worthing 2007, pp. 165–166; Prasad Varma 1965, p. 113.

[34] Mehra 2007, p. 181.

offensive operations, the Chinese army routed its Indian counterpart with an ease that even surprised Beijing.

The Indian defeat stemmed from a gross underestimation of the capability gap and the intentions gap that existed between the two sides. Indian intelligence analysts had not fully appreciated the scale of China's operational-level advantages, preferring instead to focus on the grand strategic level. This was an understandable mistake: India held some real strategic advantages over China, such as an air force which was capable of reversing the tide of ground operations if used offensively. The Indian military and political leadership forgot their own airpower advantage during the course of the war, when panic gripped them as the Chinese advanced rapidly into Arunachal Pradesh. Unsure of Chinese intentions, and still focused on the paradigm that war with China would last many months, they decided not to commit the air force to a close air support role. In retrospect, this decision was a mistake, because it allowed the Chinese to accomplish their limited campaign objectives without hindrance from air interdiction.[35]

New Delhi could also count on swift and substantial replenishment of its war stocks from the West, while Moscow would be slower and more reluctant in aiding Beijing, due to the good state of Soviet-Indian relations. Focusing on these attributes helped conceal the degree to which Indian frontline forces were logistically and doctrinally unprepared to wage a war against a larger and better-organized foe.

On the issue of intentions, the IB did not understand the mentality of the Chinese leadership, beyond having a reflexive suspicion of anything communist. This stemmed from the agency's colonial past, when it had served the British Empire in suppressing communist networks across South Asia. The IB's top officers were experts on counter-subversion, but not on military affairs or Chinese politics.[36] They did not understand that a one-party state built around a personality cult was likely to make key decisions partly based on paranoia and a more mercurial worldview than a democracy like India.[37]

Taking a long view, they believed that China valued its international reputation too much to jeopardise it for a border dispute that affected neither country's vital regions. In the process, they overlooked the medium-term temptation that Indian military weakness had presented Beijing.

Most important of all, the Indian intelligence community did not understand that the structural conditions on which it had presaged its forecasts were changing. In May 1962, the US had dispatched bombers to Laos, as part of its effort to contain communism in East Asia. This led Indian analysts to believe that China would remain preoccupied with its eastern seaboard, and especially the threat of a Taiwanese invasion. They did not take serious note of the fact that in late June, Washington quietly gave two separate assurances to Beijing that it would not

---

[35] Sukumaran 2003, pp. 341–343.

[36] Bhat 1967, p. 66.

[37] Hudson 1957, pp. 181–182.

support a Taiwanese attack.[38] At a stroke, the entire basis of Indian military planning and intelligence assessment was nullified.

With its eastern coast now secure, Beijing turned its attention to the western border with India. Chinese policymakers were determined to eliminate any prospect of a two-front threat, by using the window of opportunity they had gained, to knock out India as a military challenger. Had the Indian intelligence community been populated by more experts on military history and logistics, it is possible that New Delhi would have been more aware of its own weakness. China realised that the Indian Army was not capable of fighting a fast-paced campaign, being instead caught up in the attritional mind-set of the British colonial army. It also realised that if war came, India would initially fight alone because its policy of non-alignment would leave it isolated.[39] Only if the war dragged on for too long, or was carried into the Indian heartland, was there a risk of Western intervention on the side of New Delhi. So Beijing planned for a short lightning campaign whose results would nevertheless be irreversible. The Indian intelligence community did not know the logic behind this campaign, and so was caught off-guard when China overran both Aksai China and Arunachal Pradesh in a matter of days rather than months, as had been anticipated.

3.6 The Professionalization of Indian Military Intelligence

Within 9 years of the 1962 debacle, the Indian Army staged a spectacular comeback when it defeated its Pakistani counterpart and thereby created a new nation, Bangladesh. The turnaround was due in part to the creation of a new agency in 1968, the Research and Analysis Wing (R&AW) exclusively responsible for foreign intelligence. R&AW was a civilian agency, like the IB, but was designed to take over the latter agency's mandate of tracking overseas threats. From its inception, the agency prioritized institutional relations with the military, ensuring that a senior armed forces officer could advise the R&AW chief on all matters pertaining to adversary war readiness assessments. This intra-organizational relationship, initially strong, slowly withered during the 1990s as the threat of Pakistan-sponsored cross-border terrorism blurred the conceptual boundaries between foreign and domestic intelligence, and conventional and unconventional threats. What resulted was a tactical surprise in the Kargil sector of the Indian-administered part of Jammu and Kashmir in 1999, when Pakistani soldiers disguised as irregular fighters crossed into Indian territory and seized several hilltops.

The acrimony that followed led to the creation of a new Defence Intelligence Agency (DIA) in 2002 for the collation of all military-related intelligence, as well as

[38] Palit 1991, pp. 160–161.

[39] Central Intelligence Agency 1964, p. v.

independent technical collection. Importantly, India remained averse to allowing its military officers to collect strategic intelligence in friendly third countries. New Delhi consciously avoided creating a behemoth like the Pakistani Inter Services Intelligence, for fear this would damage its image abroad. Civilian-military divides thus remained in the human intelligence sphere. Since 75% of the R&AW's output was concerned with political intelligence and only 25% with military topics, India lacked on-ground human assets within well-guarded installations on hostile foreign territory. The shortcoming became painfully obvious when Pakistan-sponsored terrorists attacked Mumbai in November 2008. For the first time, top-ranking Indian policymakers recognized that the civilian intelligence community lacked the operational capacity to undertake retaliatory covert action. The Army's Military Intelligence Directorate was thus encouraged to build up agent networks inside Pakistan that could hit terrorist groups. Meanwhile, the IB, which had returned to its original role of being a domestic intelligence agency, took responsibility for counterterrorism coordination within India.

The biggest lesson from 1962 was the need for specialized and professionalized analysis, supported by technically advanced collection systems. India's intelligence agencies have improved on both counts, although suggestions are sometimes made for a broader recruitment process, mainly into the civilian agencies, for the purpose of tracking emerging and complex threats. To my best knowledge, such specialized expertise is already being hired on a low-key, needs-driven basis, with the emphasis being mostly on quality control. Steeped in an Anglo-Saxon (and specifically British) tradition of relying on old-boy networks, India wishes to avoid unrestricted open market recruitment to its intelligence agencies. As the country faces growing assertiveness from a Sino-Pakistani military axis, that is far more developed than it was in 1962, its spying capability, both human and technical, will have to adapt accordingly.

References

Arpi C (2004) Born in Sin: The Panchsheel Agreement. Mittal Publications, New Delhi

Askew J (2002) The Status of Tibet in the Diplomacy of China, Britain, the United States and India, 1911–1959. Thesis submitted to the University of Adelaide

Bennett G (2014) War and Intelligence. RUSI Journal 159(4):50–55

Bhargava GS (1964) The Battle of NEFA: The Undeclared War. Allied Publishers, New Delhi

Bhat S (1967) India and China. Popular Book Services, New Delhi

Brugger B (1981) China: Liberation and Political Transformation 1942–1962. Croom Helm, London

Chakravarti PC (1961) India-China Relations. Firma KL Mukhopadyay Publishers, Calcutta

Chen Jian (2006) The Tibetan Rebellion of 1959 and China's Changing Relations with India and the Soviet Union. Journal of Cold War Studies 8(3):54–101

CIA (1963a) The Sino-Indian Border Dispute. DD/I Staff Study 12 March 1963. http://www.foia.cia.gov/sites/default/files/document_conversions/14/polo-07.pdf Accessed 28 July 2014

CIA (1963b) The Sino-Indian Border Dispute DD/I Staff Study 19 August 1963 http://www.foia.cia.gov/sites/default/files/document_conversions/14/polo-08.pdf Accessed 28 July 2014

CIA (1964) The Sino-Indian Border Dispute. DD/I Staff Study 5 May 1964 http://www.foia.cia.gov/sites/default/files/document_conversions/14/polo-09.pdf Accessed 28 July 2014
Dalvi JP (1969) Himalayan Blunder: The Curtain-raiser to the Sino-Indian War of 1962. Thacker and Company Limited, Bombay
Dave AK (2006) The Real Story of China's War on India, 1962. United Services Institution of India, New Delhi
Davies PHJ (2004) Intelligence Culture and Intelligence Failure in Britain and the United States. Cambridge Review of International Affairs, 17(3):495–520
Dhar A (2009) CIA's Eye on South Asia. Manas, New Delhi
Dikotter F (2011) Mao's Great Famine. Bloomsbury, London
George RZ (2004) Fixing the Problem of Analytical Mindsets: Alternative Analysis. International Journal of Intelligence and Counter-intelligence, 17(3):385–404
Government of India (1962) Official 1962 War History, at http://www.bharat-rakshak.com/LAND-FORCES/Army/History/1962War/PDF/1962Chapter10.pdf, Accessed 28 July 2014
Grabo CM (2004) Anticipating Surprise: Analysis for Strategic Warning. University Press of America, Oxford
Guruswamy M (ed) (2006) Emerging Trends in India-China Relations. Hope India Publications, Gurgaon
Hoffman SA (2006) Rethinking the Linkage between Tibet and the China-India Border Conflict: A Realist Approach. Journal of Cold War Studies 8(3):165–94
Hoffmann SA (1972) Anticipation, Disaster, and Victory: India 1962–71. Asian Survey 12 (11):960-979
Hudson GF (1957) Communist Ideology in China. International Affairs 33(2):176–184
Karnow S (1990) Mao and China: A Legacy of Turmoil. Penguin, London
Khanduri CB (2006) Thimayya: An Amazing Life. Knowledge World, New Delhi
Mahadevan P (2008) The Failure of Indian Intelligence in the Sino-Indian Conflict. Journal of Intelligence History. 8(1):1–27
Mahadevan P (2011) The Intelligence Aspects of the 1962 War. Indian Military Review 2 (July):23–24
Malhotra I (2005) Introduction. In: Subrahmanyam K, Monteiro A (eds) Shedding Shibboleths: India's Evolving Strategic Outlook. Wordsmiths, Delhi
Maxwell N (2000) India's China War. Random House, New York
Mehra P (2007) Essays in Frontier History: India, China and the Border Dispute. Oxford University Press, New Delhi
Mullik BN (1971) My Years With Nehru: The Chinese Betrayal. Allied Publishers, New Delhi
Palit DK (1991) War in the High Himalaya: The Indian Army in Crisis, 1962. Lancer International, London
Pascovich E (2014) Military Intelligence and Controversial Political Issues: The Unique Case of the Israeli Military Intelligence. Intelligence and National Security 29(2):227–261.
Prasad Varma S (1965) Struggle for the Himalayas: A Study in Sino-Indian Relations. University Publishers, Delhi
Subrahmanyam K, Monteiro A (2005) Shedding Shibboleths: India's Evolving Strategic Outlook. Wordsmiths, Delhi
Sukumaran R (2003) The 1962 War India-China War and Kargil 1999: Restrictions on the Use of Airpower. Strategic Analysis 27(3):332–356
Verghese BG (2012) The War We Lost. Tehelka 41,9. 13 October 2012, at http://www.tehelka.com/the-war-we-lost/ Accessed 10 September 2014
Vertzberger Y (1984) Misperceptions in Foreign Policymaking: The Sino-Indian Conflict, 1959–1962. Westview, Boulder, CO
Worthing P (2007) A Military History of Modern China: From the Manchu Conquest to Tiananmen Square. Praeger Security International, London

Author Biography

Prem Mahadevan, senior researcher with the Global Security Team at the Center for Security Studies, Eidgenössische Technische Hochschule, Zürich. He specializes in the study of intelligence and sub-state conflict. He holds a doctoral degree in Intelligence Studies from King's College, London. He has advised Indian government agencies on counter-terrorist operational management, provided political risk assessments to the private sector, and been consulted by the Czech government, EUROPOL and NATO Headquarters on emerging security challenges. He has authored two books: *The Politics of Counterterrorism in India*, and *An Eye for An Eye: Decoding Global Special Operations and Irregular Warfare*. Besides lecturing at the University of Innsbruck, he has been a Senior Lecturer at the Metropolitan University Prague and trained as a foreign correspondent in the Czech Republic. He has published extensively in edited academic volumes, peer-reviewed journals and CSS security analyses.

Chapter 4
Western Intelligence and Covert Soviet Military Aid to Indonesia During the 1962 West New Guinea Crisis

David Easter

Abstract This chapter assesses the performance of Western intelligence services against the Soviet target in the 1962 West New Guinea Crisis. During this crisis the Soviet Union secretly supplied Indonesia with Soviet-manned submarines and bombers and was prepared for these units to participate in an Indonesian attack against the Dutch military in West New Guinea. American and British intelligence services managed to detect the deployment of the Soviet force and obtained some indications that they would be used in support of an Indonesian attack. However, while the Americans and British had good military intelligence they had insufficient political and diplomatic intelligence and, therefore, could not discover the motivations behind the Soviet deployment.

Keywords West New Guinea · West Irian · Sukarno · Khrushchev · Sigint · Cuban Missile Crisis

Contents

D. Easter (✉)
Department of War Studies, Kings College
London, Strand, London WC2R 2LS, UK
e-mail: david.easter@kcl.ac.uk

F. Baudet et al. (eds.), *Perspectives on Military Intelligence from the First World War to Mali*, DOI 10.1007/978-94-6265-183-8_4

4.1 Introduction

During the Cold War covert Soviet military deployments in the developing world posed a particular challenge for Western intelligence agencies. Starting in the Korean War in 1950, the USSR on several occasions secretly sent Soviet military personnel and equipment to support radical, anti-imperialist states such as Egypt and North Vietnam. Since Western intelligence agencies could not penetrate high-level Soviet decision making circles they were often taken unawares by these deployments. The Soviet military units had to be detected and evaluated when they were en route or in place in the host country, which was not an easy task. The most famous example of this was Operation Anadyr, the covert Soviet deployment of intermediate and medium range ballistic nuclear missiles in Cuba in 1962. The United States had no prior intelligence of this operation. Indeed, a Central Intelligence Agency (CIA) Special National Intelligence Estimate on 19 September 1962 forecast that the Soviet Union would not install nuclear missiles in Cuba.[1] The CIA also initially failed to spot the shipment of the missiles and their warheads to the island. It was only after an American Lockheed U-2 reconnaissance aircraft photographed a missile site under construction in Cuba on 14 October that the CIA realised was happening. From that point on American intelligence agencies closely monitored the build-up but even so their intelligence on the Soviet order of battle in Cuba was never perfect. The CIA did not know that the Soviets had also positioned tactical nuclear weapons on the island and it underestimated the size of the accompanying Soviet conventional force.[2] As the CIA lacked high-level diplomatic and political intelligence on the USSR it could not provide President John Kennedy with hard evidence about Soviet intentions or Moscow's motivations in deploying the missiles.

Over the last 20 years evidence has emerged of another covert Soviet military deployment in the developing world which was near contemporaneous with Operation Anadyr. In the summer of 1962 Indonesia and The Netherlands stood on the verge of war over the Dutch colony of West New Guinea, which Indonesia claimed as its territory. In memoirs and newspaper articles former Soviet and Indonesian military personnel and civilian leaders have revealed that during the crisis the USSR secretly provided Indonesia with submarines and bombers manned by Soviet crews to help with a planned Indonesian attack on West New Guinea.[3] Moreover, Matthijs Ooms has shown that the Dutch naval intelligence service, Marine Inlichtingendienst (MARID), received information that Soviet crews were manning Indonesian submarines.[4]

---

[1] Garthoff 1998, p. 20.

[2] Idem, pp. 28–29; Fursenko and Naftali 1999, p. 188, 210, 217.

[3] Ryzhikov 1995, pp. 52–54; Rijs 1999, pp. 1, 5; Ryzhikov 2004; Khrushchev 2007, pp. 789–790; Andriia͡nov 2003, p. 169. See also Muraviev and Brown 2008, pp. 5–6.

[4] Ooms 2012, p. 26.

Building upon these sources this chapter will assess how well Western intelligence performed in the West New Guinea case. It will examine when Western intelligence services discovered the presence of the Soviet manned submarines and aircraft and to what extent they were able to establish the purpose of this force. The main focus will be on American, British and Australian intelligence but using the works by Ooms and Bob De Graaff, Cees Wiebes and Wies Platje, reference will also be made to Dutch intelligence activity during the crisis. This study is limited by the fact that most of the relevant intelligence documents are retained by organisations such as the CIA, the National Security Agency (NSA) and the British Government Communications Headquarters (GCHQ). Furthermore, the Russian and Indonesian governments have still not released the documents relating to the Soviet military deployment, making it difficult to compare Western intelligence reports and assessments with actual Soviet and Indonesian actions and intentions. But drawing on the American, British and Australian documents that have been declassified and the fragmentary Russian and Indonesian sources available, this paper will argue that Western intelligence services did succeed in detecting the Soviet deployment and obtained some indications that the Soviet units would be used in support of the Indonesian attack. However, as in the Cuban Missile Crisis, they could not produce hard evidence on Soviet motivations in deploying the force.

4.2 War Over West New Guinea?

First of all, it is necessary to explain the background to the crisis and the Soviet deployment. The West New Guinea dispute arose from the tortuous process of Dutch decolonisation in South East Asia. After World War Two The Netherlands fought a bitter colonial war against the Indonesian independence movement led by Sukarno. Eventually The Netherlands was forced to give independence to most of the Dutch East Indies in 1949, thereby creating Indonesia, but it retained the West New Guinea portion of the colony. Sukarno, who became the Indonesian President, wished to incorporate all the territories of the Dutch East Indies within his new state and he pushed the Dutch to withdraw from West New Guinea, which the Indonesians called West Irian, and transfer sovereignty to Indonesia. The Netherlands refused. West New Guinea did not share a land border with Indonesia and the Dutch argued that the Papuan peoples in the colony were ethnically distinct from Indonesians and should in time exercise the right to national self-determination on their own. Negotiations over the issue became deadlocked so Sukarno applied escalating economic, diplomatic and military pressures on the Dutch. In 1957 he seized Dutch commercial assets in Indonesia and in 1960 he broke off diplomatic relations. The Indonesians began small-scale guerrilla infiltration into West New Guinea but the Dutch were able to maintain military control over the colony and remained obdurate.

The Soviet leader Nikita Khrushchev strongly backed Sukarno's campaign for West New Guinea. Since the mid-1950s Khrushchev had been able to expand

Soviet influence in the developing world by supporting radical states such as Egypt and Iraq in their confrontations with the declining European empires. By taking up the case of West New Guinea, he could strengthen ties with Indonesia which by virtue of its size, location and natural resources was a strategically important country in the Cold War struggle. Soviet propaganda and diplomatic statements endorsed the Indonesian claim to the territory. More importantly, Khrushchev supplied Indonesia with considerable amounts of modern weaponry, so much so that by 1962 it was the biggest non-communist recipient of Soviet Bloc military aid.[5] Between 1958 and 1961 Indonesia ordered around $700 million worth of arms from the Soviet Union, Poland and Czechoslovakia.[6] These purchases greatly expanded and modernised the Indonesian navy (ALRI) and air force (AURI). ALRI received a light cruiser, destroyers, and six Project 613 diesel-electric submarines. AURI was equipped with the latest Soviet military jet aircraft, such as Tupolev Tu-16 medium bombers and Mikoyan MiG-21 fighters. The arms were sold on credit and the terms were generous, giving a one-third discount on cost price.

Soviet Bloc instructors would have to train Indonesian personnel in how to use this advanced weaponry, limiting its immediate effectiveness, but in time it would give Sukarno the ability to launch a large scale military attack on West New Guinea. In January 1962 he therefore set up the Mandala military command to plan, prepare and execute operations to recover the colony.[7] The Mandala commanders envisaged a three-phase campaign; in phase one lasting until the end of 1962 more Indonesian guerrillas would be infiltrated into West New Guinea and 'free areas' set up.[8] At the same time naval, air and land bases in Indonesia would be developed in preparation for full-scale war. Phase two would start at the beginning of 1963 with an operation to capture and occupy the small island of Biak, just north of West New Guinea, which was central to the Dutch defences. In phase three the Indonesians would take control over the rest of the territory. The Indonesians accordingly stepped up their guerrilla infiltrations into the colony and on 15 January 1962 this led to an Indonesian-Dutch naval clash near Vlakke Hoek on the southern coast of West New Guinea.[9] Dutch destroyers intercepted Indonesian motor torpedo boats carrying infiltrators and sunk one of them, killing around 50 Indonesians. Full-scale war seemed to be edging closer.

---

[5] Webster 2009, p. 117; Boden 2006, pp. 206–216.

[6] Gale Digital Collections, Declassified Document Reference Service (DDRS) http://gdc.gale.com/products/declassified-documents-reference-system/ CIA Current Intelligence Weekly Summary, 16 February 1961; Intelligence Report, 'Indonesia's Growing Dependence on Soviet Bloc Arms', Bureau of Intelligence and Research, State Department, 24 February 1961; The British National Archive (TNA), DEFE 5/130, Memorandum COS (62) 374, 11 September 1962.

[7] Dinas Sejarah Militer TNI – Angkatan Darat 1972, pp. 462–463.

[8] Nasution 1985, pp. 295–297.

[9] Drooglever 2009, pp. 448–449.

4.3 The West's Intelligence Position

American, British, Australian and Dutch intelligence agencies monitored the flow of Soviet arms to Indonesia and the growing Indonesian military campaign. Initially the United States had good sources of information on Soviet arms supplies. Soon after two major Soviet-Indonesian arms deals were signed in early 1961 the CIA acquired '[d]ocumentary evidence' about the agreements from 'reliable Indonesian sources'.[10] The agency believed it had 'excellent contractual information' about the terms under which Soviet military technical assistance was provided to Indonesia.[11] Unfortunately poor security appears to have compromised some of these sources. The CIA complained in September 1962 that it had lost 'ease in acquisition of Indonesian arms contracts' after the State Department released the content of one contract to the South East Asia Treaty Organisation on a virtually unclassified basis.[12]

The CIA's information about Soviet arms supplies came partly from signals intelligence (Sigint). CIA reports on the arms agreements and deliveries of Soviet arms to Indonesia carried the marking 'Top Secret Dinar' and Dinar was a category III signals intelligence code word which indicated that a document contained material derived from Sigint.[13] A later American report stated that it had been 'apparent from intercepted messages' that the Soviet military aid programme to Indonesia had been subject to some delays in May 1962.[14] Almost certainly these were intercepted Indonesian rather than Soviet messages. The American and British Sigint organisations, the NSA and GCHQ, were unable to read high-level Soviet cipher systems but they had great success in the early 1960s against Indonesian ciphers.[15]

Some of the Sigint appearing in the CIA assessments may actually have come from GCHQ and its Australian counterpart, the Defence Signals Directorate (DSD), for there was close cooperation between these organisations and the NSA. A GCHQ-DSD intercept station in the British colony of Singapore collected

---

[10] DDRS, CIA Current Intelligence Weekly Summary, 16 February 1961.

[11] roquest Digital National Security Archive (DNSA), National Security Agency Collection http://www.proquest.com/products-services/databases/dnsa.html Memorandum, Guthe to Crawford, 20 September 1962.

[12] CIA Freedom of Information Act Electronic Reading Room (CIA FOIA), http://www.foia.cia.gov/ Memorandum "Further Analysis of Bloc and Western Shipping Calling at Cuban Ports", Assistant Director, Research and Reports to Deputy Director (Intelligence), 11 September 1962.

[13] DNSA, National Security Agency Collection, Memorandum, Guthe to Crawford, 20 September 1962; United States National Archives and Records Administration at College Park (NARA), CIA Records Search Tool (CREST), Memorandum, Assistant Director, Research and Reports to Deputy Director for Politico-Military Affairs, State Department, 18 September 1962. For information about the code word system see: Easter 2012, pp. 875–895.

[14] NARA, CREST, Report on the Soviet Arms Build up in Cuba, United States Arms Control and Disarmament Agency, not dated.

[15] Aid 2009 pp. 78, 130–131; Easter 2008, p. 694; Easter 2012, pp. 891–892.

Indonesian traffic and under the United Kingdom-United States Communications Intelligence Agreement (UKUSA) the three Anglo-Saxon powers shared raw intercepts and finished Sigint.[16] Moreover, the British, Americans and Australians could share intelligence in area through the British Joint Intelligence Committee (Far East) (JIC (FE)) based in Singapore. American, Australian and New Zealand representatives attended JIC (FE) meetings.[17]

The Netherlands also had good Sigint and good human intelligence on Indonesia. MARID and the Dutch Sigint agency, Wiskundig Centrum (WKC), could intercept Indonesian communications from a listening post on Biak and had broken some Indonesian ciphers.[18] The Dutch foreign intelligence service, Buitenlandse Inlichtingendienst (BID), had agents in the top echelons of the Indonesian state. Wiebes and De Graaff have claimed that one of these agents was Ruslan Abdulgani, a senior Indonesian minister who was codenamed 'Virgil' by the BID.[19] However, in March 1962 Abdulgani was removed from office in a cabinet reshuffle potentially depriving The Hague of a valuable intelligence source just as the West New Guinea crisis was starting to heat up.

The Dutch exchanged intelligence with the Americans and British, sometimes via a Royal Netherlands Navy intelligence liaison officer based in Singapore.[20] Yet this exchange of information was not as full and free as that between the Anglo-Saxon states, partly because The Netherlands was not a signatory to the UKUSA Sigint agreement.[21] For example, in the late 1950s WKC gave GCHQ the Dutch air force codes but it received little of value in return and so suspended the intelligence exchange.[22] Furthermore, although the United States and the Netherlands were NATO allies, they had differing diplomatic interests and objectives in the West New Guinea dispute and this could complicate intelligence sharing. The Dutch wished to maintain control over their colony until they chose to grant self-rule to the Papuans whereas the United States was mainly concerned with limiting Soviet influence over Indonesia. Washington feared that Khrushchev was exploiting the West New Guinea issue and lavishing Sukarno with arms in order to lure Indonesia into the Soviet camp in the Cold War. If an Indonesian-Dutch war did break out it could push Sukarno even closer to the Soviets and Indonesia might be lost to the West. Mindful of these strategic concerns, the United States favoured a negotiated settlement between Indonesia and The Netherlands even if the price of this was the handover of West New Guinea to Sukarno.[23] The Netherlands that

---

16 Easter 2008, p. 684, 694.

17 National Archives of Australia (NAA), A1838 TS690/2/2 Part 9, McDonald to Department of External Affairs, 26 March 1965.

18 Wiebes 2001, p. 257; Platje 2001, pp. 296–297, 303–304.

19 De Graaff and Wiebes 1998, p. 179. Abdulgani denied De Graaff and Wiebes' claims.

20 Ibid.; Platje 2001, pp. 300–301.

21 Wiebes 2001, pp. 258–259; TNA, CAB 159/37, 2nd Meeting, 11 January 1962.

22 Wiebes 2001, pp. 258–259.

23 Jones 2002, p. 49; Penders 2002, pp. 340–342.

sought US support for its position thus found itself in exactly the same predicament as in 1945–1949 when it had tried in vain to frame its policy toward Indonesia as a contribution to the wider struggle against communism in order to regain US support.

4.4 Assessing Soviet Intentions

In the wake of the Vlakke Hoek incident the United States made strenuous efforts to get negotiations underway and avoid further military clashes. In February 1962 American Attorney General Robert Kennedy visited Indonesia and The Netherlands and urged both sides to be more flexible. After much pressure from the Americans it was finally agreed that secret Indonesian-Dutch talks would be held in the United States with an American mediator. At the same time though Sukarno continued the infiltrations of guerrillas into West New Guinea and the preparation of Indonesian military forces and bases for large-scale warfare. A CIA report indicated that in the first three months of 1962 an additional 7,000 AURI and ALRI personnel were deployed in the 'New Guinea operations area'.[24]

The first round of Indonesian-Dutch negotiations took place in March 1962 at Middleburg near Washington with the American diplomat Ellsworth Bunker acting as mediator. The talks made little progress but they did lead to Bunker putting forward a possible formula for a settlement.[25] Under this three stage 'Bunker Plan' the Dutch would first transfer West New Guinea to a United Nations body which would administer the territory for one or two years. The United Nations would then hand over West New Guinea to Indonesia. Finally Jakarta, in cooperation with the United Nations, would give the people of West New Guinea an opportunity to exercise their right of national self-determination. The Americans recommended the Bunker Plan to the Indonesians and Dutch as a basis for further negotiations. Sukarno was receptive, although he wanted Indonesia to have control over West New Guinea by the end of 1962 which would mean shortening Bunker's timetable.[26] By contrast, the Dutch and especially the pugnacious Dutch Foreign Minister, Joseph Luns, were dismayed and indignant.[27] They saw the Bunker Plan as merely a face-saving device to cover an Indonesian take-over of West New Guinea. In addition, they did not believe that the Indonesians would ever allow the Papuans a truly free vote on self-determination. Given the importance of American support the Dutch cabinet was not able to reject the Bunker Plan outright but for weeks Luns sought unsuccessfully to water down its provisions and delay further negotiations.

---

[24] DNSA, National Security Agency Collection, CIA Current Intelligence Weekly Review, 30 March 1962.

[25] Penders 2002, pp. 360–361; Drooglever 2009, pp. 468–469.

[26] TNA, DO 169/167, Telegram 322, Jakarta to Foreign Office, 27 April 1962.

[27] Penders 2002, pp. 359–368; Drooglever 2009, pp. 469–477.

With the diplomatic process stalled and continuing Indonesian preparations for war, American and Australian intelligence analysts began to consider the likely intentions of the Soviet Union over West New Guinea. In late April Roger Hilsman, the Director of the State Department's Bureau of Intelligence and Research, examined the Soviet position in paper for Secretary of State Dean Rusk.[28] Hilsman recognised that West New Guinea had become a vehicle for Soviet entry into Indonesia. A diplomatic resolution of the dispute was therefore not in Soviet interests and the Soviet Union would oppose American-led negotiations. However, Hilsman did expect the Soviets to show some caution. His assessment was that 'Moscow probably does not seek to bring about an Indonesian attempt at an armed take-over of West New Guinea at this time.'[29] This was because if the Indonesians did attack the Dutch and got into difficulties, they might call upon the USSR for military assistance and the Soviets would then face the difficult choice of either refusing the Indonesian request and thereby losing influence and prestige, or intervening and risking a superpower confrontation with the Americans. The Australian Joint Intelligence Committee (JIC) also believed that the United States would have a deterrent effect on Soviet behaviour although it suspected Moscow might see some political advantage even in an abortive Indonesian attack on West New Guinea.[30] Still, the JIC considered that the Soviet Union 'would probably not wish to be [militarily] directly involved since this would create a danger of United States intervention.'[31]

It is now apparent from Russian sources that these American and Australian intelligence assessments underestimated the lengths to which Khrushchev was willing to go in support of Sukarno. In fact, Khrushchev was prepared to militarily intervene in the West New Guinea crisis by covertly supplying Indonesia with Soviet manned submarines and aircraft. It appears to have been the Indonesians who requested the equipment and crewmen. Khrushchev later told Rumanian communist leaders that Sukarno took the initiative and sent Foreign Minister Subandrio to the USSR to ask for 'submarines, aircraft and commanders for these things.'[32] In early May Subandrio flew to Moscow and on 8 May he signed a new arms agreement with the Soviets.[33] Through this arms deal Khrushchev gave Sukarno what he wanted. Anastas Mikoyan, the Soviet First Deputy Chairman, later recalled that:

---

[28] DDRS, State Department, Research Memorandum RSB-96, Hilsman to Secretary of State, 27 April 1962.

[29] Ibid.

[30] NAA, A1838, TS3036/6/1 Part 14, Minute Loveday to Anderson, covering JIC (AUST) (62) 49 (Revise), 26 June 1962.

[31] Ibid.

[32] Opris 2012, p. 517.

[33] TNA, FO 371/166514, Telegram 801, Moscow to Foreign Office, 9 May 1962.

> This summer, when Sukarno was getting ready to decide this issue…[h]e asked and we gave him several submarines with Soviet crews, several (I cannot cite the numbers) TU-16s with antiship missiles, so that they could destroy Dutch ships.[34]

Judging by Mikoyan's comments and the deliveries of arms after the deal was signed, the Soviets agreed to provide the Indonesians with six more Project 613 submarines and six Tu-16KS medium bombers equipped with the formidable *Kometa* anti-shipping missile. Soviet personnel would man the Tu-16KS bombers as well as the submarines. Khrushchev told the plenum of the central committee that he had supplied Indonesia with crews for submarines and added that 'Sukarno also asked for crew for missile carrier aircraft. In conversation with minister for foreign affairs Subandrio, I said very well, we will assist you.'[35] Khrushchev even seemed willing for the Soviet-piloted planes to take part in combat against the Dutch. In his memoirs he freely admitted that during the West New Guinea crisis Soviet personnel had been commanding Indonesian submarines and piloting Tu-16s.[36] Khrushchev wrote that during the Indonesian Foreign Minister's visit:

> I asked Subandrio: 'What are the chances that an agreement [with the Dutch] could successfully be reached?' He answered: 'Not very great.' I said: 'If the Dutch fail to display sober-mindedness and engage in military operations, this is a war that could to some extent serve as a proving ground for our pilots who are flying planes equipped with missiles. We'll see how well our missiles work.'[37]

Perhaps unsurprisingly, the Soviets and Indonesians did not publicly disclose the details of their arms deal.[38] Indeed, Sir Frank Roberts, the British Ambassador in Moscow, found that Soviet officials were 'very cagey' about discussing the results of Subandrio's visit.[39] On his return to Jakarta Subandrio told Howard Jones, the American ambassador to Indonesia, that he had purchased from the Soviets submarines and other military equipment worth a total of $70 million but he did not mention the use of Soviet personnel.[40] The Dutch did receive a more dramatic report from an anti-communist Indonesian army officer who had been part of the delegation to Moscow.[41] This source claimed that as well as providing a substantial amount of arms, the Soviets had promised that if a third party became involved in the West New Guinea dispute the Soviet Union would militarily intervene on behalf

---

[34] Mikoyan 2012, p. 467.

[35] Andriia͡nov 2003, p.169. Translation by author.

[36] Khrushchev 2007, p. 790.

[37] Ibid., pp. 791–792.

[38] TNA, FO 371/166514, Telegram 801, Roberts to Foreign Office, 9 May 1962; Telegram 802, Roberts to Foreign Office, 9 May 1962.

[39] Ibid, Letter Roberts to Foreign Office, 16 May 1962.

[40] John F. Kennedy Presidential Library, National Security Files, Box 113A, File Indonesia, Volume II, April–June 1962, Telegram 2014, Jakarta to State Department, 15 May 1962.

[41] Koster 1991, pp. 109–110; John F. Kennedy National Security Files, 1961–1963, Asia and the Pacific (JFK) (University Publications of America, Bethesda, 1987), Microfilm, Reel 2, Telegram 907, The Hague to State Department, 23 May 1962.

of the Indonesians. In return, the Indonesian government was ready to make Indonesia a socialist state and set up a joint Soviet-Indonesian company to exploit natural resources in the country. American diplomats were sceptical about these claims. Jones reported that none of his sources in Jakarta, including the CIA station there, had come up with anything similar.[42] The American embassy in Moscow thought that this type of politico-economic agreement was not something the Soviets would put forward.[43] Luns though did seem to give the report more credit.[44] Yet crucially, despite their intelligence sources neither the Dutch nor the Americans seemed aware at this point that Khrushchev had agreed to Soviet crews manning submarines and bombers for the Indonesians.

Although Western intelligence agencies did not know the full details of the Soviet-Indonesian arms agreement they were able to track the movement of the equipment to Indonesia.[45] In this way military intelligence could cover some of the gaps in Western diplomatic intelligence. Two Soviet Pacific Fleet Project 613 submarines left Vladivostok in May and sailed to the Indonesian port of Surabaya in Java where the crew were ordered to change into ALRI uniforms. On board one of them was Rudolf Ryzhikov, a Soviet naval officer who later wrote an account of his experiences.[46] Ryzhikov recalled that en route to Indonesia his submarine was followed by an American Lockheed Neptune maritime reconnaissance aircraft. According to a British intelligence summary, on 28 May the two Indonesia-bound submarines were spotted off the coast of Taiwan heading south.[47] Four more Soviet submarines and a support tender were seen off Japan on 16 June and reached Surabaya thirteen days later.[48] On 29 June six Soviet-manned Tu-16s landed at Jakarta airport.[49] These aircraft were the Tu-16KS variant, able to carry the *Kometa* missile.[50] Given that Subandrio had only signed the arms agreement in May, the CIA was perturbed by the speed of these deliveries, describing them as 'the quickest ever noted for such complex equipment under a Soviet arms deal with a

---

[42] NARA, Record Group 59, State Department Central Decimal File, 1960–1963, Box 89, Telegram 2071, Jakarta to State Department, 25 May 1962.

[43] Ibid., Telegram 3049 Moscow to State Department, 24 May 1962.

[44] JFK, Reel 2, Telegram 907, The Hague to State Department, 23 May 1962. No Indonesian or Soviet source has subsequently confirmed these claims.

[45] NARA, CREST, CIA, Memorandum from Assistant Director, Research and Reports to Deputy Director for Politico-Military Affairs, State Department, 18 September 1962.

[46] Ryzhikov 1995, p. 52.

[47] TNA, AIR 24/2692, FEAF Weekly Intelligence Summary, Reports Received During the Period Ending 1st June, 1962, not dated.

[48] TNA, AIR 24/2692, FEAF Weekly Intelligence Summary, Reports Received During the Period Ending 22 June, 1962, not dated; NARA, CREST, CIA Current Intelligence Weekly Summary, 6 July 1962.

[49] NARA, CREST, CIA Current Intelligence Weekly Summary, 6 July 1962; NAA, A1838, 3034/12/5 Part 7, Memorandum 1445 Upton to Department of External Affairs, Annex A, 26 July 1962.

[50] TNA, DEFE 5/130, Memorandum COS (62) 374, 11 September 1962.

non-bloc country.'[51] The agency warned that there were unlikely to be sufficient numbers of trained Indonesian personnel and if the bombers and submarines were to be used operationally within the next 6 months, many of them would have to be manned by Soviet crews.

This did appear to be the intention of the Indonesians. As the Soviet weaponry arrived at Surabaya and Jakarta the Indonesian military prepared for a large-scale attack on the Dutch. On 22 June 1962, the Mandala command issued orders for Operation Jayawijaya (Glorious Victory), a combined arms assault on Biak.[52] In the operation AURI and ALRI would first seek to establish air and sea superiority. Indonesian paratroopers would then be dropped on Biak followed by an amphibious landing. Once Biak was captured, the city of Hollandia in West New Guinea would be attacked. This was an ambitious operation, far bigger and more complex than the guerrilla infiltrations the Indonesian military had hitherto been carrying out, and it was set to take place in August, earlier than envisaged by the Mandala command back in January 1962. The forces allocated to Jayawijaya suggest that at least some Soviet personnel would take part in the operation. The planned attacking force included 12 submarines and 20 Tu-16 and Tu-16KS bombers.[53] Since the Indonesians only possessed six submarines the other six in the plan had to be the Soviet-manned submarines collecting in Surabaya harbour. Indonesia did have 20 Tu-16 and Tu-16KS bombers so on paper AURI could mount this part of Jayawijaya on its own.[54] But an Indonesian source told the Australian air attaché in Jakarta in July that AURI had trained crews for just six Tu-16s.[55]

The Soviets may also have helped draw up the plans for Jayawijaya. In his memoirs Khrushchev wrote that:

> …Sukarno was asking us to send knowledgeable staff officers to help him work out a plan for military operations in the event of a resort to arms. We agreed to this and sent our people to Indonesia.[56]

Khrushchev told a Cuban delegation in 1963 that Soviet airmen and sailors had 'helped [the Indonesians] to master Soviet weaponry and participated in working out plans for offensive operations.'[57] Significant in this context may have been the visit to Indonesia between 20 June and 2 July of Air Marshal Konstantin Vershinin, the commander of the Soviet air force.[58] Certainly Vershinin gave advice to the Indonesians. According to an American intelligence report, Vershinin complained

---

[51] NARA, CREST, CIA Current Intelligence Weekly Summary, 6 July 1962.

[52] Djamin 2001, p. 155; Nasution 1985, pp. 310–311.

[53] Nasution 1985, pp. 310–311; Dinas Sejarah Militer 1972, p. 467.

[54] TNA, DEFE 5/130, Memorandum COS (62) 374, 11 September 1962.

[55] NAA, A1838,3034/12/5 Part 7, Letter Upton to Department of External Affairs, Annex A, 26 July 1962.

[56] Khrushchev 2007, p. 792.

[57] Fursenko 2008, p. 899. Translation by author.

[58] TNA, FO 371/166514, Letter Petersen to London, 20 June 1964; Letter Petersen to London, 4 July 1964.

to AURI that its Soviet-supplied aircraft were not being handled properly.[59] He suggested and the Indonesians agreed that an additional 225 Soviet air force personnel should be quickly sent to Indonesia to work on MiG 19 and 21 fighters and Tu-16s. The Australian military attaché in Jakarta was told by a 'very reliable' Indonesian source that Vershinin had also pushed the Indonesians to take West New Guinea by force.[60]

Sukarno though had not completely abandoned negotiations. The build-up of Indonesian forces and Soviet aid would soon give him the ability to launch a full scale attack on West New Guinea but it could also be used to intimidate the Dutch and win the territory through coercive diplomacy. Encouraged by the United States, Luns had finally agreed to negotiate on the basis of the Bunker Plan and Sukarno decided to resume talks with The Netherlands. Negotiations therefore restarted at Middleburg on 13 July. Progress was difficult, mainly because by this time the Indonesians wanted better terms than those laid out in the Bunker Plan. They asked for a shortening of the two-year period for the transfer of West New Guinea.[61] Subandrio suggested to the Americans that the territory could be passed directly to the Indonesians without any intervening United Nations administration.[62] The threat of war lay in the air if they did not get their way. The CIA reported that Sukarno had given Subandrio one week to secure Dutch agreement and until 4 August to arrange the details of the transfer of West New Guinea.[63] If the Dutch had not agreed after a week, Subandrio was to return home and Sukarno would order large-scale landings in West New Guinea. The Indonesians were finalising their preparations for Operation Jayawijaya.[64] Starting on 17 July, the Mandala command began to move troops from their bases at Jakarta, Surabaya and Amahai. The invasion fleet would assemble in the waters around the Banggai Islands on the east coast of Sulawesi, in Peling Bay and Bangkalan Bay. The Indonesians planned to carry out initial air attacks on Dutch targets on 10 August. The assault on Biak would follow on 12 August.

Dutch and American intelligence were monitoring the movements of the Indonesian forces and could see that a large-scale attack was imminent. Through Sigint MARID had built up a detailed picture of the Indonesian order of battle, logistical readiness and even the timing of the planned attack but it was uncertain whether the target was going to be Biak or Sorong, further to the west.[65] The United

[59] TNA, AIR 24/2692, FEAF Weekly Intelligence Summary 27/62, Reports Received During the Period Ending 13 July, 1962, not dated.

[60] NARA, Record Group 59, Central Decimal Files State Department, 1960–63, 656.9813/5-1762 – 656.9813/8-162, Box 1356, Telegram CX-127, Jakarta to State Department, 28 July 1962.

[61] TNA, FO 371/166547, Minute by Chalmers, 18 July 1962.

[62] JFK, Reel 10, Telegram 87, Jakarta to State Department, 13 July 1962.

[63] DNSA, National Security Agency Collection, CIA Current Intelligence Weekly Review, 20 July 1962.

[64] Nasution 1985, pp. 311–312; Suharto 1989, p. 108; Drooglever 2009, pp. 505–506.

[65] Platje 2001, p. 305; NARA, Record Group 59, Central Decimal Files State Department, 1960–63, 656.9813/5-1762–656.9813/8-162, Box 1356, Telegram 270755Z, ALUSNA Hague to State

States secretly used U-2 high altitude reconnaissance planes to observe the Indonesian preparations for war.[66] These flights appear to have been flown by the United States Air Force's Strategic Air Command rather than the CIA.[67] Sukarno later claimed that U-2 aircraft overflew Indonesian military bases in the Mandala command area seven times.[68] The Indonesians also found that their invasion fleet was shadowed by an unidentified foreign submarine.[69]

By this point the United States and Britain had learnt that Soviet personnel were manning Indonesian submarines and aircraft. A weekly intelligence summary for the British air force in Singapore (probably produced by JIC (FE)) stated in mid-July that:

> According to an American secret report, the six W-class submarines which arrived in Surabaya in June were entirely Russian manned. At present all six submarines, still with Soviet crews, are stationed in Surabaya. Crews of two of these submarines are wearing ALRI uniforms without insignia. ALRI officers jokingly refer to these men as 'volunteers'.[70]

News of the Soviet presence percolated through the American administration. Robert Komer, a staffer on the National Security Council, advised Robert Kennedy on 16 July that if the talks in Middleburg failed 'Sukarno will move to military action. Our reports indicate he's poised to do so, even if he has to use subs and planes with Soviet crews.'[71] The Americans attempted to warn off the Soviets. At the Geneva Conference on Laos, William Sullivan from the State Department's Bureau of Far Eastern Affairs brought up the subject of West New Guinea on 22 July with Georgi Pushkin, the Soviet Deputy Foreign Minister for Southeast Asian Affairs. Sullivan told Pushkin that the American government was 'alarmed at the apparent wish of the Russians to bring about active fighting in the area.'[72] He added that:

(Footnote 65 continued)

Department, 28 July 1962; Telegram 301259Z, ALUSNA Hague to State Department, 30 July 1962.

66 Jones 1971, p. 210.

67 The CIA Director wanted SAC to carry out the missions and a record of CIA flights shows none having taken place over Indonesia in 1962. See NARA, CREST, Memorandum Cunningham to Director of Central Intelligence, 29 July 1962; NARA, CREST, Memorandum 'Project Idealist', nd.

68 CIA, Foreign Broadcast Information Service, Daily Report, Foreign Radio Broadcasts, FBIS-FRB-62-207, Indonesia, 23 October 1962. However, in his autobiography Sukarno stated that there were two U-2 flights 'over Irian'. See: Sukarno 1966, p. 288.

69 Suharto 1989, p. 108.

70 TNA, AIR 24/2692, FEAF Weekly Intelligence Summary 26/62, Reports Received During the Period Ending 13 July 1962, not dated. W-class stood for 'Whiskey' class, Whiskey being the NATO codename for Project 613 submarines.

71 Foreign Relations of the United States (FRUS), 1961–63, Vol. XXIII, Southeast Asia, Document 275, Memorandum Komer to Kennedy, 16 July 1962.

72 TNA, FO 371/166547, Telegram 30, Geneva to Foreign Office, 23 July 1962.

> …the only way by which the Indonesians could penetrate the Dutch destroyer screen [around West New Guinea] would be by submarine attacks. These submarines had Soviet crews and if Dutch destroyers were attacked, the United States Government would know that the Russians had taken this warlike action.[73]

Pushkin gave no substantive reply to this warning merely saying that Sullivan 'spoke like a colonialist.'[74]

4.5 Averting War

The Indonesian military build-up formed an ominous backdrop to the talks in Middleburg and Subandrio used the threat of war to extract concessions from the Dutch. He asked for West New Guinea to be transferred to Indonesia by 31 December 1962 and for minimal United Nations' involvement in subsequent consultations with the Papuans on self-determination. When the Dutch balked at these modifications to the Bunker Plan Subandrio declared that he would break off talks and return to Jakarta within three days.[75] His departure would signify war and the United States had to apply maximum pressure to keep the negotiations going. On the evening of 26 July President Kennedy and Rusk met privately with Subandrio and according to Subandrio's account of the meeting, the president warned that if Jakarta used force he would have to send units of the 7th Fleet to evacuate American citizens from Indonesia.[76] Subandrio and other Indonesian officials interpreted this as a threat that the United States would militarily intervene in an Indonesian-Dutch war.[77] At the same time the Americans pressed the Dutch to give ground. Through these efforts they managed to push the two sides into a compromise on the hand over date. On 29 July, Subandrio and the Dutch negotiators agreed that the transfer of West New Guinea could take place on 1 May 1963.[78]

Despite this breakthrough, it would take another two weeks to work out the details of a deal and during this period the Indonesians maintained the pressure by continuing their guerrilla infiltrations and preparations for Operation Jayawijaya. On 3 August Sukarno broadly accepted the agreement negotiated by Subandrio but

---

[73] Ibid.

[74] Ibid.

[75] Drooglever 2009, pp. 495–497; See: Sukarno, 1966, p. 75.

[76] FRUS, 1961–63, Vol. XXIII, Southeast Asia, Document 281, Memorandum of a Conversation between Rusk and van Roijen, 26 July 1962; Subandrio 2001, p. 77.

[77] Ibid; FRUS, 1961–63, Vol. XXIII, Southeast Asia, Document 285, Telegram Jakarta to State Department, 3 August 1962; TNA, FO 371/166548, Telegram 525, Selby to Foreign Office, 1 August 1962; DDRS, Telegram SF1007, CIA to White House, 2 August 1962.

[78] Drooglever 2009, p. 498.

the Mandala command only postponed Jayawijaya by 14 days rather than halting it altogether.[79] It was not until 11 August that the Mandala command was ordered to cancel plans for a large-scale attack. Four days later Subandrio signed a final agreement with the Dutch in New York.[80] Under the terms of this agreement the United Nations would take control over West New Guinea and transfer the territory to Indonesia on 1 May 1963.[81] The Papuans would have to rely on an ill-defined 'act of free choice' held before the end of 1969 to give their views. Essentially the Dutch had been browbeaten into handing West New Guinea over to Indonesia.

In the end then, Sukarno did not need to fight a full-scale war to recover West New Guinea. But there is evidence from Indonesian and Russian sources that if Operation Jayawijaya had been launched the Soviet-manned submarines would have participated. Admiral Sudomo, the Mandala naval commander, later revealed in a newspaper article in 2005 that six submarines with Russian crews had formed the strategic reserve of the Jayawijaya amphibious landing force and had been held ready at Bitung in east Sulawesi.[82] During a visit by Sukarno to Moscow in 1964, Khrushchev reminded him that the USSR had provided Indonesia with pilots and sailors and said that 'If you [had] faced Holland, our people were with you there. That is a fact.'[83] Soviet submarine veterans had dramatic tales of being on the verge of war. Ryzhikov recalled that on 29 July 1962 his submarine had received orders from Admiral Sergey Gorshkov, the Commander in Chief of the Soviet Fleet, to secretly patrol a combat zone west of New Guinea and sink any shipping after midnight on 5 August.[84] When 5 August came, this order was rescinded and Ryzhikov's submarine sailed on the surface to Bitung, where it spent the rest of the crisis. Gennadi Melkov, an officer on another Soviet submarine, claimed his craft had orders to attack at midnight on 15 August oil storage tanks at the port of Manokwari in West New Guinea and torpedo a Dutch frigate nearby.[85]

In the final stages of the crisis, Western intelligence services did have some indications that Soviet-crewed submarines were allocated to the Indonesian invasion fleet and might take part in the operation. On 15 August the Dutch intelligence liaison officer in Singapore reported that Sukarno had agreed to Russians manning submarines but not Tu-16 bombers.[86] The CIA's 'Current Intelligence Weekly

[79] FRUS, 1961–63, Vol. XXIII, Southeast Asia, Document 285, Telegram Jakarta to State Department, 3 August 1962; Nasution 1985, p. 313.

[80] JFK, Reel 10, Telegram 128, State Department to The Hague, 11 August 1962.

[81] Drooglever 2009, pp. 765–770.

[82] Sudomo, "Perebutan Irian Barat: Di Balik Konflik RI-Belanda 1962", Suara Pembaruan, 11 August 2005. Available at https://groups.yahoo.com/neo/groups/tionghoa-net/conversations/messages/37748 Accessed 8 March 2014.

[83] Artizov 2007, p. 153. Translation by author.

[84] Ryzhikov 1995, pp. 52–54; Rijs 1999, p. 5.

[85] Rijs 1999, p. 1, 5; Ooms 2012, p. 25.

[86] Ooms 2012, p. 26.

Review' issued on 17 August referred to 'the large [Indonesian] task force located in Bangkalan Bay in the Celebes [Sulawesi], and the six Soviet-manned submarines attached to it.'[87]

What is surprising is that despite these reports, the Dutch Cabinet was apparently not informed of the presence of Soviet personnel even though The Netherlands was on the brink of war with Indonesia.[88] It is not clear why this was. One possibility is the intelligence on Soviet involvement was fragmentary and unconfirmed. Another possibility is that the Anglo-Saxon powers did have reliable intelligence but were not fully sharing it with the Dutch because it came from Sigint. It is notable that more references to Soviet participation in the Indonesian attack force do appear in post-crisis British and American documents. A British Joint Intelligence Committee study of Soviet defence policy in October 1962 recorded that there was 'some evidence that Soviet-manned Indonesian submarines were prepared to operate in the event of an Indonesian attack on West Irian, to make up for the technical inadequacies of the Indonesians.'[89] A month later the First Lord of the Admiralty warned the Minister of Defence that 'There were indications that the Russians would have been prepared to man some Indonesian submarines for the West Irian Campaign.'[90] A CIA memorandum in November 1962 claimed that 'Soviet eagerness to embroil the Indonesians in open warfare with the Dutch' had led them 'to permit the use of Soviet personnel to operate some of the weapons being provided. Six submarines manned by Soviet crews actually conducted war patrols under nominal Indonesian command.'[91]

4.6 Conclusion

Overall, it appears that Western intelligence had a mixed performance in the West New Guinea crisis. American and Australian intelligence assessments in 1962 failed to predict that Khrushchev might provide Indonesia with Soviet-manned submarines and bombers. As in the case of Cuba, American intelligence underestimated the risks Khrushchev was prepared to take and his willingness to use Soviet military units in the developing world. Western intelligence services did not know the details of the agreement between Subandrio and Khrushchev in Moscow in May 1962 and could not give advance warning of the Soviet deployment. These were essentially failures of analysis and political/diplomatic intelligence.

---

[87] DNSA, CIA Current Intelligence Weekly Review, 17 August 1962.

[88] Ooms 2012, p. 27.

[89] TNA, CAB 158/47, Memorandum JIC (62) 81 (Final), 1 October 1962.

[90] TNA, DEFE 13/139, Minute 1st Lord of the Admiralty to Minister of Defence, 26 November 1962.

[91] NARA, CREST, Memorandum from Lehman to Executive Director, enclosing paper on 'CIA Handling of the Soviet Build-up in Cuba', 14 November 1962.

Western military intelligence was much more successful. Once the Soviet submarines and aircraft were despatched the Americans were able to track their progress to Indonesia. American and British intelligence were also aware by mid-July that the submarines were fully manned by Soviet personnel and by the end of the crisis they had information that these units might participate in Operation Jayawijaya.

It is quite possible though that American intelligence had some help from the Indonesians. When later talking about the supply of Soviet-manned submarine and bombers to Indonesia, Mikoyan made an intriguing statement that

> Indonesia was very smart – as if it was hiding something from the Americans, but in reality it actually helped the Americans to find out what Soviet weapons they had. The Americans learned about this. Now they were facing the question: Did they want to get into a confrontation with those ships on the side of Holland…? But this was very unfavourable for them: they knew what kind of forces we had that were concentrated in that area. All those forces were under the Indonesian flag. There was no Soviet flag on those ships, they had been temporarily transferred to Sukarno. And therefore, Sukarno was able, while playing with two pieces on the political chessboard, to force Holland to give up Western Irian to Indonesia through the Americans.[92]

Mikoyan's remarks raise the possibility that the Indonesians deliberately let American intelligence discover that Soviet seamen were manning some 'Indonesian' submarines. Some support for this interpretation comes from a confidant of Sukarno, Wibisana, who claimed that in 1962 he took a CIA officer to Surabaya harbour and a military airfield in east Java to show him Indonesia's Soviet supplied submarines and aircraft.[93] According to Wibisana, this had allowed the CIA officer 'to also discover that Russian crews were standing by for the submarines and aircraft.'[94] The difficulty with Wibisana's account is that he described this event as happening during Robert Kennedy's visit to Indonesia in February 1962 and as we now know, the Soviet-manned submarines and planes did not arrive in Indonesia until June. Still, it is conceivable that Sukarno believed he could derive some diplomatic advantage by surreptitiously revealing to the Americans that Soviet personnel were manning submarines for him. This would demonstrate to Washington that at least part of an Indonesian attack on West New Guinea would be militarily effective and capable of inflicting real damage on the Dutch forces. It could also play on United States' anxieties about the developing relationship between Indonesia and the USSR and make the Americans more willing to push the Dutch into a settlement.

Finally, the example of West New Guinea highlights one of the problems of being reliant upon military intelligence. The American intelligence community was able to track the movement of Soviet submarines and bombers to Indonesia and establish that they were being manned by Soviet personnel. In this way it could

---

[92] Mikoyan 2012, pp. 467–468.

[93] Giebels 2001, p. 259.

[94] Ibid. Translation by author.

make up for some of the deficiencies in Western diplomatic intelligence on the Soviet Union. But in the Cold War good knowledge of Soviet military deployments did not necessarily enable Western intelligence to understand the motivations behind these deployments. For example, after the discovery of the missiles in Cuba the CIA did not fully appreciate that one of Khrushchev's main motivations for deploying nuclear missiles was to protect the Cuban communist regime from American attack.[95] Over West New Guinea Khrushchev's motives were equally unclear. The CIA did suggest the Soviets might have encouraged Sukarno to attack West New Guinea in order to divert American attention away from the build-up taking place on Cuba.[96] But without hard evidence this was only speculation and with Russian archives closed on this topic even today, we still do not know if this hypothesis was correct. Some Cold War intelligence puzzles could not be solved with good military intelligence alone.

References

Aid M (2009) The Secret Sentry: The Untold History of the National Security Agency. Bloomsbury Press, New York

Aid M, Wiebes C (eds) (2001) Secrets of Signals Intelligence during the Cold War and Beyond. Frank Cass, London

Andriia͡nov V (2003) Kosygin. Molodaia͡ Gvardiia͡, Moscow

Artizov A (ed) (2007) Nikita Khrushchev 1964: stenogrammy plenuma TS͡K KPSS i drugie dokumenty. Materik, Moscow

Boden R (2006) Die Grenzen der Weltmacht: Sowjetische Indonesienpolitik von Stalin bis Breznev. Franz Steiner Verlag, Stuttgart

De Graaff BGJ, Wiebes C (1998) Villa Maarheeze: De Geschiedenis van de Inlichtingendienst Buitenland. SDU, The Hague

Dinas Sejarah Militer TNI – Angkatan Darat, 1972 Cuplikan Sejarah Perjuangan TNI – Angkatan Darat, Fa Mahjuma and Dinas Sejarah, Jakarta

Djamin A (ed) (2001) Ir. H. Djuanda, Negarawan, Administrator dan Teknokrat Utama. Buku Kompas, Jakarta

Drooglever P (2009) An Act of Free Choice: Decolonization and the Right to Self-Determination in West Papua. Oneworld, Oxford

Easter D (2008) GCHQ and British External Policy in the 1960s. Intelligence and National Security, 23(5):681–706

Easter D (2012) Code Words, Euphemisms and What They Can Tell Us About Cold War Anglo-American Communications Intelligence. Intelligence and National Security, 27(6):875–895

Fursenko A (ed) (2008) Prezidium TS͡K KPS. 1954–1964 Tom 3. Postanovleniia͡ 1959-1964 Rospen, Moscow

Fursenko A, Naftali T (1999) One Hell of a Gamble: Khrushchev, Castro, Kennedy and the Cuban Missile Crisis, 1958–1964. Pimlico, London

[95] Garthoff 1998, pp. 24–26.

[96] CIA FOIA, Memorandum by the National Indications Center on 'The Soviet Bloc Armed Forces and the Cuban Crisis: A Discussion of Readiness Measures', 15 July 1963.

Garthoff R (1998) US Intelligence in the Cuban Missile Crisis. Intelligence and National Security 13(3):18–64
Giebels L (2001) Soekarno President: Een Biografie 1950–1970. Uitgeverij Bert Bakker, Amsterdam
Jones H (1971) Indonesia: The Possible Dream. Harcourt Brace Jovanovich Inc, New York
Jones M (2002) Conflict and Confrontation in South East Asia, 1961–1965: Britain, the United States and the Creation of Malaysia. Cambridge University Press, Cambridge
Khrushchev N (2007) Memoirs of Nikita Khrushchev: Volume 3: Statesman (1953–1964). Pennsylvania State Press, Pennsylvania
Koster B (1991) Een Verloren Land: De Regering Kennedy en de Nieuw-Guinea Kwestie, 1961–62. Anthos, Baarn
Mikoyan S, Savranskaya S (2012) The Soviet Cuban Missile Crisis: Castro, Mikoyan, Kennedy, Khrushchev and the Missiles of November. Woodrow Wilson Center Press/Stanford University Press, Chicago
Muraviev A, Brown C (2008) Strategic Realignment or Déjà vu? Russia-Indonesia Defence Cooperation in the Twenty-First Century, Australian National University Strategic and Defence Studies Centre, Working Paper No. 411
Nasution A (1985) Memenuhi Panggilan Tugas, Jilid 5: Kenangan Masa Orde Lama. Gunung Agung, Jakarta
Ooms M (2012) Geheime Sovjetsteun in Nieuw-Guinea. Marineblad 122(5): 23–28
Opris P (2012) Romania and the Cuban Missile Crisis: Soviet Nuclear Warheads for Romania? Cold War International History Project Bulletin, 17/18:514–521
Penders C (2002) The West New Guinea Debacle: Dutch Decolonisation and Indonesia, 1945–1962. University of Hawaii Press, Honolulu
Platje W (2001) Dutch Sigint and the Conflict with Indonesia, 1950–62. In: Aid M, Wiebes C (eds) Secrets of Signals Intelligence during the Cold War and Beyond. Frank Cass, London
Rijs B (1999) Moskou beraamde in 62 aanval op Nieuw-Guinea. De Volkskrant, pp. 1, 5
Ryzhikov R (1995) Topi ikh vsekh!, Tekhnika Molodezhi, 1995–11
Ryzhikov R (2004) Na Rumbe – Okean. IPP Novik, Sint Petersburg
Subandrio (2001) Meluruskan Sejarah Perjuangan Irian Barat. Yayasan Kepada Bangsaku, Jakarta
Suharto (1989) Pikiran, Ucapan dan Tindakan Saya: Otobiografi. PT. Citra Lamtoro Guna Persada, Jakarta
Sukarno (1966) Sukarno: An Autobiography as told to Cindy Adams. Gunung Agung, Hong Kong
Webster D (2009) Fire and the Full Moon: Canada and Indonesia in a Decolonizing World. UBC Press, Vancouver

Author Biography

David Easter, lecturer in War Studies Online at King's College, London, obtained his Ph.D. from the London School of Economics and Political Science. He has been a Fellow at the Cold War Studies Centre/IDEAS. His research interests include British foreign and defence policy, signals intelligence and the Cold War, especially the interplay between Cold War, nationalism and anti-colonialism in conflicts in the Middle East and South East Asia. His book, *Britain and the Confrontation with Indonesia, 1960–1966*, was published by I.B. Tauris in 2004. He has published in *Intelligence and National Security* and *Cold War History.* He is currently writing a monograph on Indonesia in the Cold War.

Chapter 5
Postmodern Intelligence: Strategic Warning and Crisis Management

Chong Guan Kwa

Abstract This chapter argues the need for a paradigm shift in intelligence practice in the face of contemporary strategic challenges. The classic linear way to handle a crisis, as epitomized in the Cuba crisis of October 1962, is particularly ill suited in the face of contemporary non-linear challenges. The pace of events, the overload of real-time information and an increase in the number of actors—both state and non-state—that are able to present strategic challenges require a different approach both to intelligence and to the notion of strategic surprise. This approach is to be found in the analysis of multiple narratives leading to the identification of a number of possible scenarios rather than in attempts to connect the dots in time, attempts which inevitably reflect our own biases.

Keywords Crisis management · Strategic surprise · Bias · South China Sea

Contents

C.G. Kwa (✉)
S. Rajaratnam School of International Studies, Nanyang Technological University, Singapore, Singapore
e-mail: iscgkwa@ntu.edu.sg

F. Baudet et al. (eds.), *Perspectives on Military Intelligence from the First World War to Mali*, DOI 10.1007/978-94-6265-183-8_5

5.1 Introduction

> There cannot be a crisis next week. My schedule is already full.
>
> Henry Kissinger[1]

This chapter argues for a paradigm shift in our understanding of international crises and the role intelligence can play in channelling them.[2] In our current understanding of such crises, they are unexpected and surprising turns of events that threaten the survival of the nation-state, or, more generally speaking, the balance of power in a given part of the world. They erupt when one actor is able to 'strategically surprise' the other. Jones and Silberzahn define this surprise as 'the sudden realization that one has been operating on the basis of an erroneous threat assessment that results in a failure to anticipate a grave threat to 'vital' national interests'.[3] Strategic surprises are construed as a failure of strategic intelligence. This is because strategic intelligence is expected to provide the policy maker with the information which anticipates what the adversary is planning and so enable him to take appropriate pre-emptive action to deny the adversary a decisive strategic advantage.

This understanding of both international crises and the purpose of strategic intelligence is largely based on the model of the Cuba Crisis when agile US diplomacy found a way out of an impending nuclear stand-off. The US Administration's response to the discovery of ballistic missiles on Cuba in October 1962, and the role of US intelligence before and during the ensuing international crisis have been a topic of continuing interest as it is one of the few cases where an international crisis with potentially grave consequences did not end in war.[4] Based on Jones and Silberzahn's definition quoted above, the modern age has seen similar strategic surprises that have similarly been attributed to short-comings in the collection, processing, analysis and dissemination of intelligence. These include the 1973 Yom Kippur War, the 1979 Iranian Revolution—that fundamentally altered the balance of power in the Middle East and could be considered a defeat for the United States—, the collapse of the Soviet empire, and 9/11. Other instances of failure, with strategic consequences, include the issue of weapons of mass destruction in Iraq in 2003.[5]

Several of these have resulted in inquiries and in attempts to redress what went wrong. In fact, the CIA owes its existence to such an effort.[6] The same goes for a

---

[1] Attributed to Henry Kissinger and quoted with his permission in Leventhal 2011, p. 80.

[2] Cf. Gilpin and Murphy 2008 for a similar call for a paradigm shift in corporate world approach to crisis management.

[3] Jones and Silberzahn 2013, p. 5.

[4] Allison and Zelikow 1999; Fursenko and Naftali 1998; Gioe et al. 2014.

[5] Seliktar 2004; Jervis 2010; Jones and Silberzahn 2013.

[6] Jones and Silberzahn 2013, p. 1.

number of other services. These learning efforts often led to new arrangements between services, the accordance of new powers to them, and the creation of coordinating bodies or even entirely new services. However, these adaptations have not prevented the occurrence of new strategic surprises.

This chapter argues that instead of reframing intelligence architectures, we should examine how to reframe our understanding of international crises, and our expectations of intelligence in the management of such crises.[7] This is especially important in an age in which hybrid challenges abound. 'Classic' inter-state confrontations seem less likely to occur but cannot be excluded. In fact, a number of key areas could be defined in which the Great Game, the 19th century rivalry between two great powers in relation to Asia, seems to have returned. There is growing rivalry in the seas to the south and east of the People's Republic of China. There is outright tension between Russia's, the EU's and the United States' visions for Ukraine, Syria and the wider Middle East. Further east, India and China compete for influence in the Indian Ocean. In the meantime, the number of (friendly or adversarial) non-state actors whose actions may lead to strategic surprise has multiplied. Globalisation has produced an unprecedented level of interconnectedness and there seems to be considerable truth in the idea that a butterfly flapping its wings in Brazil may produce a tornado in Texas.[8] At the same time not only the generally hierarchical architecture of intelligence services, but also the mindset of intelligence personnel and policy makers is ill-suited to adequately respond to challenges, and especially to crises emanating from them. In short, what is needed is a paradigm shift.

The argument is based on an analysis of the nature of international crises, and the role intelligence is expected to play in controlling and channelling these. I will discuss a number of factors that have come to complicate the fulfilment of this expectation. Lastly I will propose a different approach to strategic warning. I will illustrate my point by referencing a number of cases.

5.2 Understanding International Crises

An international crisis can be said to occur when one party, or both, recognizes that normal diplomatic relations have broken down and events are taking an unexpected and surprising turn that precipitates a crisis that has to be managed if war is to be avoided. At this point, strategic intelligence can be said to have failed as it is expected to provide policy makers with the foreknowledge of events taking such an unpredicted turn. Given that a key element of crisis is unpredictability such a verdict seems somewhat contradictory. Nonetheless, we then enter a new phase: crisis management. As Williams reminds us, crisis management is about

[7] Compare veteran CIA analyst Davis 2003a, b and idem 2009, pp. 173–188.

[8] Lorenz 1972; for a recent discussion see Bousquet 2008.

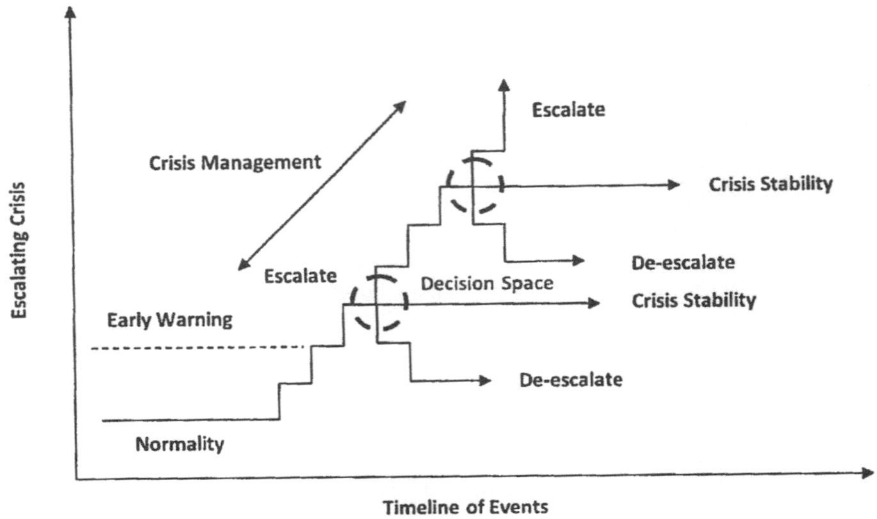

Figure 5.1 Crisis Management. *Source* Kwa 2012

maintaining control over such events. Successful crisis management is about recognizing the limits of coercive diplomacy and the necessity of moderation.[9] A diplomatic crisis can be conceived as an ascending stairway to war on which there are at every step opportunities to de-escalate and return to a normal state of affairs, or achieve a standoff with no resolution of the crisis or climb up the next step of the crisis (Fig. 5.1).

The first step of political crisis management is to achieve an understanding of what sense the adversaries are making of their rapidly changing environment. What are the motives of the other side in pursuing this course of action which has led to a crisis? This understanding, especially the resolve of the other side in holding on to their intentions, is a key to our formulation of a strategy for the settlement of the crisis.[10] The crux of successful crisis management is awareness that the degree of coercion we are prepared to exert on the adversary—often in response to our own domestic and bureaucratic politics—feeds back into the crisis. Our response then becomes the basis of the next phase of the crisis when the adversary has to decide what to do next.[11]

The Cuban missile crisis may serve as an illustration. While President Kennedy is usually praised for his handling of the crisis, the evaluations of the performance of the American intelligence community have focused on its failure to estimate the Soviet intent to deploy strategic missiles on Cuba. Special National Intelligence

---

[9] George 1991; Williams 1976.

[10] Lebow 1981.

[11] See de Montbrail 2013 for an in-depth analysis.

Estimate (SNIE 85-3-62) issued on 19 September 1962 argued against Soviet deployment of missiles on Cuba because the risks involved were 'incompatible with Soviet practice to date and with Soviet policy as we presently estimate it'.[12] At the same time US intelligence was monitoring Soviet activities on Cuba using the high-altitude U2 aerial reconnaissance plane. Subsequent analysis of the photographs indicated and then confirmed the construction of ballistic missile sites at San Cristobal, which precipitated the crisis.

For Kennedy the crisis erupted on 14 October 1962 when U2 aerial photography confirmed the construction of missiles sites on Cuba and undermined the Special National Intelligence Estimate 85-3-62 that had argued that the Soviets had no interest in deploying missiles in Cuba and therefore would not resort to it. As Kennedy and his associates had earlier been reassured by this Estimate, they now were fundamentally surprised that Khrushchev would act so irrationally against what they, the White House policy group, perceived to be Soviet national interests and clear US warnings of its interests.[13] For Soviet leader Khrushchev however a crisis would erupt if the United States discovered the deployment of missiles before the Soviets had completed it and so present the United States with a *fait accompli.* Khrushchev thought Kennedy would not react because the US was already vulnerable to Soviet intercontinental missiles and Soviet missiles in Cuba were therefore not a new or escalating threat. In addition, Khrushchev may have assessed that the Soviet Union could withstand any diplomatic pressure from the young and inexperienced US President.[14]

The Cuban missile crisis could well have sparked a nuclear war. It did not, but it cemented conventional thinking of international crises. It seemed to confirm the idea, stemming from the Japanese surprise attack on Pearl Harbor, that intelligence cannot adequately provide strategic early warning. As said, the CIA actually did consider the possibility of Khrushchev deciding to base offensive missiles in Cuba, but ruled out this prospect. 'Cuba' thus seems just another instance of intelligence failure to provide policy makers with strategic early warning, just like the predecessors of the CIA failed to provide their service chiefs and national leaders warning of the Japanese decision to go to war with the US. Declassified records now enable us to assess the high level of support US intelligence provided to their policy makers during the crisis. While they misjudged Khrushchev's intentions, they did monitor the levels of the Soviet build-up on Cuba and globally. They also attempted to estimate Soviet reactions to possible US actions against their missiles deployed on Cuba. Lastly, the intelligence community monitored the Soviets' removal of their missiles from Cuba. Incidentally, they also highlight a difference between Soviet and US decision-making. Soviet archives indicate that Soviet

---

[12] CIA History Staff 1992.

[13] Williams 1976, Chap. 7; George and Simons 1994.

[14] Fursenko and Naftali 1998.

intelligence was cut out of the Soviet decision-making including that which led to the deployment of Soviet missiles on Cuba. And during the crisis it had no information on the United States' options and response to this deployment.[15]

In formulating their response to Khrushchev's challenge, Kennedy and his associates showed they understood the dynamics of crisis management as outlined above. They were well aware of the momentous consequences of failure and their responses in the Cuban missile crisis were in large part driven by how their decisions would be judged both in Moscow, and by history a decade or a century later. In Neustadt and May's words, Kennedy and his team were 'thinking in time.'[16]

Their approach is markedly different from what we know about the American response to the al-Qaeda 9/11 attack on the New York World Trade Centre. This was driven only in part by its understandings of al-Qaeda narratives of its Islamic vision of the world. But more important to the formulation of this response was how those al-Qaeda visions fed into US visions of al-Qaeda's place and role in the world, views that were defined by a group of neo-conservative policy-makers who saw al-Qaeda's actions as an evil that the US must engage in a Manichean struggle against.

As a consequence of US post-9/11 policies, Al-Qaeda then was able to 'prove' that their own narrative on US policies and intentions was correct, which, no doubt, won it support throughout the Islamic world where narratives critical of the US had won a firm basis. This set the US on a protracted 'war on terror', that by definition cannot be won.[17]

5.3 Why Has Intelligence Failed in Anticipating International Crises?

Traditionally, the intelligence community is expected to support policy makers in the management of an (impending) international crisis. Three distinct functions come to mind. Firstly, the intelligence community is to provide the policy maker with early warning of the impending breakdown of normalcy and the possible outbreak of a crisis, or worse, surprise attack. Secondly, during the crisis, it is expected to provide the policy maker with a constant flow of estimates and assessments of the other side's intentions and response to the changing

[15] Blight and Welch 1988; Fursenko and Naftali 1998.

[16] Neustadt and May 1986, p. 14.

[17] Adam Curtis' three-part television series The Power of Nightmares (2004) brings out, in albeit simplified form for television format, this epic interplay of two cosmic visions and their moral disgust with each other. Ex-CIA analyst Michael Scheuer, writing anonymously makes the same critique of the US, that its imperial hubris will be its downfall in its war on al-Qaeda (Scheuer 2004).

environment. Thirdly, these estimates and assessments are expected to provide the policy maker with an advantage in negotiating a settlement of the crisis or prosecution of a war.[18]

The track record of the intelligence community in fulfilling these expectations during a crisis has been dismal. Prussia's victory over Austria in the battle of Sadowa (1866); the Russo-Japanese War in 1904; the Japanese attack on Pearl Harbor (1941); the North Korean attack on South Korea in June 1950, and Chinese intervention in that conflict; the Suez War of 1956; the Indo-Chinese War of 1962; crisis and surprise in three Arab-Israeli Wars (1948, 1967, 1973); the Argentinian invasion of the Falklands (1982) and Iraq's 1990 invasion of Kuwait were all strategic surprises in which the incentives and opportunities for a surprise attack in a political crisis were all overlooked. In this dismal record only the Cuban Missile Crisis and the earlier Berlin Blockade Crisis of 1948–49, and, possibly, the Sino-Soviet border crisis of 1969 stand out as examples of successful crisis management which did not lead to war even when intelligence did not provide adequate early warning.[19]

The limited number of identified instances of successful de-escalation in which strategic intelligence may (or may not) have contributed, has focused scholarly attention on failures in crisis management. Subsequent post-mortems and studies on each of these crises have generally blamed the intelligence community for not having provided their policy makers with the foresight and understanding to successfully avoid war.[20] The underlying assumption is that these failures could have been averted if only the intelligence professionals had better anticipated.

Broadly speaking, four categories of failure have been identified. The first category of failures is the inability of intelligence to see through the fog of deception generated by the adversary in the build-up to a crisis. Central to penetrating the fog of deception is uncovering the adversary's actions to cover and conceal his movements to launch a surprise attack. The Soviets successfully covered and concealed much of their shipment of their missiles to Cuba from the CIA until 14 October 1962, when they were about to complete it. Barton Whaley[21] pioneered the study of stratagems that state actors employ in a crisis to deceive and surprise their adversary for a strategic advantage. Whaley's 1973 study of the signals and warnings of the German invasion of Russia in June 1941 is still significant in that it highlights how the Allied intelligence services read very different interpretations

---

[18] See Cradock 2002 on how the Joint Intelligence Committee, which he chaired from 1985 to 1992, attempted to provide this service to British Governments.

[19] Michael Handel has distinguished military surprise as an integral part of military planning from diplomatic surprise. Surprise in military planning is to gain a strategic advantage over the adversary who must be then deceived and deprived of knowledge of moves against him. In contrast, diplomatic surprise is about moves and signals to the adversary of planned changes in foreign policy which may surprise the other. The 1971 US-Chinese rapprochement is an instance of a major diplomatic surprise de-escalating US-China tensions. See Handel 1981.

[20] Knorr and Morgan 1983; Diamond 2008, pp. 11–12. Cf. Mahadevan in this volume.

[21] Whaley 1969.

into these warnings.[22] The lesson that intelligence services have drawn is that deception and denial of information by the adversary of its intentions and actions are a major obstacle they are up against in their efforts to provide better assessments and estimates to their policy makers. Given that successful deception feeds into, and exploits the adversary's expectations and preconceptions to 'see what they expect to see', the need for counter-deception strategies seems evident. At the same time, it is justified to ask to what extent it is actually feasible or possible to successfully employ these.[23] It is easy to preach as Sunzi did some two millennia ago that success in battle depends upon knowing oneself first, but practising that maxim is not easy.

The second category of explanations for intelligence failures are the cognitive biases driving intelligence analysis. As CIA veteran Richards J. Heuer, Jr., has advised his staff, there are biases in the evaluation of evidence; biases in perception of cause and effect; biases in estimating probabilities and finally hindsight biases in evaluating the quality and value of intelligence products.[24] Studies by a generation of scholars from Roberta Wohlstetter in her 1962 classic study of Pearl Harbor to Richard Betts, Robert Jervis and a generation of post-Yom Kippur Israeli scholars led by Michael Handel and including Zvi Lanir and more recently Ariel Levite and Ephraim Kam have all lamented the inevitability of strategic surprise in a crisis which could lead to a surprise attack. For these analysts, as a result of cognitive bias, surprise is inevitable.[25] Their conclusions are largely upheld today.[26]

The third category of reasons for intelligence failures to forecast crisis and surprise attacks is believed to originate from the management and organization of the intelligence services. This has been the finding of most Commissions of Inquiry from the *Congressional Hearings* into Pearl Harbor in 39 volumes to the Agranat Commission on failures in Israeli intelligence in the run-up to the Yom Kippur War in October 1973. More recently, the *9/11 Commission Report* and the July 2004 Butler report on Iraq called for reform of not only the intelligence community, but much of the entire government.[27] In the US this produced the establishment of the DNI that, however, like the CIA before it, developed into a service of its own rather than a body that would coordinate and in a sense fuse each individual service's

---

[22] Whaley 1973.

[23] Bennett and Waltz 2007; Daniel and Herbig 1982.

[24] Heuer Jr. 1999.

[25] Wohlstetter 1962; Betts 1982; Jervis 2010 draws on a study on the Iranian Revolution he was commissioned by the CIA to undertake thirty years ago; Handel 1984; Handel 1989, pp 229–311; Levite 1987; Kam 1988. See Lanir 1983. I thank Zvi Lanir, who served in the Israeli Defense Force intelligence, for discussing his work with me in the late 1980s.

[26] Cf. Betts and Mahnken 2003.

[27] Byman 2005, pp. 145–170; Jervis 2010.

assessments. The continuing challenge in reforming the intelligence services is finding the delicate balance between over-centralisation, and decentralization and pluralism.[28]

Finally, a key to the failure of intelligence services to warn of an impending crisis may lie in their relations to their policy maker.[29] The mainstream expectation of the intelligence analyst is that he is to provide an objective and accurate picture of 'what is out there' to his policy maker. He is expected to 'tell truth to power'. In many countries the analyst is excluded from the policy process itself to ensure that his estimates and assessments are not biased and politicized. But there is a downside to this, as Richard Betts argued back in 1982.[30] Betts opined that intelligence may correctly anticipate a crisis, but policy makers may either choose to ignore warnings or be reluctant to authorize a military response. Less dramatically, separated from the policy process the intelligence analyst risks producing estimates and assessments that bear little relevance to policy needs and priorities. The challenge, as more than one intelligence analyst has recognized, therefore is how to be close to the policy maker without being caught in the policy process itself. Intelligence professionals have to withstand the pressure to produce politicized products which rationalize and justify certain policy goals, and as objectively as they possibly could advise on the possible political and military responses that these policy goals might evoke from the adversary. The British Joint Intelligence Committee epitomized this approach in that it brings together policy makers and intelligence officers in a single committee, but it, too, has not proven immune to bias, politicized intelligence, and failure.[31]

5.4 Emergent Issues in Crisis Management

The current and dominant framework for crisis management is that a crisis may be occurring once the warning signals that an international actor is out to challenge the international order and flaunting diplomatic protocols are disregarded or missed.[32] The challenge for policymakers is to recognize that the actor who challenges the international order has crossed the Rubicon, that a crisis is in progress and that contingency plans to contain the damage and limit the crisis must be launched. The

---

[28] Betts 2007, pp. 124–158.

[29] An issue that also worries strategic intelligence analysts and their managers; see for example, Davis 2002, 2003a, b and 2009. The British perspective is summed up in Omand 2010, pp. 171–208.

[30] Betts 1982, p. 4.

[31] On British intelligence failures: Bluth 2004; Fitzgerald and Lebow 2006; Lebow 2007; Morrison 2011.

[32] Boin et al. 2005. It is hardly different in business; see Harvard Business School, 1999. Compare Fink 2002. Mitroff et al. 1996 provides a more analytical approach outlining various qualitative techniques for crisis management.

successful containment and de-escalation of a crisis in large part depends upon how the policymaker makes sense of, and grasps the crisis as it unfolds.[33] For how policymakers make sense very much determines their response which in turn determines whether the crisis will de-escalate, reach some form of stability and stand-off, or escalate further.[34] What these functionaries subsequently tell their domestic and foreign audiences of what they are doing and why they are responding in this, and not another way to the situation, precludes certain courses of action and shapes the next phase of the crisis.[35]

This mechanism has changed little since Cuba and so have expectations of what intelligence should provide. The intelligence analyst is expected to provide early warning to enable the policy maker to take action and deter the opposing actor from destabilizing the status quo. Unsurprisingly, improvements in intelligence services' performance in the run-up to crises have been sought in more effective early warning systems.[36]

This persistent expectation that intelligence should provide the foresight and sufficient warning time to pre-empt strategic surprise in a crisis is based on an understanding of policy processes as rational, empirically-driven processes within which policy issues and challenges can be empirically verified and analysed. This analysis is then translated into a rational policy to solve the problem. This world-view assumes that the policy maker is in some control of his environment and assured of being able to decide his future in an orderly, stable and predictable world. Although states compete for influence and assets, they do so based on rational choices and clearly defined interests. The quote attributed to Kissinger at the start of this chapter reflects this idea of a fundamentally rational and organized world of policy making.

In this 'realist' worldview, an international crisis is precipitated by an actor who seeks to challenge and change the established order to his favour. Think of North Korea and Iran that, from the perspective of Washington and its allies, are examples of such actors due to their persistence in developing nuclear capabilities.

But while 'classic' crises involving two opposing states are still possible, the changing nature of the international system and the rise of non-state actors in it, suggest that crises increasingly may be of a different nature. In addition, in view of the rising number of audiences and potential stakeholders, crisis management is increasingly about political communication about our sense of the crisis and how

---

[33] The CIA appears to be exploring corporate practice of crisis planning in a category of "exotic" organizations called "high reliability organizations" (HROs) such as nuclear power plants, oil rigs and refineries where there is a high risk of accidents and are therefore expected to be preoccupied with warning systems and signals of breakdowns and accidents (Fishbein and Treverton 2004).

[34] See Smith 2006, pp. 301–317 and especially his Figs. 3 and 4 for a similar conceptualization of industrial crises.

[35] See Magnusson and Ottosson 2009.

[36] Note especially the declassified 40-year old CIA manual by Cynthia Grabo (who served as an US intelligence analyst from 1942 to 1980) and Jan Goldman (Grabo and Goldman 2010). An abridged version is in Grabo 2004. See also Bracken 2008, pp. 16–42, and Lavoix 2006.

we want to terminate it. Such communication is expected to do a number of things at the same time: it needs to define the crisis for a domestic audience, and bolster resolve to support a certain reaction. At the same time it needs to convince target audiences, plus those that happen to be listening, that we want to impose our solution *and* leave open the proverbial golden bridge. This sends out contradictory signals, which, in turn, complicates finding a solution.

This increased complexity underscores the need for policymakers and the intelligence community to start thinking about more sophisticated early warning systems.[37] But it is unlikely that any early warning system can anticipate the actions of, say, the skipper of a fishing vessel or the Captain of a naval patrol boat in the South China Sea when it is confronted by another naval vessel challenging its right to be where it is. Neither can intelligence anticipate the nature and extent of 'blowback' which will follow that naval confrontation or detention of a fishing vessel. Making sense of the crisis which followed the 26 March 2010 sinking of the Republic of Korea Ship Cheonan (PC-772) was difficult. The same was true of the 7 September 2010 collision of the Chinese trawler Minjinyu 5179 with Japanese Coast Guard patrol boats Yonakuni and Mizuki near the Senkaku Islands, and, more recently, of the 7 November 2011 Japanese Coast Guard detention of a Chinese fishing vessel within Japanese waters. Even today, there is considerable argument about the alternative explanations and narratives of what happened, and about the appropriateness of the responses that were intended to terminate these crises.

Similar challenges confront our attempts to better manage the political crises which erupted on 1 April 2001 over the Chinese interception of a US EP-3 surveillance plane 110 km from Hainan Island, and over the blocking on 23 March 2001 by the Chinese frigate Jianheu of the US Navy hydrographic survey vessel USNS Bowditch that collected data within China's exclusive economic zone in the South China Sea. As the South China Sea and the East China Sea are becoming increasingly contested, incidents occurring in these waters that escalate into political crises are likely to continue.[38]

What their role should be in mitigating such incidents at sea and in preventing their escalation is a key challenge for intelligence services today. The unintended consequences of an incident at sea between competing naval vessels or detention of fishing vessels are both unpredictable and indicative of a complex and chaotic world. The instinctive reaction of the skipper to being pursued by a coast guard vessel cannot be anticipated and may trigger a series of events which culminates in a diplomatic crisis which was totally unpredictable.

While such incidents themselves are hardly new,[39] what *is* new is that the policy maker today will not have the time Kennedy and his advisers had in 1962 to reflect on their proposed responses to Khrushchev. This is because information technology today has created a new matrix of real-time information flows which enable an

---

[37] Cf. Svendsen 2017.

[38] An issue argued for by Kwa 2010, pp. 227–231.

[39] A fine example is the incident that produced the War of Jenkins' Ear (1739–1748).

unprecedented number of not only participants in a crisis, but also observers to witness—and influence—what is happening.[40] The increased volume of real-time information engulfs the intelligence analyst, but also traditional media editors, whereas the speed of events unfolding further complicates both sense-making and formulating responses based thereupon. As a result, the response time for officials and policy makers to react to the detention of their fishing vessels, or collusion of their naval vessels, is contracted to single-digit hours as the unfolding crises is captured and broadcast by participants on their mobile applications. The crisis may be compounded by dormant or new stakeholders in the policy process emerging to assert a claim to the crisis for their own agendas. Non-governmental and other political movements or groups, for instance, may try to push policy makers towards their special interest.

The aforementioned incidents at sea in the South China Sea may serve as an illustration. They not only involved naval vessels of the conflicting parties, but also their coast guards and other maritime agencies with rather different agendas for how to terminate or extend the crisis. All this complicated making sense of them, as transpires from the fact that, as said, there is still considerable argument about what happened and whether the responses did not, in fact, worsen the crisis. This state of affairs suggests that strategic intelligence will probably be unable to help the policy maker in linking cause and effect. In the turbulence of a crisis these are impossible to determine. Cause and effect may be apparent only in hindsight. This makes it difficult, if not outright impossible, for the policy maker to decide how to intervene in the unfolding course of events to influence its dynamic and, hence, outcome.[41] Likewise, this makes it highly difficult for intelligence services to analyse their performance, to learn from it and to implement what they have learned.

5.5 Revising the Role of Intelligence in International Crisis Management

On 2 February 2002 Donald Rumsfeld, speaking on the absence of evidence linking Saddam Hussein to the supply of weapons of mass destruction to terrorist groups, said:

> There are known knowns; there are things we know. We also know there are known unknowns; that is to say we know there are some things we do not know. But there are also unknown unknowns — the ones we don't know we don't know.

While these words were uttered in a different context, they neatly sum up the agony faced by the policy maker in a crisis, when he is dragged out of working on

[40] Gowing 2009.

[41] Cilliers 2007.

issues which he is aware of what he knows and does not know into a world of 'unknown-unknowns'.

Dave Snowden, consultant and researcher in the field of knowledge management, currently at Hong Kong Polytechnic University, holds that decision-making on issues where we know what we know and where we can perceive cause and effect relations, is about applying standard operating procedures and best practices. Analytical systems thinking such as scenario planning by an expert community may lead to a solution based on good practice in deciding on problems where we know what we do not know. But in the chaos of a crisis where cause-and-effect-relationships cannot be established with any certainty—as said, they only may become apparent after the crisis has passed—then the

> leader's immediate job is not to discover patterns but to stanch the bleeding. A leader must first *act* to establish order, then sense where stability is present and from where it is absent, and then respond by working to transform the situation from chaos to complexity, where the identification of emerging patterns can both help prevent future crises and discern new opportunities.[42]

In Snowden's Cynefin Framework for sense-making and decision-making (Fig. 5.2), the Cuban missile crisis would be a 'Complex' situation, where what would have been 'best' or 'good' diplomatic practice for Kennedy to respond to Khrushchev no longer worked. Kennedy was into a 'complex situation: where he fortunately had the time to probe, make sense and then respond to Khrushchev. But, I argue, the crisis emerging from an unplanned encounter at sea between a Japanese, Korean or Chinese Naval vessel in the East China Sea or in the South China Sea will be more a 'chaotic' situation in which policy makers will have to act first, and then after that, try to make sense of what is happening and then respond.

There is a similar transformation of high-risk industry accidents. The 2010 Deepwater Horizon oil spill was more complex and chaotic than earlier oilrig blowouts. The catastrophe and ensuing crisis after the meltdown of the Fukushima Daiichi Nuclear Power Plant in Japan when it was hit by the 11 March 2011 earthquake and tsunami was more than a complicated situation involving attempting to make sense of 'known-unknowns' about what was happening inside the reactor core. It became a chaotic crisis decision situation involving the internal politics of the ruling Democratic Party, tensions between politicians and bureaucrats and between central and local governments. This uncertainty and unpredictability in Japanese leadership and policymaking and failure of nuclear technology and engineering to provide solutions to the accident has made for a very difficult and still incomplete crisis recovery.

In my view, intelligence has a role to play in support of policy makers *acting* to seize control of events and impose some order at the onset of a diplomatic crisis. This applies to classic 'Cuba-type' models of crisis, but especially so to the type of crisis that may emanate from any confrontation between a Japanese and Chinese coast guard vessel in the East China Sea. This role, however, will be different from the old

[42] Snowden and Boone 2007.

Figure 5.2 The Cynefin Framework—after Snowden and Boone 2007

one of attempting to provide expert judgment on worse-case/warning-focused assessments based on incoming operational intelligence. The new role for intelligence will be providing a more complex analysis, probing and trying to make sense of 'unknown-unknowns' of how the Chinese and Japanese leaders are reading the other's actions and intentions in their perception of the emerging crisis, and deciding how to respond. This new role requires fundamental adaptation.

Intelligence's role may be particularly helpful to feed the slow thinking system of the policymaker's mind. As Fig. 5.1 illustrates, a diplomatic crisis may be compared to an ascending stairway to war on which there are at every step opportunities to either de-escalate and return to a normal state of affairs, or achieve a stand-off. Alternately, with no palatable solution within sight, policy makers could also choose to climb the next step.

In crises, the decision of whether to escalate or de-escalate the crisis or go for a stand-off is shaped by a range of cognitive biases attempting to instinctively make sense of the inherent chaotic situation.[43] Our minds, as Nobel Prize Laureate Daniel Kahneman has demonstrated, are wired to think fast and slow.[44] Fast thinking enables us to balance on a bicycle without falling, multiply 2×2 or orient to the source of a sudden sound and detect hostility in a voice. It is this system of fast thinking that usually drives our reactions to the world around us, and in this case, action to try to control a crisis. The slower, more deliberative and logical system of

[43] Weick 1988, pp. 305–317 and Weick 1995.
[44] Kahneman 2011.

our mind is only activated when fast thinking confronts a problem it has no immediate response to, like multiplying 17 × 24. The role of intelligence must be to support the slow thinking reflective system of the policymaker's mind. Arguably, intelligence support for the fast thinking system of the policymaker's mind has been its nemesis when it provided the policymaker desired evidence, for example of the presence of WMD in Iraq.

Intelligence should then feed the slow thinking system of the policymaker's mind to break the instinctive fast thinking system's move to action because that action will feed into the crisis and may escalate it. But decision-making in a crisis is not a static single choice. Rather, it is a dynamic decision-making problem requiring the policy maker to make sequential risky choices in a rapidly evolving and complex environment. The policymaker has to make sense of the feedback and consequences of his choice and decide how to respond to the next round of the crisis. Further, the policymaker can try to anticipate, but cannot control how a decision he makes now will impact on his options later in the unfolding crisis. The sequential risky choices made by adversaries in a crisis create an uncertain and unpredictable environment not under their control. The challenge for intelligence is to advise their policymakers on the adversary's capacity for risk, sensitize the policymaker to the possible consequences of his own risky choices on the adversary, and open up the policymaker's mind-set to divergent outcomes of the crisis.[45]

For, as Dave Snowden has pointed out, in a complex and chaotic world there is not one future we are working towards. Rather, there are multiple futures we could work towards which we need to probe, make sense of and then respond to. This is true in times of normalcy, but the same applies to crises: there is not one predictable outcome of a crisis or aim in resolving it. Rather, there are multiple possible outcomes as competing parties in the crisis manoeuvre and act out their scenarios to contain (or prolong, if not escalate) the crisis. The Chinese term for crisis, *weiji* refers to a possible disaster or danger. But the element *ji* in it in Chinese refers to creating and utilizing opportunities, i.e., furthering one's own interests. This renders the prospect of crisis management in a crisis that involves China more complex. China concurrently chases the conflicting policy aims of both preventing the escalation of a crisis and exploiting it to maximize its national interests.[46] This conceptualization contrasts with European and American conceptualizations of *crisis* (itself from Greek *krisis* 'judgement, turning point') that imply escalation and impending catastrophe ('turn for the worse'). These conceptualizations stimulate the idea that it is pertinent to contain its dangers through mediation and when necessary, compromise.

---

[45] See Kai He's 2016 international relations theory analysis of the factors which determine whether Chinese leaders escalate or scale down their responses in a crisis situation.

[46] Compare the 2013 attempt of the Japanese National Institute for Defense Studies to understand and make sense of crisis management in China, at http://www.nids.go.jp/english/publication/chinareport/.

Following Dave Snowden, the starting point of policy is not necessarily studying the past to get a clearer picture of the present in order to define a course of action that will lead towards the knowable future. Rather, the more useful starting point may be the multiple futures that a crisis could bring about. Intelligence analysts should probe for whether there are patterns among them which can then be worked back to our present. Understanding China's position on the South China Sea will, as a first step, entail the task of identifying the various Chinese agencies that have emerged or are emerging as interested parties claiming a stake in the issue. The second step would be trying to make sense of their different claims and core interests in the South China Sea.[47] But in order to define our policy options toward China, we need to go beyond that. Discerning the bureaucratic politics of Chinese agencies is only the first phase. We need to define different sets of outcomes and establish for each of them, working backwards, whether they fit actual behaviour to see how China's actions are shaped by what it wants.

The narrative underpinning China's response to the various crises it is involved in in the South and East China Seas is the narrative of China's rise after a 'century of humiliation'.[48] China also talks about reclaiming its rightful place in opposition to a Cold War strategy of containment enacted in a series of treaties at San Francisco at the end of World War II. This at least is the mainstream understanding. But, as the historian Paul A. Cohen has argued, behind China's actions there is a deeper narrative of suffering humiliation, sometimes externally inflicted, occasionally self-imposed, 'in order to carry out an important task' enshrined in the proverb *renru fuzhong*—which translates as 'to bite the bullet'. *Renru fuzhong* stems from a story about the fifth century BCE Yue king Goujian who, to save his beleaguered kingdom, went into self-exile and servitude in his rival's kingdom to buy time to rebuild his kingdom and eventually avenge himself in conquering his rival. Cohen has demonstrated the relevance of this story to understand the policies of Chiang Kai-shek, who identified with this king. Its influence is manifest in his sensing of the political crisis of Republican China in the 1920s–1930s and, after World War II, his decamping to Taiwan.[49] It is probable that the story not only has had an appeal to Chinese nationalists, but also to Mao and his successors. Are we today experiencing China's quest for revenge for its 'century of humiliation' now that China through patience, hard work and foresight triumphed against the odds

---

[47] See the International Crisis Group 2012 on trying to make sense of Chinese policies and positions on the South China Sea. The issue may be more complex than poor or lack of coordination between China's different state agencies claiming an interest in the South China Sea, as this report suggests. Rather, it may well be that each of these agencies has a different justification and narrative for its stake in the South China Sea.

[48] See Lovell 2011 for a historiographic analysis of the myths of the Opium Wars and its legacy in shaping China's relations with the West.

[49] Cohen 2009. He has since widened his thesis to reconstruct how often forgotten stories like the fall of Masada have been recalled as a leitmotif in modern Jewish memory, or Lawrence Olivier's film re-enactment of William Shakespeare's Henry V helped restore and unify British confidence towards the end of World War II (Cohen 2014).

and is now ready to avenge the humiliations inflicted upon it during the last 150 years or so?

For the ten members of the Association of Southeast Asian Nations, situated, in a sense, between China and the United States, and in many ways stakeholders themselves, the challenge is not only to make sense of Chinese narratives of the South China Seas, but also to make sense of narratives cherished by the leadership of Unites States and how these narratives shape their perception of developments in the South and East China Seas. This is especially relevant with regard to how they support their allies Japan or the Philippines in their next confrontation with China. Sarantake, and more recently, Miller, have proposed to connect current US policies to a narrative about US identity that is thoroughly shaped by the 1960s television and movie serial *Star Trek*.[50] Perhaps intelligence services would do well to watch these rather than focus on the collection of ever-increasing amounts of data.

More generally speaking, this is the way forward though. As Max Boisot and Bill McKelvey have argued, traditional data processing is hierarchic, in which the mountain of data is processed upwards through the layers of a pyramid of 'experts' into a single agreed assessment.[51] In the intelligence world this final product is the *Intelligence Estimate*. In 1962, SNIE 85-3-62 assessed it unlikely the Soviets would deploy missiles on Cuba. But they did. After this, US intelligence provided insights that helped Kennedy to defuse the crisis.

In our increasingly chaotic and complex world, traditional data processing that underlay the initial intelligence failure and then the successful support of the policy process will no longer suffice.[52] For this reason, strategic intelligence has to revise its modus operandi of simplifying and reducing the 'number of dots' to form a pattern. Instead it ought to rather increase the number of dots and the possible patterns they could form within different narratives that adversaries produce. The challenge for the intelligence analyst is to discern how in an emerging crisis foundation narratives are being appropriated, adapted and asserted by different parties for different agendas. The processing pyramid with layers of experts will thus have to be inverted so as to allow for a search for multiple and divergent patterns that define narratives and possible scenarios based on them. Predictive warning may then be more a process of socializing the policy maker into understanding and accepting that there are multiple futures, the 'dots' of which need to be connected into various patterns that could produce probable futures or scenarios which the analyst and policy maker then need to keep in mind as they work out of their present into their preferred future.

The successful connecting of these multiple futures to a specific number of dots will be dependent upon the intelligence analyst's awareness and empathy for the different narratives that justify the initiation, continuation or termination of a crisis. This involves more than just acquiring the current intelligence which enables the

---

[50] Sarantake 2005, pp. 74–103; Miller 2014.

[51] Boisot and McKelvey 2006.

[52] Cf. Svendsen 2017; it is implied in Bousquet 2008.

analyst to reconstruct how the other side sees the world and is making sense of it. It involves a deep empathy and reading of the other side's narratives about its place in the world. It especially involves identifying potential crises embedded within these narratives. This is not about how the other side is 'learning the lessons of history', but about how the other side's self-image has evolved over time and how this played out in earlier crises. In the case of the Yugoslav wars of succession, awareness of the theme of revenge on non-orthodox 'renegades', recurrent in Serbian nationalism, could have alerted intelligence analysts to potential scenarios should the safe areas fall, whereas actionable intelligence that Srebrenica's male inhabitants were about to be slaughtered was absent.

To sum up, the conventional reductive analysis in which a range of data is processed to recognize patterns cannot help policy makers when it comes to identifying potential crises. It will have to change to a more open warning system that probes and attempts to make sense of possible multiple crises. Analysts and policy makers will have to judge and assess together which are the more probable crises scenarios they should be responding to. This requires an intelligence architecture that resembles the British one. More importantly, however, is a change in modes of thinking: strategic intelligence should not be (nor believed to be) about connecting the dots in time, based on the assumption that the opponent is rational. Instead it should be about connecting different scenarios based on a variety of narratives to an emergent pattern of dots. This requires redundancy, as analysts will have to devote time to thoroughly research these narratives; it will require imagination to develop scenarios. Lastly, it will require policy makers that can spare the time to play out such scenarios. Such a change amounts to a paradigm shift in intelligence practice.

5.6 Conclusion

This chapter has argued for a paradigm shift in our understanding of international crises[53] and the role of strategic intelligence in the termination of these crises on three grounds. The first is the dismal record of intelligence in providing their policy makers with sufficient warning time of the onset of a crisis. A variety of explanations and justifications for the failure of intelligence to warn of a crisis, which escalates into a surprise attack, have been discussed.

Second, and more problematic, is that intelligence is still expected to provide early warning of a crisis within a policy framework that assumes an orderly, controllable and predictable world populated by rational actors working to maximize their gains. This view of human society and its nature is embedded in an Enlightenment vision of the world. It was further theorized in the work of at least two if not three generations of 20th century social and behavioural scientists who believed that the understanding of human society can be modelled after the physical and natural sciences.

[53] Cf. Gilpin and Murphy 2008.

But this view of our physical and natural world as an orderly and predictable reality that can be grasped by scientific investigations and codified in theories was undermined by new experiments and theorizing about our physical world from the beginning of the 20th century. In Thomas Kuhn's felicitous phrase, it was a paradigm shift from the Newtonian view of the physical world to a more uncertain, complex and chaotic world of sub-atomic particles of quantum physics.[54] The implications of this shift from the orderly, predictable and deterministic world of Newtonian physics to the uncertainties and relativity of the world of quantum physics is reaching the social and behavioural sciences today.

At least one of these, behavioural economics challenges the rationality of *homo economicus* and the rational actor assumed in political science.[55] The conundrum for intelligence agencies is how to convince themselves and their policy-makers that the rationality they assume they, and their adversary, bring to managing a crisis may be misleading them into believing that they have more control over the course of events than is often the case in the uncertainty and unpredictability of a crisis.

Third is how post-Cold War globalisation is drawing us closer and making us more interdependent in a tightly-networked and complex world. Information technology is dragging us from our current world to a new 'internet-of-things' world of more complex flows of information and knowledge that is changing our worldview and how we relate to each other, to governments and to markets. Unforeseen events, this chapter has argued, can reverberate through our tightly-networked world with catastrophic consequences, escalating minor events or issues into a crisis. In such situations, an overload of fragmentary and contradictory information enabled by the exponential development of information technology, contributes to confusion as it drowns analysts. Paradoxically, then, this information overload challenges the power and effectiveness of governments that in view of increasing public scrutiny need to be more transparent, responsive and accountable. It does not strengthen governments nor does it offer guidance in emerging crises.

References

Allison G, Zelikow Ph (1999) Essence of Decision. Explaining the Cuban missile crisis. Longman/Addison-Wesley, New York

Anonymous [Scheuer M] (2004) Imperial Hubris: Why the West is losing the war on terror. Bassey's, London

Bennett M, Waltz E (2007) Counter deception principle and applications for National Security. Artech House, Boston

Betts RK (1982) Surprise attack: Lessons for defense planning. Brookings Institution, Washington, D.C.

[54] Well analysed in the classic Castells 1996.

[55] See, for example, the collection of essays in Michel-Kerjan and Slovic 2010. For how behavioural economics is shaping public policy making in Singapore, see Low 2012.

Betts RK (2007) Enemies of intelligence: Knowledge and power in American National Security. Columbia University Press, New York

Betts RK, Mahnken T (2003) (eds) Paradoxes of strategic intelligence. Essays in honor of Michael I. Handel. Routledge, New York

Blight JG, Welch DA (eds) (1998) Intelligence and the Cuban missile crisis. Frank Cass, London

Bluth C (2004) The British road to war. Blair, Bush, and the decision to invade Iraq. International Affairs 80(5):851–872

Boin A, 't Hart P et al (2005) The politics of crisis management: Public leadership under pressure. Cambridge University Press, Cambridge

Boisot M, McKelvey B (2006) Speeding up strategic foresight in a dangerous and complex world: A complexity approach. In: Suder G (ed) Corporate strategies under international terrorism adversity. Edward Elgar, Cheltenham

Bousquet A (2008) Chaoplexic warfare or the future of military organization. International Affairs 84(5):915–929

Bracken P (2008) How to build a warning system. In: Bracken P, Bremmer I, Bordon D (eds) Managing strategic surprise: Lessons from risk management and risk assessment. Cambridge University Press, Cambridge. pp. 16–42

Byman D (2005) Strategic surprise and the September 11 attacks. Annual Review of Political Science 8:145–170

Castells M (1996) The Information Age: Economy, society and culture. Blackwell Publishers, Oxford

CIA History Staff (1992) CIA documents on the Cuban missile crisis 1962. CIA, Washington, D.C.

Cilliers P (2007) Making sense of a complex world. In: Aaltonen M (ed) The third lens: Multi-ontology sense-making and strategic decision-making. Ashgate, Aldershot, pp. 99–110

Cohen PA (2009) Speaking to history: The story of King Guojian in twentieth-century China. University of California Press, Berkeley

Cohen PA (2014) History and popular memory: The power of story in moments of crisis. Columbia University Press, New York

Cradock P (2002) Know your enemy: How the Joint Intelligence Committee saw the world. John Murray, London

Curtis A (2004) The Power of Nightmares (television series)

Daniel DC, Herbig KL (1982) Strategic military deception. Pergamon Press, New York

Davis J (2002) Improving CIA analytic performance: Analysts and the policymaking process. Sherman Kent Center for Intelligence Analysis, Occasional Papers vol. 1/ii

Davis J (2003a) Strategic warning: If surprise is inevitable, what role for analysis? Sherman Kent Center for Intelligence Analysis, Occasional Papers, vol. 2/i

Davis J (2003b) Tensions in analyst-policy maker relations: Opinions, facts and evidence. Sherman Kent Center for Intelligence Analysis, Occasional Papers vol. 2/ii

Davis J (2009) Strategic warning: Intelligence support in a world of uncertainty and surprise. In: Johnson LK (ed) Handbook of intelligence studies. Routledge, London, pp. 173–188

de Montbrial T (2013) Action and reaction in the world system: The dynamics of economic and political power. UBC Press, Vancouver

Diamond JM (2008) The CIA and the Culture of Failure: U.S. Intelligence from the End of the Cold War to the Invasion of Iraq. Stanford University Press, Stanford

Fink S (2002) Crisis management: Planning for the inevitable. Authors Guild, Cincinnati, Ohio

Fishbein W, Treverton G (2004) Making sense of transnational threats. Sherman Kent Centre for Intelligence Analysis, Occasional Papers, vol. 3/I

Fitzgerald M, Lebow RN (2006) Iraq. The mother of all intelligence failures. Intelligence and National Security 21(5):884–909

Fursenko AA, Naftali T (1998) "One hell of a gamble". Khrushchev, Castro, and Kennedy, 1958–1964. WW Norton & Co., New York

George AL (ed) (1991) Avoiding war: Problems of crisis management. Westview Press, Oxford

George AL, Simons WE (1994) (eds) The limits of coercive diplomacy. Westview Press, Boulder, CO

Gilpin DR, Murphy PJ (2008) Crisis Management in a complex world. Oxford University Press, Oxford

Gioe D, Scott L, Andrew C (2014) An International History of the Cuban Missile Crisis: A 50-year Retrospective. Routledge, London

Gowing N (2009) 'Skyful of Lies' and Black Swans: The new tyranny of shifting information power in crises. Reuters Institute for the Study of Journalism/ University of Oxford, Oxford

Grabo C (2004) Anticipating surprise: Analysis for strategic warning. University Press of America, Lanham, MD

Grabo C, Goldman J (2010) Handbook of warning intelligence: Assessing the threat to National Security. Scarecrow Press, Lanham, MD

Handel M (1981) The diplomacy of surprise: Hitler, Nixon, Sadat. Harvard University Press, Cambridge, MA

Handel M (1984) Intelligence and the problem of strategic surprise. Journal of Strategic Studies 7 (3):231–232

Handel M (1989) Diplomatic surprise. In: Handel M (ed) War, strategy and intelligence. Frank Cass, London pp. 282–309

Harvard Business School Publishing (1999) 'Harvard Business Review' on crisis management. Harvard Business School, Boston

He K (2016) China's crisis behaviour: Political survival and foreign policy after the Cold War. Cambridge University Press, Cambridge

Heuer Jr. RJ (1999) Psychology of intelligence analysis. Center for Study of Intelligence, CIA, Washington D.C.

International Crisis Group (2012) Asia Report no. 223, 23 April 2012, 'Stirring up the South China Sea' (Part I)

Jervis R (2010) Why Intelligence Fails: Lessons from the Iranian Revolution and the Iraq War. Cornell University Press, Ithaca, NH

Jones M, Silberzahn Ph (2013) Constructing Cassandra: Reframing Intelligence Failure at the CIA, 1947–2001. Stanford University Press, Stanford

Kahneman D (2011) Thinking, fast and slow. Penguin/Allen Lane, London

Kam E (1988) Surprise attack: The victim's perspective. Harvard University Press, Cambridge, MA

Knorr K, Morgan P (1983) (eds) Strategic military surprise: Incentives and opportunities. Transaction Books, New Brunswick, NJ

Kwa CG (2010) Cooperation and confidence building: A Southeast Asian perspective. In: Bateman S, Ho J (eds) Southeast Asia and the rise of Chinese and Indian naval power: Between rising naval powers. Routledge, London/New York. pp. 227–231

Kwa CG (2012) Role of Intelligence in International Crisis Management. RSIS working paper 243 https://www.rsis.edu.sg/wp-content/uploads/rsis-pubs/WP243.pdf

Lanir Z (1983) Hahafta'a habsisit: Modi'in Bemashber [Fundamental surprise: The national intelligence crisis]. Hakibutz Hama'ukhad, Tel Aviv

Lavoix H (2006) Developing an early warning system for crises. In: Ricci A (ed) From early warning to early action Brussels. European Commission, Brussels

Lebow RN (1981) Between peace and war: The nature of international crisis. John Hopkins University Press, Baltimore

Lebow RN (2007) Revisiting the Falklands intelligence failures. The RUSI Journal 152(4):68–73

Leventhal M (ed) (2011) The hand of history: An anthology of history, quotations and commentaries. Greenhill Books, Elstree

Levite A (1987) Intelligence and strategic surprise. Columbia University Press, New York

Lorenz EN (1972) Predictability: Does the Flap of a Butterfly's Wings in Brazil set off a Tornado in Texas? Paper presented at the AAAS Annual Meeting, 29 December 1972

Lovell J (2011) The Opium War: Drugs, dreams and the making of China. Picador, London

Low D (2012) (ed) Behavioural economics and policy design: Examples from Singapore. World Scientific/Civil Service College, Singapore

Magnusson L, Ottosson J (2009) (eds) The Evolution of Path Dependence. Edward Elgar, Cheltenham

Michel-Kerjan E, Slovic P (2010) (eds) The irrational economist. Making decisions in a dangerous world. Public Affairs/Perseus Books, New York
Miller AD (2014) How Star Trek's Prime Directive explains Obama's foreign policy. Foreign Policy 8 Jan 2014
Mitroff II et al (1996) The essential guide to managing corporate crises. Oxford University Press, Oxford
Morrison JM (2011) British intelligence failures in Iraq. Intelligence and National Security 26 (4):509–520
National Institute for Defense Studies, Japan (2013) NIDS China Security Report 2013, http://www.nids.go.jp/english/publication/chinareport/ Accessed 15 April 2015
Neustadt RE, May ER (1986) Thinking in time: The uses of history for decision makers. Free Press, New York
Omand D (2010) Securing the state. Hurst, London
Sarantake NE (2005) Cold War pop culture and the image of US foreign policy: The perspective of the original Star Trek series. Journal of Cold War Studies 7(4):74–103
Seliktar O (2004) Politics, paradigms and intelligence failures. Why so few predicted the collapse of the Soviet Union. ME Sharpe, Armonk, NY
Smith D (2006) The crisis of management: Managing ahead of the curve. In: Smith D, Elliott D (eds) Key readings in crisis management: Systems and structures for prevention and recovery. Routledge, London, pp. 301–317
Snowden DJ, Boone ME (2007) A leader's framework for decision making. Harvard Business Review, https://hbr.org/2007/11/a-leaders-framework-for-decision-making
Svendsen ADM (2017) Intelligence Engineering: Operating Beyond the Conventional. Rowman & Littlefield, New York
Weick KE (1988) Enacted sensemaking in crisis situations. Journal of Management Studies 25 (4):305–17
Weick KE (1995) Sensemaking in organizations. Sage, Thousand Oaks, CA
Whaley B (1969) Stratagem: Deception and surprise in war (reprint 2007). Artech House, Boston, MA
Whaley B (1973) Codeword Barbarossa. MIT Press, Cambridge, MA
Williams Ph (1976) Crisis management: Confrontation and diplomacy in the nuclear age. J Wiley, New York
Wohlstetter R (1962) Pearl Harbor: Warning and decision. Stanford University Press, Stanford

Author Biography

Chong Guan Kwa, Senior Fellow at the S. Rajaratnam School of International Studies, Nanyang Technological University, Singapore; Adjunct Associate Professor at the History Department, National University of Singapore and Visiting Fellow at the Archaeological Unit of the Nalanda-Sriwijaya Centre, Institute of Southeast Asian Studies. Earlier he worked on policy analysis in the Ministry of Foreign Affairs and on early warning for the management of strategic surprise in the Ministry of Defence. His publications includes *Early Southeast Asia Viewed from India: An Anthology from the Journal of the Greater India Society* (2013); *China-ASEAN Sub-regional Cooperation: Progress, Problems and Prospects* (2011), co-edited with Mingjiang Li; *Energy Security: Asia Pacific Perspectives* (2010), co-edited with Virendra Gupta; *Singapore: A 700-Year History; From Early Emporium to World City* (2009), co-authored with Derek Heng and Tan Tai Yong; and *Maritime security in Southeast Asia* (2007), co-edited with John K. Skogan.

Chapter 6
The Revolution in Intelligence Affairs: Problem Solved?

Minne Boelens

Abstract The end of the Cold War and the 9/11 attacks spurred a still inconclusive debate concerning the necessity and the extent of a Revolution in Intelligence Affairs in order to adapt to a new security context of what we now call hybrid warfare. Experiences with hybrid opponents in recent conflicts have produced two innovations that effectively render the RIA debate superfluous. First, the 2006 conflict between Israel and Hezbollah, and the follow-on Israeli operation against Hamas in 2008, revealed that an intelligence-led integrated approach is of paramount importance to effectively counter hybrid opponents. Second, US experiences with interagency teams in counter-narcotics operations and in the conflicts in Afghanistan and Iraq showed that the fusing of all-source interagency intelligence efforts with operational capabilities creates remarkable results against hybrid opponents. The responsibility now lies with the intelligence community to effectively implement these innovations.

Keywords Revolution in Intelligence Affairs · Hybrid warfare · Innovation · Hezbollah · Hamas · Afghanistan · Iraq

Contents

M. Boelens (✉)
Ministry of Defence, The Hague, The Netherlands
e-mail: MA.Boelens@mindef.nl

F. Baudet et al. (eds.), *Perspectives on Military Intelligence from the First World War to Mali*, DOI 10.1007/978-94-6265-183-8_6

6.1 Introduction

One week after the attack on the Pentagon and the World Trade Center on 11 September 2001, National Security Advisor Condoleeza Rice told the press: 'This isn't Pearl Harbor'.[1] According to Melvin Goodman, she was right. It was much worse. At the time of Pearl Harbor, the United States (US) did not have a Director of National Intelligence plus sixteen intelligence agencies or a combined budget to the equivalent of more than 50 billion dollars to provide early warning of an enemy attack. But despite all this organizational mass and capabilities the attack of 9/11 succeeded to a large extent. The National Commission on Terrorist Attacks Upon the United States that was tasked by Congress and the President to prepare a full and complete account of the circumstances surrounding the 9/11 attacks concluded that before 9/11, the US tried to solve the Al Qaeda problem with the capabilities it had used in the last stages of the Cold War and its immediate aftermath. These capabilities were insufficient and little had been done to expand or reform them.[2] Rather, the US intelligence community (IC) struggled throughout the 1990s and up to 9/11 to collect intelligence on, and analyse the phenomenon of, transnational terrorism. The combination of an overwhelming number of priorities, flat budgets, an outmoded structure, and bureaucratic rivalries resulted in an insufficient response to this new challenge.[3]

The 9/11 attacks and the subsequent conclusions about the failures within the IC expedited the debate about the so-called Revolution in Intelligence Affairs (RIA). Ever since the end of the Cold War, politicians, academics and intelligence practitioners have debated about the necessity of evolutionary or revolutionary changes within the IC. The debate revolves around the general realization that the political context and the strategic and operational environment in which the IC operates has significantly changed in recent years. Authors such as Lahneman, Moore, George and Vandepeer have argued that in order to stay relevant and effective the IC must adopt a new intelligence paradigm and change its practices and analytical processes.

---

[1] Goodman 2005, p. 59.

[2] The 9/11 Commission Report: Executive Summary 2004, p. 10.

[3] Idem, p. 12. Budinger and Smith 2011, p. 1.

Important elements that have changed the context for the IC are the decline of inter-state war and the pressure on the state-centric international system due to broad developments, such as globalisation and the information revolution. These developments and actual conflicts have resulted in thinking about so-called new wars.[4] Many approaches are possible in defining these new manifestations of warfare but a suitable concept is hybrid warfare as defined by Frank Hoffman in his 2007 Potomac Institute for Policy Studies report 'Conflict in the 21st century: The rise of hybrid wars',[5] because it corresponds well to recent and current conflicts.[6] Most of these are characterised by a blurring of modes of war, of who is fighting and of what technologies are brought to bear resulting in a higher level of complexity than classical inter-state warfare.[7]

While much has been written on these developments, more than a decade after 9/11 the literature concerning RIA is still inconclusive. It focuses mainly on the strategic level of intelligence and the restructuring of national intelligence services. By contrast, there seems to be only a limited academic debate and analysis concerning the intelligence process at the operational and tactical levels in which military forces are actually confronted with this changed context. The latter is remarkable as recent conflicts show that fielded innovative interagency intelligence concepts and processes combined with revised operational tactics are crucial for successfully countering non-state actors and their hybrid tactics.[8]

Therefore, the main question in this chapter is to what extent the Revolution in Intelligence Affairs debate is still valid considering the intelligence developments that have taken place on the operational and tactical levels of warfare aimed at countering non-state actors in hybrid wars. I argue that the intelligence communities of, in particular, Israel and the United States have started to adapt to the new context of hybrid warfare. They analysed earlier failures and drew valuable lessons from them that enabled them to cope with the hybrid nature of their adversaries. The main lessons for these communities were the necessity of the integration, rather than the compartmentalization, of the intelligence and operations domains and the remarkable results of interagency cooperation. Therefore, intelligence communities in other states should study these and focus on improving their performance and institutionalizing these lessons at all levels.

I will focus on two combined cases: the Israel—Hezbollah war of 2006 and its follow-on Operation Cast Lead in 2008 and, secondly, the use of interagency teams and concepts in the conflicts in Afghanistan and Iraq from 2001 onwards. These cases are specifically chosen because they are exemplary of the challenges on the operational and tactical levels of warfare in the post Cold War context of hybrid

---

[4] See for example Kaldor 2012, pp. 4–5 and 72–78.

[5] Hoffman 2007.

[6] De Wijk 2012, pp. 358–359.

[7] Hoffman 2007, p. 14. See also Williams 2001; Williams 2003; Hammes 2006, p. 35; and Malis 2012, pp. 187–190.

[8] See for example Rosenbach 2008, p. 134; Lever 2012, pp. 239–241; Johnson 2011, p. 128; Matthews 2009, p. 26; Marrero 2009, pp. 91–95; Munsing and Lamb 2011, pp. 18–31.

warfare and non-state actors. The case studies are also mutually supportive. The Israeli case study defines the overall scope concerning the necessary focus in hybrid warfare such as interagency cooperation and the relevance of modern military technologies and concepts.[9] The case study on interagency teams in Afghanistan and Iraq further illustrates the principal and successful innovations that took place at the operational and tactical levels in countering hybrid opponents.

6.2 The Second Lebanon War and Operation Cast Lead

6.2.1 A Changing Strategic Outlook for the IDF

In the run-up to the second Lebanon war the Israeli Defence Forces (IDF) were confronted with a changing strategic outlook. Three trends may be identified that influenced the strategic context for Israel. These are the influence of the end of the Cold War on the Israeli security context, the proliferation of missile technology throughout the Middle East directly threatening the security of Israel and the growing importance of Low Intensity Conflicts (LIC) at the expense of large-scale war.[10] These trends have led to an unstable region with many Arab states remaining politically volatile while at the same time maintaining a collective hostility towards Israel. Additionally, the growing importance of several non-state entities such as the Palestine Liberation Organization (PLO), Hamas and Hezbollah has also contributed to the instability. In countering these threats the IDF embraced military-technological developments and concepts and it was convinced that the technological dominance over the opponents was its main advantage.[11] IDF's analysts found support for this view in the 1999 Kosovo war that seemed to vindicate the validity of standoff attack in order to reduce casualties and collateral damage.[12]

Adding to the challenges of the changed security context were internal changes in the Israeli society. In the 1980s Israel's society became more individualistic and the people became more interested in globalisation and the economy than in

---

[9] The technological and conceptual advancements achieved by Western military forces are usually referred to as the Revolution in Military Affairs (RMA). The main innovations within the RMA can be divided into three separate streams: information technology, surveillance and sensor capabilities and precision guided munitions. See Osinga et al. 2010, pp. 21–23. Cf. Sinterniklaas 2013 and Shimko 2010, pp. 35–37.

[10] Kainikara and Parkin 2007, pp. 11–15. Low Intensity Conflict (LIC) can be defined as political-military confrontation between contending states or groups below conventional wars and above the routine, peaceful competition among states. See http://www.nids.go.jp/english/publication/kiyo/pdf/bulletin_e2001_3.pdf.

[11] Petrelli 2013, pp. 4–12. Cf. Kreps 2007, pp. 75–79, Kober 2008, pp. 17–21; Adamsky 2010, pp. 93–130.

[12] Johnson 2011, pp. xvi–xvii; Matthews 2008, p. 23–24; Petrelli 2013, pp. 672–673 and Rapaport 2010, pp. 4–6.

security issues. Because Israelis worried more about their personal well-being, the political costs of casualties grew and the loss of Israelis in conflict came under greater scrutiny, Kober and Berman argue. As the possibility of a conventional, existential war drew ever more remote in the minds of ordinary Israelis, they became less ready to sacrifice, bodily and financially, for the Israeli Defense Forces (IDF).[13] The IDF itself reflected this change in that it moved away from its classic doctrine in the decades before the 2006 war, relying more on the already mentioned standoff power instead of ground manoeuvre and it started to focus more on the containment of opponents instead of engaging them actively.[14]

The changing strategic outlook and social situation resulted in budgetary cuts for the armed forces, a reduced focus on training and a reduced integration of air and ground operations. Because of the focus on Low Intensity Conflict, especially regarding the Palestinians, there seemed to be no need for high-end combat training. Also, the pace of technological innovation within the armed forces against real life threats was hampered by the reduced budgets for example concerning the defence against short-range rockets systems and systems for the protection of Israeli armour.[15] All of these developments were on-going when in 2006 Israel was confronted with the very capable hybrid opponent Hezbollah.

6.2.2 *Hezbollah: The Hybrid Opponent Baseline*

The Shia Hezbollah (Party of God) was founded in 1982 in response to Israel's invasion of Lebanon in that same year, the euphoria created by the 1979 Islamic Revolution in Iran and the marginalization of the Shia population in Lebanon in general. Besides being nowadays a primarily political movement, Hezbollah also has a military force, equipped with a wide range of weaponry, including weapons normally associated with nation states, and it uses the full range of conventional, terrorist and guerrilla tactics.[16]

In preparation for future conflicts, at the tactical level Hezbollah addressed the IDF's precision weapons capability by reducing its own weapon signature and target-appearance time and by building hardened defensive positions. Hezbollah also focused on concealing its military infrastructure inside densely populated civilian areas hereby complicating Israeli attack options because of the high risk of collateral damage. Knowing very well that the IDF desired to generate effects on its systems, Hezbollah created a network of autonomous cells with little inter-cell systemic interaction.[17]

---

[13] Berman 2012, p. 125. Cf. Kober 2008, pp. 10–14.

[14] Petrelli 2013, p. 15; Matthews 2008, pp. 16–17.

[15] Berman 2012, pp. 127–128; Kaplinsky 2009, pp. 27–30; and Johnson 2011, pp. xvii, 16–44.

[16] See Exum 2006, pp. 5–6; Rudner 2010, p. 237.

[17] Matthews 2008, p. 21.

On the strategic level, Hezbollah also predicted that the IDF would attack with long-range precision weapons on its strategic centres of gravity. To counter this, Hezbollah simply did away with them. In any future war with Israel, there would be no critical strategic assets to attack. In addition, Hezbollah had a well-devised media strategy based on redundant capabilities in order to be able to keep broadcasting its narrative of victory during the war. By using the media it succeeded in turning tactical events, such as for example collateral damage by Israel, into strategic and even political affairs.[18] By the summer of 2006, Hezbollah had assembled a well-trained, well-armed, highly motivated, and highly evolved war-fighting machine on Israel's northern border.[19]

The hybrid characteristics of Hezbollah, combined with the changed strategic outlook as detailed in the previous paragraph, were the most important factors influencing the outcome of the Second Lebanon War for Israel as will be shown in the next paragraphs.

6.2.3 The Second Lebanon War

The actual casus belli of the Second Lebanon War took place on 12 July 2006 when an Israeli ground patrol was ambushed by Hezbollah in a carefully planned action. The ambush resulted in several Israeli deaths and wounded and also the hostage taking of two Israeli soldiers. Hassan Nasrallah, the leader of Hezbollah, declared after the action that the abduction of the Israeli soldiers was aimed at forcing negotiations concerning the release of numerous Islamic terrorists who were held captive by Israel. As a reaction to this incident Israel started the first military operation against Hezbollah in Lebanon since 2000 and its largest military action since the First Lebanon War of 1982.[20]

It soon became clear that the preferred approach of the Olmert government, at least initially, would be to rely exclusively on executing standoff attacks, primarily from the air, on a variety of targets. This approach was completely in accordance with the IDF doctrine at that time aimed at preventing casualties of its own as much as possible. In return, and completely as expected, Hezbollah responded with an extensive rocket campaign against Israel resulting in large-scale evacuations of the Israeli civilian population, hereby disrupting public life. Although in many occasions the rocket launch positions and launchers were destroyed by IAF's quick time-sensitive targeting, the IDF failed in completely negating the rocket attacks until the end of the war.

[18] Johnson 2011, p. 21; Rid and Hecker 2009, pp. 147–148 and 155–161.

[19] Matthews 2008, p. 21, Sharp 2006 pp. 10–11, Berman 2012, p. 124; Haloutz 2009, p. 63.

[20] The main outline of the description of the Second Lebanon War in this paragraph is based on Johnson 2011, pp. 9–90, Berman 2012, pp. 131–133, Kainikara and Parkin 2007, pp. 51–62, Matthews 2009, pp. 6–24, Arkin 2007b, pp. 39–55, Matthews 2008, pp. 33–56, Lambeth 2012a, pp. 85–91 and Lambeth 2011, pp. 13–71; Arkin 2007a, pp. 106–122.

Although the air campaign and its result in itself were impressive, within the government doubts emerged about the military course. Therefore, despite worries of the ground commanders about heavy losses, a ground offensive was launched to supplement the air campaign. However, IDF leadership emphasized that it would be limited and the operational focus would remain with the execution of standoff attacks.

As soon as the tank and infantry units moved into Lebanon they met fierce resistance by dug-in Hezbollah elements that changed the fight into a full-contact and face-to-face operation. The terrain of South Lebanon offers defending forces, like Hezbollah, numerous tactical advantages by channelling armoured manoeuvre and by creating ideal circumstances for ambushes and the employment of mines and Improvised Explosive Devices (IED).[21] In addition, the battlefield was well prepared by Hezbollah by building an extensive network of sophisticated bunkers, trenches, tunnels and fighting positions in the area. Finally, the Hezbollah forces were locally experienced, well trained and they formed decentralized (self-organizing and distributed) units that combined the weapons normally associated with states with guerrilla tactics.

Hezbollah's mission on the ground was to remain intact as a fighting force while at the same time inflicting as many enemy casualties as possible. The tactics used by Hezbollah were tailored to this mission. The rocket teams had the mission of launching a steady stream of rockets into Israel in order to create casualties and create the appearance that the Israeli campaign was unsuccessful. The mission of the teams in the villages and in the border fortifications was to slow down IDF movement in order to protect the rocket systems.[22]

Rather than having to react faster than the IDF's decision cycle, the Hezbollah teams could largely ignore it, waiting out Israeli attacks, staying in positions, re-infiltrating or re-emerging from cover, and choosing the time to attack or ambush.[23] The weapons, equipment and sophisticated measures far exceeded the level of routine equipment and training generally used by terror and guerrilla organizations around the world.[24]

When the Israeli forces entered Lebanon it soon became apparent that despite their technological advantage they lacked current intelligence and they were ill-prepared for facing a hybrid opponent such as Hezbollah within a high-intensity conflict. Israeli forces were unable to sufficiently seize the terrain in South Lebanon and they were also unable to prevent Hezbollah from executing rocket attacks on Israel. Further adding to the complexity for the Olmert government was the fact that on 13 August 2006 UN Security Council Resolution 1701 came into effect which called for the withdrawal of Israeli troops and the disarming of Hezbollah and any other armed group in Lebanon not being the Lebanese Army or the UN Interim Force in Lebanon (UNIFIL).

---

[21] See Exum 2006, pp. 3–4, Matthews 2008, p 17.

[22] See Exum 2006, p. 8, Matthews 2008, p. 18; Siboni 2007, p. 62.

[23] Cordesman and Sullivan 2007, p. 136.

[24] Schweitzer 2007, p. 125.

In the last 72 hours of combat, the IDF tripled its number of troops in Lebanon and significantly increased the level of standoff attacks. The IAF for example flew almost 45% of its total number of missions during these last 3 days. Not surprisingly, the IDF also suffered its highest casualty rate during these last days of intense fighting. The overall performance however, especially on the ground, was not convincing. The ground operations lacked an identifiable operational pattern and they revealed shortcomings in combat expertise and coordination between the various air and ground units.

The war turned out to be a disaster for Israel and the IDF's reputation as a competent military force, a key element of Israeli deterrent power, suffered significantly. The Israeli shortcomings were a result of the lack of preparation for the hybrid war in which it found itself. Nasrallah immediately claimed a strategic and decisive victory, further adding to Israeli fears. On the other hand, it can be questioned if the Israeli forces were really that unsuccessful. Nasrallah stated afterwards that had he known the full scale and intensity of the Israeli attacks he would not have risked the war by kidnapping the two soldiers.[25] Chief of Staff Halutz claimed that the war dealt a significant blow to Hezbollah by firmly etching the price for challenging Israel into the minds of the Lebanese people.[26]

Nevertheless, both Olmert and Halutz admitted to shortcomings in the planning and conduct of the war and that important lessons had to be learned. In order to do so the Olmert government installed the Winograd Commission that would make a full inquiry into the Second Lebanon War.

6.2.4 The Lessons from the Second Lebanon War

The Winograd Commission found that Israel failed to achieve a decisive victory in the war. According to the commission, the negative outcome of the war was a result of flawed political and military leadership, poor performance by the IDF as a whole but especially the ground forces, and of deficient Israeli preparedness.[27] The Israeli Air Force had performed better, but Winograd warned against excessive expectations of airpower against a hybrid opponent such as Hezbollah. The campaign of standoff attacks was the result of a growing belief in the military-technological superiority of Western armed forces. According to this belief strategic objectives can be achieved by targeting leadership and infrastructure, especially from the air, with precision weapons, with only limited involvement of ground forces, and under the umbrella of various Intelligence, Surveillance and Reconnaissance (ISR) assets and a robust Command and Control system. The Winograd Commission found this belief erroneous as it underestimated the versatility of the opponent.[28] General Yossi Peled

[25] Exum 2006, p. 9; Cordesman and Sullivan 2007, p. 35; Elran and Brom 2007, p. 19.

[26] Haloutz 2009, p. 67–68.

[27] An overview of the main unclassified findings can be found in Winograd 2007 and Winograd 2008.

[28] See for example Lambeth 2011, pp. 210–213; Kainikara and Parkin 2007; Arkin 2007b, pp. 129–136.

(retired) illustrated the overreliance on technology as follows: Something very bad has happened to the IDF in recent years. We have lost the balance between the arms, giving credit to the IAF's ability to solve any problem. A golden calf was created and named technology; many believed it could win the war.[29]

The Winograd Commission attributed the negative performance of the ground component to successive IDF chiefs concentrating training, readiness and equipment acquisition on countering the Palestinian terrorist threat on the premise that the likelihood of a major war was low and that the main focus needed to be placed on the asymmetrical threats posed by the Palestinian intifada.[30] Furthermore, the ground campaign revealed serious problems in the level of planning and execution. This was not confined to technical aspects. Although the war was a limited one, it exposed the fact that while the IDF consists of two branches, the air force and the ground forces, there was an insufficient level of integration and unity in concepts, training and operations between the air force and the ground forces before and during the war.[31]

Several authors have argued that another important aspect of the problem was that the Israeli government lacked understanding of the special nature of the war with the Hezbollah organization. Because Israel has achieved conventional military supremacy, enemies look for asymmetrical solutions. Israel needs to develop the strategy, military doctrine and forces needed to deal with such scenarios.[32] However, based on the assumptions before the war that for the foreseeable future the focus would be LIC, the Israeli defence establishment saw no urgent need to update in a systematic and sophisticated way the overall strategy and to consider how to mobilize and combine all its resources and sources of strength to address the totality of the challenges it faces.[33]

One constant lesson of war is that the quality of war fighting depends heavily on the quality of intelligence analysis before, during, and in terminating the war. Cordesman and Sullivan claim that the war with Hezbollah has shown that nations must learn to fight in asymmetric ways that deprive conventional forces of their technical advantages and give the enemy the initiative. However, they emphasize that fighting asymmetric wars not only requires altering tactics and targeting but also enabling an effective intelligence process by funding suitable ISR assets and by putting human intelligence (Humint) in the loop.[34]

---

[29] Quoted in Kober 2008, p. 19.

[30] Lambeth 2011, p. 203. Cf. Zagdanski 2007, p. 35 and Niva 2010.

[31] Romm 2007, p. 60; Rapaport 2010, p. 21 and Berman 2012, p. 138.

[32] Elran and Brom 2007, p. 22; Cordesman and Sullivan 2007, p. 85; Lambeth 2012a, p. 98. Cf. Kalb and Saivetz 2007.

[33] Quoted in Cordesman and Sullivan 2007, p. 75.

[34] Idem, pp. 49–50, 107 and 141. Both authors also emphasize the importance of learning what intelligence can and cannot do in order to prevent setting unrealistic operational and strategic goals.

6.2.5 Implementing the Lessons Identified

The Second Lebanon War and the conclusions of the Winograd Commission proved to be a wakeup call for the IDF. In the years after the war, the IDF actively implemented a number of changes. The first important change was the creation of a new doctrine. In the years before the war, the long-established and combat proven IDF modus operandi had been replaced by a conceptual framework, called Systemic Operational Design, which resulted in a doctrine that relied on precise standoff fire, mostly from the air and using ground manoeuvres only as a last resort. The IDF discarded the complexity of this most recent doctrine and it returned to basics by focusing on combined-arms fire and manoeuvre tactics and skills. The IDF also reinstated simple terms as attack and defend, and improved the quality of mission orders by clearly defining missions and objectives.[35]

The second important change was a renewed emphasis on joint-integration and training for high and low intensity conflicts. In the period before the war each service planned and trained as if the other did not exist. After the war this unhealthy approach was positively altered. The air and ground forces hosted several joint command post exercises aimed at establishing a new pattern of joint contingency planning and training while focusing on large-unit manoeuvre and joint combined-arms integration. In a concurrent effort on the working-floor level both the IDF and the IAF also started to frequently visit each other in order to receive orientation of the host unit's mission, operations, capabilities and support needs. Also the leadership of both organizations entered into regular meetings and discussions in order to discuss capabilities and joint issues.[36]

All these changes and improvements, some more complete than others, were put to the test in 2008 when the IDF launched military operations against Hamas in the Gaza Strip in Operation Cast Lead.

6.2.6 Operation Cast Lead: Vindication for the IDF?

In August 2005 the IDF pulled out of the Gaza Strip ending 38 years of occupation. Thereafter Hamas gained control over the Gaza Strip and gradually stepped up its rocket and mortar attacks on Israel. As a result, Israel found itself in the same dilemma as at the beginning of the Second Lebanon War. Israel would have to respond decisively, with all the risks associated with such a confrontation, or it would be seen as failing to defend itself again. Israel chose the first option and on 27 December 2008 Israel started air attacks on Hamas positions; Operation Cast Lead had begun.

[35] See Johnson 2011, pp. 26–31, 99–100 and Matthews 2009, pp. 22–23.

[36] See Lambeth 2011, pp. 226–227 and Johnson 2011, pp. 98–101.

Taking a closer look at Operation Cast Lead is relevant because it shows what has been done with the lessons drawn from the Second Lebanon War. The operation itself will not be described; other authors, notably Johnson, Farquhar and Cordesman, have already done so extensively from various perspectives. Here, the focus is on the lessons implemented by the IDF from the Second Lebanon War on the tactical and operational level that proved to be successful in this operation. The analysis of Operation Cast Lead also identifies several important lessons in the context of hybrid warfare.

Israeli's primary opponent in the 2008 operation was the Palestinian Sunnite Hamas (Islamic Resistance Movement) movement, a hybrid opponent comparable to Hezbollah. It has committed itself to driving Israel out of the occupied territories and over the years has become a major factor of influence in the occupied territories. Comparable to Hezbollah, Hamas has organized itself in a political section, a social section focusing on providing basic social services, and a militant section: the Izzedine al-Qassam Brigades. The core of these brigades consists of skilled fighters that have been trained by Hezbollah, Syria and Iran and they have a full range of weapons at their disposal.[37] It is important to note that Hamas as a threat was not a hybrid opponent at the same level as Hezbollah was in 2006. Hamas was not as well-trained, organized and equipped as Hezbollah and the intelligence position on the Gaza Strip and Hamas was much better because it had been the focus of attention for the IDF for decades.

The Gaza Strip is a small (360 km^2), densely populated and urbanized area bordering Israel and Egypt. Compared with the complex terrain of South Lebanon the Gaza Strip is flat and sparsely vegetated which was advantageous for the IDF. Because the strip is under constant observation by the IDF, Hamas has had to make good use of the urban areas for concealment and it has created an extensive tunnel network especially near the border with Egypt in order to smuggle weapons and supplies.[38]

The success of the operation was to a large extent based on its foundation: much effort was put into the planning and the objectives were clear from the outset and militarily achievable.[39] In the timeframe between 2006 and 2008 the IDF had also heavily invested in planning joint operations with the air force, and training for them.[40]

An additional reason for success was that Prime Minister Olmert settled for more modest and achievable campaign goals while also much effort was put into controlling public expectations. This was done by working especially hard to ensure that the operation would be as brief as possible, for example by rejecting all temptations to seek regime change or completely disarming Hamas once and for all.[41]

---

[37] See for example IICC 2008; Kulick 2009, p. 54; Pelletiere 1999, pp. 716–735 and Zuhur 2008.

[38] Johnson 2011, pp. 102–103, 140–144. See also Lambeth 2012b, p. 103.

[39] Johnson 2011, p. 124.

[40] See for example Kaplinsky 2009, p. 36.

[41] Lambeth 2012b, pp. 106–107.

The successful and massive air campaign was based on an extensive interagency intelligence study that had identified more than 600 Hamas related targets. In the initial phase of operations the IAF attacked hundreds of these targets and prepared the battle space for the ground forces.[42] In addition, in another novelty, not seen before on this scale, the IAF and the intelligence agencies merged their capabilities to create new sources of real-time intelligence for hunting down a variety of time-sensitive targets. Israel's Internal Security Service Shin Bet embedded its personnel in various IDF command posts, as well as in forward-deployed combat units. The forward-deployed operators gathered valuable human-source inputs to supplement what the Military Intelligence Service Aman and the IAF were collecting by means of ISR assets. Compared with the 2006 conflict, this time the IDF had a better intelligence-based understanding of the opponent, which proved to be the essential foundation for success.[43]

Another important success factor was the fact that the ground offensive was integrated in the operation from the beginning and the army, navy and air force had a joint approach. Most of the combat effectiveness displayed by the IDF throughout the operation resulted from the greatly improved force integration that had been forged in the 2 years that followed the end of the 2006 Lebanon war. The combination of overwhelming firepower, an adequate intelligence-based situational awareness and rapid manoeuvres overwhelmed Hamas.[44]

A ceasefire proposed by Egypt was accepted on 18 January 2009; all IDF forces had left the Gaza Strip 3 days later. Although the operation did not completely stop the rocket attacks on Israel, the level of attacks after the war was significantly lower and Israel succeeded, at least temporarily, in severely disrupting Hamas's capabilities. Maybe the most important result for the IDF was the validation of the changes that were implemented after the war in 2006. Of course no two conflicts are exactly the same but the new focus on high-intensity warfare, a meticulous intelligence-based preparation of the battle space and the full integration between the air and ground component did prove its worth.

6.2.7 Concluding Remarks

The Second Lebanon War of 2006 was a significant defeat for the IDF. A competent and well-prepared hybrid, non-state opponent was able to withstand a numerical and technological superior army. However, the lessons from the war were identified and implemented by the IDF leading to a more successful campaign in Gaza in 2008. The most important lesson for the debate surrounding RIA is that the conflicts have

[42] Cordesman 2009, pp. 16, 18–27; Lambeth 2012b, p. 95.

[43] Lambeth 2012b, pp. 108–112.

[44] Matthews 2009, pp. 108–109; Kulick 2009, pp. 55–56.

proven that countering hybrid opponents requires exquisite interagency intelligence efforts and a comprehensive strategic approach. In Johnson's words: 'There are no single-service solutions to the challenges posed by hybrid adversaries'.[45] The case also highlights the relevance of military-technological advancements for hybrid warfare but at the same time warns against the notion that technology in itself can achieve a quick victory.[46]

6.3 Interagency Teams

When General Petraeus assumed command in Iraq in 2007 he stated that warfare has never been more complex and never has it required more imaginative leadership. He emphasized the need to empower subordinates and to push decisions, resources, and authorities to the lowest level possible, to provide appropriate right and left limits for the leaders (the boundaries in which to operate) and to give them the flexibility to be imaginative and adaptive.[47] What Petraeus was referring to is a new concept that was employed against criminals, insurgents and terrorists with considerable success, as various authors hold. The new capability in itself is far from high-profile. It is nothing more than an underappreciated organizational innovation: interagency teams.[48] Interagency teams are empowered and self-synchronizing teams with members originating from different agencies. As the following paragraph will show, US experiences indicate that this innovation is especially suited for dealing with complex hybrid challenges.

6.3.1 Joint Interagency Task Force—South

Interagency teams in Afghanistan and Iraq were modelled on the Joint Interagency Task Force-South (JIATFS), which is tasked with countering drug trafficking from South America to the United States.[49] Its origins can be traced back to the 1980s, when powerful Colombian drug cartels brought large quantities of drugs and the associated crime to the US. The US government realized that these drug cartels could not be countered with traditional means. It therefore decided to

---

[45] Johnson 2011, pp. 176–177. See also Jones 2007, who argues the relevance of preparing for war in conventional and unconventional environments and the importance of intelligence based on pre-2006 Israeli experiences.

[46] Kober 2008, p. 38.

[47] As quoted in Lamb and Munsing 2011, p. 42.

[48] Idem, p. 5.

[49] Munsing and Lamb 2011, p. 3; Pope 2011.

establish Joint Task Forces (JTF) in which law enforcement agencies are supported by the military.[50] After several less successful initiatives the JIATFS was created in 1994.

JIATFS focused on improving its intelligence fusion process, one of the main deficiencies of earlier JTF initiatives, resulting in tactical intelligence products that operators could use to great effect. These products were based on multiple intelligence sources ranging from imagery intelligence provided by the Coast Guard, signals intelligence provided by the National Security Agency (NSA), human intelligence provided by the Drug Enforcement Agency (DEA) and by agents and sources in foreign countries.

While the task force faced periods of declining resources and assets, for example, because the assets were redirected to support the war on terror after the 9/11 attacks, continuing improvements in intelligence networks and operational practices allowed it to increase its success in interdiction and arrests. The latter is a clear indication that organizational processes are of paramount importance regarding interagency cooperation; to a certain extent improving processes can even compensate for scarcity of resources.

Even though its enemy has proven elusive and adaptable—typical characteristics of a hybrid opponent—JIATFS has maintained its record of success. JIATFS has generated increased levels of interdictions and arrests in its first decade.[51] But its success is completely dependent on its interagency partnerships. The intelligence-driven operations would not be possible without the partners delivering the intelligence, the platforms and the authority while using the military organizational backbone as provided by the Department of Defense (DOD). The next paragraph will indicate which performance variables enabled JIATFS to become and remain so successful.

6.3.2 JIATFS Performance Variables

The success of JIATFS has been examined by Munsing and Lamb using ten variables originating from the organization and management literature on cross-functional teams. All of these ten variables are attributes of the team but they can be grouped on three levels of scope: the organization as a whole, the team itself and the individual. In a later study these authors have also applied the same performance variables in describing the success of interagency teams in Afghanistan and Iraq but the descriptions are to a large extent interchangeable.[52]

---

[50] This description is based on Munsing and Lamb 2011, pp. 3–30 unless indicated otherwise.

[51] Idem, p. 69; Dawes 1996.

[52] Munsing and Lamb 2011, pp. 30–69; Lamb and Munsing 2011, p. 35–49; Orton and Lamb 2011; Hull 2008.

The organizational level variables are team purpose, empowerment and support.[53] Within JIATFS it is completely clear to all participants what the purpose of the task force is and this unifies the team and it provides direction to all the participants.

For the success of JIATFS it is essential that the teams are empowered, meaning that they have control over the resources they need to succeed. This makes them also accountable for their success or failure. However, participating agencies are often reluctant to handover full control over their assets to another organization. Therefore, it has been arranged between JIATFS and its partners that JIATFS gains tactical control over the units, including the related funds and personnel, while the operational control over the units remains with the partnering agency.[54]

Finally, on the organizational level JIATFS also needs support from the various organizations and political actors in the national security system, in order to gain the necessary authority, funds and (political) direction.

The team-level variables that Munsing and Lamb describe are team structure, decision-making, culture and learning.[55] The team-level variables, unlike organizational-level variables, are all under control of the team and they help to explain day-to-day performance.

The structure of the team is directly related to its productivity. Research has shown that teams designed to tackle specific tasks are usually small (typically fewer than 10 people), collocated and they have a strong internal and external communications framework. For JIATFS the complexity of the subject of narcotics requires several functional competencies in its teams, and therefore also several partnering organizations. It also requires a focus on intelligence collection and fusion so that actionable intelligence drives operations. Within JIATFS the tenure of personnel is also an important issue because it is relevant that team members stay long enough to really get to know their job and reach higher performance levels. Especially the military leadership of JIATFS and the military members of the teams typically have a shorter tenure than civilians. On the other side, a long tenure can also lead to resistance to change and becoming 'part of the problem.' JIATFS now balances the turnover of interagency personnel with a core of long-term civilians.

Concerning decision-making for the basic plans, JIATFS focuses on collaborative decisions, based on consensus, in order to benefit from the often-diverging viewpoints that exist as a result of the interagency composition of JIATFS. Collaborative decision-making takes longer than an authoritative model but it produces better solutions and maintains the support of interagency and international

[53] Munsing and Lamb 2011, pp. 34–46.

[54] Tactical Control (TACON) is defined by the DOD as the authority over forces that is limited to the detailed direction and control of movements or maneuvers within the operational area necessary to accomplish missions or tasks assigned. Operational control is defined by the DOD as the authority to perform those functions of command over subordinate forces involving organizing and employing commands and forces, assigning tasks, designating objectives, and giving authoritative direction necessary to accomplish the mission. (DOD Dictionary of Military Terms)

[55] Munsing and Lamb 2011, pp. 46–59.

partners. During the actual execution of operations the decision-making process becomes directive because real-time operations require rapid decisions that cannot be hampered by consensus-building debates.

Creating a positive team culture, which means the shared values, norms and beliefs, requires time in an interagency context because members must overcome their personal and agency's views in order to work as a new and integrated team.[56] It is, however, an important variable because it strengthens the member's commitment to the team.

In order to remain effective the teams must also be able to adapt and learn quickly. Therefore, a lot of emphasis is placed on passing existing knowledge to new members. This is done informally by more experienced members acting as mentors for newcomers and formally through training programs and standard operating procedures.

The individual-level variables are team composition, rewards and leadership.[57] JIATFS must obtain the full range of skills necessary for achieving success in its fight against narcotics by recruiting a diverse group of members and ensuring the individuals work together well. The JIATFS consists of temporary personnel from the various participating agencies supplemented by permanent civilians and contractors. The civilians provide stability and institutional knowledge while the rotating military and other agency personnel provide new ideas and a periodic review of how business is done.

JIATFS supports the idea that individuals need to be rewarded for their responsibilities as team members but also that teams should receive joint awards. Therefore the task force provides a range of recognitions and monetary rewards to its members and it also communicates these appraisals with the parent organizations. The combination of empowering team members and giving immediate feedback on their performance creates a satisfying work environment within JIATFS.

The shared leadership model has proven to be the most beneficiary for JIATFS. This model is well suited for countering adaptive enemies because authority (leadership) is pushed down to a low level so team members can make decisions rapidly without having to consult their superiors, hereby enabling the teams to quickly adapt and act on developing situations. In the shared leadership model, JIATFS leadership must ensure that team members, as well as their parent agencies, always know their contributions are valued and that they are empowered to take actions.

The effort that JIATFS has put into the interagency cooperation and the organizational, team and individual performance variables are the foundation for the task force's success and have provided valuable lessons for other interagency efforts.

---

[56] Bogdanos 2007, p. 3.

[57] Munsing and Lamb 2011, pp. 59–69.

6.3.3 *Interagency Initiatives in Afghanistan and Iraq*

In response to the 9/11 attacks the United States started military operations against the Taliban and Al Qaida in Afghanistan. The operation was not founded on the extensive use of conventional ground forces but on a new interagency concept, as proposed by the CIA, in which airpower teamed up with SOF, USAF combat controllers, intelligence personnel and indigenous Afghan forces.[58] More specifically: airpower was used to degrade enemy communications while small teams of SOF joined up with indigenous forces in order to pin down and amass enemy forces so they could be attacked by precision air strikes. The concept of ad hoc interagency teams was able to engineer a swift victory over the Taliban and has since then been known as the Afghan model.[59] This experience suggests that relatively small forces enabled with advanced technologies and adjoining concepts, such as interagency teams, with new approaches to intelligence and operations are able to significantly alter the status quo in a hybrid battle space.[60]

Based on this initial interagency success in Afghanistan, several other interagency team initiatives were launched. US Central Command for example established the Joint Interagency Task Force—Counter Terrorism (JIATF-CT) that opened its doors to as many interagency partners as it could find.[61] It focused on unravelling the Taliban and al Qaeda networks and it combined intelligence fusion with direct operational support of SOF.

The increase of US activities and troops in the 2001–2004 timeframe also supported a further expansion of interagency developments because commanders wanted to replicate the successful interagency partnerships that had spearheaded the initial American response. Although the various interagency teams gained success, several problems also emerged.[62] The first problem was that conventional forces were wary of working too closely with SOF (and therefore with interagency teams) and were not culturally inclined toward intelligence-operations fusion. However, they did appreciate and use the fusion cells as all-source intelligence staff support. Thus, the conventional forces maintained the traditional split between intelligence and operations in the conventional military command and staff structure.

A second problem that emerged was the frequent tensions between the operations (usually SOF) and intelligence domains. The SOF were often focused on hitting targets as soon as possible while intelligence wanted to protect sources and collect information for as long as possible. Adding to this dilemma was the fact that SOF teams were weak in exploitation and analysis of sites and targets after actions.

---

[58] See Scahill 2013, Chapter 3 specifically.

[59] Andres et al. 2005, pp. 124–131. See also Boot 2007, Chap. 11; Mazzetti 2013, p. 1; McInnes 2005, pp. 116–119; Kaldor 2012, p. 155; Lamb and Munsing 2011, pp. 8–11.

[60] The model has also received criticism, see for example Biddle 2003, pp. 45–46 and Shimko 2010, p. 138.

[61] Lamb and Munsing 2011, p. 11. See further Bogdanos 2007.

[62] Munsing and Lamb 2011, pp. 12–14; Cf. Mansager 2006.

Although the FBI did train some teams in site exploitation, a lot of intelligence was actually lost.

Finally, there were differences between the focus of the interagency teams and the conventional forces. The teams were focused on taking down terrorist leadership, which resulted in kinetic actions that often conflicted with the focus of the conventional forces on counterinsurgency and winning the hearts and minds of the local people.

In conclusion it can be said that in Afghanistan the US military pioneered with the use of interagency teams in war but, apart from the initial swift victory over the Taliban, the overall effectiveness of the teams could have been higher. There were still too many fissures between all the actors required for an integrated effort: between SOF and conventional forces, between SOF and diverse intelligence disciplines and between conventional forces and the intelligence fusion cells. The war in Iraq provided another opportunity to test the validity of interagency teams.

At the operational and tactical level, the variety of interagency task forces that pioneered in Afghanistan migrated to Iraq in 2003 for Operation Iraqi Freedom. Although the previously described impediments were still present, the various interagency high-value target teams were tactically successful; however, they did not yet make a strategic difference.[63] When the security situation in Iraq deteriorated after 2004, several US commanders further experimented with the use of interagency teams.[64] Examples include Task Force Freedom (TFF) in Mosul, the 3rd Armored Cavalry Regiment (3ACR) in Tal Afar and the 1st Brigade Combat Team (1BCT) in Ramadi whose commanders built organizations and tactics capable of conducting classic counterinsurgency warfare. They were able to target insurgents and terrorists with sufficient discrimination to put them on the defensive, while population-centric security measures and influence operations pacified the broader population.[65]

After their arrival in the operational area, TFF started working with various military and civilian actors making them all partners in the security process. The TFF commanders also pushed mission authority down to their company commanders. As a result, the subordinate units were made responsible for their respective areas of operations, intelligence collection and targeting decisions. This approach led to an increased number of self-initiated missions and more actionable intelligence. The advanced communications architecture available to TFF and the decentralized leadership model made it possible to rapidly redirect units in response to new information and 'swarm' the enemy by having nearby units quickly surround the insurgents. Finally, TFF also began combining unique intelligence assets for massed electronic and human monitoring of the opponent with network

---

[63] Lamb and Munsing 2011, pp. 15–16; Bogdanos 2007.

[64] Munsing and Lamb 2011, p. 18.

[65] See McCulloh and Johnson 2013, pp. 13–4 for details about the US approach to hybrid warfare in Iraq.

targeting; based on extensive intelligence operations, SOF and conventional forces put persistent pressure on the opponent's network until it collapsed.[66]

3ACR focused on first getting a clear understanding of their operational environment, including detailing the opponent's networks, before actually retaking the city of Tal Afar. In order to gain as much intelligence as possible 3ACR also chose an interagency approach by cooperating for example with NGO's, local authorities, key leaders and other military units in the area. At the same time they also actively collected intelligence by using ISR assets, checkpoints, biometric registration and checks of individuals while at the same time supporting local governance initiatives in order to strengthen the community.[67]

1BCT was made responsible for Ramadi in June 2006, which at that time was one of the most dangerous places in Iraq and by some it was even regarded as a lost cause. However, eventually it became one of the biggest success stories of the American operations in Iraq. 1BCT had a less extensive organic intelligence architecture available to work with compared to the previous examples and also the interagency options were more limited because there were fewer partners in the area to cooperate with. They did make extensive use of the experiences of other units in Iraq and 1BCT started by building a common picture of the enemy networks in the area. Eventually the cooperation between the IC, SOF and 1BCT and local militia led to a seamless targeting process through liaisons officers and the intelligence fusion centre that was created. As a concurrent effort, also the local government and police forces were supported and improved. For example, in a matter of months the Ramadi police force increased in size from 150 to 4000. The combination of the interagency approach, the targeting of the opponents' networks and the strengthening of local authorities resulted in a significantly safer environment.[68]

The success of these examples can be traced back to three separate innovations which all required interagency collaboration. The first innovation was network-based targeting. A narrow characterization of this innovation is that insurgent and terrorist cells and their supporters were analysed in order to be able to attack them. This approach is often summarized as find, fix, finish, exploit, analyse and disseminate (F3EAD). Within F3EAD persistent ISR and all-source intelligence efforts find the target amidst civilian clutter and fix the exact location. Based on this exact location surgical finish operations are possible. Finishing does not only mean kinetically removing a target from the battlefield but also gaining more information on the opponent. Exploit and analyse is the main effort of F3EAD because it provides insight into the enemy network and offers new lines of operations[69] A broader characterization is that all-source intelligence provides situational awareness of the local environment, its social networks, key decision makers and

---

[66] Lamb and Munsing 2011, pp. 18–20; Flynn 2012a, p. 22.

[67] Lamb and Munsing 2011, pp. 24–28.

[68] Idem, pp. 28–31.

[69] Flynn et al. 2008, p. 57; Builta and Heller 2011, pp. 6–7. Cf. Bousquet 2009, pp. 203–210.

their motivations. With such knowledge commanders were able to influence the population even without lethal measures.[70]

The second innovation was the fusion of improved all-source intelligence with operational capabilities. Having intelligence and operations working together co-located on a sustained basis produced persistent surveillance and improved discrimination (between friend, foe and locals).[71] Removing the organizational seams between intelligence and operations results in having an unblinking eye on high-value targets and a completely integrated F3EAD process. It also improves decision-making on the difficult trade-offs between developing sources and taking down targets because operators get to appreciate the intelligence value of sources and intelligence analysts better understand operations and their need to deliver relevant support.[72]

The third and final innovation was the integration of counterterrorist (the interagency teams) and counterinsurgency efforts and the proliferation of that same integration. When the success of the interagency teams and their intelligence fusion cells became clear they were frequently located in close proximity of the enemy network in order to increase the speed of analysis and the F3EAD cycle. The cooperation with conventional forces also increased in support of their population-centric counterinsurgency efforts.[73]

6.3.4 Concluding Remarks

Despite their success the interagency teams have received surprisingly little attention and study.[74] Lamb and Munsing underline their concern by stating that interagency teams are not well understood and respected, are not significantly present in literature and have not been codified into military doctrine and best practices. The latter is remarkable because the authors also state that virtually every recent major national security study has identified inadequate interagency cooperation as a glaring systemic deficiency.[75] Interagency teams are no magical solutions for hybrid conflicts. However, the philosophy of intensive interagency cooperation focused on a common purpose has proven to be an essential tool in the hybrid warfare toolbox.

---

[70] Lamb and Munsing 2011, p. 33.

[71] See Flynn 2012b who emphasize the relevance of intelligence fusion and the integration of intelligence and operations.

[72] Lamb and Munsing 2011, p. 33.

[73] Idem, p. 34.

[74] Rosenbach 2008, pp. 137–141 and McConnell 2007.

[75] Lamb and Munsing 2011, pp. 7 and 56. Cf. Pope 2011, p. 117; Flynn 2012b, p. 26.

6.4 Conclusion

In the preceding pages I argued that the rise of a new type of conflict after the Cold War stimulated debate within the intelligence community and among politicians and scholars about how to react to this change. Some called for a new paradigm that should guide intelligence practitioners, but after two decades the debate on the Revolution in Intelligence Affairs is still inconclusive. This is all the more remarkable because a number of intelligence communities, and the armed forces they serve, have taken up the challenge the change poses. In the process they have seriously erred at times but they came up with a number of innovations suited to counter or stymie adversaries that displayed characteristics of Hoffman's hybrid warfare paradigm. Two of these learning processes and the innovations they produced have been discussed in this chapter.

The first is the Israel-Hezbollah war of 2006. The IDF is generally said to have lost the war. The main reason for this loss was the inadequate level of preparation for war with a well-trained and highly motivated opponent that employed hybrid tactics. Extensive analyses after the war indicated deficiencies within the IDF in the run-up to the war related to doctrine: the IDF was so much focused on fighting Low Intensity Conflicts against the Palestinians, that it neglected preparing to fight more sophisticated opponents. The active and reserve forces displayed an inadequate level of training and the IDF leadership paid insufficient attention to the integration of ground, air and naval forces. After the war, the IDF entered into a process to actively correct these deficiencies and the successful operation against Hamas in 2008 can be seen as a positive result of that learning process. My analysis of the 2006 Israel-Hezbollah war and the 2008 Israel-Hamas war indicates that countering hybrid opponents requires an intelligence-led integrated approach that is supported by doctrines and tactics specifically tailored to the hybrid opponent.

While the Israel-Hezbollah 2006 war provides details about the main outline of how to counter hybrid non-state actors, the case study concerning interagency teams zooms in on a new approach to the intelligence and operations process on the tactical and operational levels. Interagency teams build on US experiences in countering illegal narcotics trafficking from South America. The original Joint Interagency Task Force South (JIATFS) consisted of personnel from various organizations that are all stakeholders in countering illegal drugs trade. All personnel is organized into small, empowered and diverse teams. This promoted adaptability and flexibility and made JIATFS an important and successful asset in countering illegal drugs trade.

Because of its success, similar interagency initiatives were used in Iraq and Afghanistan. Its overall success was inspiring, although there were also setbacks. The integration of operational personnel (often Special Forces) with intelligence analysts and subject matter experts on various disciplines into small self-synchronizing teams proved to be effective in countering the hybrid opponents. Interagency teams and interagency cooperation are the actual quintessence of the developments on the tactical and operational levels that have taken place, and have proven successful, in countering hybrid opponents.

While further research is necessary—study of the learning experiences during operations in Libya, and Syria may be particularly enlightening—it seems correct to conclude that the operational and tactical lessons the US and Israel have drawn in hybrid conflicts they were engaged in, have effectively rendered the RIA debate and its academic approaches to the new paradigm superfluous. In other words, the characteristics of the new threats are known and new concepts and approaches that are effective in countering these threats have been identified. The task at hand for the intelligence community is to truly incorporate this new intelligence paradigm into its organizations and processes.

Still, caution is in order. While success on the tactical and operational level against hybrid opponents is achievable, this does not guarantee strategic success. Battlefield success may prove to be Pyrrhic when the hybrid opponent succeeds in swaying public opinion. Hybrid warfare and non-state actors require a comprehensive strategic, operational and tactical approach firmly supported by a well-devised narrative. Such a comprehensive approach can only be made possible by an intelligence community that actively implements the new intelligence paradigm and the successful innovations learned from hybrid conflicts. As the very nature of hybrid opponents dictates that every opponent and every situation will be different, there is no standard solution to a hybrid scenario. While the military must learn to master different types of soldiering, intelligence communities will need to be imaginative, adaptive, networked and innovative.

References

Adamsky D (2010) The Culture of Military Innovation: The Impact of Cultural Factors on the Revolution in Military Affairs in Russia, the US, and Israel. Stanford University Press, Stanford

Andres RB, Wills C, Griffith TE Jr (2005) Winning with Allies: The Strategic Value of the Afghan Model. International Security 30(3):124–160

Arkin WM (2007a) Divine Victory for Whom? Airpower in the 2006 Israeli-Hezbollah War. Strategic Studies Quarterly 1(2):98–141.

Arkin WM (2007b) Divining Victory: Airpower in the 2006 Israel-Hezbollah War. Air University Press, Maxwell Air Force Base

Berman L (2012) Capturing Contemporary Innovation: Studying IDF Innovation Against Hamas and Hizballah. Journal of Strategic Studies 35(1):121–147

Biddle S (2003) Afghanistan and the Future of Warfare. Foreign Affairs 82(2):31–46

Bogdanos M (2007) Transforming Joint Interagency Coordination: The Missing Link Between National Strategy & Operational Success. Center for Technology and National Security Policy, Washington DC

Boot M (2007) War Made New: Weapons, Warriors, and the Making of the Modern World. Gotham Books, New York

Bousquet AJ (2009) The Scientific Way of War of Warfare: Order and Chaos on the Battlefields of Modernity. Hurst & Co Publishing, London

Budinger Z, Smith J (2011) Ten Years After 9/11: A Status Report on Information Sharing Statements before the Senate Committee on Homeland Security and Governmental Affairs

Builta JA, Heller EN (2011) Reflections on 10 Years of Counterterrorism Analysis. Studies in Intelligence 55(3):1–15

Cordesman AH (2009) The Gaza War. Center for Strategic and International Studies, Washington DC

Cordesman AH, Sullivan WD (2007) Lessons of the 2006 Israeli-Hezbollah War. CSIS Press, Washington DC

Dawes SS (1996) Interagency Information Sharing: Expected Benefits, Manageable Risks. Journal of Policy Analysis and Management 15: 377–394

de Wijk R (2012) Hybrid Conflict and the Changing Nature of Actors. In: Lindley-French J, Boyer Y (eds) The Oxford Handbook of War. Oxford University Press, Oxford, pp 358–372

DOD Dictionary of Military Terms http://www.dtic.mil/doctrine/dod_dictionary/ Accessed 19 August 2015

Elran M, Brom S (2007) The Second Lebanon War: Strategic Perspectives. Institute for National Security Studies, Tel Aviv

Exum A (2006) Hizballah at War: A Military Assessment. Washington Institute for Near East Policy, Washington DC

Flynn GJ (2012a) Decade of War, Volume 1: Enduring Lessons From the Past Decade of Operations. Joint Staff J-7, Joint and Coalition Operational Analysis (JCOA), Suffolk

Flynn MT, Flynn CA (2012b) Integrating Intelligence and Information: Ten Points for the Commander. Military Review 92(1):4–8

Flynn MT, Juergens R, Cantrell TL (2008) Employing ISR SOF Best Practice. Joint Force Quarterly 50 (3rd Quarter 2008):56–61

Goodman M (2005) 9/11: The Failure of Strategic Intelligence. In: Wark WK (ed) Twenty-first Century Intelligence. Routledge, London, pp. 59–71

Haloutz D (2009) The Second Lebanon War: Achievements and Failures. Military and Strategic Affairs 1(2):61–71

Hammes TX (2006) The Sling and the Stone: On War in the 21st Century. Zenith, Minneapolis

Hoffman FG (2007) Conflict in the 21st Century: The Rise of Hybrid Wars. Potomac Institute for Policy Studies, Arlington

Hull J (2008) We're All Smarter Than Any One of Us: The Role of Inter-agency Intelligence Organizations in Combating Armed Groups. Journal of Public and International Affairs 19 (Spring 2008):28–50

Intelligence and Terrorism Information Center at the Israel Intelligence Heritage & Commemoration Center (IICC) (2008) Hamas's military buildup in the Gaza Strip, Ramat Hasharon

Johnson DE (2011) Hard Fighting: Israel in Lebanon and Gaza. Rand Corporation, Santa Monica

Jones SG (2007) Fighting Networked Terrorist Groups: Lessons From Israel. Studies in Conflict & Terrorism 30(4):281–302

Kainikara S, Parkin R (2007) Pathways to Victory: Observations From the 2006 Israel-Hezbollah Conflict. Air Power Development Centre, Canberra

Kalb M, Saivetz C (2007) The Israeli Hezbollah War of 2006: The Media As a Weapon in Asymmetrical Conflict. The Harvard International Journal of Press/Politics 12(3):43–66

Kaldor M (2012) New and Old Wars: Organized Violence in a Global Era, 3rd edn. Stanford University Press, Stanford

Kaplinsky M (2009) The IDF in the Years Before the Second Lebanon War. Military and Strategic Affairs 1(2):25–37

Kober A (2008) The Israel Defense Forces in the Second Lebanon War: Why the Poor Performance? The Journal of Strategic Studies 31(1):3–40

Kreps SE (2007) The 2006 Lebanon War: Lessons Learned. Parameters 37(1):72–84

Kulick A (2009) "Lebanon Lite": Lessons From the Operation in Gaza and the Next Round Against Hizbollah. Military and Strategic Affairs 1(1):51–66

Kuperwasser Y (2007) Lessons From Israel's Intelligence Reforms. The Brookings Institution, Washington DC

Lamb C, Munsing E (2011) Secret weapon: High-value target teams as an organizational innovation. National Defense University Press, Washington DC

Lambeth BS (2011) Air Operations in Israel's War Against Hezbollah: Learning From Lebanon and Getting It Right in Gaza. Rand Corporation, Santa Monica

Lambeth BS (2012a) Learning From Lebanon: Airpower and Strategy in Israel's 2006 War Against Hezbollah. Naval War College Review 65(3):82–104

Lambeth BS (2012b) Israel's War in Gaza – A Paradigm of Effective Military Learning and Adaptation. International Security 37(2):81–118

Lever P (2012) Intelligence and War In: Lindley-French J, Boyer Y (eds) The Oxford Handbook of War. Oxford University Press, Oxford, pp 228–241

Malis C (2012) Unconventional Forms of War. In: Lindley-French J, Boyer Y (eds) The Oxford Handbook of War. Oxford University Press, Oxford, pp 185–198

Mansager TB (2006) Interagency lessons learned in Afghanistan. Joint Forces Quarterly 40(1st Quarter 2006):80–84

Marrero AF (2009) The Tactics of Operation Cast Lead. In: Farquhar SC (ed) Back to Basics: A Study of the Second Lebanon War and Operation Cast Lead. Combat Studies Institute Press, Fort Leavenworth, pp 83–99

Matthews M (2008) We Were Caught Unprepared: The 2006 Hezbollah-Israeli War. Combat Studies Institute Press, Fort Leavenworth

Matthews M (2009) Hard Lessons Learned. In: Farquhar SC (ed) Back to Basics: A Study of the Second Lebanon War and Operation Cast Lead. Combat Studies Institute Press, Fort Leavenworth, pp 5–34

Mazzetti M (2013) The Way of the Knife. The CIA, a Secret Army, and a War at the Ends of the Earth. Scribe Publications, London

McConnell M (2007) Overhauling Intelligence. Foreign Affairs 86(4):49–58

McCulloh T, Johnson R (2013) Hybrid Warfare, JSOU Report 13–4. Joint Special Operations University, MacDill Air Force Base

McInnes C (2005) A different kind of war? September 11 and the United States' Afghan War. In: Duyvesteyn I, Angstrom J (eds) Rethinking the Nature of War. Frank Cass, New York, pp 109–134

Munsing E, Lamb C (2011) Joint Interagency Task Force-South: The Best Known, Least Understood Interagency Success. National Defense University Press, Washington DC

Niva S (2010) Drawing the Wrong Lessons From Israel's 2006 War. Middle East Report 255: 30–33

Orton JD, Lamb C (2011) Interagency National Security Teams: Can Social Science Contribute? Prism 2(2):47–64

Osinga F, Terriff T, Farrell T (2010) The Rise of Military Transformation, a Transformation Gap? Stanford University Press, Stanford

Pelletiere S (1999) Hamas and Hizbollah: The radical challenge to Israel in the occupied territories. In: Almond HH, Burger JA (eds) The History and Future of Warfare: Selections From the Professional Readings in Military Strategy. Strategic Studies Institute, Carlisle

Petrelli N (2013) Deterring Insurgents: Culture, Adaptation and the Evolution of Israeli Counterinsurgency, 1987–2005. Journal of Strategic Studies 36(5):666-691

Pope RS (2011) Interagency Task Forces: The Right Tools for the Job. Strategic Studies Quarterly 5(2):114–152

Rapaport A (2010) The IDF and the Lessons of the Second Lebanon War. Begin-Sadat Center for Strategic Studies, Ramat Gan

Rid T, Hecker M (2009) War 2.0: Irregular Warfare in the Information Age. Praeger Security International, Westport

Romm G (2007) A Test of Rival Strategies: Two Ships Passing in the Night. In: Elran M, Brom S (eds) The Second Lebanon War: Strategic Perspectives. Institute for National Security Studies, Tel Aviv, pp 49–60

Rosenbach E (2008) The Incisive Fight: Recommendations for Improving Counterterrorism Intelligence. The Annals of the American Academy of Political and Social Science 618 (1):133–147

Rudner M (2010) Hizbullah: An Organizational and Operational Profile. International Journal of Intelligence and CounterIntelligence 23(2):226–246

Scahill J (2013) Dirty Wars: The World Is a Battlefield. Nation Books, New York

Schweitzer Y (2007) "Divine Victory" and Earthly Failures: Was the War Really a Victory for Hizbollah? In: Elran M, Brom S (eds) The Second Lebanon War: Strategic Perspectives. Institute for National Security Studies, Tel Aviv, pp 123–134

Sharp JM, Blanchard C, Katzman K, Migdalovitz C, Prados A, Gallis P, Rennack D, Rollins J, Browne M, Bowman S (2006) Lebanon: The Israel-Hamas-Hezbollah Conflict. Congressional Research Service, Washington DC

Shimko KL (2010) The Iraq Wars and America's Military Revolution. Cambridge University Press, New York

Siboni G (2007) The Military Campaign in Lebanon. In: Elran M, Brom S (eds) The Second Lebanon War: Strategic Perspectives. Institute for National Security Studies, Tel Aviv, pp 61–76

Sinterniklaas R (2013) Airpower and Irregular Warfare Thinking (1991–2011). Netherlands Defence Academy, Breda

Thompson PG (2014) Armed Groups: The 21st Century Threat. Rowman & Littlefield, London

Williams P (2001) Non-state Criminal Networks. In: Arquilla J, Ronfeldt D (eds) Networks and Netwars: The Future of Terror, Crime, and Militancy. Rand Corporation, Santa Monica

Williams P (2003) Preface: New Context, Smart Enemies. In: Bunker RJ (ed) Non-state Threats and Future Wars. Frank Cass, New York

Winograd Commission (2007) Winograd Commission Submits Interim Report at http://www.mfa.gov.il/mfa/pressroom/2007/pages/winograd%20inquiry%20commission%20submits%20interim%20report%2030-apr-2007.aspx

Winograd Committee (2008) Winograd Committee Submits Final Report at http://www.mfa.gov.il/mfa/mfa-archive/2008/pages/winograd%20committee%20submits%20final%20report%2030-jan-2008.aspx

Zagdanski JD (2007) Round 2 in Lebanon: How the IDF Focused Exclusively on COIN and Lost the Ability to Fight Maneuver War. Infantry 96(1): 32–35

Zuhur S (2008) Hamas and Israel: Conflicting strategies of group-based politics. Strategic Studies Institute, Carlisle

Author Biography

Major Minne Boelens graduated from the Royal Netherlands Defence Academy (NLDA) in 2003 and subsequently held several intelligence positions within operational air force units and at staff level. He currently works at the Defence Staff in The Hague in the air operations branch of the plans directorate. In 2015 he obtained his NLDA Military Strategic Studies master's degree in Intelligence and Security. This chapter is an adaptation of his master thesis.

Chapter 7
Blindfolded in the Dark. The Intelligence Position of Dutchbat in the Srebrenica Safe Area

Cees Wiebes, Jeoffrey van Woensel and Aad Wever

Abstract The attack on and the full conquest of the Safe Area of Srebrenica on 11 July 1995 caught everyone by surprise. This did not only go for Dutchbat, but for all intelligence services concerned. This cannot merely be explained by the fact that it was just shortly before the attack on the enclave that the Bosnian Serbs took the decision to conquer it completely, but it also has to do with the extremely weak intelligence position of the UN and with the absence of sufficient capacity and the right means to gather and analyse intelligence. Because of this, the fall of Srebrenica can be attributed to the failure of military intelligence. The Netherlands can be blamed as well. In the Dutch cabinet, in the Dutch Army and in Parliament an anti-intelligence attitude prevailed. Among them the idea had taken root that a peacekeeping operation did not require intelligence. Dutchbat command made serious mistakes and did not seize all available opportunities improve the intelligence position inside the enclave.

Keywords Srebrenica · Bosnia-Herzegovina · Military intelligence · Peacekeeping intelligence · Dutchbat · UNPROFOR

C. Wiebes (✉)
Institute of Security and Global Affairs (ISGA), University of Leiden, The Hague, The Netherlands
e-mail: ceeswiebes@gmail.com

J. van Woensel
Centre of Research and Expertise, Veterans Institute, Doorn, The Netherlands
e-mail: jtwh.v.woensel@veteraneninstituut.nl

A. Wever
Enschede, The Netherlands
e-mail: ajmwever@hotmail.com

F. Baudet et al. (eds.), *Perspectives on Military Intelligence from the First World War to Mali*, DOI 10.1007/978-94-6265-183-8_7

Contents

7.1 Introduction

In 1996, the Dutch government gave the *Nederlands Instituut voor Oorlogsdocumentatie* (Dutch Institute for War Documentation, NIOD) the assignment to investigate the events during the fall of Srebrenica.[1] This event, in which some 8,000 Muslim men were killed, is a national trauma which has haunted The Netherlands to this very day. The director of the NIOD presented the voluminous report[2] to the then-Minister of Education, Culture and Science on 10 April 2002. The sub-report *Intelligence en de oorlog in Bosnië, 1993–1995* deals with the role of the intelligence and security services during the fall of the enclave.[3]

In this chapter we will take an extensive look at the conclusions of the NIOD-report and the sub-report and in this we will include the current theories on military intelligence. We will try to answer the question what the intelligence and security services exactly knew about the attack on Srebrenica. When answering this question the following sub-questions will be dealt with: what intelligence requirements does a military unit have and in what way are they collected? Why did the UN not collect intelligence? Why did The Netherlands not collect intelligence? What did the allies do in the field of intelligence? What did Dutchbat's intelligence position in the enclave look like? Did opportunities present themselves to strengthen the intelligence position? Can the fall of Srebrenica be called an *intelligence failure*?

---

[1] Nederlands Instituut voor Oorlogsdocumentatie (NIOD) 2002a.

[2] Nederlands Instituut voor Oorlogsdocumentatie (NIOD) 2002b.

[3] Wiebes 2002; for the English-language version, see Wiebes 2003.

7.2 Military Intelligence

In order to establish what intelligence and security services knew about the attack on Srebrenica it is important to know a military unit's intelligence requirements. It should be noted that we sketch the way military intelligence was collected, analysed and made available as customary in the early nineties when the civil war in Yugoslavia started.

First of all a military unit wants to know their (potential) opponents' plans and capabilities. Therefore, it is important to collect and process data on foreign powers, potential enemy regular forces, irregular warring parties, but also data on areas and conditions for current or future operations. Put simply, intelligence deals with weather, terrain and enemy. The aim of the intelligence system in peace, armed conflict or war is supplying processed information to enable commanders and headquarters to formulate policy and plans. In addition, the intelligence system provides information about targets that can be attacked in order to realize plans. An intelligence section has to collect data and produce intelligence reports that meet the commander's and headquarters' requirements. Therefore, it is important that the commander or headquarters clearly state their information requirements. In addition to intelligence about weather, terrain and enemy, a commander or headquarters also need information on aspects like location, activities and operational readiness of friendly forces, civilian organisations and knowledge about groups of population in the area of operations. Under information we understand all knowledge about the situation, including intelligence about weather, terrain and enemy. Rapidly changing situations in an operations area make timely and correct information essential for a commander. There is a continuous battle for information: the *information battle*.[4]

There is an essential difference between intelligence and military intelligence. In order to show this a definition follows for both intelligence and military intelligence.

> Intelligence is the product of systematic efforts to collect, confirm, evaluate, and correlate information from a variety of sources. The resulting conclusions are often subjective and tentative, representing the best informed estimate by the analysts involved.[5]

Military intelligence, however,

> is concerned primarily with the armed force of enemy or potential enemy powers, but also includes analysis of the terrain, weather, industrial production, weapons development, local diseases, and many other factors that affect military operations quite as much as the enemy force in the field.[6]

---

[4] Doctrinecommissie van de Koninklijke Landmacht 1996, pp. 128–130; see also: Nederlandse Defensiestaf 2012, pp. 12–13.

[5] House 1993, p. 2.

[6] House 1993, p. 3.

Within a military organization several levels collect and analyse various levels of information in varying levels of detail for diverging objectives. 'A head of state or commanding general is interested in a broad picture of the situation, while junior commanders need to know in detail the immediate threat in their own area.'[7] There are four different levels: Strategic Intelligence, Operational Intelligence, Tactical Intelligence en Combat Information. The political-strategic level and the military-strategic level are supported by strategic intelligence, the operational, tactical and executive by, respectively, operational intelligence, tactical intelligence and Combat Information.[8] As the various levels play a part in this chapter, we will list them here:

> *Strategic Intelligence* is intelligence that is required for forming policy and military plans, decisions and operations at national and theatre levels and over a longer period of time. The collection of Strategic Intelligence often requires integrating information concerning politics, military affairs, economics, societal interactions, and technological developments.[9]
>
> Operational Intelligence is an intermediate level (..) of intelligence that will affect the campaign plan or contingency plan intended to accomplish strategic or national objectives. It is concerned with current or near-term events.[10]
>
> Tactical Intelligence (also called Combat Intelligence) is the traditional focus of military intelligence, seeking to understand the composition, disposition, doctrine, and if possible intentions of enemy units that immediately threaten friendly tactical units.[11]
>
> Combat Information may be considered a subset of Tactical Intelligence. In this case, the term 'information', rather than 'intelligence' implies that little if any effort is expended on verifying or analyzing that information. It is composed of raw reports rather than evaluated intelligence.[12]

Intelligence and security services have at their disposal various means to collect information and intelligence. A number of (important) collection methods, of which most play a role in this article, will be dealt with briefly. Firstly, OSINT (Open Source Intelligence): this concerns intelligence obtained from publicly accessible sources, such as radio, television, internet, press and other information. Secondly, HUMINT (Human Intelligence): this is a class of intelligence obtained from all forms of information collected from or supplied by human sources. Obtaining the required information can take place by direct observation, such as reconnaissance or observation, debriefing and interrogation and by using more indirect methods, such as employing recruited sources. All information thus obtained is normally collected

---

[7] House 1993, p. 3.

[8] House 1993, p. 3; Nederlandse Defensiestaf 2012, pp. 38–39.

[9] See: The Interagency OPSEC Support Staff 1996, p. 2-1.

[10] House 1993, p. 3; The Interagency OPSEC Support Staff 1996, p. 2-1; see also: Nederlandse Defensiestaf 2012, p. 40.

[11] House 1993, p. 4; see also: Nederlandse Defensiestaf 2012, p. 40.

[12] House 1993, p. 4; see also: Herman 1996, pp. 121–124.

and forwarded to the intelligence officer, who will attempt to synthesize a more complete view of the opposing force.[13] IMINT (Imagery Intelligence) is acquired by analysing and interpreting imagery. Finally, there is SIGINT (Signals Intelligence). It is a generic term to describe intelligence obtained from the electromagnetic spectrum. SIGINT comprises COMINT (Communications Intelligence) and ELINT (Electronic Intelligence).[14]

One more category of intelligence should be mentioned, namely basic intelligence (Basic Intelligence, more commonly called Order of the Battle Intelligence or OB). This is intelligence and validated information about any possible subject. They are the basis for processing freshly available information or intelligence. 'Order of the Battle involves comparing a host of intelligence reports against the known organization, equipment, strength, leadership, training, doctrine, and past performance of an enemy force, in order to develop a fuller picture of enemy dispositions and possible actions. OB is the basis for intelligence analysis in almost any unit or agency, and is often a simple matter of common sense.'[15] Take for instance the position of the artillery. Moving artillery is a time-consuming process that soldiers wish to avoid, especially if artillery support is needed. If a military unit wants to defend a certain location, it will position the artillery relatively far behind the frontline to make sure that the artillery pieces will not suddenly have to be repositioned to keep them from being conquered by the enemy should they succeed in penetrating the line of defence. When a military unit is planning an offensive, they will locate the pieces close to the front line so as to provide the best possible fire support at the maximum distance. 'The knowledge of the battlefield positions and maximum effective range of particular artillery unit may be an important indication to the order of the battle analyst that the enemy is expecting to attack or to defend.'[16] Such an indication in itself does not mean anything, but combined with other information it can be used to obtain a more complete survey of the enemy. When one knows that a certain number and calibre of weapons belong to a certain unit (brigade, division or other unit) localising a certain artillery unit may be an indication of the possible strength of the opposing enemy. 'The knowledge that this artillery unit is located at a particular place may come from reconnaissance, imagery, signals intercept, or human intelligence, but that knowledge must be confirmed by other sources and compared to the enemy's known organization and habits of operation.'[17]

The intelligence process in its entirety is called intelligence cycle: 'If a commander wishes to know certain information about the enemy, his intelligence officers decide what indications they must look for, then direct different functional organizations to seek those indications. Once the raw information has been

[13] House 1993, pp. 5–6.

[14] Nederlandse Defensiestaf 2012, pp. 44–45; see also: House 1993, pp. 4–9.

[15] House 1993, p. 9.

[16] House 1993, p. 10.

[17] House 1993, pp. 9–10.

collected, it must be processed by comparing, evaluating, and interpreting different reports to develop the best available picture of the enemy. The absence of an expected indication may be useful as negative information, suggesting what the enemy is not planning to do.'[18] The picture thus arising is shared with the commander and other levels in the military organisation. 'The cycle of directing collection, collecting information, processing the data, and disseminating the results of such analysis, is continuous.'[19] In theory this looks simple, but in practice it is rather more complicated, '...and the results both subjective and ambivalent at best.'[20]

7.3 The Tension Between Peacekeeping and Intelligence Collection

For a long time the UN was opposed to collecting intelligence. The UN was an open and impartial organisation and for that reason the collection of intelligence was strictly forbidden. Especially the humanitarian component of the UN (UNHCR, UNDP, UNICEF, etc.) was strongly opposed. The humanitarian community has always expressed its concerns about the fact that the safety of its staff will be endangered if a humanitarian organisation is associated with collecting intelligence. For the operational part of the UN this is, of course, slightly more nuanced. The UN Secretariat in New York, notably the Department of Peacekeeping Operations (DPKO) and the Department of Political Affairs (DPA), were directly involved in preparing and executing peace support operations (PSOs). Still, also the UN Secretariat had always been opposed to intelligence collection in support of peace operations: 'it was just not done'. In addition, it was not deemed necessary for traditional peace operations where consent by all participants was the leading principle.[21] In the UN a discussion was going on that can be summarized as follows: 'The controversy is fuelled by disreputable stereotypes surrounding intelligence as spying, and the UN-held view that peacekeeping's benevolent presence, welcomed by all sides in a conflict, supposedly eradicates any requirement for intelligence.'[22]

In the mid-nineties this was certainly still the case. In the UN 'intelligence' was not an accepted word, activity or process. Euphemistically, 'military information' was used instead of 'military intelligence'. In accordance with UN practice, the Dutch military used this phrase when dealing with peace operations. The *Militaire*

---

[18] House 1993, p. 10.

[19] Ibidem.

[20] House 1993, p. 10; for a theoretical approach of the *intelligence cycle* see for instance: De Graaff 2010, pp. 349–358.

[21] Van Kappen 2003, pp. 3–4; see also Carment et al. 2006, pp. 1–2.

[22] Martyn 2006, p. 23.

Doctrine (Military Doctrine) of the *Koninklijke Landmacht* (Dutch Army) (1996) enters on the sensitivities: 'Instinctively 'intelligence systems' refer to the opposing side. In an operation with mutual consent, where impartiality is one of the founding principles, the use of the phrase 'intelligence' may endanger the perception of impartiality in the conflict.' It is for that reason that in the case of peace support operations the Military Doctrine uses 'military information'. In this case, of course, intelligence in meant, but using certain sources of information (such as interrogating prisoners of war) are not frequent here. Opposed to this is the fact that other sources can be used on a large scale, such as non-military organisations (e.g., NGOs).[23] In the army doctrine publication *Vredes-operaties* (Peace Operations), published in 1999, a changing view can be observed. This doctrine still speaks of military information, but it equals intelligence. No distinction is made between collecting intelligence and military information, and between the ways in which this is done. In principle, the same procedure goes for a peace operation (Collecting data on the terrain, the weather and the enemy), with the addition that in case of peace operations 'information on less tangible matters such as opinions, visions, feelings, tensions etc. are also needed.'[24] 'This doctrine also states that the information flow in peace operations should go two ways: 'It is in the importance of peace operations that all parties are aware of information about the operations of the peace-keeping force. This does not mean that all details can always be revealed fully, but that in news releases the truth may not be violated.'[25] This 'open' approach, inspired by the UN, has completely disappeared in the *Nederlandse Defensie Doctrine* (2005) (and the new 2013 version) and the *Joint Doctrine Publicatie 2 Intelligence* (2012). The notion 'military information' within the framework of peace operations has disappeared; collecting intelligence is a standard activity in all military operations and missions, and the terminology is no longer phrased in euphemistic terms.[26]

Although the army's Military Doctrine dates back to 1996, is obvious that it was written in another era. In the course of the nineties the UN carried out operations in, among other places, Rwanda en Somalia, which showed that the starting point not to collect intelligence posed great problems.[27] In the Former Yugoslavia as well the UN had to deal with a situation that was completely different from what they were used to. UNPROFOR's assignments and responsibilities multiplied as a consequence of the rapid deterioration of the situation in Bosnia–Herzegovina. The moment that the political leadership was in need of good intelligence to make a proper assessment of the situation, there was an absence of adequate sources: 'Mandates, tasks, and responsibilities were changed and upgraded in an ad hoc fashion, indicating that comprehensive analysis and intelligence had not been

23 Doctrinecommissie van de Koninklijke Landmacht 1996, p. 130; see also: Cammaert 2003, pp. 14–15.

24 Doctrinecommissie van de Koninklijke Landmacht 1999, p. 118.

25 Ibid.

26 Defensiestaf 2005; Nederlandse Defensiestaf 2012; Ministerie van Defensie 2013.

27 Theunens 2001, p. 598.

carried out during the planning stages.' Moreover, the UN troops were sent to a region where fighting could break out any moment and where they had to support an UN plan (for the enclaves) that in fact was not accepted by the local population. 'The frequent absence of unambiguous consent, on the part of the parties in the conflict, to the deployment of external forces made the operation increasingly dangerous and the need for tactical intelligence increasingly evident.' The UN operations in the nineties showed that the current peace support operations (PSOs) 'demand a level of intelligence capability, coherence, and coordination that is unparalleled'.[28] In 2010 the former director-general of the MIVD, (Dutch) Military Intelligence and Security Service, major-general, Royal Marines (ret.) J.A. van Reijn (1999–2002), phrased the need for good intelligence in peace operations as follows: '[…] effectively carrying out military operations in distant areas, often in politically, militarily and culturally complex and opaque situations, sometimes with considerable risk for the participating troops, puts great demands on, especially, operationally useful intelligence reports that will benefit the commander on the spot.'[29]

By then the UN themselves had already found out so. In 2000, UN leading diplomat Lakhdar Brahimi published his *Report of the Panel on United Nations Peace Operations,* in which he discusses the causes of the failure of many UN peace missions. One of his recommendations was that UN peace missions required a more robust and realistic mandate to achieve their objectives.[30] The direct result of this was establishing an *Information and Strategic Analysis Secretariat* within the DPA 'to collect and manage 'strategic information', an acceptable euphemism for intelligence'.[31] But what intelligence was in fact available in the case of Srebrenica? What was known and what was unknown?

7.4 Dutchbat and the Attack on Safe Area Srebrenica

Towards the end of the Cold War, Yugoslavia started to disintegrate. In 1991 Slovenia and Croatia declared independence and civil war broke out. In order to prevent further escalation of the fighting the UN Security Council decided in March 1992 to establish the peacekeeping force *United Nations Protection Force* (UNPROFOR). Initially, UNPROFOR's emphasis lay on Croatia, but this shifted to Bosnia–Herzegovina[32] when fighting broke out there as well. In Bosnia fighting was heaviest and the population suffered most under 'ethnic cleansing'. There was little UNPROFOR could do. In the beginning of 1993 Bosnian Serbs harassed a

[28] Carment et al. 2006, p. 2.

[29] Van Reijn 2010, p. 87.

[30] See for instance Leurdijk 2006.

[31] Carment et al. 2006, p. 2; see also Leurdijk 2006.

[32] Hereinafter, the term "Bosnia" will be used to denote the entire area of Bosnia–Herzegovina.

number of Muslim enclaves in what was, at that moment, predominantly Bosnian Serb territory. In reaction, in April and May 1993 the UN Security Council declared six Muslim enclaves (Srebrenica, Sarajevo, Tuzla, Žepa, Goražde and Bihać) Safe Areas. According to the UN an additional 34,000 troops were required to protect these areas. The UN member states promised 7,600, of which in the end only half did arrive in Bosnia. In June 1993 the UN Security Council provided UNPROFOR with the mandate to use force against an attack on a safe area. In practice this especially meant threatening with air power. The lightly armed UNPROFOR ground troops lacked the military power to withstand an attack by the Bosnian Serbs.[33]

Since March 1992, The Netherlands had contributed to UNPROFOR in the form of staff officers, a communications battalion and, together with the Belgians, a transportation battalion.[34] In September 1993, the Dutch minister of Defence Relus ter Beek offered the UN an air assault infantry battalion for participation in UNPROFOR. Although Relus ter Beek and army commander lieutenant-general Hans Couzy, had preferred stationing the battalion in central Bosnia, they eventually agreed to stationing it in the isolated *safe areas* of Srebrenica and Žepa in the east of Bosnia. Srebrenica was surrounded by mountains controlled by the Bosnian Serb Army (*Vojska Republike Srpske*, VRS). Fighting had been going on in the surroundings since 1992 and because of the arrival of refugees the population had increased from 5,000 to over 30,000. Among them were thousands of soldiers of the Bosnian government army (*Armija Bosne i Hercegovine*, ABiH).

On 12 November 1993 the Dutch government formally agreed to deploy the infantry battalion, called Dutchbat for short. In March 1994, Dutchbat-I commander lieutenant colonel C.H.P. Vermeulen took over command from the commander of the Canadian detachment (Canbat), which had been in Srebrenica since April 1993. The most important task of Dutchbat-I, 11 infantry battalion (air assault), complemented among others with a reconnaissance platoon of the Korps Commandotroepen and a detachment of the Explosives Ordnance Disposal Service, was assuring a safe enclave where no military activities would be taking place. (One company of the subsequent battalions, incidentally, was always stationed in Simin Han near Tuzla). Muslim troops had to hand in their weapons with the Dutch, who would then store them in so-called Weapon Collection Points (WCPs). By patrolling the enclave and establishing and manning observation posts Dutchbat had to survey the security situation in the enclave, especially the disputed borders of the enclave. Social patrols were meant to maintain contact with the civilian population.[35]

---

[33] Van Woensel 2004, pp. 261–263; Klep and Van Gils 2005, pp. 298–301.

[34] For this, see for instance: Ten Cate and Van Woensel 2008, pp. 256–272; Ten Cate 2014, pp. 232–235.

[35] Van Woensel 2004, pp. 263–264; Klep and Van Gils 2005, pp. 309–311; Ten Cate and Van der Vorm 2016, pp. 70–71.

Because of the continuous siege by the Serbs, disarming the Bosnian government troops was not realized. The Bosnian government troops did not hand in all their weapons, but were hiding them. The weak mandate did not allow the Dutch to search houses. The refusal to hand in weapons and the supply of new weapons through the neighbouring enclave of Žepa strengthened in their turn the Bosnian Serbs' persistence to continue the siege of the enclave to prevent a possible break-out by Bosnian government troops. The siege of Srebrenica worsened the humanitarian situation in the enclave. A great part of the inhabitants relied on external help, but this was stopped by the Bosnian Serbs who controlled the access roads. The refugees preferred to leave the enclave, but this was prevented by the ABiH and the local authorities. The inhuman situation in the enclave and the international attention thus created was a cynical method of the Bosnian government to keep control of the area.[36]

Dutchbat as well had to endure the whims of the Bosnian Serb army. Political or military developments elsewhere in Bosnia regularly caused the VRS to stop Dutch convoys with supplies and troops returning from leave. In due course this would only get worse and lead to grave consequences for the operational capability of Dutchbat. In July 1994 lieutenant colonel P.L.E. Everts of Dutchbat-II, 12 Infantry battalion (air assault), took over command from lieutenant colonel Vermeulen. Everts, too, had to deal with the suffocating stranglehold of the Bosnian Serbs. After a few weeks already the supplies of Dutchbat-II had been reduced so much that a shortage of fuel and spare parts was looming. Everts introduced the so-called '*minimize programme*' aimed at reducing the operational use of fuel and spare parts. For the Dutch blue helmets this meant that they used their vehicles as little as possible and patrolled on foot. UN-ordered NATO Air attacks on Serbian positions in Croatia and Bosnia gave the Serbs an excuse to take hostage for a week over a hundred Dutch troops going on leave at the end of November 1994.[37]

In January 1995, Dutchbat-III, 13 infantry battalion (air assault), commanded by lieutenant commander T.J.P. Karremans, replaced Dutchbat-II. During the rotation of Dutchbat-II to Dutchbat-III a crisis arose. The Bosnian government army accused the Bosnian Serb troops of having taken up new positions at an illegal location near the demarcation line. The ABiH was of the opinion that Dutchbat had to react. If Dutchbat did not react, the Bosnian government troops would take action themselves. When Dutchbat indicated that they would not meet the demands of the Bosnian government troops, the ABiH told Dutchbat they could no longer enter the southwest of the enclave. Karremans did not accept this and decided to enforce freedom of movement in the area in question by sending out patrols and establishing a new observation post. At the end January of 1995 this led to a four-day

[36] Ten Cate and Van der Vorm 2016, pp. 71–72.

[37] Van Woensel 2004, pp. 266–268; Ten Cate and Van der Vorm 2016, pp. 73–75; see also Ten Cate 2014, pp. 236–241.

hostage-taking action of almost one hundred Dutchbat-troops by the ABiH, supported in this by the local Muslim population.[38]

In the meantime the Bosnian Serbs had ceased giving permission for the transport of fuel to the enclave. Troops returning from leave were not allowed to return to the enclave. Slowly the number of Dutch blue helmets in the enclave was reduced to 430. Owing to the shortage of manpower, equipment and supplies Dutchbat was not able to carry out its assignments properly. For the Muslim population in Srebrenica itself the situation was even much worse: only one third of the required food supply was present. Many civilians and ABiH-troops attempted to escape from the enclave. In retaliation of the NATO bombardment on their 'capital' Pale, from 26 May 1995 the Bosnian Serbs hermetically sealed off the enclave of Srebrenica from the outside world. In early June, the VRS occupied the Dutch observation post Echo in the far south of the enclave.

On 6 July 1995, the Bosnian Serbs again attacked the south of the enclave. UNPROFOR was convinced that the target was the strategically important road through the south of the enclave. This, however, turned out not to be the case. The VRS pushed through, during which Dutch blue helmets in observation posts were taken prisoner or were forced to withdraw. In this chaos private-I R. van Renssen was killed on 8 July when a Bosnian Muslim soldier threw a hand grenade at the withdrawing *YPR* 765 AIFV of which he was the gunner. The remaining well over four hundred lightly armed Dutchbat soldiers were no match for the advancing Bosnian Serbs, especially not when it became clear that (massive) air support could not be counted on. Only Close Air Support (CAS) could be given but this to no avail. On the evening of 11 July the enclave had in fact fallen. Tens of thousands of refugees were seeking refuge on and around the *compound* in Potočari where degrading scenes could be observed. Part of the Muslim population and the greater part of the Muslim fighters started on a trek through the mountains in the hope of forcing a breakthrough to Tuzla. During this trek many were captured by the VRS and subsequently murdered, or died from exhaustion or in the fighting on their way. The men and boys of military age who had stayed behind in Srebrenica and Potočari were taken away by the Bosnian Serbs and were killed as well. The Bosnian Serbs murdered around 8,000 men. Women and children were transported by bus by the Bosnian Serbs to the government-held area in Central Bosnia. Dutchbat-III left the enclave on 21 July and returned to The Netherlands via Zagreb.[39]

---

[38] Van Woensel 2004, pp. 268–269; Ten Cate and Van der Vorm 2016, p. 75.

[39] Van Woensel 2004, p. 271; Klep and Van Gils 2005, pp. 315–317; Ten Cate and Van der Vorm 2016, pp. 76–77.

7.4.1 Strategic Intelligence

The political and military leaders believed that at some time the enclaves had to be given up. In 1994 it was already obvious in diplomatic circles that the enclaves were an obstacle to the peace process. The Bosnian government itself was willing to give up the enclaves, but certain ministers wanted to use the enclaves as bargaining material. The enclaves had a military value as a base of Muslim hit-and-run operations against the VRS and could be used in war propaganda. Although the Bosnian government would have liked to see this differently, Srebrenica was not able to 'survive' in a humanitarian and military sense. The enclave was in a stranglehold by the VRS. For political reasons the VRS had not yet invaded the enclave. The main reason was that the VRS did not know what to do with the population and feared house-to-house fighting. We may conclude that policy makers and analysts assumed that either in the short run or in the long run the enclaves would disappear anyway via a political way (as part of a peace process) or via a military way (conquest by the VRS). Srebrenica was simply tolerated by VRS; 'Nothing more and nothing less.'[40]

7.4.2 Tactical Intelligence

Strategic intelligence is completely different from tactical intelligence. What did the intelligence services concerned know about the Serbs' real plans? According to some authors the Americans were aware of plans for the attack on Srebrenica as early as three weeks before the attack.[41] This is not supported by any evidence. How could they have known of such a plan? In the VRS-plan *Krivaja '95*, produced only a few days before the beginning of the attack, the conquest of Srebrenica is mentioned, but it was not until the evening of 9 July that the decision was taken to conquer the enclave in its entirety. Therefore, advance knowledge of the attack was impossible. It would only have been possible to collect information about the preparations for the attack. Still, one should not forget that this was not a large-scale operation such as the June 1944 Normandy invasion. It was a modest military operation with only a limited number of infantry (three light battalions and two reinforced companies), no air support, some ten tanks, supported by about twelve artillery pieces and mortars which were already positioned in the surroundings of the enclave. As the troops and weapons, with the exception of the tanks, were already in position, there was nothing to warn against. An analysis by the U.S. Interagency Balkan Task Force (BTF) on 1 June 1995 confirms the above. It also reported that the VRS needed large-scale reinforcements in order to be able

---

[40] De Graaff and Wiebes 2014, pp. 157–158.

[41] Andreas Zumach 1995. See also: Nederlands Dagblad, 13 October 1995 and De Gelderlander, 13 October 1995.

to conquer the enclave. As these reinforcements were not observed, the Americans did not expect an attack. The British Defence Intelligence Staff held a different view: 'the BSA do not need to move troops and equipment into the area to take the enclaves, the local troops are sufficient in number for the task'. Bosnian government troops saw some military activity on 5 July; one day later they passed on these vague indications to Dutchbat. Also the JCO/SAS-teams (about which later more) operating in the surroundings did not raise the alarm. Until the end the VRS maintained complete radio silence, so there was nothing to be intercepted.[42]

Suppose that new troops, tanks and artillery had been discovered in time. Then it would still not have been clear for what purpose. Dutchbat had no intelligence whatsoever. Limited information came from SAS patrols, observation posts, convoy commanders, the local population and authorities, and UNPROFOR headquarters in Sarajevo and Zagreb. Dutchbat itself was not able to carry out patrols owing to lack of fuel. There was no HUMINT, because the Dutchbat-III commander Karremans had forbidden all contacts with the population. All sources had dried up: 'no ears, no eyes'. Reconnaissance flights would have been a solution, but after the downing of an American F16 on 2 June 1995 and the reinforcement of the air defence around Srebrenica by the VRS these flights were reduced.[43] The absence of larger numbers of Bosnian Serb troops, their limited strength and firepower on the one hand, and the lack of heavy weapons with the ABiH on the other hand led analysts to the conclusion that there would be no warning for a possible attack. 'It could happen any minute and this situation had existed since 1993. In short, there were no clear indications.' At the end of June there were a few indications that something was about to happen, but nobody knew exactly what. UNPROFOR was of the opinion that the commander of the Bosnian Serb army, Ratko Mladić, was only interested in the southern part of the enclave. Not until 12 July did it become clear to everyone that the VRS had conquered Srebrenica.[44]

During the fall of the enclave Dutch brigade-general Cees Nicolai was chief of staff of the UNPROFOR-command in Bosnia (*Bosnia Herzegovina Command*) in Sarajevo. In 2008 he confirmed in an interview with a researcher of the Dutch Veterans Institute the picture sketched above: 'In fact we had few intelligence collection means of our own. So we got most through the Americans who carried out reconnaissance flights, often with unmanned aerial vehicles.[45] From the moment an American fighter had been downed, they were not very keen any more

---

[42] De Graaff and Wiebes 2014, p. 158.

[43] While patrolling the no-fly zone over Bosnia, the aircraft was hit by an SA-6 Gainful SAM. The aircraft came down near the town of Banja Luka, Bosnia. Captain Scott O'Grady was able to safely eject. However, O'Grady spent six days on the ground in enemy territory before being rescued by a Marine Corps CH-53 and support aircraft. Scott was picked up near the town of Mrkonjić Grad. Scott O'Grady's story made headlines around the world, becoming a celebrity. He is one of the better-known F-16 pilots.

[44] De Graaff and Wiebes 2014, pp. 158–159.

[45] The authors have some doubts as to whether the UAVs' range was great enough to cover Eastern Bosnia.

on flying over Serb territory.' The U2 simply continued its flights. UNPROFOR did receive information from the Americans, but they had no tangible information about the Bosnian-Serbs' plans:

> […] do they want to grab the enclaves or do they only want to reduce them in size, it all remains a matter of guesswork. […] We thought that they only wanted to have the southern point of Srebrenica because a major road passed through. But that they wanted to get hold of the whole enclave, we had not thought of that. Perhaps that was not even a pre-determined objective, but that the Serbs smelled their opportunity at that moment and seized it.[46]

Dutch analysts as well thought that the VRS would be satisfied with the southern part of the enclave. This turned out to be correct, as was shown later by VRS documents. The Dutch knew that the British intelligence services were worried, but the Brits did not have solid intelligence. For instance, the UK Joint Intelligence Committee doubted the reliability of their VRS sources. It was not until after the fall of Srebrenica that the Dutch received the reports by the UK Defence Intelligence Staff (DIS) and the CIA. But there was no solid intelligence in these reports either. No intelligence was received from other foreign services. The Dutch ministry of defence received no intelligence. Later, the US Secretary of Defense emphatically stated to his Dutch colleague that the Pentagon had no form of beforehand knowledge whatsoever. The Americans denied that the NSA or the CIA had intercepted conversations in which, before the attack, buses were ordered to deport the population: 'No surprise: these buses were only called in by Mladić after the collapse.'[47]

7.4.3 Signals Intelligence

In the field of SIGINT it is known that the Americans, the British, the French, the Germans and other services intercepted military and political communication in Central-Bosnia. They did not share these intercepts: intelligence services want to prevent at any price that the world finds out that they are intercepting, what and whom they are eavesdropping on and in what way they practise intercepts. This may lead to the conclusion that these intercepts were probably not 'hot'. Only in extreme cases, namely when dealing with solid intelligence, services may be willing to share SIGINT (thus partly exposing themselves). SIGINT did not give the western intelligence services indications for a possible attack either.[48]

In fact, SIGINT coverage of East-Bosnia was extremely bad. On the one hand, the NSA especially targeted Central-Bosnia and did not pay much attention to

---

[46] Veteraneninstituut (Vi), Interviewcollectie Nederlandse Veteranen (ICNV), interviewnummer ID: 516, C.H. Nicolai, 13 oktober 2008, [2:23–2:25].

[47] De Graaff and Wiebes 2014, p. 159.

[48] De Graaff and Wiebes 2014, pp. 159–160.

Srebrenica; on the other hand, the Americans were limited in intercept possibilities. Moreover, the VRS stuck to strict radio protocols. Could it have been done better? The CIA and NSA have tried to improve the situation. As many as five or six times these services requested Dutchbat to smuggle advanced espionage gear (COMINT suitcases) into the enclave to intercept communication of the Bosnian government army (ABiH) and the Bosnian Serb army (VRS). From this it may be deduced that they were desperately looking for possibilities to improve SIGINT coverage in this part of Bosnia. Every time again the Dutch army staff refused the request, without, incidentally, informing the minister of defence. After every failed attempt the CIA tried again. The Agency was not able to intercept the short-wave radio traffic of the warring parties by using satellites, U2 reconnaissance aircraft or other systems. For the Americans this was a major reason to establish a dedicated intercept base in Italy—de Deployed Shed Facility in Naples. If Dutchbat command had complied with this request the CIA would have done everything possible to establish friendly cooperation with the Dutch. It would probably have improved the Dutch intelligence position greatly: 'It would have resulted in giving Dutchbat 'ears' and perhaps also 'eyes'.'[49] The ears could have followed the VRS and ABiH radio- and walkie-talkie traffic in and around Srebrenica and the eyes could have been supplied by the CIA, which, in exchange for placing COMINT suitcases, certainly had wanted to share aerial photographs. In that case the 'Quid-pro-quo'-position between two unequal partners would have reached a certain balance. Moreover, the Netherlands would have obtained a means to 'pressure' the Americans into sharing intelligence. If there was no sharing, then 'turning off the SIGINT switch would have been an effective threat'.[50] Refusing this offer was rather short-sighted.[51]

7.4.4 Imagery Intelligence

We have seen there was no reliable HUMINT or SIGINT. What about IMINT? In hindsight images were available on which could be observed the buses in Potocari (for deporting the civilian population), prisoners who had been herded together and disturbed soil (where executed prisoners had been buried). Unfortunately, no real-time IMINT was available. Also for the IMINT analysts Srebrenica had no high priority. 'Large-scale killings were foreseen, albeit some analysts anticipated some revenge, but the final score of thousands of dead was far beyond imagination.'[52] Only the UK Defence Intelligence Staff (DIS) had used IMINT to identify VRS reinforcements in the enclave, but this did not ring a bell because the VRS had

[49] De Graaff and Wiebes 2014, p. 161.

[50] De Graaff and Wiebes 2014, p. 161.

[51] De Graaff and Wiebes 2014, pp. 160–161; see also: Wiebes 2002, pp. 299–300, and Brouwers and Kranenberg 2002, 'Inlichtingen rond Srebrenica faalden'.

[52] De Graaff and Wiebes 2014, p. 159.

sufficient numbers of troops on site to be able to conquer the enclave without any problems. The US services did not possess permanent real-time IMINT and because of this they could not observe what was happening in and around the enclave. Even two weeks after the enclave had fallen, when most executions had already been carried out, the images still had not been analysed and they did not report anything about the events that had already taken place, while it turned out that the IMINT had already been in their possession for some time. The imagery that did turn up was of a very bad quality, and not everything was shared. With the excellent IMINT technology it has at its disposal, the Dutch can also be blamed. Their Air Force had excellent IMINT capabilities in Bosnia and nobody prevented them from using their F-16's of 306 reconnaissance squadron. A U.S. intelligence official stated: 'no NATO commander would stand in the way of such action.'[53] Still, the Dutch F-16s were not used. The last flight was on 27 May. The fear of the VRS anti-aircraft units was probably too great. It can be concluded that IMINT was available from US satellites, U2 reconnaissance aircraft and from UAVs Unmanned Aerial Vehicles (UAV). Allegedly, this IMINT covered events before, during and after the attack on the enclave, but the information was not analysed in time and, therefore, was in fact useless, with the exception of later recording of war crimes.[54]

When the VRS attacked the American analysts had no idea that they would conquer the whole enclave. Until then they had assumed that the VRS would refrain from this for fear of heavy losses, air attacks and unmanageable flows of refugees. They could imagine that the Bosnian Serbs would put heavy pressure on Srebrenica to gain control over the higher grounds, but not that they would conquer the whole of the enclave. The VRS would suffer too large losses if they attacked the ABiH that had more infantry. The analysts, however, forgot that local circumstances could play a role as well. There was, for instance, an order by the VRS general staff in March 1995, which said that Srebrenica had to be separated from Žepa. In addition the Muslim fighters were pestering the Bosnian Serbs with their hit-and-run operations from Srebrenica and the continual penetrations into Bosnian Serb territory. The western services were not aware of these local circumstances and of the effect that they had on Mladić's way of thinking. They were not familiar with the VRS plan to conquer only a part of the enclave. The same thing went for the decision on 9 July to push through and to conquer the whole enclave because the ABiH put up hardly any resistance, and because the Bosnian Serbs were quite certain of the fact that UNPROFOR and/or NAVO-air forces would not act.[55] The British intelligence community concluded 'It was only the rapid and unexpected collapse of government defences which led them to push on and take the enclave at that point.'[56]

A single reason for the decision to attack the enclave and choose 6 July as the date has never been found. In hindsight, a number of reasons has been given:

[53] Cited in: Wiebes 2003, p. 366.

[54] De Graaff and Wiebes 2014, pp. 161–162.

[55] De Graaff and Wiebes 2014, pp. 162–163; see also Wiebes 2003, p. 367.

[56] Cited in: Wiebes 2003, p. 363.

irritation caused by the ABiH-activities outside the enclave, the fall of the enclave would free a large number of Bosnian Serb infantry for deployment elsewhere by the VRS, who were short of infantry, a victory would benefit the morale of the Bosnian Serb troops and it would create new opportunities for political negotiations because it would change the balance of power in Bosnia.[57]

7.4.5 'Cry Wolf' Syndrome

Whatever may have been the case, the western intelligence services claimed that they had not foreseen the attack. The ABiH, however, stated that they had warned for the attack in time, but that Dutchbat and UNPROFOR did not believe them. The ABiH knew about the strengthening of military forces on 4 and 5 July through HUMINT, but reports by Dutchbat, the UN Military Observers (UNMOs) and SAS units show that this HUMINT was shared only after the attack had started on 6 July. The ABiH claim is not supported by any facts and does not appear to be based on truth.[58]

Suppose that the Bosnian government troops had warned in time. Why was this warning not heeded? The UN had a fairly reliable idea of the VRS capabilities and of the order of battle[59] of the Bosnian Serb troops but did not know—as established before—what their intentions and plans were. The Bosnian Serb commander Mladić and the leader of the Serb Republic of Bosnia and Herzegovina, Radovan Karadžić, repeatedly announced that they would reduce the enclaves in size or would conquer them. The main question was: when? In the beginning of 1995 there were frequent warnings of an imminent attack. Every time again the alarm was false. Did this not unwillingly create the so-called 'Cry Wolf' syndrome?[60] It is conceivable that every false warning led to less alertness and finally to negligence. That this might have been the case is evidenced by the CIA report 'Srebrenica: Background and Battle' from 1999, which enters into the indications that new Bosnian Serb troops had been observed in the surroundings of Srebrenica: 'Similar troop movements had been recorded around the enclave dozens of times in the past, and the VRS was constantly adjusting its forces all across Bosnia. There was no special indicator, which would particularly distinguish these reports among hundreds of reports over the months and across the country.'[61] In May 1995 the SAS

[57] De Graaff and Wiebes 2014, p. 163.

[58] Ibidem.

[59] The 'order of battle' shows the hierarchical organisation, command structure, strength, disposition of personnel, and equipment of units and formations of the armed force.

[60] *Information repetition* or the '*Cry Wolf*' syndrome occurs when certain intelligence is presented again and again, does not appear to be true again, thus causing *warning fatigue*: because similar intelligence was false the last few times it must be false again. De Graaff 2010, p. 559; see also: Metselaar 1997, p. 32 ff.

[61] Cited as such in: De Graaff and Wiebes 2014, p. 164; CIA 1999, p. 15.

reported that 'there were constant rumours at this time from the ABiH that the Bosnian Serb Army was planning to attack the Enclave'.[62] The SAS, however, heard rumours so often that it became more and more problematic to take the warnings seriously. Strangely enough the Bosnian Serb build-up of troops on 4 and 5 July did not produce serious warnings by the Bosnian government troops.[63]

7.4.6 *Noise Barriers*

Have certain assumptions led to so-called Noise Barriers that influenced the information analysis? This is the case if '[...] the 'right' signals are frequently distorted if not overwhelmed by 'noise''.[64] Mladić repeatedly told that he wished to have more control of the southern tip of Srebrenica, but did not tell how and when he wanted to achieve that. Analysts got used to this, involved it in their analyses and assumed that the Bosnian Serbs would restrict themselves to conquering the south of the enclave. Within the UN the idea had taken root that Mladić did not know what to do with the refugees in Srebrenica. Additionally, the most important political players were mainly concerned with the strategic level; for them and the Western intelligence services the enclave had a low priority. Analysts, therefore, could not figure out whether Mladić wanted to conquer only a part of the enclave or the whole of the enclave. This is strange because soldiers always have to start from the worst-case scenario. But not one analyst hit upon the cynical idea—'the blackest scenario' as phrased by Frank Westerman and Bart Rijs[65]—that the VRS might solve the refugee problem by killing the major part of the male population.[66]

The most important self-generated Noise Barrier was the very idea that the VRS did not dare to attack (the so-called 'sheer nerve scenario'), causing the political leaders to make the wrong estimate of the Serb intentions. An attack simply did not fit in their general expectations. Although Mladić and Karadžić frequently told that they wanted to get rid of the enclaves, most political leaders expected this to happen through diplomatic negotiations, under the assumption that threatening with air attacks would scare the Bosnian Serbs sufficiently. By sticking to this idea, the view of the political leaders became opaque. Information showing otherwise was assessed wrongly in an attempt to prevent cognitive dissonance (the uneasy tension between new intelligence and in-rooted patterns of thinking).[67] The same also

[62] Cited in De Graaff and Wiebes 2014, p. 164.

[63] De Graaff and Wiebes 2014, p. 164.

[64] Metselaar 1997, p. 36.

[65] Westerman and Rijs 1997.

[66] De Graaff and Wiebes 2014, p. 164.

[67] Cognitive dissonance is a psychological term for the uneasy tension that arises when learning facts or opinions contrary to one's own conviction or opinion, or behaviour that does not match one's own conviction, values and norms. According to this theory people feel a strong urge to reduce that dissonance by adapting or rationalising their opinion or behaviour.

occurred at Dutchbat's headquarters. On 7 July Dutchbat was still of the opinion that the attack intended to provoke and intimidate the ABiH. Signals were continually interpreted wrongly and intentions observed were brushed aside as unlikely. Everyone believed that Mladić 'would not dare to go to such brutality and thereby provoke the whole international community',[68] but that is exactly what happened.[69] As the German General Von Moltke once said: 'Gentlemen, I notice that there are always three courses (of action) open to an enemy and that he usually takes the fourth.'[70]

Still, one cannot blame the international intelligence community for the fact that their analysts did not predict the attack, because they allowed themselves to be guided by the 'Cry Wolf' syndrome and/or Noise Barriers. A so-called hit, in this case predicting the attack, only occurs if an analyst has at his disposal adequate intelligence.[71] The preparations should have been noticed in time. And this, as established earlier, was not the case. For this, both the Dutch and other services can be blamed. If Dutchbat had had at its disposal 'eyes and ears', the preparations for the attack might have been discovered in time. If the commander of Dutchbat-III had actively supported information collection, had asked his men to gather HUMINT among the local population, and had given permission to the JCO/SAS-teams to move freely inside and outside the enclave, his information position would have improved considerably. Therefore, it is no use blaming other services for what the Dutch themselves did not do.[72]

7.5 Dutchbat's Intelligence Position Inside the Srebrenica Enclave

Dutchbat and the political and military leaders in The Netherlands had prepared themselves badly for things to come in the enclave. Dutchbat was sent abroad without obtaining extensive information from their Canadian predecessors. Beforehand, no or hardly any enquiries were made with Canbat or the Canadian government about Canbat's experiences in the enclave. Already from the moment his unit was deployed Dutchbat-I commander Vermeulen complained with the Dutch Army's crisis staff and with Sector North East (the regional UN sector covering the enclave) about the absence of a three-dimensional intelligence overview which severely limited his view of the surroundings. Because of this, Dutchbat

[68] Metselaar 1997, p. 43.

[69] De Graaff and Wiebes 2014, pp. 164–165.

[70] Citeds as such in: Wiebes 2002, p. 387.

[71] Ofri 1983, pp. 822–827.

[72] De Graaff and Wiebes 2014, p. 165.

could not anticipate developments outside the enclave and could not validate information supplied by the warring parties. Dutchbat's intelligence view mainly consisted of information supplied in the enclave itself.[73]

Of course (social) patrols and the observation posts played an important part in collecting HUMINT inside the enclave. Also the special forces of 108 reconnaissance platoon of the Korps Commandotroepen, which was assigned to Dutchbat, were engaged in collecting information. The first thing the commandos did after arrival was mapping the enclave. In addition they carried out patrols, especially in areas not covered by Dutchbat's static observation posts. By daytime this was done overtly, in accordance with the UN policy of 'open operations'. As a consequence they were frequently fired upon by both warring parties who wanted to keep outsiders away. The commandos also scouted new routes, accompanied in this by EODS personnel because of the danger of mines and booby traps. Furthermore they collected information about the local population, the warring parties, weapon storage places and smugglers' routes. Smuggling in and around the enclave especially took place at night. In order to catch smugglers red-handed the commandos established secret observation posts at night. This information was passed on to Dutchbat's section S2 (intelligence). They also recorded on camera armed Muslims in the enclave and border crossing of the enclave by Bosnian Serbs. This imagery was used by section S5 (plans and strategy) in discussions about a cease-fire with the fighting parties. Due to the fuel shortages during Dutchbat-II and –III the commandos were forced to leave behind their jeeps and carry out patrols on foot, which limited their range.[74]

Lt-Col Vermeulen could not count on support from army commander Couzy. He was convinced that intelligence did not play a part in peace operations. Couzy was not the only person in the army adhering to this line of thought. In the preparation for Dutchbat's deployment intelligence had never been discussed. Among those responsible in the Dutch Army the idea prevailed that a peace mission in the Former Yugoslavia was a classic peace operation and that intelligence was not needed. This is and remains a remarkable attitude. UN troops taking part in the peacekeeping operation in the Former Yugoslavia badly needed a strong information position because they operated in a complex environment where irregular troops were ruling. The fact that in The Netherlands, when the mission started, the idea prevailed that it was a classic peace operation and that there was no need of intelligence, can in a way be understood, but this does not go for the fact that this anti-intelligence attitude did not change when Vermeulen raised the subject. As contrasted to other NATO countries—battalions from Scandina via, Canada and Great Britain had organic intelligence capacity at their disposal—The Netherlands stuck to the idea that a peacekeeping operation and intelligence collection should not go together.[75]

[73] Nederlands Instituut voor Oorlogsdocumentatie (NIOD) 2002b, II, p. 1388.

[74] Van Woensel 2004 p. 264; Ten Cate and Van de Vorm 2016, pp. 72–73; see also De Weger 2011, p. 61.

[75] Nederlands Instituut voor Oorlogsdocumentatie (NIOD) 2002b, II, pp. 1389–1390.

Couzy refused to give Dutchbat its own intelligence capacity, but also prohibited exchanging information between Dutchbat and the Military Intelligence Service/Koninklijke Landmacht. Of course this had far-reaching consequences for the battalion's intelligence position. Dutchbat did not receive intelligence from the Netherlands about the situation in the Former Yugoslavia, it did not have its own intelligence cell and was therefore unable to collect, process or analyse information. It must be added, however, that the Dutchbat staff mainly kept complaining and made no efforts to free personnel for this task and did not insist on extra capacity for this purpose.[76]

Dutchbat needed general intelligence about developments in the whole of Bosnia to obtain a good overview of the general political and military context in which the battalion could interpret developments in the enclave itself. Little was to be expected from UNPROFOR headquarters itself: staff members from NATO countries did not want to share their intelligence with colleagues from non-NATO countries. The Indian UNPROFOR commander lieutenant-general Satisch Nambiar (1992–1993) did not have access to NATO intelligence that his NATO staff members did have. This did not improve much under one of his successors, French lieutenant-general Bernard Janvier (1995–1996), because his senior intelligence officer, Colonel Jan-Inge Svensson, was from Sweden, a non-NATO member.[77] Of more importance, however, was knowledge of events in the immediate surroundings of the enclave, at some 5–10 km distance. The regional UN command (Sector North East and Bosnia Herzegovina Command) did not supply this information because they did not have it themselves. Sector North East was, as they stated themselves, 'Blindfolded in the dark'. The Dutch G2 (head of intelligence) of Sector North East (at the time of the fall of the enclave) said in an interview with a researcher of the Dutch Veterans' Institute that it took him an awful lot of trouble to obtain information. Regularly he had to produce an intelligence assessment: 'If reports came in with no information whatsoever, how in the world could one produce an assessment?'[78] The sporadic reconnaissance patrols outside the enclave by the Dutch commandos of 108 reconnaissance platoon—as practised during Dutchbat-I and II—could not meet that information requirement. Neither could the UN Military Observers. Their freedom of movement was limited and in Bosnian Serb territory they were definitely *persona non grata*.[79]

Initially though Dutchbat was not totally devoid of intelligence. Through regular contacts with the warring parties and refugees in the enclave Dutchbat-I possessed much information which was also analysed. To the situation reports Vermeulen

[76] Nederlands Instituut voor Oorlogsdocumentatie (NIOD) 2002b, II, p. 1390.

[77] Martyn 2006, p. 23; see also Svensson 2003, pp. 41–46.

[78] Veteraneninstituut (Vi), Interviewcollectie Nederlandse Veteranen (ICNV) [interview collection Dutch veterans], interviewnummer ID: 1411, F. Heuberger, 3 May 2011, [1:17–1:23].

[79] Nederlands Instituut voor Oorlogsdocumentatie (NIOD) 2002b, II, pp. 1390–1391.

often added a so-called Commander's assessment in which he evaluated developments inside the enclave, a possible relation with external events and a short-term expectation. Through, among other reasons, the deteriorating relation with the Bosnian government army, far fewer of these commander's assessments were written for Dutchbat-II. During Dutchbat-III this was discontinued. For reasons of security the commanders of Dutchbat-II and III (Everts and Karremans) prohibited all contacts between the local population and Dutchbat troops. This eliminated a number of important sources of information. Not all Dutchbat troops, incidentally, adhered to this prohibition: several observation posts (OP-A, OP-M en OP-E) as well as the EODS troops, who could move around the enclave to clear UXOs (unexploded ordnance) for humanitarian reasons, maintained regular contacts with the local population.[80]

7.5.1 *Joint Commission Observers*

Dutchbat III-commander Karremans acted in the line of Couzy. He prohibited the commandos of 108 reconnaissance platoon to execute reconnaissance operations outside the enclave, thus limiting the possibility to gather additional intelligence. He also ordered the group of British Joint Commission Observers (JCOs), who were active in Srebrenica, to stop doing their work outside the enclave. The JCOs had been the 'invention' of lieutenant general Michael Rose, UNPROFOR commander in Bosnia (Bosnia Herzegovina Command). 'A few good Brits…', that was what he asked the British government to support him in carrying out his assignments. Rose needed 'directed telescopes' for a 'frank, true assessment of the situation on the ground' (among other things by verifying information or intelligence from other sources).[81] What he referred to were soldiers of the Special Air Service (SAS), a legendary Special Forces unit. In 1979–1982 Rose was SAS commander and as such involved in the liberation of the hostages in the Iranian embassy in London (1980). During the Falklands war in 1982 he was responsible for Special Service Operations, also involving the SAS. Rose divided the SAS troops into small teams who carried out their work under the euphemistic name of Joint Commission Observers. 'Their primary mission was to act as military emissaries of the UNPROFOR Commander but these military professionals proved useful in a wide range of operations. These included escorting important UN relief convoys and providing eyewitness assessments to the Commander as required.'[82] They also acted as Forward Air Controllers (FACs), for instance in Goražde but also in

[80] Nederlands Instituut voor Oorlogsdocumentatie (NIOD) 2002b, II, p. 1391; Van Woensel 2004, pp. 269–270.

[81] Ramirez 2004, no page.

[82] Cleveland 2001, p. 5.

Srebrenica.[83] The JCOs met a necessary requirement and Rose's successor, lieutenant-general Rupert Smith, continued the programme. When UNPROFOR departed and IFOR commenced its mission, the British JOC-programme was one of the few holdovers.[84]

Karremans considered the JCOs mainly as possible Forward Air Controllers and not so much as convenient tools for obtaining additional intelligence. During the attack on the enclave the JOC team, together with a number of operators of 108 reconnaissance platoon, acted as FACs. They collected information about possible targets, but first came effectively into action on 11 July when the three JCOs and 3 commandos guided two Dutch F16s to a number of selected targets, during which one of the bombs dropped put a tank or an armoured vehicle out of action.[85] Karremans and the JCOs clashed several times, after which Karremans also limited their freedom of movement. Karremans made no efforts either to obtain British intelligence through the JCOs in his enclave from Bosnia Herzegovina Command. There was, however, cooperation between Dutchbat and UNMOs. In a few cases UNMOs and commandos of 108 reconnaissance platoon reconnoitred positions of the Bosnian-Serb army. Nevertheless the intelligence position of Dutchbat in the enclave remained limited. Dutchbat had hardly any information about the area just outside the enclave so that the Dutch soldiers had the feeling of living and working in isolation.[86]

7.6 Conclusion

Can one speak of an intelligence failure in the case of Srebrenica? Let us establish first and foremost that an intelligence failure is mostly not due to just one cause, but often has a range of causes. We can speak of an intelligence failure when afterwards it turns out that somewhere in the intelligence cycle a signal could have been discovered in time, but that the signal has not been discovered, with negative

[83] Rose dispatched a JOC team to Goražde to check on rumours about Serbian cruelties against the muslim population. They set up an observation post in the town centre from where they started patrols in the vicinity of the town. In April 1994 one of the JOCs was killed when his Land Rover was fired on by the Serbs. In the same month the JOC team called in air support against an attack by Serb artillery and tanks. During the air attacks a British Fleet Air Arm (Royal Navy) Sea Harrier was downed by the Bosnian Serbs. The pilot was able to eject safely and managed to join the JOC team in town. Meanwhile the team was beleaguered by the local muslim population because they felt underprotected. JOC team decided to exfiltrate from Goražde under the cover of darkness. On foot the SAS soldiers, with a number of wounded colleagues and the pilot, succeeded in reaching a safe spot, where they were picked up by a helicopter. See Mackenzie 2011, pp. 227–228 and De Weger 2011, pp. 63–64. For a detailed account: Spence 1998.

[84] Cleveland 2001, p. 5; Ramirez 2004; Mackenzie 2011, pp. 227–228; see also Wiebes 2002, pp. 219–211, and De Weger 2011, pp. 63–64.

[85] Ten Cate and Van der Vorm 2016, pp. 65–67; see also: Wiebes 2002, p. 221.

[86] Nederlands Instituut voor Oorlogsdocumentatie (NIOD) 2002b, II, p. 1391; Wiebes 2002, pp. 220–221.

consequences for the decision-making process. In other words, if an intelligence or security service (unintentionally) fails in its mission to warn political leadership in time for dangers. In that case we speak of a miss: there is a signal, but it has not been noticed by an intelligence or security service. In general, we do not speak of an intelligence failure when the opponent suddenly changes plans so that his act could not be foreseen.[87] As the Bosnian Serbs decided only at the very last moment to attack and occupy the enclave, nobody was able to foresee these plans. Moreover, it was a relatively small-scale operation involving only relatively small number of troops, no air support, a small number of tanks, artillery pieces and mortars. There was no large-scale building up of troops and no moving of, for instance, artillery and mortars—they were already in the area. In this case one could speak of a correct rejection: there was no (direct) indication for an attack on the enclave and the intelligence services made no observations pointing at an attack.

One cannot really speak of a '100%' intelligence failure—a miss—but still a number of circumstances can be mentioned that point at a failure by the intelligence services. One reason for an intelligence failure can be deception by the enemy. In addition, an intelligence failure may occur in any phase of the intelligence cycle: when directing collection, collecting information, processing the data, and disseminating the results of the analysis to the customers. In the case of Srebrenica we can point at a few cases where things went wrong. It is obvious that things already went awry in the control: Eastern Bosnia and Srebrenica, in particular, did not figure prominently among the international political leadership. In other words: 'Srebrenica fell simply off the priority list.'[88] The Dutch government and the military in their turn took the deliberate decision to not to carry out intelligence activities in and around the enclave.[89] 'This decision was based on the argument that intelligence collection should not go together with blue UN peace operations.'[90] Of course, this had consequences for the extent to which and the way in which intelligence collecting was practised in East-Bosnia. For Dutchbat-III commander Karremans, for instance, this meant that he ordered the commandos of 108 reconnaissance platoon and the JOC SAS teams not to execute out recces in and just outside the enclave, thus drastically limiting the possibilities to collect HUMINT. In this light, also refusing the CIA offer to improve the SIGINT position by smuggling COMINT suitcases into the enclave must be considered a downright intelligence failure.

Moreover, setting priorities when processing data had major consequences. To give one example, there was enough IMINT from American reconnaissance flights over Bosnia, but we cannot speak of real-time IMINT so it was only months later

---

[87] De Graaff 2010, p. 554.
[88] De Graaff and Wiebes 2014, p. 166.
[89] Wiebes 2002, pp. 113–114, 161–162.
[90] Van Reijn 2010, p. 87.

that it could be determined that there were images of men waiting for their execution.[91] The Dutch themselves missed a chance in the field of IMINT by not employing the available Dutch F16s with special photo equipment. Additionally, a number of intelligence failures can be established in the analysis process. First, the so-called 'Cry Wolf' syndrome played a part. The Muslims had already warned so often for a possible attack on the enclave without anything in fact happening that nobody listened or took the warnings seriously. The most important noise barrier or analysis failure concerned mirror imaging: 'projecting on the opponent estimates and intentions that exist in one's own country or culture.'[92] The intelligence services were obviously hampered by mirror imaging; for the Western analysts it was simply unimaginable that Bosnian Serbs would slaughter around 8,000 male Muslims of the military age.

What if the intelligence on the attack on Srebrenica had been known? Imagine that there had been intelligence about the VRS plans, that preparations for an attack had been observed and that the analysts had analysed everything correctly, then UNPROFOR and NATO would probably have had time to react 'for Mladić and Karadžić were not always insensitive to international pressure.'[93] In hindsight, the UN arrives at the same conclusion—albeit without committing themselves: 'Had the Unites Nations been provided with intelligence that revealed the enormity of the Bosnian Serbs' goals, it is possible, though by no means certain, that the tragedy of Srebrenica might have been averted'.[94]

Although the fall of Srebrenica can certainly not exclusively be blamed on an intelligence failure, it will have become clear that systematically neglecting the collection of intelligence by the UN and some countries (among which the Netherlands) had major consequences.[95] Fortunately, the policy on intelligence has been changed; not only the UN learned from the fall of Srebrenica (UN 2000), but also The Netherlands. The importance attached by The Netherlands to supporting the international rule of law has changed the demands on the army's operations and, through this, support by intelligence as well. 'In this respect the lessons from Srebrenica were sufficiently clear: high-quality intelligence can to a large degree determine the success of military operations, no matter whether they are large-scale operations or operations other than war.'[96]

[91] See also: De Graaff 2010, pp. 558–559.

[92] De Graaff 2010, p. 560.

[93] De Graaff and Wiebes 2014, p. 166.

[94] Quoted as such in De Graaff and Wiebes 2014, p. 166 [United Nations 1999, § 487].

[95] De Graaff and Wiebes 2014, p. 166.

[96] Dimitriu and Tjepkema 2010, p. 229.

References

Brouwers A, Kranenberg A (2002) Inlichtingen rond Srebrenica faalden. De Volkskrant, 29 April 2002 http://www.volkskrant.nl/archief/inlichtingen-rond-srebrenica-faalden~a617155/ Accessed 14 October 2016

Cammaert PC (2003) Intelligence in Peacekeeping Operations: Lessons for the Future. In: De Jong B, Platje W, Steele RD (eds) Peacekeeping Intelligence. Emerging Concepts for the Future. OSS International Press, Oakton, VA. pp. 11–30

Carment D, Rudner M (eds) (2006) Peacekeeping Intelligence. New Players, Extended Boundaries. Routledge, London

Carment D, Rudner M, Heide RL (2006) Peacekeeping intelligence. Extending partnerships and boundaries for peacekeeping. In: Carment D, Rudner M (eds) 2006, Peacekeeping Intelligence. New Players, Extended Boundaries. Routledge, London, pp. 1–14

CIA (1999) Srebrenica: Background and Battle

Clevland CT (2001) Command and Control of the Joint Commission Observer Program U.S. Army Special Forces in Bosnia. Research paper Army War College, Carlisle Barracks, PA

Defensiestaf (2005) Nederlandse Defensie Doctrine

De Graaf BA, Muller ER, Van Reijn JA (eds) (2010) Inlichtingen en veiligheidsdiensten. Kluwer, Alphen aan de Rijn

De Graaff BGJ (2010) Die eeuwige, onvermijdelijke Intelligence failures. In: De Graaf BA, Muller ER, Van Reijn JA (eds) Inlichtingen en veiligheidsdiensten. Kluwer, Alphen aan de Rijn, pp. 553–570

De Graaff BGJ, Wiebes C (2014) Fallen off the Priority List. Was Srebrenica an Intelligence Failure? In: Walton TR (ed) The Role of Intelligence in Ending the War in Bosnia in 1995. Lexington Books, London, pp. 151–168

De Jong B, Platje W, Steele RD (eds) (2003) Peacekeeping Intelligence. Emerging Concepts for the Future. OSS International Press, Oakton, VA

De Weger M (2011) Steeds ergens anders. De organisatie en de operaties van de Nederlandse militaire speciale eenheden. Faculteit Militaire Wetenschappen van de Nederlandse Defensie Academie, Breda

Dimitriu GR, Tjepkema AC (2010) Inlichtingenondersteuning bij handhaving en bevordering van de internationale rechtsorde. In: De Graaf BA, Muller ER, Van Reijn JA (eds) Inlichtingen en veiligheidsdiensten. Kluwer, Alphen aan de Rijn, pp. 225–253

Doctrinecommissie van de Koninklijke Landmacht (1996) Militaire doctrine. Landmacht Doctrinepublicatie deel I

Doctrinecommissie van de Koninklijke Landmacht (1999) Vredesoperaties. Landmacht Doctrinepublicatie deel III

Herman M (1996) Intelligence Power in Peace and War, Cambridge University Press, Cambridge

House JM (1993) Military Intelligence, 1879–1991. A Research Guide. Greenwood Press, Westport

Kappen F van (2003) Strategic Intelligence and the United Nations. In: De Jong B, Platje W, Steele RD (eds) Peacekeeping Intelligence. Emerging Concepts for the Future. OSS International Press, Oakton, VA, pp. 3–9

Klep C, Van Gils R (2005) Van Korea tot Kaboel. De Nederlandse militaire deelname aan vredesoperaties sinds 1945, 3rd revised edn. SDU, The Hague

Leurdijk DA (2006) Robuuste vredeshandhaving. Nieuwe doctrine voor VN operaties. Internationale Spectator 70(7–8):376–379

MacKenzie A (2011) Special Force: The Untold Story of 22nd Special Air Service Regiment (SAS) IB Tauris, London and New York

Martyn R (2006) Beyond the next hill: the future of military intelligence in peace support operations. In: Carment D, Rudner M (eds) Peacekeeping Intelligence. New Players, Extended Boundaries. Routledge, London, pp. 17–31

Metselaar MV (1997) Understanding failures in intelligence estimates – UNPROFOR, the Dutch, and the Bosnian-Serb attack on Srebrenica. In: Soeters J, Rovers JH (eds) NL Arms. Netherlands Annual Review of Military Studies. The Bosnian Experience. Netherlands Defence Academy, Breda, pp. 23–50

Ministerie van Defensie (2013) Nederlandse Defensie Doctrine, revised edn.

Nederlands Instituut voor Oorlogsdocumentatie (NIOD) (2002a) 'Dutchbat moest vrede handhaven waar geen vrede was', Press release Srebrenica report, 10 April 2002 http://www.niod.knaw.nl/nl/srebrenica-rapport/persbericht Accessed 12 October 2016

Nederlands Instituut voor Oorlogsdocumentatie NIOD (2002b) Srebrenica, een 'veilig gebied'. Reconstructie, achtergronden, gevolgen en analyses van de val van een Safe Area. Volume I-III. Boom, Amsterdam

Nederlandse Defensiestaf (2012) Joint Doctrine Publicatie 2. Inlichtingen

Ofri A (1983) Crisis and Opportunity Forecasting. ORBIS, 26(4):822–827

Ramirez AJ (2004) From Bosnia to Baghdad: The Evolution of US Army Special Forces from 1995–2004. Naval Post Graduate School Monterey, CA

Roozenbeek H (ed) (2008) In dienst van de troep. Bevoorrading en transport bij de Koninklijke Landmacht. Boom, Amsterdam

Schoenmaker B (ed) (2014) 200 jaar Koninklijke Landmacht 1814–2014. Boom, Amsterdam

Soeters J, Rovers JH (eds) (1997) NL Arms. Netherlands Annual Review of Militairy Studies. The Bosnian Experience. Netherlands Defence Academy, Breda

Spence C (1998) All Necessary Measures. Penguin Books, London

Svensson J-I (2003) Peacekeeping and Intelligence Experiences with UNPROFOR 1995 In: De Jong B, Platje W, Steele RD (eds) Peacekeeping Intelligence. Emerging Concepts for the Future. OSS International Press, Oakton, VA, pp. 41–46

Ten Cate A, Van der Vorm M (2016) Callsign Nassau. Dutch Army Special Forces in Action in the 'New World Disorder'. NIMH/Leiden University Press, Leiden

Ten Cate A (2014) De landmacht expeditionair 1989–2014 In: Schoenmaker B (ed) 200 jaar Koninklijke Landmacht 1814–2014. Boom, Amsterdam, pp. 220–273

Ten Cate A, Van Woensel J (2008) Logistiek na de val van de Muur 1989–1996 In: Roozenbeek H (ed) In dienst van de troep. Bevoorrading en transport bij de Koninklijke Landmacht. Boom, Amsterdam, pp. 238-273

The Interagency OPSEC Support Staff (1996) Intelligence Threat Handbook https://www.books.google.nl/books?id=V0Xy77qQ624C&printsec=frontcover&dq=The+Interagency+OPSEC+Support+Staff+1996+Intelligence+Threat+Handbook&hl=nl&sa=&ved=0ahUKEwj7rvXR1qXRAhWCChoKHfVSAaEQ6AEIIzAA#v=onepage&q=The%20Interagency%20OPSEC%20Support%20Staff%201996%20Intelligence%20Threat%20Handbook&f=false Accessed 16 October 2016

Theunens R (2001) Intelligence en vredesoperaties. Militaire Spectator 170(11):598–603

United Nations (1999) Report of the Secretary-General pursuant to General Assembly Resolution 53/55 (1998) 'Srebrenica Report'. United Nations, New York

Van Reijn JA (2010) Militair of civiel centraal of decentraal: De wordingsgeschiedenis van de MIVD In: De Graaf BA, Muller ER, Van Reijn JA (eds) Inlichtingen en veiligheidsdiensten. Kluwer, Alphen aan den Rijn, pp. 71–94

Van Woensel J (2004) Vrij van Explosieven. De geschiedenis van het EOCKL en zijn voorgangers. Boom, Amsterdam

Walton TR (ed) (2014) The Role of Intelligence in Ending the War in Bosnia in 1995. Lexington Books, London
Westerman F, Rijs B (1997) Srebrenica: het zwartste scenario. Atlas, Amsterdam
Wiebes C (2002) Intelligence en de oorlog in Bosnië 1992–1995. De rol van de inlichtingen en veiligheidsdiensten. Boom, Amsterdam
Wiebes C (2003) Intelligence and the war in Bosnia 1992–1995: The role of the intelligence and security services. http://www.niod.nl/sites/niod.nl/files/C.%20Wiebes%20-%20Intelligence%20en%20de%20oorlog%20in%20Bosni%C3%AB%201992-1995.%20De%20rol%20van%20de%20inlichtingen-%20en%20veiligheidsdiensten%20-%20Engels.pdf Accessed 19 October 2016
Zumach A (1995) US Intelligence knew Serbs were planning an assault on Srebrenica. Basic Reports, No. 47

Author Biographies

Cees Wiebes, Ph.D., is a Senior Research Fellow with the Institute of Security and Global Affairs (ISGA), University of Leiden. He also worked at the Expertise and Analysis Department of the Dutch National Coordinator for Counterterrorism, and at the University of Amsterdam. He was a member of the Dutch team researching circumstances before, during and after the fall of the enclave Srebrenica in Bosnia. Recent publications: *Intelligence and the war in Bosnia 1992–1995* (2004), (with Bob de Graaf), 'Fallen off the Priority List: Was Srebrenica an Intelligence Failure?' in: T.R. Walton (ed), *The Role of Intelligence in Ending the War in Bosnia in 1995* (2014) and *Samen met de CIA (about Joint Dutch-CIA-MI6 clandestine intelligence operations* (2016). A founding member of the Netherlands Intelligence Studies Association, he is a member of the Editorial Board of *Intelligence and National Security*.

Jeoffrey van Woensel is an MA graduate and reserve first lieutenant of the Regiment Technical Troops (retired), studied history at the Radboud University in Nijmegen. After his studies he was conscripted as ROAG (academically trained reserve officer) in the Royal Netherlands Army. From 2001 to 2015 he worked at the Netherlands Institute for Military History, The Hague. He has published books on a number of topics including chemical warfare, the Explosive Ordnance Disposal Service of the Dutch armed forces, logistics, and the Royal Netherlands Marechaussee. He currently works at the Centre of Research and Expertise of the Veterans Institute on secondment from the Ministry of Defence. Since 2012 he is the Secretary of the Netherlands Intelligence Studies Association.

Aad Wever, a graduate of Utrecht University, taught information security and intelligence at Saxion University of Applied Sciences, Enschede, The Netherlands, and at Ferris State University, Big Rapids, Michigan, USA, until his retirement in June 2016. He has contributed to several publications on the history of the Royal Netherlands Air Force during the Cold War. Since 2004 he has been engaged in educational cruises at Spitsbergen in the Norwegian Arctic. Wever is a member of the Board of the Netherlands Intelligence Studies Association.

Chapter 8
Achieving Understanding in Contemporary UN Peace Operations: The Joint Mission Analysis Centre

Reynaud Theunens

Abstract This chapter discusses the current status of intelligence in UN peace operations by examining the Joint Mission Analysis Centre (JMAC), and makes proposals for the further development of this concept. After a brief historical overview, I will make the argument that rather than using the potentially controversial expression '(military) intelligence', the UN should adopt contemporary terminology by employing the term 'understanding'. I will then explain why JMAC is such an important step in the development of effective 'intelligence' support for decision-making support in peace operations. Finally, I will make some proposals, which are based on my experience as a military information officer in the former Yugoslavia in the 1990s and Chief JMAC (UNIFIL), for the further development of the JMAC concept, by elaborating options for its relations with military intelligence structures like U2 and the All Sources Intelligence Fusion Unit (ASIFU); and the use of social media for situational awareness and understanding.

Keywords Peacekeeping intelligence · JMAC · ASIFU · UN intelligence reform

Contents

R. Theunens (✉)
Burg. S. De Rijcklaan 58/22, B-3001 Heverlee, Belgium
e-mail: theunensr@un.org

F. Baudet et al. (eds.), *Perspectives on Military Intelligence from the First World War to Mali*, DOI 10.1007/978-94-6265-183-8_8

8.1 Introduction[1]

This chapter discusses the current status of intelligence in UN peace operations by examining the Joint Mission Analysis Centre (JMAC) concept, and makes proposals for the further development of this concept. After a brief historical overview, I will make the argument that rather than using the potentially controversial expression '(military) intelligence', the UN should adopt contemporary terminology by employing the term 'understanding'. I will then explain why JMAC is such an important step in the development of effective 'intelligence (i.e. understanding)' support for decision-making in peace operations. Finally, I will make some proposals, which are based on my experience as a military information officer (UNPROFOR/UNPF; UNTAES) and Chief JMAC (UNIFIL), for the further development of the JMAC concept, by elaborating options for its relations with military intelligence structures like U2 and the All-Sources Intelligence Fusion Unit (ASIFU) and the use of social media for situational awareness and understanding.

8.2 To Intelligence or not to Intelligence?

At the time of writing, there is no UN definition for 'intelligence', nor 'peacekeeping intelligence'. Irrespective of on-going discussions to develop a UN 'framework policy' on intelligence in peace operations, the expression 'intelligence' is rarely used in UN doctrinal documents. Instead, preference is given to the potentially confusing expression 'information'. At peace-mission level, it is often implied that 'intelligence' is the prerogative of the military component, hence the use of the term 'military information'. Both among member states as well as (senior) civilian and military UN personnel, there continues to be confusion or even controversy about what 'intelligence' is and what it is not. Some still believe that 'intelligence' equals espionage and that therefore intelligence is not done in UN peace operations, as it violates the principles of consent of the parties and of

[1] Disclaimer: the views expressed herein are those of the author and do not necessarily reflect the views of the United Nations.

impartiality.[2] At the same time, there is a widely shared concern for the security of personnel. The need for adequate situational awareness and comprehensive understanding of the operational environment for mission planning and mandate implementation is increasingly acknowledged, albeit without specifying how this is to be achieved. Irrespective of this dichotomy, information sharing by member states continues to be determined by national considerations rather than the information needs of the UN, raising the question as to when an international security issue becomes a national one[3] (and vice versa).

Given the debate that continues to surround 'intelligence' in a UN context, the experiences of several member states in recent (non-)UN-led crisis management operations may provide a way out. These operations have revealed the limitations of the traditional (military) intelligence approach; more is needed: 'understanding'. 'Understanding' is defined as 'the perception and interpretation of a particular situation to provide the context, insight and foresight required for effective decision making'.[4] Insight means knowing why something has happened or is happening, while foresight refers to what may happen. Intelligence is the processed[5] information that is required for understanding.

'Understanding' expresses more accurately what is required for effective decision making in a UN peace operation irrespective of its mandate and the operational context. 'Understanding' also offers a better description of JMAC's role and contribution, and is clearly less controversial than 'intelligence'. To put it in a more concrete way: 'intelligence is knowing that a tomato is a fruit, understanding is not putting it in a fruit salad'.[6]

8.3 Background—Where Do We Come from?

The lessons concerning intelligence support for civilian and military decision-makers during recent (and current) stability[7] or peace operations are very similar to those of UN-led peacekeeping operations during the 1990s like UNAMIR, UNOSOM, and UNPROFOR.[8] Decision-makers need first and foremost information that gives them a 'comprehensive' understanding covering all aspects (political, military, security, historical, economic, sectarian, ethnic, cultural, etc.) of the operational environment. The parties' perceptions and intentions are more important than their capabilities. One of the main lessons of UN-led peacekeeping

[2] United Nations, DPKO/DFS 2008, 2010, p. 33.

[3] Dorn 2010, p. 294.

[4] NATO 2014, p. 3-1.

[5] Processing of information consists of collation, evaluation, analysis, integration, interpretation.

[6] Ministry of Defence, UK Development, Concepts and Doctrine Centre 2010, p. 2-1.

[7] Flynn et al. 2010; Norheim-Martinsen and Ravndal 2011, p. 454.

[8] Theunens 2003, pp. 61–70.

and stabilization operations, in particular those conducted in 'asymmetric environments',[9] is that the political, economic, social, security, cultural, historical, religious, ethnic/sectarian, atmospherics (i.e., the 'human terrain'[10]) etc. context and dynamics are of far greater relevance than military aspects.[11]

Without understanding the local actors—who may pursue political, criminal and ideological interests—conflict causes, drivers, and dynamics, outside actors (i.e., peace operations) risk exacerbating conflicts, even when acting with the best of intentions.[12] As can be derived from the definition of '*understanding*', this means that in order to be successful in peace operations, we need to apply a much broader approach to (military) intelligence than in traditional settings like interstate conflicts. Contemporary Western military intelligence doctrine therefore emphasizes the importance of a multi-dimensional approach through the use of the acronym X-PMESII, a cross-approach covering Political, Military, Economic, Socio-cultural, Infrastructure, and Information.

8.4 Where Do We Stand: The Joint Mission Analysis Centre (JMAC)

8.4.1 Why JMAC?

The experiences from missions like UNAMIR, UNOSOM, and UNPROFOR demonstrate the importance of comprehensive situational awareness and understanding (insight, context, foresight), and the potentially disastrous effects if these are lacking. Contemporaneous multidimensional peace operations conduct a wide range of activities in fluid and unpredictable, increasingly asymmetric environments where they face challenging climates, geography and infrastructure.[13] This demands an enhanced operational capacity to monitor (i.e. '*situational awareness*'), assess and predict (i.e. '*understanding*') political, military, security, economic and other pertinent events and developments that influence the operational environment on a continuous basis, as a pre-requisite for senior mission leaders' decision-making. Missions must be able to identify, forecast and respond (mitigate, prevent) to emerging threats to mandate implementation including the security of UN personnel, equipment and facilities.

Contemporary (post) conflict situations are characterized by an increasingly prominent role of non-state actors, who are often acting as 'proxies' of internal or external state actors. The distinction between the different levels (tactical;

---

[9] Lollesgaard 2015.

[10] Ministry of Defence Development, Concepts and Doctrine Centre 2011, paras 437–444.

[11] Roux 2008, p. 22.

[12] United States Institute for Peace 2011, p. 2.

[13] Roux 2008, p. 22.

operational; strategic) of decision-making is mostly irrelevant or even counter-productive: tactical developments may have strategic implications and vice versa.

Taking a closer look at UNIFIL, a mission with a comparatively limited and mainly military mandate,[14] the volatile geopolitical situation in its area of interest is characterized by close and constant interaction between political, military, security, sectarian, economical, religious, historical, and other factors and considerations. Regional tensions and conflicts are reflected in Lebanon's internal dynamics. Few issues, events, developments or trends that can impact on mandate implementation originate from within UNIFIL's (small) area of operations (AO). Regional developments, including international concern over these developments, can have (in) direct implications for UNIFIL's mandate implementation and security. UNIFIL has to be able to understand the potential ramifications of these (apparently) remote issues.[15] Focusing on military aspects only would not allow achieving this.

According to the 2008 Capstone doctrine, drafted by the Department for Peacekeeping Operations, department of Field Support (DPKO/DFS), a peacekeeping operation should continuously analyse its operating environment to detect and forestall any wavering of consent. A peacekeeping operation must have the political and analytical skills, the operational resources, and the will to manage situations where there is an absence or breakdown of local consent.[16] The 2009 UN New Horizon paper adds: 'Assessment capacities must systematically collect and analyse threats to the civilian population. Mission leaders need to draw together political, military, police and civilian assets in integrated protection strategies or integrated teams to support implementation'.[17] Furthermore,

> The peacekeeping partnership is put to the test most in crises. A critical priority for missions is to prepare in advance for such eventualities. Timely, accurate and detailed analysis of the situation on the ground can provide early warning of an emerging threat. Early warning is also critical to enhancing the safety and security of United Nations personnel and to improving the Organization's ability to predict a crisis.[18]

Units on the ground, military observers, civilian personnel, other UN agencies, NGOs are usually more familiar with the environment in which they operate than the higher Command. Accordingly, it is critical that field-level information is made available to the mission Headquarters (through 'vertical fusion'), and that the latter is able to 'fuse' information originating from a wide range of sources with

---

[14] UNIFIL's mandate is laid out in UNSCR 1701 and subsequent resolutions renewing the mandate, most recently Resolution 2305 (2016).

[15] For an interesting discussion of the challenges, the Middle East poses for (intelligence) analysis see Kam 2015.

[16] UN DPKO/DFS 2008, 2010.

[17] UN DPKO/DFS 2009, p. 20.

[18] Idem, p. 24.

information concerning (potential) developments and trends at the national, regional and international level (or ‘horizontal fusion’).

JMACs have been created to achieve this horizontal and vertical ‘fusion’.[19]

8.4.2 *What Is JMAC?*

The 2003 UN Handbook on Multidimensional Peacekeeping Operations states that JMACs are responsible for the management (collection, coordination, analysis and distribution of information and reports) of the mission’s civil and military information in order to support the Special Representative of the UN Secretary General (SRSG)’s and Force Commander’s decision-making process.[20] The first JMACs were created in 2005,[21] followed by the first DPKO/DFS Policy and Guidelines on JMAC in 2006.

According to the 2015 DPKO/DFS policy, ‘JMACs are joint entities established to support mission planning and decision-making through the provision of integrated analysis and predictive assessments.’[22] The 2015 policy furthermore states that JMACs are responsible for managing information requirements from the Head of Mission and the Mission Leadership Team, including through the development of an information Collection Plan to support mission-leadership decision-making; collect and analyse multi-source information, including intelligence-related material; and prepare integrated analysis and predictive assessments that are timely, accurate, comprehensive and relevant to support decision-making; mission strategic, operational and contingency planning; and crisis management.[23] JMACs also identify threats and challenges to mandate implementation.

JMACs are complementary to Joint Operation Centres (JOCs). JOCs ensure 24/7 situational awareness and act as the mission’s integrated operations information hub, including facilitating integrated operations coordination.[24] JMACs can be best compared to ‘Fusion Centres’. The general principles governing the role, structure and functioning of Stability Operations Information Centres (SOIC) that existed in Afghanistan,[25] as well as the views General Michael Flynn expressed in a January 2012 article apply[26] to a large extent to JMACs. Although SOICs operated in settings that are very different from those of a UN-led peace operation, a number of

---

[19] This statement is based on the experience of the author; cf. Norheim-Martinsen and Ravndal 2011.

[20] UN DPKO 2003, p. 69.

[21] Abilova and Novosseloff 2016, p. 25.

[22] Idem, p. 14.

[23] Ibid.

[24] UN DPKO/DFS 2015, p. 65.

[25] Flynn et al. 2010, pp. 19–20.

[26] Flynn and Flynn 2012, p. 4, 7.

insights like the kind of intelligence (or understanding) support mission leaders need in stability operations; the profile of Information Analysts; the importance of information exchanges with NGOs; the significance of 'white' (population, economy, development, government) information as opposed to 'red' activity (the enemy) are pertinent to the further development of the JMAC concept. The June 2011 USIP paper 'Conflict Assessment and Intelligence Analysis' presents important views on the evolving nature of intelligence analysis in stability (and peace) operations, highlighting the need for convergence towards conflict assessment whereby tools from both approaches have to be used in tandem.[27]

8.4.3 How Does JMAC Operate?

Even if the JMAC concept is still evolving and there is no 'one size fits all', i.e. the specific role, size (from approx. 10 to 30 persons), structure and composition, interaction with its partners (JOC; U2; Political Affairs, Security, others) will vary in accordance with the mission's mandate and the views of the Head of Mission (HoM) on JMAC's role, a number of common features can be identified.

JMACs are integrated teams consisting of civilian and uniformed personnel, led by a civilian officer. Information Analysts include a mixture of civilian and uniformed personnel who have an analytical background covering different fields to ensure a multi-disciplinary approach that incorporates all mandate-related perspectives (political; military; civil affairs; security; police; rule of law; demobilization; demilitarization and reintegration (DDR); security sector reform (SSR); electoral; humanitarian; gender; child protection; etc.).

The importance of JMAC's integrated structure (i.e. civilian and military personnel cooperating in the same team) cannot be overestimated. Civilian personnel, in addition to their UN experience, have the regional and other expertise that is needed to understand, analyse and assess mandate-relevant issues. As they usually stay in the same post for several years, they can build specialized knowledge of their subject area as well as an effective information network with other UN actors and with local communities. The continuity in the civilian personnel's service is a prerequisite for the creation of an institutional memory, backed up by databases. Uniformed personnel, who usually have limited tours of duty, bring specific military or police expertise to JMAC and facilitate liaison (and information sharing) with the uniformed mission components.

There are persistent clichés concerning the (alleged) difficulties of civilian and military personnel to work together in integrated teams like JMACs. Clashing corporate cultures or distrust between uniformed and non-uniformed personnel, are not unique to the UN.[28] It would be overly simplistic to reduce silo-thinking, turf

[27] UN DPKO/DFS 2015.

[28] Lacquement 2010.

wars, lack of information sharing, and other resistance to integration or change in general, to a question of civilian versus military. Integrated structures like JOCs and JMACs where civilians and military personnel work together are actually important steps towards improving civil-military relations.

Irrespective of the importance of the quality of the information that is made available to JMAC, the skills[29] and expertise of the Information Analysts play an even more significant role, highlighting also that notwithstanding the benefits of analytical tools and databases, JMAC will always be a people–centric team. The complexity and fluidity of contemporary (post) conflict situations require highly skilled and intellectually-fit analysts who are able to give a meaning to the information that has been gathered and answer the ‘So what?’ question. Relying on their extensive regional and/or analytical expertise, they are able to identify, analyse, and predict all aspects of the operational environment that may affect mandate implementation. Larger JMACs may make a distinction between information collectors and analysts. Still, in most operational contexts, it is advisable not to separate these closely related activities, as most information outside the regular UN circuit is obtained through informal exchanges of views with counterparts in other organizations, instead of simply asking questions to a source.[30]

JMACs report directly—or through the mission Chief of Staff (CoS)—to the Head of Mission (HoM). HoM supervision allows for the shortest communication lines and most effective understanding of his/her information needs. HoM supervision is also important for a proper awareness among the other mission components of JMAC’s role. Whereas JMAC products are usually only shared with a small number of clients, procedures need to be put in place so that other mission components can also benefit from JMAC’s work, and create the conditions for two way information sharing.

8.4.4 What Kind of Information Does JMAC Need?

UN Chapter VI (and Chapter VII) peace operations require the consent of the parties and the confidence of the local population. This applies equally to information gathering (and analysis). Given the usually high degree of suspicion among host nation actors and (parts of) the population, information-gathering activities that could be perceived as intrusive are likely to have serious consequences for the mission’s reputation, and consequently, its ability to implement its mandate. There is a fundamental difference between, on the one hand, the mostly passive information gathering to ensure situational awareness and understanding in a Chapter VI

---

[29] “The best, most extroverted and hungriest analysts”, and “Analysts must absorb information with the thoroughness of historians, organize it with the skill of librarians and disseminate it with the zeal of journalists. They must embrace open-source, population-centric information as the lifeblood of their analytical work.” (Flynn et al. 2010, p. 23).

[30] Siman-Tov and Ofer 2013, pp. 36–37.

setting, and, on the other hand, aggressive (or even covert) information collection that could be confused with espionage, in peace enforcement/making settings. A Chapter VI peace operation needs to ensure that information gathering and analysis are conducted (and understood as such) in support of mandate implementation, rather than being perceived as directed against a party, or, worse, that the peacekeeping force (or its troop contributing countries) attempt(s) to gather information to which it is not entitled.

Accordingly, situational awareness and understanding for decision-making should focus, through the Head of Mission's Critical Information Requirements and the Priority and Specific Information Requirements derived from them, on the information that is required to implement the mission's mandate. The mission's mandate will also determine what kinds of assets are available for information gathering. Hence, access to information in a Chapter VI mission is more restricted than in a Chapter VII operation. While it could be argued that information gathering is not simply a question of quantity (i.e., more does not necessarily mean better), it should also be recognized that given the more limited mandates of Chapter VI operations, their information requirements will be less wide. Still, due to the more restricted capabilities to gather information, there are likely to be more information gaps, and additional challenges to mitigate the impact of these gaps.

As the population is the centre of gravity[31] in a peace operation, population-centric information will be the focus of information gathering. It may sound contradictory that the mission needs to know 'everything' about the population, and, at the same time, needs the latter's trust and its leaders' consent to succeed. For the largest part, however, this population-centric information is in the open domain or available from other mission components, i.e., anyone in the mission who interacts with the local population. Compared to non-UN crisis management operations that usually have a heavy military (i.e., uniformed) footprint and a small civilian component, UN peace operations' mandates include a wide range of activities conducted predominantly by civilian personnel in close interaction with the local population. While information gathering is not (and should never be) the priority of such interactions, the impressions on local atmospherics and other information obtained during contacts with members of local communities are a key component of situational awareness, and, consequently, vital for comprehensive understanding. Hence the importance of properly coordinated Key Leader Engagement (KLE), including recording, archiving, and analysis (and sharing of the latter) of the information gathered through any interaction with members of local communities.

The challenge will be to ensure that information can (i.e., technologically) and will (i.e., culturally or attitudinally) be shared in a timely manner and a user-friendly format. Technology remains a challenge too: how to create a system that gives Information Analysts access to information avoiding information overload?

Irrespective of the fact that JMAC Policies and Guidelines state that Missions are expected to make arrangements for effective information sharing with JMAC,

[31] Graziano 2007.

the latter continues to be a challenge. One would expect that human behaviour can be influenced to a certain extent (e.g., sharing usually works better when all parties involved are convinced that they gain from it), but a lot remains to be done. In addition to the controversy surrounding intelligence; turf-issues; a lack of trust; other factors may also cause problems. Uniformed personnel may be discouraged to share information with JMAC because they doubt the mission's capacity to protect sensitive information given the absence of secure communication means and the UN's lack of 'intelligence-culture'.

8.4.5 What Does JMAC Produce?

JMACs operate like fusion centres, relying on information shared by the other mission components: open sources; (if applicable) relations with host nation services; and JMAC's own information network. This information is transformed into actionable predictive integrated (or multi-dimensional or comprehensive) analysis that provides an answer to at least the following question: What does the (past, on-going, future) event, development, trend or pattern mean for mandate implementation, now and in the future? The added value of JMAC products resides in their integrated analysis (i.e., context and insight) and (forward-looking) assessment (i.e., foresight). JMAC products have to identify options for courses of action, flagging potential pitfalls, and historical analogue situations that can provide important contextual insights in current or future situations. Scenario papers identifying at least the worst-case scenario, the best-case scenario and the most likely scenarios are a good practice. Avoiding surprise among decision-makers should be JMAC's prime objective. Forward-looking integrated (or multi-dimensional) assessments are crucial for early warning. As JMAC is not burdened by routine reporting, it can cast a more general bird's eye view on emerging issues, in the widest possible manner (i.e., covering all mandate-relevant aspects), including potential threats or opportunities, long before these issues develop (potential) mandate implications.

8.4.6 Robust Peacekeeping—Peace Enforcement

Robust peacekeeping (i.e., the limited use in time and/or space of force to restore peace and security with the consent of the host nation and/or the main parties to the conflict, e.g. for POC) requires enhanced situational awareness and risk analysis to better anticipate and prepare for potential challenges.[32]

MONUSCO's Force Intervention Brigade (FIB), which was first deployed in May 2013 following the adoption of UNSCR 2098, is the 'first-ever United Nations

[32] UN DPKO/DFS 2009, p. 21.

'offensive' combat force intended to neutralize and disarm the rebel groups'.[33] Wider and more aggressive mandates require that missions, in addition to more robust and/or sophisticated means to implement them, also have corresponding tools for information gathering and analysis. After all, their requirements for situational awareness and understanding are more extensive.[34] This need for deeper situational awareness and understanding will have an impact on the role and structure of JMAC.

When conducting robust peacekeeping, the basic principle of JMAC as the (only) mission structure that produces the integrated (or fused) multi-sourced and multi-dimensional information picture (i.e. comprehensive 'understanding'), should be preserved. Alternatively, when several mission entities produce 'understanding', procedures should be established to achieve a maximum degree of integration or at least coordination. This may be easier said than done as the use of more robust and/or sophisticated means for mandate implementation and information gathering may be the subject of Troop Contributing Country (TCC)-imposed caveats, potentially restricting JMAC's access to information gathered through these means.

8.5 The Way Ahead: Options for the Future?

8.5.1 Use of Technology

The Final Report of the 2015 Expert Panel on Technology and Innovation in UN Peacekeeping emphasizes the importance of secure communications and of analytic support tools for JMACs. The lack of secure means of communication, even in a Chapter VI-setting like UNIFIL, seriously hampers information sharing. Given the vulnerability of non-secure communication means to intrusion, the absence of secure means also creates vulnerabilities in relation to perception management (e.g. damage to the credibility of the mission in case of leaks of sensitive information) and force protection.[35]

The development of IT-tools for JMACs (and JOCs) should be coordinated with UN partners, in particular the Department for Safety and Security (DSS); the Department for Political Affairs (DPA); the Department for Field Support (DFS); the Department for Public Information (DPI) and other potential stakeholders, to facilitate 'interoperability' and ensure the efficient use of resources. 'Less is more' definitely applies when it comes to databases and other IT tools in peace operations. Those developing the tools should make sure that they understand the requirements of users in the field as opposed to the field adjusting its requirements to what technicians think is good for them.

[33] Cammaert 2013, p. 2.

[34] Cammaert 2013, p. 10.

[35] UN DPKO/DFS 2015, p. 64; Abilova and Novosseloff 2016, p. 5, 23.

Since the use of observation technology in a Chapter VI mission requires the same level of consent of the parties as the other aspects of mandate implementation, the deployment of such technology is subject to the same caveats. UNIFIL's land and sea (Maritime Task Force)-based radars are used to detect violations of Lebanon's airspace, and the trajectory of outgoing/incoming rocket, artillery or mortar fire in violation of the cessation of hostilities. Accordingly, radars are an essential tool to monitor compliance by the parties with the mission's mandate.

For JMACs, the use of monitoring technology by the mission implies that there are specialized (technical) analysts, ideally within JMAC, who can interpret observation data and compile a quantitative and qualitative analysis that can be fused into the other layers of JMAC's multi-dimensional analytical picture. JMACs should be entitled to request the use of monitoring assets for their specific information requirements.

8.5.2 Social Media: A Tool for Situational Awareness and Understanding?

In 2015, every minute, 3.3 million posts were added on Facebook; 422,340 tweets recorded on Twitter; 44.4 million messages sent via Whatsapp; 2.05 million e-mails sent; 55,555 pictures uploaded on Instagram; 400 h of video uploaded on Youtube; etc. According to Flynn, in 2014, 'we create as much information in an hour today as we could download in all of 2004'.[36] The number of terrorist websites has increased from 12 in 1998 to more than 9,800 in January 2014.[37] The Final Report of the Expert Panel on Technology and Innovation in UN Peacekeeping states: 'Given the demands on today's missions, peacekeeping can simply no longer afford to be the last to know'.[38]

Social media can provide near real-time situational awareness of unfolding events. They can also be a vital source of information for humanitarian organizations in case of natural disasters.[39] Social media are used by activists to disseminate their views and mobilize supporters.[40] Statistics concerning the use of social media can provide a unique insight into the degree of influence activists or others have on public opinion, including the traction gained by calls for civil unrest or other mobilization.

Social media proved to be a key tool for mobilization during the Arab Spring and the crises that subsequently unfolded in the Middle East. They have also become the favourite means of public communication for extremist groups to

[36] Prism 2014, p. 185; Allen [s.a.].

[37] Weimann 2014.

[38] UN DPKO/DFS 2015, p. 67.

[39] OCHA 2015.

[40] See Omand et al. 2012.

propagate their cause and views, gather funds, intimidate opponents, recruit members, etc. According to a January 2014 USIP study, the conflict in Syria has been the most socially mediated civil conflict in history, whereby 'an exceptional amount' of what the outside world knows-or thinks it knows-about Syria's nearly three-year-old conflict has come from videos, analysis, and commentary circulated through social networks.[41]

Accordingly, information disseminated via social media is an essential component of situational awareness and understanding in peace operations, at least in the Middle East. As far as UNIFIL is concerned, social media has been an essential source to monitor and understand the potential implications for mandate implementation of the intentions and activities of the warring parties on the neighbouring Golan Heights.

While it may seem strange that the UN have not yet developed a capacity to use social media as a tool for situational awareness and understanding in peace operations, this may well provide an unique opportunity for the future. Given the sheer scale at which social media operate, the volume of (dis)information that is generated, and the (human) resources that are required to monitor; select (including verification: reliability of the source; credibility of the information) and analyse potentially relevant information, there is a need for a coordinated approach that goes beyond mission-level. While at mission level, JMAC, in close cooperation with the Press Information Media Monitoring unit, appears to best-placed to act as a coordinator, counterparts in neighbouring missions and at UN HQ-level should participate, too.

Accordingly, based on its importance for situational awareness and understanding; the fact that it relies exclusively on open source information (i.e., there should be no obstacles to sharing information); and the need for cooperation, including a division of labour, social media would be an ideal starting point to develop cooperation for the provision of comprehensive (integrated) understanding within and between different peace operations as well as with relevant departments at UN Headquarters (DPKO; DPA; DSS; DFS; DPI); and funds, agencies and programs. In the absence of such a coordinated approach, 'we are missing what these new voices are telling us'.[42] A successful integrated approach to monitoring social media and the analysis and assessment of information they disseminate could create a momentum that could also facilitate progress in other areas where situational awareness and understanding would benefit from cooperation and coordination, including information sharing within and between missions, and with UN Headquarters.

---

[41] Lynch et al. 2014, p. 5.

[42] Prism 2014, p. 184.

8.5.3 More Integration?

Ideally, organizational structures are based on the desired output and on the processes to produce this output. In the context of the provision of 'understanding' for decision-making in peace operations, this would ideally imply that all the mission's Information Collectors and Information Analysts are part of one single, integrated structure, i.e., an expanded JMAC encompassing all sections, uniformed and non-uniformed, which gather and analyse information. While this approach would seem ideal from a theoretical point of view, it is probably unrealistic.

Factors internal to the UN like a lack of intelligence mind-set; a lack of culture to share information; the absence of secure means of communication; and external factors, like a lack of trust among troop contributing countries in the UN's capacity to maintain confidentiality; discrepancies in their own capabilities; legal constraints stemming from domestic arrangements; and 'facts of life' like resistance to integration and change; in addition to the fact that JMAC-concept is still developing, all suggest that it is most probably too early to seek full integration.

No contemporary peace operation is acting in an exclusively military (or civilian) (post) conflict environment or with a military (or civilian) mandate only. Contemporary (post) conflict environments involve a mixture of sectarian, historical, ethnic, political, economic, etc. causes, factors and dynamics. It is these, together with the widening role of non-state actors (including organized crime), that determine developments, rather than traditional military considerations and/or state actors (only). Mission mandates do not only consist of the traditional observing and reporting, but usually involve a wide range of other tasks like stabilization; humanitarian assistance; SSR; DDR; safeguarding electoral processes and reconstruction; etc., requiring the permanent close cooperation of uniformed and non-uniformed personnel. A traditional Napoleonic (military) staff structure for peace operations hinders the implementation of an integrated approach as civilian counterparts in the mission are structured in a different manner.

Limiting 'understanding' to military aspects will generate incomplete (i.e., inaccurate) assessments, and, consequently, flawed decision-making, reducing the added value of these assessments, as decision-makers will probably increasingly rely on other sources (the media?) rather than on the work of their U2. Even if, as discussed earlier, recent western military intelligence doctrine emphasizes the importance of a multi-dimensional approach (X-PMESII), most other Troop Contributing Countries (TCCs) have not (yet?) made this leap.

In the context of UN peace operations that have a JMAC and/or ASIFU, the relevance of maintaining a separate U2 structure can be questioned. In addition to the 'integrated' nature (i.e. X-PMESII) of contemporaneous (post)conflict situations, the high rotation rates of uniformed personnel prevent continuity and the creation of an institutional memory in the U2 branch. Troop contributing countries are not always in a position to deploy personnel with the required analytical and/or regional expertise, and/or sustain this effort during several years. In case they also provide staff, in addition to U2, to ASIFU and/or national intelligence liaison elements, Troop contributing countries are likely to give priority to their national assets or ASIFU, to the detriment of the U2, making it even harder for it to provide a meaningful contribution.

If the U2 and JMAC are integrated in one team, cross-fertilization between experienced civilian JMAC Information Analysts and their uniformed counterparts will be greatly enhanced, shortening the learning time for uniformed personnel and mitigating the impact of high rotation rates. Integration will also facilitate the building of mutual trust and the creation of an institutional memory. Close cooperation with their uniformed colleagues will make it easier for civilian JMAC personnel to grasp the specific requirements of the military and police aspects of the mission's mandate, enhancing client orientation of JMAC's products. Such an integrated JMAC-U2 can maintain functional relations with both the Special Representative of the Secretary General (SRSG) and with the Force Commander (FC) to ensure that the latter's information requirements (which should in any event be very similar to those of the Special Representative, as both officials are implementing the same mission mandate) are effectively met.

Taking into account the similarity of information requirements for 'understanding' and for 'force protection', and the importance of properly appreciating the importance of ideology and other thought processes behind terrorism, including factors and grievances leading to radicalisation and violence,[43] there is a need for close cooperation between JMAC and civilian security information analysts. Depending of the nature of the security threats in which the mission operations, the integration of Security Information Analysts in JMAC, while maintaining functional links with the Security Department, as a means to achieve synergies should be examined.

Although at least theoretically there should be no unwanted duplication between JMAC and the Political Affairs Division (PAD), as their respective focus of work is different, 'turf issues' may arise. Given the specific role of PAD personnel, their integration into JMAC is not advisable. Still, arrangements need to be made to regulate information sharing between PAD and JMAC: both overlap and information gaps are to be avoided. Political Affairs Officers should be given the opportunity to contribute to JMAC products in order to ensure that political aspects are covered most effectively.

Cooperation between (JMAC) Information Analysts; U2 Military Information Analysts; Political and Civil Affairs Officers; and Security Information Analysts will benefit from common training. A common understanding of information analysis and its role in mission planning will contribute to creating an 'understanding' mind-set among civilian UN staff in the long term. In the short term, common training facilitates the creation of informal networks enhancing mutual understanding and cooperation at intra- and inter-mission level.

In the absence of the integration of all those who contribute to producing (comprehensive) understanding, a more realistic alternative consists of developing

[43] Boutelis and Chowdhury Fink 2016, pp. 1, 25.

close functional relations between them. To this effect, UNIFIL has created an 'Information Community'. The 'Information Community' is a functional network, coordinated by JMAC, linking all mission assets who gather information and conduct information analysis. This network is not an additional hierarchical layer, but connects the Community's (core and regular)[44] members along functional lines with the objective of producing a single, fused multi-dimensional analytical picture by applying an integrated approach to information gathering and analysis.

The integrated multidimensional (analytical) picture (i.e. comprehensive understanding), the 'Information Community's' main deliverable, covers the full spectrum of aspects that are relevant to Head of Mission or Force Commander's 'understanding' for mandate implementation, in order to answer the following two 'So What?' questions:

- What does it (i.e., event, development, statement, etc.) mean (for UNIFIL)?
- What is the impact (of the event, development, statement, etc.) now and in the future (for UNIFIL)?

Through the Information Community, members can focus on their area of expertise and avoid unwanted duplication or information gaps, enabling also a far greater degree of cooperation and involvement. Accordingly, Information Community analytical products reflect the expertise, knowledge and insights of all members, rather than relying solely on one pillar/component or only JMAC. De-conflicting is done before the final product is shared with the clients, i.e., potentially contradictory or otherwise inconsistent analytical conclusions will only be presented after they have been verified by the Community and the reasons for the differing views have been checked.

The degree of implementation of the 'Information Community'-concept has varied, in particular in relation to information gathering. In the absence of similar procedures outside UNIFIL, leadership buy-in, which is essential to ensure cooperation of Community Members (i.e., the mission pillars), needs to be re-established with each change of personnel/rotation. While military personnel are usually familiar with concepts like Priority Information Requirements (PIR), Specific Information requirements (SIR) or Requests for Information (RFI), this is not the case with civilian personnel. Integrated information gathering requires coordination and management by dedicated qualified personnel supported by specific IT-tools. These are not (yet) available.

JMAC's coordinating role in the Information Community has occasionally been challenged, as pillar heads are reluctant to grant JMAC a tasking authority, fearing that it could interfere with their authority. From a JMAC point of view, tasking of Community members should be limited to (i.e., be consistent with) Head of Mission

---

[44] Core members are those for whom analysing information concerning the Head of Mission's Collection and critical information requirements (CIR) is their core business (i.e. Political Affairs; U2; Security; JMAC). Regular members while contributing to mandate implementation in their respective areas may come across information that is relevant to these requirements and should be made available to the Information Community.

or Force Commander's direction as expressed through his/her information requirements. Coordination by no means implies that JMAC will be in charge of each Information Community project; the leading role will reside with the pillar or component in whose domain the project falls.

The implementation of the Information Community-concept has been most successful as far as the preparation of integrated analysis is concerned. The 'Situational Awareness Cell (SAC)' is an example of a JMAC-led Information Community platform. SAC is a non-permanent body consisting of representatives of the Information Community's Core and Regular members who meet on a regular basis to share and discuss analytical views on past, current or future issues that are relevant to the Head of Mission or Force Commander's situational awareness and understanding (i.e. mandate implementation). JMAC subsequently prepares a report summarizing these analytical discussions (i.e., fusion) which, after review by the Community members, is disseminated as a SAC report to the mission leadership. SAC reports' analyses (context, insight) and assessments (foresight) focus on the implications for UNIFIL, reflecting the views of all the Community members including, if applicable, (de-conflicted) dissenting opinions.

UNIFIL's 'Threat Assessment Group (TAG)' creates the conditions for an integrated approach to the sharing, evaluation, analysis, assessment, and dissemination of security threat information. The TAG's purpose is to enhance the mission's capacity to adopt preventative or mitigating measures, and avoid the 'cry wolf'-syndrome, without interfering with the legal accountability defined in DSS's Security Risk Management (SRM) System.

8.5.4 JMAC-ASIFU Relations

The question of integration between U2 and JMAC applies also to the All-Source Information Unit (ASIFU) in missions with such a structure. The example of MINUSMA is discussed in detail the next chapter but a few remarks are needed here. ASIFU is intended to provide 'fused, relevant, timely, *actionable and integrated analysis based on a comprehensive approach*', in support of the Force Commander's priority information requirements and MINUSMA force protection.[45] It gathers information on armed groups, political, military, economic, social, infrastructure and Information issues, and has its own Analysis Fusion Cell (AFC) and Osint capability.[46] ASIFU relies on the capabilities of specific, European troop contributing countries.

Under-Secretary-General Hervé Ladsous, (then) Head of the UN Department of Peacekeeping Operations, in an October 2014 interview discussing the situation in Mali, provided important insights on what he described as 'fusion cells'. Ladsous

[45] Karlsrud and Smith 2015, p. 11.

[46] Van Dalen 2015, p. 311.

also highlighted the shift that has taken place in the attitude at the UN towards 'intelligence', including Humint and Sigint.[47] In his October 2014 statement to the UN's Fourth Committee on Peacekeeping, Ladsous described ASIFU as an 'unprecedented' ability to gather and analyse information relating to threats to UN peacekeeping personnel and to the local population.[48]

Several research papers discuss the lack of clarity in ASIFU's role and its relations with other mission components that gather and analyse information, in particular JMAC, despite ad hoc coordination mechanisms like the Joint Coordination Board (JCB).[49] The question of duplication between ASIFU's AFC and JMAC arises, since according to DPKO/DFS Policy and Guidelines, JMAC is supposed to be the mission's integrated all-source fusion unit. In the absence of proper coordination between ASIFU and JMAC, there has been overlapping, duplication, or other inefficient use of resources.[50] There is also a need to ensure that the UN mission leadership knows how to use ASIFU's added value to improve planning and decision-making.[51]

While the progress described by Under-Secretary-General Ladsous in relation to the acceptance of 'intelligence' in the UN and the creation of 'fusion cells' (i.e., the ASIFU) is laudable, it is paramount that the role of JMAC as the mission's only structure producing integrated all-source analyses and assessments is preserved, for at least five reasons.

First, JMAC is a UN-proper integrated structure that can rely on the continuity of its (civilian) staffing. This is important given the scarcity of properly qualified and experienced information analysts (and the high rotation rate of uniformed personnel in peace operations; see also the fifth reason). Second, as a result of its successful implementation in an increasing number of missions, the understanding and acceptance of the JMAC concept have progressively widened, and it is now even applied in non-DPKO missions. Creating the impression now that other, new capacities like ASIFU, are the preferred option would send the wrong signal.

Third, while ASIFU's unique capabilities; the flexibility and operability of the concept; and the skills of its staff are undeniably important assets supporting its wider application in UN peace operations, the latter requires the participation of countries that are able to provide these capabilities and skilled staff to peace operations throughout missions' life spans. ASIFU's sophisticated sensors and other advanced information gathering tools (which are cost-intensive to acquire and to operate), are not available to all troop contributing countries, i.e., there will be an increased reliance (or even dependency) on a specific number of them. What happens if the troop contributing countries on whose tools ASIFU relies, are not

---

[47] Crossette 2014.

[48] Ladsous 2014.

[49] Van Dalen 2015; Abilova and Novosseloff 2016, pp. 17–19. Handelingen Eerste Kamer der Staten-Generaal 2015, p. 12.

[50] Van Dalen 2015.

[51] Abilova and Novosseloff 2016, p. 24.

interested in participating in a peace mission, or in case they were participating, reduce or withdraw their participation? Within missions, the discrepancy in capabilities may create frictions[52] with mission components that do not have access to such systems (and accordingly, the information they gather).

Fourth, the difficulties troop contributing countries face with the deployment of properly qualified uniformed staff due to high rotation rates also apply to the ASIFU. If the data provided by ASIFU's sophisticated sensors cannot be transformed into actionable understanding due to a lack of qualified analysts, the ASIFU's added value will erode, or worse, flawed assessments may lead to 'bad' decisions. Missions that have ASIFU also need to have the staffing capacity to make better use of the analyses and assessments produced by ASIFU.[53]

Fifth, last but not least, the deployment of ASIFU requires the consent of host nations or other parties or stakeholders to the conflict/mandate. It can be expected that the host nation or other stakeholders will (try to) impose caveats that will (in) directly impact on ASIFU's capabilities, as they may well fear that ASIFU could be used against them.

If it is decided to deploy ASIFU in a peace operation, procedures to regulate relations (information sharing, division of labour, tasking, other) between the JMAC and ASIFU need to be agreed upon between DPKO and countries that provide personnel for this Unit prior to its deployment. A differentiation between ASIFU and JMAC, whereby JMAC focuses on 'strategic' aspects whereas ASIFU (and U2) supports the 'operational' and 'tactical' level is counter-productive as these levels are most often closely intertwined in contemporaneous (asymmetric) (post) conflict environments, and events or incidents can easily change dimension in the course of their development.

Instead of attempting to maintain separate (and in practical terms duplicating) analytical capabilities, options for achieving synergies should be explored, by focusing on the complementarity of JMAC and ASIFU's Analysis Fusion Cell (AFC). Given the role of (specific) troop contributing countries in ASIFU, the full integration of ASIFU's AFC in JMAC is probably wishful thinking. More realistic options could be to have ASIFU's non-technical (i.e., other than Sigint or Imint) analysts integrated in JMAC, or to exchange liaison officers between JMAC and ASIFU. If this is not feasible, protocols for analytical cooperation, including production should be developed. Rather than ASIFU duplicating the work of JMAC (or vice versa), or competing with the latter, JMAC and ASIFU's AFC could prepare joint assessments or develop other forms of analytical cooperation.

If indeed ASIFU's and JMAC's analytical capabilities were (partially) merged, it would seem appropriate to rename ASIFU as 'Military Information Collection Unit (MICU)' to avoid misunderstandings about JMAC's status as the mission's (only) fusion unit. Maximizing the contribution of ASIFU (i.e., MICU) to mandate implementation would mean that it concentrates on gathering information through

---

[52] Karlsrud and Smith, p. 12.

[53] Lollesgaard 2015, p. 2.

means that are not accessible to JMAC. The MICU's analytical capacity would only consist of technical analysts who can provide a meaning to the data gathered by the unit's sensors and share their analysis (even if this may require sanitization) with JMAC to allow the latter to fuse it into its comprehensive analytical picture.

Closer relations between ASIFU and JMAC could also improve ASIFU's access to civilian sources in the mission, agencies and others who may well be reluctant to engage with a military structure and rather interact with civilian UN counterparts. Such cooperation will not only reinforce ASIFU's Humint (which should focus on other sources than JMAC) capacity,[54] but will also ensure better coordinated key leader engagement between ASIFU and JMAC.

Another area where synergies could be achieved is Osint, including social media. Instead of ASIFU and JMAC, in addition to PIO or even U2 monitor (social) media in an uncoordinated manner, a coordinated approach would allow all to rely on each other's experience and expertise.

Closer cooperation between ASIFU and JMAC requires that the UN create the basic conditions that allow for such cooperation by introducing secure communication networks and procedures for the ownership and sharing of information The participation in ASIFU of countries that have a more advanced approach to information management than the UN could create a momentum to push the latter to move ahead with the development of secure electronic archives, databases, etc. as has also been recommended by the UN Expert Panel on Technology and Innovation,[55] not only for JMAC and ASIFU, but for all mission components that handle information that is pertinent to the mission's critical information requirements (and decision-making for mandate implementation).

8.6 Conclusion

With the introduction of the JMAC concept, the UN has come a long way from the situation in the 1990s when the credibility of UN peacekeeping was seriously damaged by what is commonly portrayed as 'intelligence failures'[56] in Rwanda (UNAMIR) and Srebrenica (UNPROFOR). The introduction of the JMAC concept more than 10 years ago has given mission leaders a tool that allows them to achieve comprehensive understanding (insight, context, foresight) of the operational environment in support of mandate implementation, including early warning.

Under-Secretary-General Ladsous in his statement for the Fourth Committee on Peacekeeping in October 2014, identified 'improved intelligence and situational

---

[54] Van Dalen 2015, p. 318; Abilova and Novosseloff 2016, p. 11.

[55] UN DPKO/DFS 2015, p. 65.

[56] Roux 2008, pp. 18–19.

awareness' as the fourth 'critical' priority to strengthen peacekeeping.[57] Ladsous reiterated these views in October 2015, stating

> As peacekeeping faces new threats posed by transnational organised crime and violent extremism, we must leverage the technological tools at our disposal to support greater situational awareness and analysis. Ultimately, we must seek to have reliable, actionable intelligence to guide our actions and take informed decisions at the tactical, operational and strategic levels. It is time to de-mystify the term 'intelligence'. Without it, we will not be able to protect ourselves and others.[58]

UN Secretary General Ban Ki-Moon's September 2015 report on 'The future of United Nations peace operations: implementation of the recommendations of the High-level Independent Panel on Peace Operations' states:

> An effective system for the acquisition, analysis and operationalization of information for peace operations in complex environments is lacking. I have tasked the Secretariat with developing parameters for an information and intelligence framework that can support field missions in operating effectively and safely. I welcome further discussions with Member States on that urgent capability gap.[59]

The UN leadership's recognition of the importance of 'intelligence' (i.e., understanding) for mandate implementation raises high expectations for the future.

Still, the experience from the first deployment of ASIFU shows that the UN and the member states now need to make a choice as to how to move forward. This choice is not about JMAC *or* ASIFU but about how JMAC and ASIFU can achieve synergies for the benefit of mandate implementation. Should priority be given to proceeding with the development of a 'UN-owned' fusion capacity that can operate in any mandate setting, by further investing in the JMAC concept including a policy framework and procedures that confirm its leading role as peace operations' (only) fusion units, or, alternatively, should the emphasis be on new units like ASIFU that depend on capacities of individual member states and can only be deployed in specific mandate settings?

In addition to organizational difficulties that the creation of new units generates, the main reason why such a choice needs to be made is that troop contributing countries and the UN do not have enough skilled and experienced information analysts to allow for the proper functioning throughout a mission's lifecycle of both structures in a way that effectively assists mandate implementation. Irrespective of the quality of the information that has been gathered, poor analyses will harm the JMAC and ASIFU's credibility and, consequently, have a negative impact on their added value to decision making.

Accordingly, more than 10 years after the first DPKO/DFS Policy and Guidelines for JMACs, there is a need for a proper UN doctrine on the provision of comprehensive 'understanding' in peace operations, across all relevant departments (i.e., not only DPKO but also DPA and DSS), in close coordination with interested

---

[57] Ladsous 2014.

[58] Ladsous 2015.

[59] UN Doc A/70/357–S/2015/682 2015, para 94.

member states. Such a doctrine should emphasize the role of JMAC as the mission's (only) fusion centre, whereby, depending on the mission's mandate and operational environment, specific information gathering units (like the MICU) could be established.

There is a need for a cultural shift (or change in mind-set), whereby all stakeholders agree on what is required (i.e., comprehensive understanding), how this can be achieved (i.e., the JMAC concept), and how mission leaders should use this unique capability (i.e., appropriate training). While such a doctrine may seem like a rather ambitious endeavour, it seems more feasible than attempting to work out a common (and meaningful) definition for 'intelligence'.

Based on the increasing importance of social media in contemporary (pre-) (and post-) conflict situations, and the resources they require for monitoring and analysis, a common approach towards social media as a tool for situational awareness and understanding could be the starting point for this cultural shift towards such a common doctrine. At the latest when all stakeholders realize the benefits of information sharing and of the creation of integrated common situational awareness and understanding, a change in mind-set, or, in the absence of a better expression, 'culture of understanding'[60] can be achieved.

References

Abilova O, Novosseloff A (2016) Demystifying Intelligence in UN Peace Operations: Toward an Organizational Doctrine. International Peace Institute, New York https://www.ipinst.org/2016/07/demystifying-intelligence-in-un-peace-ops Accessed 30 October 2016.

Allen R (undated) What happens online in 60 seconds? Blog post on Smart Insights Digital Marketing Advice. http://www.smartinsights.com/internet-marketing-statistics/happens-online-60-seconds/ Accessed 8 February 2017.

Boutelis A, Chowdhury Fink N (2016) Waging Peace: UN Peace Operations Confronting Terrorism and Violent Extremism. https://www.ipinst.org/wp-content/uploads/2016/10/1610_Waging-Peace.pdf Accessed 30 October 2016.

Cammaert P (2013) The UN Intervention Brigade in the Democratic Republic of the Congo. https://www.ipinst.org/wp-content/uploads/publications/ipi_e_pub_un_intervention_brigade_rev.pdf. Accessed 30 October 2016.

Crossette B (2014) UN Peacekeeping Upgrades Its Reactions to Conflicts and Adds Surveillance Tools. http://passblue.com/2014/11/11/un-peacekeeping-upgrades-its-reactions-to-conflicts-and-adds-surveillance-tools/ Accessed 30 October 2016.

Dorn AW (2010) United Nations Peacekeeping Intelligence. In: Johnson, LK (eds) The Oxford Handbook of National Security Intelligence. Oxford University Press, Oxford, pp. 275–295.

Flynn MT, Flynn CA (2012) Integrating Intelligence and Information, Ten Points for the Commander. http://usacac.army.mil/CAC2/MilitaryReview/Archives/English/MilitaryReview_20120229_art005.pdf Accessed 30 October 2016.

Flynn MT, Pottinger M, Batchelor PD (2010) Fixing Intell: A Blueprint for Making Intelligence Relevant in Afghanistan. Center for a New American Security, Washington. http://online.wsj.com/public/resources/documents/AfghanistanMGFlynn_Jan2010.pdf Accessed 30 October 2016

[60] Abilova and Novosseloff 2016, p. 24.

Graziano C (2007) Militants challenge UN Force in Lebanon. Press statement. 3 July 2007 http://reliefweb.int/report/lebanon/militants-challenge-un-force-lebanon-general Accessed 30 October 2016.

Handelingen van de Eerste Kamer der Staten-Generaal (2015) Brief van de Minister van Buitenlandse Zaken en van Defensie en de Minister van Buitenlandse Handel en Ontwikkelingssamenwerking, Nederlandse Deelname aan vredesmissies. https://www.eerstekamer.nl/behandeling/20151218/brief_inzake_voortgangsrapportage Accessed 30 October 2016.

Kam E (2015) The Middle East as an Intelligence Challenge. www.inss.org.il/uploadImages/systemFiles/The%20Middle%20East%20as%20an%20Intelligence%20Challenge.pdf. Accessed 30 October 2016.

Karlsrud J, Smith AC (2015) Europe's Return to UN Peacekeeping in Africa. Lessons from Mali. http://www.ipinst.org/2015/07/europes-return-to-un-peacekeeping-in-africa-lessons-from-mali Accessed 30 October 2016.

Lacquement RA (2010) Integrating Civilian and Military Activities. http://strategicstudiesinstitute.army.mil/pubs/parameters/Articles/2010spring/40-1-2010_lacquement.pdf Accessed 30 October 2016.

Ladsous H (2014) Statement of Under-Secretary-General for Peacekeeping Operations Debate of the Fourth Committee on Peacekeeping. http://www.un.org/en/peacekeeping/documents/USG-Ladsous-4C-Statement28102014.pdf Accessed 30 October 2016.

Ladsous H (2015) Statement of Under-Secretary-General for Peacekeeping Operations, Debate of the Fourth Committee on Peacekeeping. http://www.un.org/en/peacekeeping/documents/HL%20statement%20to%204th%20CommitteeAS%20DELIVERED30Oct2015.pdf Accessed 30 October 2016.

Lollesgaard M (2015) Operating in an Asymmetric Environment in a Peacekeeping Operation, Force Commander's speech in the Security Council. https://www.defensie.nl/binaries/defensie/documenten/toespraken/2015/06/22/toespraak-commandant-minusma/speech.pdf Accessed 30 October 2016.

Lynch M, Freelon D, Aday S (2014) Syria's Socially Mediated Civil War. http://www.usip.org/publications/syria-s-socially-mediated-civil-war Accessed 30 October 2016.

Ministry of Defence Development, Concepts and Doctrine Centre (2010) Joint Doctrine Publication 04 Understanding. www.gov.uk/government/publications/jdp-04-understanding Accessed 30 October 2016.

Ministry of Defence Development, Concepts and Doctrine Centre (2011) Joint Doctrine Publication 2-00 Understanding and Intelligence Support to Joint Operations. https://www.gov.uk/government/uploads/system/uploads/attachment_data/file/311572/20110830_jdp2_00_ed3_with_change1.pdf Accessed 30 October 2016.

NATO (2014) AJP-3.4.1 Allied Joint Doctrine for the Military Contribution to Peace Support http://nso.nato.int/nso/zPublic/ap/AJP-3.4.1%20EDA%20V1%20E.pdf Accessed 30 October 2016.

Norheim-Martinsen PM, Ravndal JA (2011) Towards Intelligence-Driven Peace Operations? The Evolution of UN and EU Intelligence Structures. International Peacekeeping 18(4):454–467.

OCHA (2015) In a disaster, we can't do anything without information. www.unocha.org/ochain/2014-15/stories/disaster Accessed 30 October 2016.

Omand D, Bartlett J, Miller C (2012) Introducing Social Media Intelligence (SOCMINT). Intelligence and National Security 27(6):801–823.

Prism (2014) An Interview with Lieutenant General Mike Flynn. http://cco.ndu.edu/Portals/96/Documents/prism/prism_4-4/Interview_LTG_Mike_Flynn.pdf Accessed 30 October 2016.

Roux A (2008) Intelligence and Peacekeeping - Are We Winning? Conflict Trends 3: 18–25.

Siman-Tov D, Ofer G (2013) Intelligence 2.0: A New Approach to the Production of Intelligence. http://www.inss.org.il/uploadImages/systemFiles/Intelligence%202.0-A%20New%20Approach%20to%20the%20Production%20of%20Intelligence.pdf Accessed 30 October 2016.

Theunens R (2003) Intelligence and Peace Support Operations, Some Practical Concepts. In: De Jong B, Platje W, Steele RD (eds) Peacekeeping Intelligence: Emerging Concepts for the Future. OSS International Press, Oakton, pp 61–70.

UN Doc A/70/357–S/2015/682 (2015) UN General Assembly. Report of the Secretary-General, The Future of United Nations Peace Operations: Implementation of the High-level Independent Panel on Peace Operations. http://www.un.org/en/ga/search/view_doc.asp?symbol=S/2015/682 Accessed 30 October 2016.

United Nations, Department of Peacekeeping Operations, Department of Field Support (2009) A New Partnership Agenda, Charting a New Horizon for UN Peacekeeping. http://www.un.org/en/peacekeeping/documents/newhorizon.pdf Accessed 30 October 2016.

United Nations, Department of Peacekeeping Operations, Department of Field Support (2015) Performance Peacekeeping, Final Report of the Expert Panel on Technology and Innovation in UN Peacekeeping. http://www.performancepeacekeeping.org/offline/download.pdf Accessed 30 October 2016.

United Nations, Department of Peacekeeping Operations, Department of Field Support (2008 and 2010) UN Peacekeeping Operations Principles and Guidelines Capstone Doctrine. http://www.un.org/en/peacekeeping/documents/newhorizon.pdf Accessed 30 October 2016.

United Nations, Department of Peacekeeping Operations, Peacekeeping Best Practices Unit (2003) Handbook on Multidimensional Peacekeeping Operations. http://www.un.org/en/peacekeeping/documents/Peacekeeping-Handbook_UN_Dec2003.pdf Accessed 30 October 2016.

United States Institute for Peace (2011) Conflict Assessment and Intelligence Analysis, Commonality, Convergence, and Complementarity Special Report. http://www.usip.org/sites/default/files/Conflict_Assessment.pdf Accessed 30 October 2016.

Van Dalen JA (2015) ASIFU: Baanbrekend inlichtingenexperiment in Mali. [ASIFU: A pioneering intelligence experiment in Mali]. Militaire Spectator 184(7/8):306–320.

Weimann G (2014) When Terrorism Met the New Media. https://www.wilsoncenter.org/sites/default/files/terror%20and%20social%20media%20PPT.pdf Accessed 30 October 2016.

Author Biography

Reynaud Theunens, M.Sc., is a former Belgian Army Officer who has been the Head of the Joint Mission Analysis Center, UN Interim Force In Lebanon (UNIFIL) since 2009. Having worked as an intelligence analyst, between 1994 and 1999, he served during a total of two years as a military information/intelligence officer in the UNPROFOR/UNPF (Zagreb, Croatia), UNTAES (Vukovar, Croatia) and SFOR headquarters (Sarajevo, BiH). Between 2001 and 2009 he worked at the Office of the Prosecutor (OTP) at the International Criminal Tribunal for the Former Yugoslavia (ICTY) as an Intelligence Analyst (Military) conducting in-depth research and analysis on *de jure* and *de facto* (para) military command, control and communication structures. He testified in ten trials as a military expert witness called by the Prosecution.

Chapter 9
The Evolution of Peacekeeping Intelligence: The UN's Laboratory in Mali

Sebastiaan Rietjens and A. Walter Dorn

Abstract This chapter looks at how peacekeeping intelligence expanded in MINUSMA and how it worked in practice. Apart from reviewing the main innovations and structures, and the means for information gathering, processing, dissemination and direction, the chapter identifies many challenges and summarizes these by means of three dichotomies. First, the European countries brought in the innovative intelligence capabilities, heavily based on advanced NATO procedures, but the main force was mostly populated with African soldiers who had the greater cultural familiarity and knew more of the locally spoken languages. Marrying the Western and African capabilities turned out to be challenging due to incoherent procedures, systems, levels of experience as well as reporting mechanisms. In addition, information-sharing from classified NATO databases proved difficult. Second, whereas several innovative intelligence units produced comprehensive intelligence reports focusing on the longer term, MINUSMA's military leadership valued current and security-related intelligence more, but that was insufficiently available within the organization. Third, the contributions of military and civilian actors were largely stovepiped and lacked sufficient sharing, coordination and integration. The reasons underlying this were organizational, political as well as technical in nature. Coordination boards were installed but these were not fully effective due to a lack of directive powers.

Keywords Minusma · ASIFU · JMAC · Peacekeeping intelligence · Stovepiping

---

S. Rietjens (✉)
Netherlands Defence Academy, Breda, The Netherlands
e-mail: Sjh.rietjens@mindef.nl

A.W. Dorn
Defence Studies at the Royal Military College of Canada and the Canadian Forces College, Toronto, Canada
e-mail: dorn@cfc.dnd.ca

F. Baudet et al. (eds.), *Perspectives on Military Intelligence from the First World War to Mali*, DOI 10.1007/978-94-6265-183-8_9

Contents

9.1 Introduction

Most modern military missions take place in complex environments with mandates that are often broad in scope and involve a multitude of political, socio-economic and security challenges. As a result conventional intelligence aimed at information regarding states, militaries, and target individuals is no longer sufficient. Rather, armed forces have to gain extensive knowledge of local populations and their societies as well. In their study 'Left of Bang', US Lieutenant General Michael Flynn and two colleagues[1] stressed this:

> The lesson of the last decade is that failing to understand the human dimension of conflict is too costly in lives, resources, and political will … a new [intelligence] concept should seek to explain how populations understand their reality, why they choose either to support or resist their governments, how they organize themselves socially and politically, and why and how their beliefs transform over time.

Many researchers and practitioners have focused on the rise of such new forms of intelligence, based mostly on the recent missions in Iraq and Afghanistan—missions that were dominated by US and NATO troops.[2] These studies reflected new initiatives that were labelled as population-centric intelligence,[3] cultural intelligence[4] and ethnographic intelligence,[5] among other names. These initiatives have contributed to our understanding of how to gain a wider and more comprehensive intelligence picture that covers multiple and interrelated domains including but not limited to political, socio-economic and security issues.

Ironically, before the United States and NATO learned of the importance of stability operations and the need for new forms of intelligence, the United Nations

---

[1] Flynn et al. 2012, p. 14.

[2] See e.g., Flynn et al. 2010; Kitzen et al. 2013, pp. 159–191.

[3] Kitzen 2012.

[4] Spencer and Balasevicius 2009.

[5] Perugini 2008, pp. 213–227.

had been evolving its own practice of intelligence in peace and stability operations, focusing also on the wider population-centric approach. Because of the array of UN actors in the field, from peacekeepers to humanitarian workers to development personnel, the United Nations was pre-disposed to take a comprehensive approach, though certainly not in a systematic fashion.

Though the United Nations is less equipped with monitoring technology and other resources than NATO or coalition forces formed by Western nations, the world organization has shown innovation over time that can benefit the wider understanding and practice of intelligence. To increase our appreciation and understanding of the UN's approach, case studies of specific missions can show the expansion in the scope and capability of UN intelligence, gradually moving towards what we call 'comprehensive intelligence'. What sources, methods and architectures have UN missions used to gather, process and disseminate intelligence? The United Nations is evolving towards a comprehensive approach as it incorporates large civilian components to complement its military instruments, though the methods and means to integrate them have proven challenging.[6] Separate agencies are tasked to care for refugees, internally displaced persons, children, women, all loosely networked with a plethora of non-governmental organizations. These UN agencies and organizations have the advantage of experience: they are in the field long before the peacekeeping mission arrives and will stay long after the mission leaves. They have built long-term relationships with the local populations that they serve, and can benefit by gaining information and situational awareness.

In part because of these relationships, the United Nations has been hesitant to even use the term intelligence. In traditional peacekeeping, as practised during the Cold War, the use of the term 'intelligence' was banned.

> Initially the United Nations even shunned all types of intrusive gathering of information because it felt it could not afford to lose credibility or tarnish its image as an impartial mediator by opening itself to accusations of employing covert or misleading techniques to gather information.[7]

The United Nations altered its stance towards the term and practice of intelligence, mainly due to the complex and dangerous environments in which many post-Cold War UN peacekeeping missions took place. As a result UN peacekeeping missions gained new capabilities,[8] and intelligence in peacekeeping has become more accepted, as well as increasingly professionalized.

In looking at the recent evolution of peacekeeping intelligence, the mission in Mali stands out. The Multidimensional Integrated Stabilization Mission in Mali

---

[6] Norheim-Martinsen and Ravndal 2011.

[7] Dorn 2010, p. 277.

[8] In the twenty-first century, the United Nations added new "intelligence" components to its missions, though avoiding the term explicitly. For instance, in 2005–06, it instituted "Joint Mission Analysis Centres" and the "Joint Operations Centres" in its peacekeeping operations and formulated a general policy for them (United Nations, Department of Peacekeeping Operations 2006).

(MINUSMA) has shown the greatest expansion of intelligence of any peacekeeping mission in the twenty-first century. It has significant and innovative intelligence capabilities, illustrating the UN's attempt to gain greater intelligence, moving in the direction of comprehensive intelligence. This chapter looks at how peacekeeping intelligence evolved in the mission, particularly within the military component. It focuses on the key innovation: the All Sources Information Fusion Unit (ASIFU). It examines its main activities and structures, the means for information gathering, processing, dissemination, as well as the direction that is provided.

9.2 MINUSMA and Its Intelligence Design

The establishment of MINUSMA by the UN Security Council in Resolution 2100 on 25 April 2013 was the result of a number of intertwined events. The northern regions of Mali had long complained of a lack of democratic power-sharing, leading to resentment and a loss of state control. Furthermore, the region became increasingly unstable due to illicit trafficking of arms, drugs and people, especially with heavily armed Tuareg fighters returning from Libya after the fall of the Gaddafi government in 2011. This explosive cocktail led to mutinies in the country, a military coup in March 2012 before some democratic order was restored and a marginalization of the Armed Forces of Mali (FAMA), which constantly lacked ammunition and reinforcements to fight in the North. At the invitation of the government, France deployed forces to push back advances by rebels, who were based in the North, and by some other groups widely labelled as 'terrorists.' A peace process was fostered with the rebels. An African Union mission was temporarily deployed in early 2013[9] before the United Nations took over the peacekeeping duties, even as an Ebola crisis hit other countries in West Africa.[10] In broad terms, it was MINUSMA's task to promote a stabilization of key population centres, and guide the political/peace process. It also carries the mandate for 'protection of civilians,' which had become standard in twenty-first century peacekeeping operations.

By 2015, MINUSMA consisted of close to 9,000 military personnel, 1,000 police, 500 international civilians, and 120 UN volunteers, along with many local hires.[11] The military troops originated from 41 different countries including European countries (e.g., Denmark, Germany, Sweden, and The Netherlands), African countries (e.g., Egypt, Gambia, and Niger) and others, notably China. In

---

[9] The African-led International Support Mission to Mali (AFISMA) was authorized by the UN Security Council in resolution 2085 of 20 December 2012. It was a military mission of the Economic Community of West African States (ECOWAS), led by Nigeria. The first forces arrived on the ground in January 2013.

[10] Fortunately, the Ebola epidemic did not spread to Mali, though about eight fatalities occurred in the country, including in Mali's capital, Bamako. World Health Organization 2015.

[11] United Nations 2015a, b. The site gives currently authorized figures (August 2016) of 13,300 military personnel and 1,920 police.

addition to the Force Headquarters (FHQ) in the capital Bamako, MINUSMA had three sector headquarters (SHQs) that commanded approximately 4,000 military personnel each. SHQ-West was headquartered in Timbuktu, whereas SHQ-East operated from Gao. A SHQ-North was created in 2014, based in Kidal and covering a smaller but very turbulent region.

African forces contributed the majority of troops on the ground, conducting patrols and seeking to maintain security. By contrast, European countries contributed key enabling forces that played to European strengths: command units, communications, special operations, attack helicopters and intelligence units.

MINUSMA's force design contained the typical military intelligence units (designated by the number 2, according to standard military staff convention) within its battalions (S2), Sector headquarters cells (G2) and Force Headquarters cell (U2). These units were supposed to provide MINUSMA's commanders with current intelligence, especially relating to security.

In addition, a civil-military Joint Mission Analysis Centre (JMAC) was established in accordance with standard UN procedures for missions since 2006 to produce mission-wide and longer-term analysis for the senior management.[12] Also a Joint Operations Centre (JOC) kept track of the situation on the ground, focusing on unfolding events and the immediate future. However, these mechanisms were not enough, since little active processing and analysis of information was done by the relatively small units listed above. These civilian structures were understaffed at the regional level. To make matters worse, a significant proportion of the civilian and local military personnel were illiterate. To help address the deficiencies, Under-Secretary-General for Peacekeeping Hervé Ladsous requested that MINUSMA be enhanced by an additional military intelligence unit that was coined ASIFU, the All Sources Information Fusion Unit, a term borrowed from NATO. After finding European countries willing to provide the personnel and forces, the ASIFU was deployed from March 2014.

The main mission of ASIFU was to provide intelligence capacity and 'contribute especially to traditionally non-military intelligence analysis, such as illegal trafficking and narcotics-trade; ethnic dynamics and tribal tensions; corruption and bad governance within Mali and MINUSMA area of interest'.[13] This wide range of topics was often referred to as X-PMESII, indicating that information was to be gathered and analyzed on Political, Military, Economic, Social, Infrastructure and Information domains (again, following NATO conventions). The X (cross) implied that these domains were interconnected and could not be seen separately. Doing this, ASIFU's role is

> …to improve the processing and production of MINUSMA broad information and intelligence in order to have accessible and useable information on time. This will support the decision-making processes on the operational (force headquarters) and tactical (sector

---

[12] For an elaboration on JMACs, see Ramjoué 2011. See also Chap. 8 by Theunens.

[13] PowerPoint presentation by representative of UN Department of Peacekeeping Operations, Carlisle Barracks, United States, 28 January 2015.

headquarters) level. But ASIFU should also be able to support the strategic level: the special representative of the secretary-general through the JMAC and UNDSS.[14]

ASIFU would also collect and analyze information in order to support MINUSMA activities such as:

- The provision of humanitarian aid;
- The recovery and stabilization efforts;
- The facilitation of peace dialogue.[15]

ASIFU headquarters was attached to the UN's mission headquarters in the capital, Bamako, and fell under direct command of MINUSMA's Force Commander. ASIFU's capacity consisted initially of 30 military officers from seven European countries (Denmark, Estonia, Finland, Germany, Norway, Sweden and The Netherlands). In time this capacity would increase to approximately 70 by the end of 2015. The primary units within ASIFU HQ were an Analysis Fusion Cell (AFC), a Collection Coordination and Intelligence Requirements Management (CCIRM) section, several liaison officers and one civilian advisor from the Dutch Ministry of Foreign Affairs.

In addition, ASIFU HQ had two ISR (Intelligence, Surveillance and Reconnaissance) companies under its command that focused on intelligence gathering and analysis. The first company consisted of 55–65 mostly Dutch soldiers[16] and was deployed in the eastern province of Gao from March 2014 onwards. As such it was worked within MINUSMA's Sector East, based at the SHQ. The company had several distinct capabilities including human intelligence (HUMINT), civil-military interaction and Unmanned Aerial Vehicles (UAVs). The second unit was the Swedish ISR Task Force. Its intelligence capacity was approximately twice the size of the Dutch unit and started to operate a year later, in March 2015. It was situated in the western province of Timbuktu and attached to MINUSMA's SHQ West. The capabilities of the Swedish Task Force included, amongst others, military reconnaissance personnel, a weapons intelligence team, and small UAVs.

Finally, MINUSMA's Force Commander had two other important assets largely dedicated to the intelligence process, though not under ASIFU. The first was the Special Operations Land Task Group (SOLTG), a unit of approximately 90 Dutch Special Forces. The second unit was a Dutch helicopter detachment consisting of Apache and Chinook helicopters. Both units operated throughout the entire country but were co-located with the Dutch ISR company in Gao. Figure 9.1 presents the organizational structure of MINUSMA, emphasizing the intelligence components. Figure 9.2 presents a map of the most relevant geographical locations.

---

[14] First Commander ASIFU, Col. Keijsers, cited in Karlsrud and Smith 2015, p. 11.

[15] 1 NLD ISR COY Information Brief. PowerPoint presentation, 13 September 2014.

[16] Several other countries contributed soldiers to the ISR Company, including Belgium, Denmark, Estonia and Switzerland.

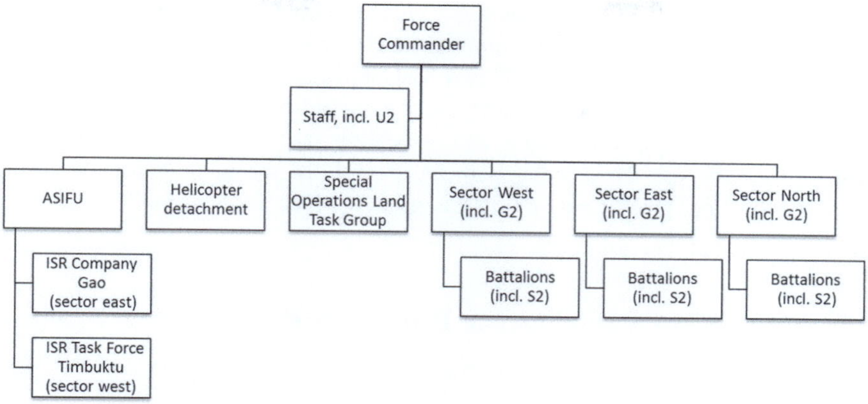

Figure 9.1 MINUSMA Force Intelligence Organisational Structure in 2014–2015. *Source* Compiled from relevant sources by Sebastiaan Rietjens

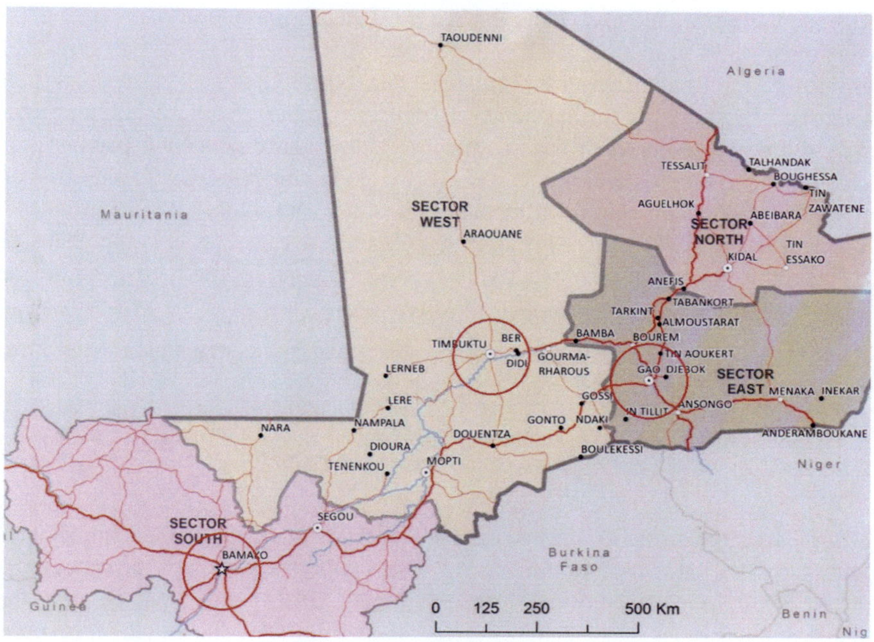

Figure 9.2 Map of Mali with relevant geographical positions. *Source* MUNISMA ASIFU briefing 2015

In order to understand the operation of ASIFU and the mission's other military intelligence units, the researchers on this project conducted 93 semi-structured interviews with key MINUSMA personnel (mostly from The Netherlands) who had been deployed between March 2014 and December 2015. We also analyzed documents from the mission, such as available intelligence reports, standard operating procedures and meeting reports. Lastly, the first author attended several pre-deployment exercises of ASIFU and SOLTG personnel and made a 2.5 week field visit to Mali in late 2015 to observe the mission firsthand. From these various sources, and subsequent feedback and validation, an account of the mission's evolution can be presented along with an analysis of the intelligence cycle (direction, collection, processing and dissemination) within the mission.[17]

9.3 MINUSMA's Intelligence Process in Practice

9.3.1 Direction

When MINUSMA first took over from an African Union force in 2013, the mission's first Force Commander, Major General Jean Bosco Kazura of Rwanda, provided very limited intelligence direction. As there was also no overall campaign plan, the various intelligence units did not have clear information requirements on which they could focus their intelligence efforts. As time progressed, the number of 'top-down' information requirements from the Force Commander and his staff increased. These requirements, however, remained quite broad, ad hoc and generally did not seem to result from a structured intelligence collection plan.

Because of this lack of direction, ASIFU took the initiative to develop an intelligence collection plan based upon the most relevant information requirements that it identified for the Force Commander. Mainly because of its comprehensive character this collection plan had a very broad scope and lacked focus. One of the respondents to our survey described the situation:

> With the best of intentions HQ ASIFU created an ICP [Intelligence Collection Plan] of 75 pages that was not workable in any way. In their ICP they deconstructed the entire Malian society along the lines of each of the PMESII factors [Political, Military, Economic, Social, Infrastructure and Information] and presented that as their information need, very much in line with the traditional intelligence officer sending a request saying 'give me everything about…'

Soon after the arrival of the second Force Commander, Major-General Michael Lollesgaard of Denmark, in May 2015, the intelligence process became more focused. The priority information requirements (PIR) were updated and the underlying questions were better structured. Despite this, the intelligence units found it often very challenging to meet the ambitious information requirements. Moreover, while MINUSMA's regular intelligence capacities (i.e., at the battalions,

[17] To ensure internal validity, four officers and one civilian analyst from The Netherlands and two civilians from Canada who were all closely involved in the mission reviewed draft versions of the paper. The draft versions were met with responses of recognition, as well as reactions indicating that important issues had been revealed.

the sector headquarters and the force headquarters) were tasked to provide current and security-related intelligence, in practice they were largely incapable of doing so, according to a large majority of the respondents. While the units accumulated a wealth of knowledge, the intelligence branches lacked experienced officers, had almost no analysis capacity and did not have adequate technical equipment such as computers. Without sufficient storage and archiving means, each new rotation (typically every 6–8 months) had to start its information collection almost from scratch.

As a result MINUSMA's Force Commander and his sector commanders did not receive proper current intelligence, which was particularly needed on safety and security issues such as the threats along MINUSMA's main supply routes and the presence of armed groups. The fact that from 2013 to 2015 more than 50 peacekeepers had died in Mali and 200 were injured only underlined the call for such intelligence.[18] The lack of current intelligence also affected ASIFU; as a result, ASIFU was pushed to fill this gap, although its mandated task was to provide PMESII-wide intelligence for the mid- and long-term. It remained a challenge to collect and process the required information, despite the fact that the mission had the most elaborate intelligence structure and information-gathering means of any UN mission to date.

9.3.2 *Collection*

To collect information MINUSMA had a great variety of sensors at its disposal. These sensors varied from the typical military battalions to innovative newcomers such as ASIFU and SOLTG. Many African nations contributed troops to MINUSMA, including battalions from Burkina Faso, Chad, Guinea, Niger, Senegal and Togo. These units had great potential to collect relevant information, mainly due to the cultural similarities they had with the Malian population. Language skills were an important part of this, though the extent to which African soldiers mastered French or any of the local languages differed. Furthermore, most of the MINUSMA battalions provided poorly detailed information to their superiors in the Sector Headquarters. This was because these battalions mainly focused on their own convoys and force protection, and executed few patrols or operations. Other reasons that contributed to this were: the illiteracy amongst many African soldiers; their unfamiliarity with Western-style intelligence gathering; and their practice of reporting though their national chains of command rather than sharing information with UN, Malian or international actors. ASIFU put much effort into improving the

[18] MINUSMA fatality statistics: 6 (2013), 39 (2014); 29 (2015), with most fatalities from malicious acts. Statistics available at http://www.un.org/en/peacekeeping/resources/statistics/fatalities.shtml Accessed 8 February 2017; cf. BBC 2015.

information flow coming from some battalions by providing training and handing them tools, such as village assessment formats. These initiatives had mixed results as one of the ASIFU members recalls:

> We have provided many units with [intelligence] training. Together with the French G2 of SHQ East in Gao we went to Nigerbat [the battalion from Niger], and provided the entire intelligence section as well as the platoon commanders with a basic intelligence training. Doing this we hoped that Nigerbat started to report since they didn't do that at all. Unfortunately, this training did not help either. We also provided training to the Bangladesh Riverine Unit. They do report and asked us for [intelligence] formats when they navigate the rivers. We gave these to them and this improved the quality of the incoming information.

The difficulty of getting national peacekeeping troops to contribute to the overall intelligence picture is a long-standing problem in UN missions.[19] It is also one of the main reasons that new and innovative units were brought into MINUSMA. ASIFU was the prime exponent of this development. ASIFU was designed from a Western intelligence perspective. Its headquarters was based in the capital Bamako, but most of its sensors were located within the Dutch and Swedish ISR units. In general, the sensors of the Dutch ISR Company, located in Sector East, focused on PMESII-wide intelligence for the mid- and long-term. The ISR Company put much effort into deriving information from human sources. To do this the ISR Company possessed human intelligence teams, civil-military interaction teams (which was more open with the local population) and mission review and advisory teams (more discrete), as well as liaison personnel. But these were entirely manned by Europeans. Due to their limited capacity and freedom of movement these 'sensors' mainly operated in and around Gao city whereas the entire area of operation was far larger, approximately 170,000 km^2, corresponding roughly with four times the size of Switzerland. However, as Gao city was the central regional hub it attracted many visitors, which enabled the sensors to also collect information from other regions.

The great cultural differences between the European soldiers of the ISR Company and the Malian actors further complicated the gathering of intelligence. Many soldiers were not fully aware of the complexity of the conflict, the history of Mali and the ethnic sensitivities.[20] This hampered them in unravelling the dynamics of the environment and addressing the information requirements they were tasked with. Also, language management greatly influenced the collection of information. There was a lack of interpreters that could speak the many local languages such as Bambara and Tamasheq, and only a few soldiers of the ISR Company had an adequate command of French.

In addition to human intelligence, the ISR Company collected much imagery intelligence. Satellite imagery provided a basis but ASIFU found the available

[19] See e.g. Cammaert 2003.

[20] One of MINUSMA's former field officers commented: "Most of the challenges faced by MINUSMA in the regions were, indeed, mostly linked to local community issues (e.g., economic and political rivalries within and between communities and individuals) and not directly to the peace process. Hence formal institutional frameworks, by themselves, only gave a partial understanding, which impacted MINUSMA activities." Email of 28 August 2016.

imagery too low in resolution so it petitioned for higher resolution imagery.[21] On the ground, imagery was gained by a force protection unit that patrolled with small cameras on their cars and helmets. In the air, imagery came from rail-launched ScanEagle UAVs that had a range of approximately 90 kilometres (limited by line-of-sight communications) and the hand-launched Raven which had a range of 10 km at most. The heat and dust of Mali posed problems for flying and image quality. In addition, the UAV systems suffered from the bureaucratic regulations that the UN enforced.[22] According to these regulations the Dutch Ministry of Defence was reimbursed for deploying the UAVs only after they had been thoroughly checked and approved by the United Nations. The organization had very little experience with UAVs and checked them as if they were standard flying platforms. Questions that were thus asked included: does the pilot of the UAV fulfil his training requirements? Or, does the rear wheel of the UAV function well? Although the UAVs did not have an on-board pilot or a rear wheel, it took the Dutch contingent almost half-a-year to get the UAVs approved and operational. When the UAVs became operational the system was able to collect imagery intelligence that supported many of the units.

In Sector West, in contrast to the Dutch ISR Company, the sensors of the Swedish ISR Task Force were mostly geared towards security-related intelligence for the short term. The Task Force's most important sensors were a reconnaissance platoon, a small UAV squad, an electronic warfare section as well as a 'Weapons Intelligence and Improvised Explosive Device (IED) Disposal Squad,' a term drawn from NATO practice, like ASIFU.

At its headquarters in Bamako, ASIFU only had a few direct sources and sensors to complement the information provided by Dutch and Swedish ISR units. The most prominent was a small Open Source Intelligence (OSINT) section. Rather than relying on classical open sources such as newspapers, radio and television, this section emphasized web-based communities such as Facebook, Twitter, wikis and internet fora.[23] By means of well-structured queries through software programs such as Silobreaker[24] the OSINT section was able to obtain a great amount of relevant information. This included live updates on events such as the Bamako hotel attack in November 2015, video and photo material that was posted on social media (Instagram, Facebook, Twitter), but also more general reports that scholars or think tanks had written on certain topics. Based on this information, the OSINT

---

[21] ASIFU found that it possessed high-resolution (<1.5 m) satellite imagery for only 8 small locations and that for its imagery covering all of Mali the best resolution was 150 m, hardly enough to do intelligence-led peacekeeping, especially within a city or to guide a helicopter or a UAV to a particular target. Especially for automated change detection and to identify emerging threats, higher resolution imagery integrated into a Geographical Information System (GIS) was deemed to be essential. MINUSMA ASIFU 2014.

[22] Van Dalen 2015.

[23] MINUSMA ASIFU PowerPoint presentation, September 24, 2015. Bamako.

[24] Silobreaker is a browser-based tool that structures open source information available on the internet.

section was frequently able to get in-depth information on specific issues, locate individuals such as local leaders by analysing the geo-tags of their posts on social media, as well as to get indications of the public opinion on certain matters or events (e.g. through twitter analyses).

In addition to ASIFU, the helicopter detachment and the SOLTG (special forces unit) contributed significantly to the mission's information gathering. The Apache helicopters of The Netherlands are, arguably, the most sophisticated helicopters ever placed in a UN mission. They were equipped with advanced Forward-looking Infra-Red (FLIR) sensors and a Target Acquisition Designation Sight (TADS), with an excellent detection range, both forward and peripheral. The attack helicopters saw their first combat on 20 January 2015 in response to rebels firing close to peacekeepers and civilians while conducting an offensive on the town of Tabankort.[25] After firing warning shots and seeing no diminution of rebel fire, the helicopter engaged and successfully destroyed the rocket launcher. Unfortunately, less than 2 months later, an Apache helicopter crashed in an accident owing to a technical cause and resulting in the loss of the two crew members.[26]

The helicopters were able to cover large distances in short periods of time, which was a crucial capability given Mali's difficult terrain. Helicopter personnel and sensors collected some very important pieces of information (e.g., the positions of armed groups) that the Special Representative of the Secretary-General (SRSG) and the Force Commander could use during the peace negotiations. Executing covert operations, however, proved to be nearly impossible for the helicopter detachment as there were insufficient hiding places and the solid ground (usually thinly covered by sand) meant that the sound of helicopters reverberated tremendously. Moreover, due to the high costs to deploy helicopters, UN Headquarters restricted the monthly hours these helicopters spent on ISR flights.

The SOLTG collected much information through multiday operations.[27] During these operations the Special Forces visited several communities at long distances from their base in Gao. This was a task that few other UN units could perform, given the remote locations of some of these communities, far from UN bases and normal patrol routes. The Special Forces held many meetings with a variety of people, including military commanders, police chiefs, political leaders, leaders of 'terrorist' armed groups and local villagers. In addition to these multiday operations some SOLTG soldiers collected open source intelligence (OSINT) by following a number of well-informed journalists, both local and international, on Twitter. A third way the SOLTG collected data was through telephone exchange with locals. A unit commander remarked:

> We gave them [the local people] our telephone numbers. And when we were in the [general] neighbourhood and they called us because of banditry or something like that, a French-speaking person in Gao answered the phone. We were then informed and could pass

---

[25] United Nations 2015; Lewis and Farge 2015.

[26] New York Times, 17 March 2015.

[27] For a detailed analysis see Rietjens and Zomer (forthcoming).

> by one day later. By this we established a telephone circle of which we retrieved much information from political and local leaders.

Since both the helicopter detachment and the SOLTG were under direct command of MINUSMA's Force Commander and the battalions were under command of the Sector commanders (see Fig. 9.1), ASIFU did not have the authority to send out data collection taskings to these units. The information flow from the SOLTG and the helicopter detachment to ASIFU was thus not self-evident and heavily relied on informal agreements and relationships (depending on 'who you know'). At times this situation proved to be detrimental to the intelligence structure's effectiveness as decisions on whether and when to share information with ASIFU were made on a case-to-case, ad hoc basis. The mission brought in new Standard Operating Procedures (SOPs) to help with information gathering, sharing and analysis.

There were, however, also positive aspects to the direct command and control that the Force Commander had with both the SOLTG and the helicopter detachment. The speedy communication enabled the Force Commander in several instances to react promptly to the incoming intelligence. The chief of SOLTG's intelligence section illustrated this as follows:

> We received information from the field that two parties were at the brink of fighting each other. This had not yet happened since we [the SOLTG] were present in the area. This kind of information will be reported [to the Force Commander] immediately with the following comment: 'we assess that when there are no UN troops in the area to take our positions, heavy fighting will take place… possibly with civilian casualties.

A final innovation for information collection that should be mentioned is the aerostat. This tethered balloon was deployed for the first time in the history of UN peacekeeping and was sent aloft with a high-resolution camera as the payload. The French company Thales was contracted to assemble the system, including the large balloon above the UN's base in Kidal to observe in a persistent fashion, observing 24/7 unlike UAVs. The primary purpose of the aerostat was to warn of attacks.[28] One such attack came at daybreak on 12 February 2016 in a complex attack on the Kidal camp using mortars, rockets and a ground attack. Soldiers from Mali and MINUSMA intervened to neutralize the attackers but not in time to prevent significant casualties: six peacekeepers from Guinea were killed and 30 others were wounded. Furthermore, major damage occurred to the camp[29] and the shrapnel from the explosions damaged the aerostat that was flying over 300 m in the air.[30] Still the balloon stayed aloft. But this highlighted the vulnerability of aerostats not only to direct fire but also to attacks

---

[28] "With all the new information coming in, one of the main problems was to interpret the data. For instance, 'how do you know if a vehicle heading towards MINUSMA is a vehicle-borne improvised explosive device (VBIED) or a contractor's car?'" Email from former MINUSMA civilian staff member, 28 August 2016.

[29] A photograph of the damage is available at http://www.unmultimedia.org/photo/detail.jsp?id=664/664068. A video taken the day after shows the aerostat still in the air. MINUSMA 2016.

[30] United Nations 2016.

on the ground. The contracted company, Thales, was not able to repair the balloon for many months. Later, the aerostat succumbed to a sand storm. The United Nations realized that the overall expense of the large aerostat (especially to transport helium) meant that smaller balloons would be preferable in the future.

In sum, it is clear that MINUSMA units collected a tremendous amount of information, and had the inherent capability to collect more. Processing all this turned out to be quite challenging.

9.3.3 Processing

MINUSMA contained several different intelligence staff branches that were tasked to process the information collected by the sensors. These staff branches were at the battalion level (S2), the sector headquarters level (G2) and the force headquarters level (U2), as mentioned above. According to many interviewees (both from these branches themselves as well as from outside units) most of these branches had great difficulty adding much value to the incoming information. There were several reasons for this. Most intelligence staff branches had very limited personnel, let alone experienced intelligence personnel. Within the battalions and at the sector headquarters this problem was most prevalent. At MINUSMA's headquarter the U2 branch consisted of approximately 15 persons, but most of them did not have experience in the field of intelligence. Meanwhile, ASIFU HQ had expanded to a total of 70 persons. Most of these were trained European intelligence officers. However, according to MINUSMA's organizational structure, the U2 was supposed to direct the work of ASIFU on behalf of the commander. This resulted in much friction between the intelligence staff of the U2 branch and ASIFU HQ as both units believed themselves to be in charge of MINUSMA's intelligence activities. For ASIFU this was because of its qualitative and quantitative advantage, while the U2 branch believed itself to be in charge because of its position in the hierarchy.

Also, at the lower levels the command and control structure was not functioning properly. The fact that in mid-2015 the G2 section of Sector HQ East did not even know the S2 officers of its own battalions was a clear example illustrating this problem.[31] Rather than processing the incoming information within western-style intelligence branches, many African troop contributing countries considered intelligence to be a matter for commanding officers only. A respondent of the U2 formulated this as follows:

> As soon as a patrol discovers something, they immediately tell their chief. This chief reports it to his commander – even if he is the battalion commander. This commander immediately calls the commander of the sector headquarters. And if you are unlucky the Sector commander reports it to the Force Commander. And when the Force Commander sits in the daily morning briefing and listens to the U2 he might say: 'no way, because I heard this and that.'

---

[31] Interview with a captain of the ISR Company by one of the authors.

There was also a major problem with the databases used to store and share information. Like many UN missions, MINUSMA employed the UN's standard database, SAGE (Situational Awareness Geospatial Enterprise), which is based on the Ushahidi software platform for incident tracking and visualization. It was available mostly to headquarters unit and some officials with access, including within the JOC and JMAC, viewed it as cumbersome, inflexible, and insufficient for creative analysis. ASIFU employed a Dutch system, TITAAN,[32] and the two databases could not 'talk' to each other, unable to convey information in real time. Also the Dutch database had classification requirements that SAGE could not meet. This meant that data would have to be entered twice, which was unacceptable to the already burdened mission. Also TITAAN required specific computer terminals and systems, which rarely existed in field locations. Most troublesome was that, TITAAN information could not be shared with other mission units but only with persons from NATO countries with the appropriate level of clearance. This meant that sharing could only be done officially after information was declassified or downgraded ('sanitized' in intelligence speak), placing an additional strain on ASIFU and diminishing its utility for various members of the mission leadership.[33] Still, some valuable intelligence could be passed on after appropriate processing.

To help process all the information that it obtained, ASIFU contained analysis fusion cells,[34] one at ASIFU HQ and the other at the Dutch ISR Company. Both cells consisted of 12–16 persons and included collators, technicians and different kinds of analysts including military analysts, geospatial analysts and human terrain analysts. These often highly-educated officers composed many different and thorough intelligence reports. Most of these reports were aimed at mid- to long-term.

The most prominent intelligence report that ASIFU made was the so-called the 'Quarterly Outlook.' Based on an extensive scenario analysis every 3 months ASIFU produced this intelligence report to predict the future status of Mali.[35] The reports tended to be very comprehensive in nature, including not only information about the armed groups, but also about tribal tensions, smuggling routes and the perception of the Malian population towards MINUSMA. ASIFU made assessments of the likely places of 'greatest potential for violence' and of civil unrest. Furthermore, ASIFU reports included some creative scenario-building, e.g., for the possible outcomes of peace negotiations held in Algiers.

---

[32] When the original system was created in the US, TITAAN stood for "Theatre Independent Tactical Army and Air Force Network" but in The Netherlands version it was renamed "Theatre Independent Tactical Adaptive Armed Forces Network," with the same acronym.

[33] For example, the Under-Secretary-General for Peacekeeping, Hervé Ladsous, obtained agreement in 2014 from Mauritania's President to provide two intelligence officers for the Mali mission but only realized later that they could not be put into ASIFU because the unit held information and equipment that only NATO countries were allowed to access (Ladsous 2016).

[34] Within the Dutch ISR Company this cell was coined the All Sources Intelligence Cell (ASIC), while at ASIFU HQ such a cell was named the Analysis Fusion Cell (AFC).

[35] ASIFU information brief, PowerPoint presentation, November 2015, Bamako.

However, unlike the expectations, very little sharing took place between the analysts of ASIFU's fusion cells and the many civilian experts that worked within other parts of the MINUSMA intelligence sections. According to many respondents more collaboration could have significantly increased the quality of ASIFU's comprehensive reports. This would be even more true if collaboration was gained with experts in the 'country team,' i.e., the UN agencies and programmes outside MINUSMA. Also, the traditional tension between the peacekeeping mission and UN humanitarian actors remains an obstacle.[36] Still, efforts at overcoming these obstacles were made. For instance, in Gao, weekly meetings were eventually initiated between the Dutch military ISR analysts and a number of civilians to gain a broader understanding.

The Swedish Task Force, operating from the Sector West, was also part of ASIFU but it did not have a similar comprehensive focus. As mentioned, this unit emphasized short-term security-related intelligence. To process its information it had a *military source information cell* consisting of a few military analysts. The intelligence reports this cell made therefore focused at the security threats such as the situation along the main supply routes and the disposition and leadership of armed groups. In an attempt to increase the comprehensiveness of their reports, the Swedish Task Force creatively tasked some of its support staff. The legal advisor, for example, made an extensive overview of the rule of law in Sector West, while its pastor composed a report on tribal groups.

As opposed to the Dutch ISR Company, the Swedish Task Force did not share its single-sensor reports with ASIFU HQ. The United Nations considered this as a national caveat and the Dutch commander of ASIFU was simply not able to enforce information reporting upon his Swedish subordinate, the commander of the ISR Task Force. As a result ASIFU HQ only received the processed reports of the Swedish unit and could not collate the raw data in ASIFU-Sector West's database. Tensions arose between the intelligence officers from The Netherlands and Sweden, something even noted by UN officials at UN Headquarters in New York.[37] Despite a major bottleneck for single-sensor information within ASIFU, the passage of information from ASIFU, including the Swedish contributions, to the Force Commander was steady.

9.3.4 Dissemination

Since ASIFU was a new concept within the UN, the leadership of ASIFU put great effort in creating awareness about its role and the potential added value. ASIFU produced several types of reports, which were primarily disseminated to the Force

---

[36] For a more general overview of the tension between military and humanitarian actors during peacekeeping operations, see Lucius and Rietjens 2016.

[37] UN official in New York in correspondence with one of the authors in 2016.

Commander. These reports were rarely shared downwards and only sometimes shared upwards, with the SRSG. But by doing so, ASIFU tried to position itself as an intelligence unit that produced valuable reports at the strategic level and to improve its integration into MINUSMA's decision-making processes. On several occasions, however, ASIFU's initiatives to disseminate its intelligence products directly to the SRSG led to friction with other units at the MINUSMA's headquarters. Such friction was most obvious with MINUSMA's JMAC that was tasked to deliver analytical reports directly to the SRSG.

To improve this situation and better coordinate all intelligence-related activities MINUSMA installed a Joint Coordination Board in 2015. This board is chaired by the chief of JMAC and includes representatives of JMAC, ASIFU, U2, United Nations Department of Safety and Security (UNDSS), U3 (the Force Commander's operations staff), United Nations Police (UNPOL), JOC and the office of the SRSG. The weekly meetings of the JCB facilitate communication as well as prevent duplication of effort between the different actors. The JCB, however, is a coordinating body only and has no directive powers, which clearly limits its effectiveness.

The Dutch company as well as Swedish ISR units disseminated their analytical products to ASIFU HQ as well as to their respective Sector Headquarters. In particular the Dutch ISR Company also disseminated many of its comprehensive products to civilian UN components within the Sector Headquarters who, over time, developed a strong interest in the company's intelligence products. The weekly civil-military coordination meetings that the ISR company organized and to which it invited several civilian MINUSMA representatives,[38] clearly facilitated this and increased the attention paid to the ISR company's activities, products and potential. The Swedish Task Force provided much valuable information on IEDs and weapons that the armed groups used. By making use of their weapons intelligence lab, Swedish forensic experts were able to identify several suspects as well as preventively disarm explosives, which most probably saved lives of MINUSMA personnel and others.[39]

Apart from disseminating full reports ASIFU also provided answers to specific questions that many outsiders had. The extensive database that ASIFU had developed over time proved to be of great value. As one UNPOL representative argues:

> We do not have a decent database. I'm still waiting for an iBase-structure with adequate search functions. As long as we do not have that, I'm very happy that ASIFU is able to structurally record the information. We can then make requests to get information such as names.

All in all, the extent to which 'customers' (intelligence-speak for the receivers of intelligence reports) appreciated the intelligence products of ASIFU and its subunits

[38] These included amongst others representatives of JMAC, Stabilization and Reconstruction and Protection of Civilians.

[39] This information was retrieved from several interviews with Dutch respondents as well as with Swedish representatives at ASIFU HQ.

varied considerably. Several civilian components of MINUSMA such as Protection of Civilians and Human Rights Division frequently expressed their gratitude and admiration for the tailor-made reports they received.[40] And as expressed above, also ASIFU's database was widely considered to be of substantial value.

On the other hand, ASIFU's reporting frequently did not satisfy the intelligence needs of its main client, the Force Commander, or of the sector commanders. These officers emphasized their need for current and security-related intelligence as this affected MINUSMA's force most,[41] while ASIFU's products were often comprehensive in nature and had a longer-term focus. This heavily impacted the extent to which ASIFU's products were taken into account in MINUSMA's decision-making process. A second main reason why the Force Headquarters in Bamako made only limited use of ASIFU's intelligence products was because it simply lacked the means to follow-up ASIFU's comprehensive and mid- to long-term intelligence estimates. Most UN troops had a hard time sustaining and protecting themselves and therefore had only limited possibilities and interest to carry out intelligence-driven operations.

9.4 Challenges as Dichotomies

MINUSMA's intelligence capacity was (and remains) unprecedented within the history of the United Nations. In addition to the regular intelligence organizations (like JMAC and U2), MINUSMA added several innovative units: ASIFU (with two ISR units), the helicopter detachment and the SOLTG. MINUSMA's intelligence capacity made significant contributions to the military as well as the civilian actors within MINUSMA. However, despite the extensive intelligence capacity, the analysis shows that the attempt to gain comprehensive intelligence has not been without its challenges. These can be expressed as three dichotomies. The first is that of the regular intelligence capacities and the innovative newcomers. While the European countries brought in the innovative intelligence capabilities including technologies and tactics, techniques and procedures (TTPs), these were heavily based on NATO procedures and standards, and requiring systems to uphold information security. The systems were linked to classified NATO intelligence systems and meant that peacekeepers from non-NATO countries could not have direct access to them. By contrast, the regular intelligence capacities of the main force were densely populated with African soldiers who had the cultural familiarity and mastered many of the locally spoken languages. Finding ways to better marry the Western and African capabilities could lead to many future improvements.

---

[40] Van Dalen 2015.

[41] At the morning briefs of the Force Commander's staff at MINUSMA headquarters, the U2 was tasked with describing the "Opposing Forces Situation" while the U3 would deal with the "Friendly Forces."

The second dichotomy is that of intelligence related to current security threats versus mid- to long-term comprehensive intelligence. The analysis shows that several intelligence units, most notably ASIFU HQ and the Dutch ISR Company, produced wide-ranging reports focusing on the longer term. Meanwhile, however, MINUSMA's military leadership valued current and security-related intelligence most, but that was insufficiently available within the organization. The case showed that when the operational environment became more dangerous the military had a tendency, naturally, to prioritize current and security-related intelligence at the cost of mid- to long-term comprehensive intelligence. This accords to the commonly observed tension in peace operations between an orientation on mission success versus an orientation on force protection. Michael Walzer[42] refers to this as the 'risk dilemma' in which he poses the critical question: 'how much risk must our soldiers take to reduce the risks they impose on civilians when they respond to those [insurgent and terrorist] attacks?'

The third and last dichotomy is that of the military and civilian actors within MINUSMA's intelligence process (counting police as civilians). The contributions of both sides were largely stovepiped and lacked sufficient sharing, coordination and integration. This applies to the relationship between ASIFU and JMAC as well as to the interaction between the military intelligence capacities and the civilian analysts that worked within MINUSMA's civilian organizations. The reasons underlying this were organizational (e.g. civil and military organizations operated in different command and control structures), political (e.g. both JMAC, ASIFU and UNDSS were eager to be the first to provide MINUSMA's leadership with relevant information) as well as technical (e.g. technical systems such as TITAAN hampered smooth sharing of information between ASIFU and the civilian organizations).

9.5 Conclusions

The Mali mission has served as an important 'intelligence laboratory' for the United Nations, as the world organization tied out more advanced intelligence concepts (NATO-style) and capabilities than ever employed before in UN missions, in particular ASIFU. With its authorized strength totalling some 450 personnel, ASIFU had two dedicated ISR companies under its command, located in Gao and Timbuktu. It conducted sophisticated analyses of trends and people/social networks, developed scenarios, and managed advanced GIS-platforms. It made predictive estimates, from near-term to 3 years in the future.

At this point, however, the experiment can only be called a mixed success. ASIFU was considered an 'outsider' within the mission, mostly because the information coming from its database (TITAAN) could not be readily shared with the rest of the mission, especially mission leaders and peacekeepers from

[42] Walzer 2016, pp. 289–293.

non-NATO countries who formed the bulk of MINUSMA's troops.[43] Also the United Nations lacked the secure communications system needed to transfer and store TITAAN information. Thus ASIFU took in much more information than it could release. In addition, it used NATO procedures and analysis methods (X-PMESII) that were foreign to the world organization, especially to military personnel from non-NATO countries (including the first force commander). The UN is seeking in 2016/17 to reform MINUSMA's intelligence architecture to allow for better information sharing and less isolated stove-pipes in the mission.

MINUSMA has already made important steps to overcome the disjunction in its disparate intelligence units. As mentioned earlier MINUSMA created a Joint Coordination Board (JCB) in 2015 to better coordinate intelligence-related activities. Another helpful step is the upcoming colocation of ASIFU and the force headquarters, and ASIFU's placement under the U2. Until mid-2016 ASIFU HQ was located close to Bamako airport, while the force headquarters resided within MINUSMA headquarters in downtown Bamako (Hotel L'Amitié). Transportation took at least 30 min, but (far) more during peak hours, which greatly hampered interaction. With the move of MINUSMA's force headquarters to a newly built super-camp at the airport, this is expected to improve. The downside to this development is that MINUSMA's civilian organizations remain located in downtown Bamako, which will probably increase the challenge of civil-military coordination. To further overcome the institutional stovepipes, the mission will need to move from 'need to know' to one of 'need to share', given that MINUSMA is a multidimensional peace operation. As a step forward, the TITAAN system has already been replaced by a UN-contracted Mali Mission Secure Network.

There is also room for technological improvement, even though the intelligence sections were the best equipped of any UN mission to date. In future, the image intelligence (IMINT), gathered by the military, UAVs and from commercial satellites, could be disseminated in real-time and funnelled directly to ground troops, with real-time analysis to assist in current operations.

Some persons in MINUSMA felt there was too much information in the mission and that intelligence was over-resourced, an unusual complaint in peacekeeping. But the fault lay more in the interface with the mission, and within ASIFU, where even the components did not share the most important or relevant information seamlessly. As mentioned, the most glaring problem was the inability to share information directly from ASIFU database to non-NATO countries, including Sweden that was the second largest contributor to ASIFU. Sweden, in return, did not share its single-sensor intelligence reports. Similarly inhibitions existed with JMAC and the French counterterrorism operation Barkhane that operated in large parts of northern Mali and the larger Sahel region. At both interfaces there were, apart from the technical reasons, also political, organizational as well as personal

[43] Abilova and Novosseloff 2016.

reasons that determined how much information was being shared.[44] In the give-and-take of the intelligence world, the more information is given to a partner unit, the more the unit is willing to provide information in return. As in many UN missions, stovepiping became the norm for the mission.

This was also true for the smaller intelligence units, such as the U2 or the battalion intelligence units. They had much more rudimentary data-sharing systems, mostly based on Excel spreadsheets, and Word/pdf files and depended on keyword searches of thousands of files. A more centralized common database, with the coordinated management of information would help considerably (e.g., similar to the UN's Sharepoint or NATO's WISEPAGE).

A lack of intelligence integration can have fatal consequences on the ground, both for the UN peacekeepers and the population they are mandated to protect. For early warning and quick response, e.g., for attacks on mission personnel and civilians, rapid information-sharing is needed. Not only mission personnel, but the local population can benefit from information sharing. In population-centric operations, a 'coalition of the connected' can be formed to provide 'protection through connection.' Also needed is the capacity for deeper analysis, which ASIFU amply demonstrated, including scenario-building and predictive analytics. For both purposes, the use of new software tools could be further explored.[45] In conclusion, a mission-wide approach is needed within MINUSMA to leverage the capabilities of intelligence in peace operations. But significant progress has been made to demonstrate how intelligence can be used in a peace operation. Despite the flawed incorporation of ASIFU into the mission, the unit showed how deeper analysis can be done in the field. The quest for comprehensive intelligence will continue both in MINUSMA and the United Nations more generally, as the international community seeks ways to field effective peace and stability operations in the challenging environments of war-torn lands.

References

Abilova O, Novosseloff A (2016) Demystifying Intelligence in UN Peace Operations: Toward an Organizational Doctrine. International Peace Institute, New York, https://www.ipinst.org/2016/07/demystifying-intelligence-in-un-peace-ops Accessed 3 August 2016.

---

[44] The interviews revealed that there was very little communication between Barkhane and the Dutch ISR Company. Most of the communication with Barkhane went through the SOLTG that was co-located with the ISR Company in Gao. Both Barkhane and SOLTG were special operations units and as a result their people trusted each other much more. Still, personal connections depended to a large extent what and how much information was being shared between Barkhane and SOLTG. In general Barkhane was very reserved in sharing information. And if they did, it was mostly for "SOLTG eyes" only. In some cases the SOLTG shared information they had received from Barkhane with their ISR colleagues, but this was incidentally.

[45] MINUSMA was one of several UN mission selected to trial i2 software. It was being rolled out in early 2016. Other software can be adopted from NATO but the lesson from TITAAN is that such software needs to be adequately customized and re-purposed for the United Nations.

BBC (2015) World's most dangerous peacekeeping mission, 20 November 2015 http://www.bbc.com/news/world-africa-34812600 Accessed 31 July 2016.

Cammaert PC (2003) Intelligence in Peacekeeping Operations: Lessons for the Future. In: De Jong B, Platje W, Steele RD (eds) Peacekeeping Intelligence: Emerging Concepts for the Future. OSS International Press, Oakton, pp. 11–30.

Dorn AW (2010) United Nations Peacekeeping Intelligence. In: Johnson LK (ed) Oxford Handbook of National Security Intelligence. Oxford University Press, Oxford, pp. 275–295.

Flynn MT, Pottinger M, Batchelor PD (2010) Fixing Intell: A Blueprint for Making Intelligence Relevant in Afghanistan. Center for a New American Security, Washington.

Flynn MT, Sisco J, Ellis DC (2012) Left of Bang: The Value of Sociocultural Analysis in Today's Environment. Prism 3,4:13–21.

Karlsrud J, Smith AC (2015) Europe's Return to UN Peacekeeping in Africa? Lessons from Mali. Providing for Peacekeeping, No. 11. International Peace Institute, New York.

Kitzen M (2012) Close encounters of the tribal kind: The implementation of cooption as a tool for de-escalation of conflict: the case of the Netherlands in Afghanistan's Uruzgan province. In: Journal of Strategic Studies 35(5):713–734.

Kitzen M, Rietjens SJH, Osinga F (2013) Soft Power, the Hard Way: Adaptation by the Netherlands' Task Force Uruzgan. In: Farrel T, Osinga F, Russell J (eds) Military adaptation in Afghanistan. Stanford University Press, Stanford, pp. 159–191.

Ladsous H (2016) Policy Forum on Demystifying Intelligence in UN Peace Operations. International Peace Institute, 18 July 2016, www.ustream.tv/recorded/89734943, 1:16:00.

Lewis D, Farge E (2015) Dutch UN attack helicopters strike Mali rebels in north. http://www.reuters.com/article/us-mali-fighting-un-idUSKBN0KT29520150120 Accessed 27 August 2016.

Lucius G, Rietjens SJH (2016) Effective Civil-Military Interaction in Peace Operations –Theory and Practice. Springer, Berlin.

MINUSMA (2016) Visite au camp de la MINUSMA à Kidal le lendemain de l'attaque du 12 février 2016 (published 18 February 2016) https://www.youtube.com/watch?v=vP5Dnm1s5L4 Accessed 8 February 2017.

MINUSMA ASIFU (2014) Why is satellite imagery important for MINUSMA? Special Report, 2 September 2014.

New York Times (2015) Mali: 2 Peacekeepers Die in Crash. 17 March 2015. http://www.nytimes.com/2015/03/18/world/africa/mali-2-peacekeepers-die-in-crash.html?_r=0 Accessed 8 February 2017.

Norheim-Martinsen PM, Ravndal JA (2011) Towards Intelligence-Driven Peace Operations? The Evolution of UN and EU Intelligence Structures. International Peacekeeping 18(4):454–467.

Perugini N (2008) Anthropologists at War: Ethnographic Intelligence and Counter-Insurgency in Iraq and Afghanistan. In: International Political Anthropology 1(2):213–227.

Ramjoué M (2011) Improving UN Intelligence through Civil–Military Collaboration: Lessons from the Joint Mission Analysis Centres. International Peacekeeping 18(4):468–484.

Rietjens SJH, Zomer J (forthcoming) In search for intelligence: The Dutch Special Forces in Mali. In: Glicken Turnley J, Michael K, Ben-Ari E (eds) Special Operations Forces (SOF) around the World: Perspectives from the Social Sciences. Routledge, London.

Spencer E, Balasevicius T (2009) Crucible of success: cultural intelligence and the modern battlespace. Canadian Military Journal 9(3):40–48.

United Nations (2015a) MINUSMA Facts and Figures. http://www.un.org/en/peacekeeping/missions/minusma/facts.shtml Accessed 15 April 2015.

United Nations (2015b) Report of the UN Secretary-General on the Situation in Mali. UN Doc. S/2015/219, 27 March 2015.

United Nations (2016) Security Council Press Statement on Mali 12 February 2016, UN Doc. SC/12240-AFR/3322-PKO/561 http://www.un.org/press/en/2016/sc12240.doc.htm Accessed 1 August 2016.

United Nations, Department of Peacekeeping Operations (2006) DPKO Policy Directive on Joint Operations Centres and Joint Mission Analysis Centres, Ref. POL/2006/3000/04, 1 July 2006]. United Nations, New York.
UNmultimedia.org (2016) Head of MINUSMA Visits Kidal Following Fatal Attack http://www.unmultimedia.org/photo/detail.jsp?id=664/664068. http://www.un.org/en/peacekeeping/resources/statistics/fatalities.shtml Accessed 8 February 2017.
Van Dalen JA (2015) ASIFU: Baanbrekend inlichtingenexperiment in Mali. [ASIFU: A pioneering intelligence experiment in Mali]. Militaire Spectator 184 (7/8):306–320.
Walzer M (2016) The Risk Dilemma. In: Philosophia, 44(2):289–293.
World Health Organization (2015) 'Ebola Situations Report,' 21 January 2015 http://apps.who.int/iris/bitstream/10665/149314/1/roadmapsitrep_21Jan2015_eng.pdf?ua=1. Accessed 1 July 2016.

Author Biographies

Sebastiaan Rietjens is an associate professor at the Netherlands Defence Academy and a reserve major in the Netherlands army. He has done extensive fieldwork in military exercises and operations (Afghanistan, Mali) and has published in *Disasters, Armed Forces and Society, International Journal of Public Administration* and *Construction Management and Economics*. His main research focus is on civil-military interaction, intelligence, effectiveness of military operations as well as humanitarian and military logistics. Sebastiaan is a member of the editorial boards of *Armed Forces and Society,* the *Journal of Humanitarian Logistics and Supply Chain Management* and editor of volumes on civil-military interaction (Ashgate, 2008; Springer, 2016), research methods in the military domain (Routledge, 2014), and organizing safety and security (TMC Asser Press, 2016).

A. Walter Dorn, professor of Defence Studies at the Royal Military College of Canada and the Canadian Forces College. He specializes in arms control, peace operations, just war theory, international criminal law, and the United Nations. As an 'operational professor' he participates in field missions and assists international organizations. For instance, he was a UN Electoral Officer for the 1999 referendum in East Timor and a Visiting Professional with the International Criminal Court (ICC) in 2010. He also served as a consultant with the UN's Department of Peacekeeping Operations, including on the Expert Panel on Technology and Innovation in UN Peacekeeping. His two most recent books are *Air Power in UN Operations: Wings for Peace (Ashgate, 2014)* and *Keeping Watch: Monitoring, Technology, and Innovation in UN Peace Operations* (UNU Press, 2011).

Chapter 10
Intelligence Accountability in a Globalizing World. Towards an Instrument of Measuring Effectiveness

Eleni Braat and Floribert Baudet

Abstract This chapter discusses the 'accountability gap' with regard to international intelligence cooperation. As a result of globalisation, and especially after 9/11, this cooperation has become vital for national security. But as mechanisms of oversight and accountability are national only, they have had trouble keeping track of these developments. The chapter discusses the reasons why intelligence accountability is problematic, and proposes an innovative analytical instrument for closing this gap.

Keywords Accountability · Globalisation · Historical research

Contents

E.C. Braat (✉)
Utrecht University, Utrecht, The Netherlands
e-mail: e.c.braat@uu.nl

F. Baudet
Netherlands Defence Academy, Breda, The Netherlands
e-mail: FH.Baudet@mindef.nl

F. Baudet et al. (eds.), *Perspectives on Military Intelligence from the First World War to Mali*, DOI 10.1007/978-94-6265-183-8_10

10.1 Introduction

Democracies are embedded in the rule of law and in the principle of transparency. Security and intelligence agencies[1] often require exemptions from domestic law, and a substantial amount of operational secrecy. This exceptionalism risks isolating intelligence agencies from the political, public and legal realm. Moreover, as we know that power may corrupt its holder, the isolated and inward-looking environment of intelligence agencies further increases the risk of corruption. Democracies need oversight or review instruments, which increase the political and public accountability of intelligence. Oversight and review instruments assume the task of keeping intelligence under democratic control when transparency conflicts with intelligence capability to the extent of thwarting intelligence work. The resulting accountability serves three purposes: first, it enables citizens to control and monitor government conduct. Second, it prevents executive abuse. And three, it enhances effectiveness and a learning capacity with the executive branch.[2]

However, the marked increase in international intelligence cooperation after 9/11 has contributed to disengagement of the intelligence sector from existing accountability mechanisms, which remain mostly nationally oriented. Intelligence laws in Europe are often more demanding concerning agencies' activities within the national borders, while the collection of intelligence abroad is not regulated with the same rigor. Cooperation between agencies could well serve to circumvent domestic legislation. Citizens increasingly display mistrust about the effects of globalisation both on security and on intelligence agencies. Some argue that in insecure times privacy needs to come second, whereas others fear a Big Brother-type apparatus that needs to be curtailed and controlled.

We argue that the ensuing accountability deficit is partly due to the large transnational variations in degrees of intelligence accountability. In this chapter we develop an instrument to systematically assess the effectiveness of intelligence accountability mechanisms. By 'effective' accountability mechanisms we mean those that are concerned with the requirements of both intelligence agencies, which tend toward greater secrecy, and democratic institutions, which tend toward greater openness. Our instrument will facilitate transnational comparisons and contribute to a smaller accountability deficit.

We first analyse obstacles to intelligence accountability and how the 9/11 attacks outpaced the development since the 1970s towards firmer accountability mechanisms. We then develop an instrument for systematically assessing effective intelligence accountability, drawing on criteria in the fields of internal oversight and review (control), which focuses on the executive, and external oversight and review, which regards external actors.

---

[1] Henceforward, we will refer to 'intelligence agencies', meaning both security and intelligence agencies.

[2] Aucoin and Heintzman 2000, pp. 244–245.

Within internal oversight and review instruments we distinguish the relevance of (a) a clear ministerial responsibility for the intelligence community, (b) ministerial expertise regarding intelligence issues, (c) internal historical research as a means of providing accountability in retrospect, (d) contractual academic research, and (e) the declassification of archives that allows others to draw conclusions on the agencies' past.

Within external oversight and review instruments we stress the relevance of (a) sufficient powers and independence of external oversight and review committees, (b) their professional attitude vis-à-vis secrecy, and (c) a proactive stance of committee members.

This model contributes to a rationalization of the debate on intelligence accountability, transcending more common and popular debates on accountability overloads and deficits. It facilitates comparisons of national accountability mechanisms and suggests how to deal with these national variations, by proposing a number of requirements of effective intelligence accountability. The innovative character of this chapter is twofold: first, it focuses on both external actors outside the executive and the executive itself, as players who can both contribute to making intelligence agencies more accountable. Surprisingly, the share of the executive in making itself accountable is largely glossed over in the existing literature on intelligence accountability.[3] Second, this chapter proposes to look beyond the traditional and current judicial character of oversight and review instruments, and explore the merits of historical research as a form of accountability in retrospect with temporally and thematically broader perspectives than the judicial approach.

The morally high reputation of the concept of accountability makes us believe that accountability is a worthy goal to pursue no matter what.[4] However, accountability, in the field of intelligence more particularly, has both advantages and disadvantages. Rendering an agency accountable increases the political trust in its functioning and strengthens its political legitimacy.[5] Political 'outsiders' will arguably feel more involved in intelligence matters, developing a sense of ownership regarding the topic. Lastly, greater accountability may also lead to less corruption and incompetency, as it renders malfunctioning more transparent. However, accountability mechanisms, especially in the field of intelligence, may be expensive. Means for secure communication, security clearances, and investment in joint technological equipment are costly and may hamper effectiveness.

Critics refer to a growing 'accountability industry' and an 'accountability overload', paralyzing the effectiveness of organisations and, in the intelligence sector, reducing the operational clout. As Bovens, Schillemans and 't Hart note

---

[3] Born and Leigh 2007; Eskens et al. 2015; Ott 2003; Phythian 2007.

[4] Bovens 2010.

[5] On the relationship between trust and acceptance from a socio-psychological perspective, see: Malone and Fiske 2013; Terwel et al. 2011.

regarding public accountability arrangements in general, both supporters and critics of intelligence accountability are largely driven by impressions and incidents.[6] In the field of intelligence the significance of impressions and incidents may be even greater due to the secrecy involved. From the public and legislative perspective, secrecy may lead to irritation, suspicion, distrust and curiosity vis-à-vis those who have the secret, instigating calls for transparency and accountability.[7]

From the perspective of intelligence agencies, public challenges to their use of secrecy may lead to reactions of feeling misunderstood and underestimated, widening the rift with 'politics' and society, and strengthening a feeling of indignation and resistance regarding the principle of accountability.[8]

Some have tried to overcome this ideal-typical divide of supporters and critics of intelligence accountability, by proposing requirements of effective intelligence accountability on the basis of specific (national) case studies. Ott departs from the US system of intelligence oversight by Congress. He concludes by briefly suggesting that 'the intelligence community must be ready and willing to support, not resist, oversight.' His other suggestions concern four criteria that relate to the role of Congress.[9] Phythian focuses on the British parliamentary Intelligence and Security Committee and, as Ott, he concludes with suggestions to strengthen the Committee.[10] Born and Leigh follow Ott and Phythian in putting the large burden for improved intelligence accountability with those external actors who exert oversight.[11] This chapter draws upon this first step towards a more integrated division of responsibilities of both those who control the agencies and the agencies themselves.

10.2 Obstacles to Intelligence Accountability

The 1970s intelligence accountability mechanisms in most Western democracies have made great progress and brought agencies closer to 'politics' and society. The 'transparent' 1990s have further accelerated this process. Since 9/11, however, accountability mechanisms face several obstacles: international intelligence cooperation has become more complex, involving more actors and more diffuse threats; a changing perception of transparency has facilitated agencies' justification of secrecy; international intelligence cooperation tends to thrive in deep secrecy, and intelligence accountability mechanisms show strong transnational variations. These

[6] Bovens et al. 2008, p. 226.

[7] See further Braat 2016b, pp. 534–538.

[8] Braat 2012, pp. 185–201.

[9] Ott 2003.

[10] Phythian 2007.

[11] Born and Leigh 2007.

obstacles strengthen the need for a more rational approach to the effectiveness of intelligence accountability mechanisms.

Control over the activities of intelligence and security services had long been the exclusive domain of the head of service or his political or military bosses. The intelligence accountability revolution in the 1970s has been a result of growing public distrust toward security and intelligence agencies, and the rise of the human rights paradigm.[12] This led to public and national introspection regarding violations of human rights at home. The decades running up to 9/11 saw a rise in formal legislation that placed these services on a statutory footing that allowed at least a modicum of external control, be it parliamentary, judicial or extra-parliamentary. This development can be seen in Western democracies and in a number of post-authoritarian states. As regards the Western democracies, Gill proposes to connect this development with a number of scandals that prompted inquiry and subsequently led to a desire to curtail excessive powers of the executive and protect the privacy and constitutional rights of citizens.[13] In the United States, the Watergate scandal and the outrage over the suspected involvement of the CIA in the 1973 coup d'état in Chile led to the establishment by the Senate of the Church Committee. A number of Western states, such as Canada and Australia, faced similar inquiries, which resulted in mechanisms of oversight and review being put in place. Faced with these developments in key partner states, and fearing a domestic backlash resulting from these inquiries, the United Kingdom's Secret Service began pressing for formal legislation that would shield it from accusations of wantonness. Its leadership argued that a statutory footing would in fact enhance the effectiveness and efficiency of the service, since such a footing would delineate the formal boundaries of what was admissible and what was not. The old 'royal prerogative' could not.[14]

Elsewhere, in countries where dictatorships gave way to democratic forms of government, the key instruments of repression—the security services—became the object of public scrutiny. Cases in point are Spain, South Africa, Brazil, and the former communist states in Central and Eastern Europe.[15] Here too, the focus was on increasing legality, even if the outcome was not straightforward in each case. Hungary, the first of the Soviet satellites to rid itself of communist rule, found it difficult to force the former regime's security apparatus into submission. Initial legislation put privacy of security apparatus personnel first and it was left to the agency to decide on what to declassify. From 2003, there was more stress on public accountability but the agency retained the right to decide on declassification, which undermined accountability. The Czech Republic by contrast followed a different trajectory and undertook a process of lustration that, it was hoped, would ensure the loyalty of its security apparatus to the new democratic order. It banned all former

---

[12] Baudet 2011; Baudet 2016; cf. Eckel 2014.

[13] Gill 2003, p. 1.

[14] Lander 2004, pp. 484–485. Cf. Gill 2003, p. 2.

[15] Gimenez-Salinas 2002; Rzeplinski 2002.

officials from politics and other positions of influence.[16] The complexities of re-forming the security sector in post-communist states stimulated commitment on the part of a number of Western European security services to engage in promoting Western professional standards, including democratic accountability. Somewhat later, Security Sector Reform was included as one of the foci of NATO's Partnership for Peace Programme.

In many cases, the new statutes and legislation stipulated that their security apparatus, as part of the wider state apparatus, should have to conform to the European Convention of Human Rights. This had symbolic meaning as much as practical. In symbolic terms it reaffirmed the commitment of the European states to a human rights-based identity: in the 1950s the signatories of the ECHR proclaimed the Convention was a statement to the totalitarian countries on the continent that 'Europe' was a community of states built on human rights and the rule of law. The accession of new member states implied (or at least suggested) they too adopted this notion. Back in the 1950s some signatory states, such as Italy and West Germany, had believed that the ECHR itself could function as a bulwark against totalitarianism and help them establish a functioning democracy. It may well be that after the Cold War, accession helped cement new democracies as well. In practical terms, the ECHR forced signatories to uphold certain standards, and through its First Additional Protocol granted the right to individual application to inhabitants of signatory states. This allowed external review by the European Court of Human Rights of a signatory state's actions.[17] The court still plays an important role as a watchdog and so does the Council of Europe that sponsored the ECHR.

The relaxation of Cold War tensions in the late 1980s and the ensuing evaporation of familiar bipolar threats problematized the rationale behind the need for intelligence agencies and bolstered political demands for greater accountability. During the 'decade of openness' of the 1990s the general push towards greater transparency in public administration further strengthened incentives both from the executive and the legislative perspective to make the intelligence sector more accountable.[18] Social movements' demands for more open, democratic and responsive governments were largely successful. For example, in the 1990s twenty-six countries introduced freedom of information acts that recognized their citizens' right of access to government information, creating a new norm for any government to be considered a democracy.[19] Former Russian President Boris Yeltsin opened a part of the Soviet archives; the UK formally acknowledged the existence of its Security Service (1989) and the CIA launched its 'openness project'. In The Netherlands the Dutch Security Service and its successor, the General Intelligence and Security Service, commissioned an official history with an unprecedented amount of operational details. Under President Clinton the American

---

[16] Stan 2009, pp. 8, 116–123.

[17] Baudet 2011. Cf. Cameron 2005, pp. 34–56.

[18] Blanton 2009; idem 2003.

[19] Blanton 2002, pp. 50–58.

government declassified many more government documents, dating from the First World War to the Vietnam War.[20]

Since 9/11 the accountability mechanisms that Western democracies had built between the 1970s and 2001 face new obstacles. The changing pace and nature of intelligence cooperation has challenged existing systems of intelligence accountability. First, international intelligence cooperation has become more complex, including more actors and more diverse threats. While international intelligence cooperation during the Cold War was primarily a matter of external intelligence services and their liaisons, in the beginning of the 21st century it has come to include domestic security services, police and other actors. Differences blur between domestic and foreign security threats, between intelligence and investigation.[21] Threats have become as diverse as jihadi terrorism, cyber espionage and war, the proliferation of weapons of mass destruction, radicalization, and extremism. The process of globalisation since the 1990s and the terrorist attacks in September 2001 have increased bilateral, multilateral and supranational intelligence cooperation. Agencies exchange nationally owned intelligence products and/or produce intelligence jointly, mostly based on reciprocity. Examples in Europe include the Club de Berne, the Middle European Conference, the Counter Terrorism Group, and the Situation Centre of the EU (SITCEN).

A second obstacle is the changing concept of transparency in public administration. Fung et al. distinguish three generations of transparency. The rise of freedom of information acts around the world in the 1990s belongs to the first generation of transparency. This generation focused on the right to know and the need to make information available without, however, the ambition to change government or companies' behaviour. By contrast, the second generation did aim at changing behaviour through 'targeted transparency', which is characterized by mandatory disclosure of standardized information to serve a specific public interest. The third and current generation of transparency is 'collaborative' in the sense that the internet (i.e., social media) serves as a 'marketplace' of information.[22] Characteristic of this present generation of transparency is that government institutions do not necessarily play a role in the process of publicity and have moved to the background as providers of information. Instead, citizens have assumed a more important role in providing and disclosing information.[23] This shows that transparency does not automatically lead to greater degrees of accountability and

[20] Blanton 2003, pp. 51–52.

[21] Aldrich 2011, pp. 18–41.

[22] Fung et al. 2007, pp. 6, 24–25; Braat 2016a, p. 394.

[23] A striking example is the Dutch private foundation Argus. On the basis of the Dutch freedom of information act it files requests and collects information on 'secret' organisations with the intention of making this information accessible to the public and encouraging new research. See http://www.stichtingargus.nl (last visited 6 December 2016).

democracy and that the current notion of transparency can run parallel to growing governmental secrecy. The paradox facilitates intelligence's justification of secrecy, but it will likely not moderate public responses to secrecy.[24]

A third obstacle to intelligence accountability is the secretive nature of international intelligence cooperation. The tendency towards greater secrecy increases as agencies cooperate with their foreign counterparts, which puts international intelligence cooperation—bilateral, multilateral or supranational—largely outside the realm of public accountability. 'Bureaucratic administration always tends to exclude the public, to hide its knowledge and action from criticism as well as it can', Max Weber states. Moreover, there is a natural tendency to think that what is withheld from the many has a special value,[25] especially under norms of transparency where the secret appears an exception. This tendency towards secrecy extends far beyond the areas of functionally motivated secrecy.[26] It is difficult to avert and easy to encourage. We therefore assume that secrecy in the field of international intelligence cooperation may risk leading to greater operational secrecy in general, which in turn can easily spread over to (unnecessary) secrecy in the policy domain.

We add a last, more structural reason for the current challenge to systems of intelligence accountability, namely the international variations in oversight mechanisms. International intelligence cooperation tends to thrive in deep secrecy because foreign counterparts are generally not keen on making their information available to foreign national oversight and review committees they are unfamiliar with. As such, they may sense drawbacks to cooperate with intelligence and security services that are subjected to robust accountability mechanisms. This, in turn, may restrain national intelligence agencies in sharing information with review committees regarding their cooperation with foreign partners. Consequently, transnational differences in the quality of national accountability mechanisms present a significant obstacle to intelligence accountability. Supranational bodies are not likely to be the answer as agencies cooperate not as friends but as parties that share an interest. As interests change, agencies will not readily submit to supranational review. Non-specialized bodies such as the Council of Europe or the European Court of Human Rights may step in, and indeed have done so, at times sharply criticizing state practice, but it is difficult to ascertain (a) whether their involvement is incident-driven, and (b) whether their criticisms are taken to heart. Likewise, although the ruling, on 21 December 2016, of the European Court of Justice in Luxembourg on data retention is binding, it is conceivable that agencies from EU member states will obtain data they can no longer amass themselves from non-EU state agencies.

As new technologies both generated the need for real-time intelligence, and for the first time offered real opportunities in this respect, these developments

---

[24] Braat 2016a, pp. 394–395.

[25] Simmel 1906, p. 464.

[26] Weber 2013, p. 992.

combined to create a situation in which 'the institutional mechanisms that were designed to provide accountability and oversight (…) were outpaced'.[27] Aldrich, who is quoted here, is hardly alone in this judgment. Others refer to an 'oversight gap' or deficit. Such terms suggest that oversight and accountability of international intelligence cooperation is highly problematic yet necessary. Why is this so? If it is admissible to explain by analogy, then a key reason must be popular distrust, fed, no doubt, by revelations about such programs as Echelon and PRISM. The detention without trial of suspected terrorists in Guantánamo Bay may well have contributed to this, and so may the CIA-run renditions program in which a number of European services acted as accomplices.[28]

A number of remarks must be made here. The outcry does not seem to focus on the fact that there is international liaison between services. In an average Western country, about 80% of the intelligence that is produced stems from liaison with other, mostly foreign services.[29] Rather, people seem to take issue with the fact that there is a form of cooperation, such as renditions in which torture is used to get detainees to talk, that run counter to Western democratic values and human rights ideology. Added to this, there is concern over privacy issues resulting from the indiscriminate collection and sharing of bulk data. Whether or not the assessment that cooperation between services as such is largely acceptable to the general public, is correct, the revelations about indiscriminate interception of communications, and torture, produced significant outcry in Europe and elsewhere in the Western world, and calls for improved oversight.

Interestingly enough, this concern about faltering oversight of intelligence liaison seems to be virtually absent with most intelligence and security services that feel that current oversight mechanisms—in their widest sense—function satisfactorily. According to some personnel of the Dutch Intelligence and Security Service, the first Law on Intelligence and Security Services (1987)[30] led, to 'over-regulation' of daily work. Mandatory approval by the legal department diminished creativity and freedom in operational work, according to some.[31] Some current Dutch intelligence personnel for instance stated that they spend much time discussing with their service's legal advisors about issues of proportionality and legality, which in their view paralyzes their organization. Others affirm that they frequently discuss with the legal advisors and claim this ensures the legality of what they are doing, and contributed to their service's efficiency as well as its effectiveness.[32] Some inside and outside of Britain's foreign policy elite have argued that the current oversight arrangements are so restrictive as to hamper the effectiveness of British

[27] Aldrich 2011, p. 133.

[28] See Committee on Legal Affairs and Human Rights of the Parliamentary Assembly of the Council of Europe 2006.

[29] Personal communication by a high-ranking Dutch intelligence official.

[30] The Wet op de Inlichtingen- en Veiligheidsdiensten (WIV).

[31] Braat 2012, p. 190.

[32] Personal communications to the authors by Dutch intelligence personnel.

services. Proponents of Brexit claim that their country would be safer if its intelligence and security services were freed from limitations imposed by the ECHR.[33] If there is any truth in these statements, this would indeed suggest that current oversight mechanisms function effectively. The question of course remains who will be the judge of that.

10.3 Towards an Instrument for Effective Intelligence Accountability

The secretive working environment of intelligence and the relatively weak politicization of intelligence, particularly prior to 9/11, may foster the misleading belief within agencies that they are 'immune from the plague of politics'.[34] However, secrecy provides only a fragile shield against this plague of politics as it protects agencies from both public criticism and public support. Accordingly, it leaves much leeway to the public perception of whether intelligence agencies function effectively, efficiently, and legally. Intelligence accountability has an important role to play in mitigating the significance of such volatile public perceptions and normalizing the power base of intelligence agencies.

In order to measure the extent of intelligence accountability, we propose a number of criteria that relate to the requirements of both internal and external oversight mechanisms. This model allows for transnational comparisons of oversight mechanisms and, consequently, contributes to a better understanding of the 'accountability deficit' of international intelligence cooperation (Fig. 10.1).

Figure 10.1 Requirements for effective intelligence accountability

Internal	Ministerial responsibility
	Ministerial expertise
	Internal historical research
	Contractual academic research
	Declassification of archives
External	Sufficient powers and independence
	Professional attitude vis-à-vis secrecy
	Proactive stance of committee members

[33] Technically speaking this is not true. For the UK to be freed from obligations stemming from the ECHR it would not only need to leave the EU, but the Council of Europe, the actual sponsor of the Convention, as well.

[34] Long 1949, p. 257.

10.4 Internal Oversight (Control)

Well-functioning internal oversight is a precondition for effective external oversight and accountable intelligence agencies; if internal control does not function properly,[35] external oversight committees will have a hard time getting a grip on the chain of events within the agency. Though hardly visible to citizens and their representatives, internal oversight mechanisms are better informed on day-to-day practices with the agencies than external oversight committees. As criteria of effective intelligence accountability we distinguish clear ministerial responsibility and expertise, the structural practice of internal historical research, the willingness to engage in contractual academic research, and the declassification of archives.

10.4.1 Ministerial Responsibility

Accountability mechanisms and their instruments of oversight and review should ideally be structured simply enough for the non-initiated to understand them at a glance. However, the confidentiality involved in oversight of the intelligence sector complicates the related accountability 'industry' and blurs its clarity. For example, parliamentary oversight committees may meet secretly and report sporadically, obscuring their presence and role in monitoring the agencies. Likewise, the differences in powers and function with independent oversight committees and, say, an Ombudsman may be not easy to grasp by the majority of people.

We, therefore, consider it democratically beneficial if the ultimate responsibility for agencies' conduct lies clearly with the responsible minister(s) for the agencies. Although the minister's personality will impact his or her ability to control the agency, this is no different with other government agencies. A possible proliferation of oversight and review committees risks overruling the position of the minister, thereby depriving the electorate of a clearly responsible individual for the agencies' conduct. For example, a recent proposal for a revision of the Dutch Intelligence and Security Services Act (WIV) introduces a new Review Committee on the Use of Special Powers (TIB). It would consist of two former judges and a 'technical expert' and it would independently verify the legal use of the recently expanded powers of the Dutch agencies, each time the agencies make use of their new powers. Despite the undeniable advantages of independent oversight, the new committee would have the power to lapse previously made decisions by the minister on the use of special

[35] For example, a well functioning internal documentation system which archives all internal documents, including emails; a legal department that oversees all operational activities and the use of special powers; managers who assume responsibility over their departments, etc.

powers, thereby blurring and complicating his responsibilities for the agencies and fragmenting the entire intelligence accountability mechanism.[36]

10.4.2 *Ministerial Expertise*

A responsible minister should be an equal partner to a head of service, on whom he depends for his information on the agency. Even if the minister has the right to know everything regarding operational activities of his agency, he finds himself in a disadvantaged position because he may not know what information to ask for, for two reasons. First, regarding most topics he depends entirely on what his head of service decides to tell him. The historical context and organisational culture of an agency decide whether the minister is considered a fellow insider, with whom much is confided without second thoughts, or rather an outsider, whose knowledge of operational work and priorities is considered of secondary importance. Second, the intelligence sector and operational work are complex matters most people are not acquainted with. Most probably, the responsible minister is not an expert in intelligence matters. Thus, if he should be an equal partner to the head of service, he will greatly benefit from support staff with an expertise in intelligence matters, independent of the agencies themselves.

10.4.3 *Internal Historical Research*

Historical research on intelligence and security services is a type of accountability in retrospect.[37] Consequently, it is a valuable addition to oversight committees, which focus on the present, and review committees, which focus on the near past. Its added value derives from both its temporal and methodological focus. Historians do not merely collect facts, but they interpret and analyse them. Their (written or oral) sources provide information on, for example, operational, legal, socio-cultural, financial and ethical aspects of agencies' histories. As such, their scope is much broader than common oversight and review committees, which usually have members with a legal background.[38]

The end of the Cold War saw a growing interest with intelligence agencies to recruit in-house historians or strengthen their historical staff. Examples are CIA's Center for the Study of Intelligence and the Dutch Intelligence and Security

[36] See also the advice of the Dutch Council of State on the new law and the TIB in particular: Raad van State 2016, Advies W04.16.0097/I, Kamerstukken II 2016/2017, 34 588, nr. 4, 21 September 2016.

[37] Blom 2013, pp. 94–98. Cf. De Baets 2009.

[38] Both in public administration and in academia there is much support for the continuing important role of lawyers in intelligence accountability. For example, see Eskens et al. 2015.

Service's recruitment of an internal historian in 1990.[39] These two examples have led to significant publications. However, most internal historical research remains classified and of less democratic, academic and practical use than published work. Historical research within the agencies—'internal historical research'—faces both more opportunities and obstacles than historical research on the agencies done by outsiders.[40] In-house historians have broader access to the agencies' archives and (former) personnel but they often lack institutional protection of their academic integrity. As their topic of research concerns their own employer they may easily find themselves in an uncomfortable position: important academic criteria may clash with norms in public administration and political incentives of the agencies. For example, academic independence does not naturally match with the principle of ministerial responsibility, the isolated environment of intelligence hampers the required openness in academic research (publication of research results and peer-review), and agencies' general distrust of the media does not correspond to academics' view of the media as a vehicle of stimulating historical debate beyond peers. Another reason for the possibly thorny position of an in-house historian is the difference in perception of the purpose of historical research and of its methodological challenges. Whereas academic historians usually seek to engender debate on past events, public administration usually seeks 'lessons learned' from the past. In other words, whereas the former seeks to diversify and clarify our knowledge of the past, the latter prefers clear-cut conclusions that are straightforward to apply to the present. This preference is visible in the establishment of committees of inquiry. For actors in public administration, historical research often has a morally high connotation, proving their eagerness to face past mistakes and learn from them. Their expectations of historical research, however, do not often correspond with what academic historical research has to offer. Arguably, this may subject (parts of the) publication of internal historical research to political preferences or sensitivities on the part of the agency. It is similar with military establishments.[41]

Even if the two parties need to find ways to come closer to one another, academic standards of historical research have important benefits to intelligence agencies. Of course, there are limits to academic independence: in-house historians and the agencies' management will inevitably need to agree on the topic of research, historians need to respect a minimum of operational secrecy regarding human sources and methods, and historians cannot decide independently on the publication of their research. However, academic criteria make agencies publicly accountable for their past actions, far beyond the reach of oversight and review committees. Moreover, the publication of historical research may increase public understanding of the intelligence sector and the working circumstances of agencies.

---

[39] The first in-house historian of the Dutch Intelligence and Security Service, Dick Engelen, published two significant operational histories of the service: Engelen 1995, and Engelen 2007. His successor, Eleni Braat, published a socio-cultural history of the service: Braat 2012.

[40] De Jong 2015.

[41] Cf. Baudet 2013.

And finally, agencies can participate in the academic and political debate on their own history.[42]

Consequently, if intelligence agencies choose to make internal historical research into an asset, both from the lessons-learned perspective and from the perspective of public accountability, they need to offer their in-house historians strong institutional protection in order to conduct their work according to academic standards. Such protection should, from the political perspective, ideally reach until the ministerial level and, from the academic perspective, include an independent academic supervisory committee with unrestricted access to the agencies' archives.[43]

10.4.4 Contractual Academic Research

Since the end of the Cold War intelligence agencies have increasingly engaged with the academic world in the form of contractual research. In such cases an independent researcher, affiliated to an academic institution and thus not a member of the agency, conducts research on behalf of the intelligence agency. Contrary to internal historical research, this type of research usually gets published, as most academics do not have an interest in conducting classified research. The best-known cases concern historical research. Examples are the official histories of the Norwegian Security Service, the Politiets Sikkerhetstjeneste (PST), and the Danish Security Service, the Politiets Efterretningstjeneste (PET) at the end of the 1990s, the research group for the history of the German foreign intelligence service 'Geschichte des Bundesnachrichtendienstes' (BND) since 2011, a comparable research group for the history of the German security service Bundesamt für Verfassungsschutz (BfV), the official histories of MI5 and MI6 in 2009 and 2010 respectively,[44] and three volumes on the history of the Australian Security Intelligence Service (ASIO) in 2014, 2015 and 2016.[45]

To both agencies and citizens and their representatives, contractual academic research has many of the same merits as internal historical research. It makes agencies more accountable for their actions, it increases public knowledge and understanding of the intelligence sector, and it allows agencies to better participate in academic and political debates on intelligence. More so than internal historical

---

[42] The CIA is a good example of an agency which actively and structurally participates in the (academic) debate on its own history, for example through publications, conference papers, and education.

[43] Such was the case with Dick Engelen, the first official in-house historian of the Dutch Security Service and one of the first worldwide to publish his work. The responsible minister of the Interior supported his academic independence and an academic supervisory committee had full access to the entire archive.

[44] Andrew 2009; Jeffery 2010.

[45] Horner 2014; Blaxland 2015; Blaxland and Crawley 2016.

research, independent academics are institutionally better protected against possible consequences of 'inconvenient findings', such as refraining from publication.

10.4.5 Declassification of Archives

Intelligence agencies tend to suffer from a 'secrecy reflex', regarding both the present and the past.[46] By 'secrecy reflex' we mean a tendency to excessively classify or insufficiently declassify information. The right to access government information is essential to participation in the democratic process, trust in the executive power, and informed decision-making by citizens and their representatives.[47] Intelligence agencies can make themselves more accountable by conducting a generous policy of declassification of their documents, transferring them to their respective national archives, and allowing independent historians to do research on their past.[48]

Naturally, (the identity of) sources and working methods, and current operationally relevant knowledge need to remain classified if an intelligence agency needs to properly do its job. For example, Christopher Andrew's official history of MI5 becomes particularly succinct as his research period approaches the present. However, as the two main criteria for operational classification—the protection of sources and methods—recede to the past, they should logically become less strict. Even if the American Freedom of Information Act (FOIA) and comparable acts in other countries spell out some mandatory disclosure procedures, intelligence agencies still have some leeway in deciding for themselves when to disclose historical material. For example, in 2015 the Dutch Intelligence and Security Service (AIVD) transferred its archives between 1946 and 1949 to the Dutch National Archives. No historical material of subsequent years has yet been transferred, despite the presence of a freedom of information act. Some Western democracies such as Belgium do not even have a freedom of information act.

How can we explain this secrecy reflex? First, from a practical point of view, declassification, the processing of an archive and its transfer to the national archives require trained staff. The operational, hands-on organizational culture of intelligence agencies does generally not prioritize the labour-intensive and long-term process and benefits of preparing an archive to be transferred to the national archives.[49] Second, classification of information is a contagious process. It rarely limits itself to its merely functional aspects, and easily spreads over to policy

---

[46] Blom 2013, pp. 94–98.

[47] Jaeger and Bertot 2010.

[48] As the British government introduced the Intelligence Service Act in 1993 it committed itself to more openness. It subsequently transferred a considerable amount of declassified documents to the British National Archives. Aldrich 2010 made use of this move towards greater openness.

[49] Braat 2012, pp. 107–128, 151–158.

matters and other matters that do not deserve to be classified. Third, fear of publicity and scandals: intelligence agencies are in a difficult position to defend themselves and are generally not very comfortable with publicity.

10.5 External Oversight

Most academic attention on intelligence accountability has focused on external oversight. By external oversight we mean oversight or review committees outside the executive realm, such as parliamentary committees and independent committees. As we restrict ourselves in this chapter to structural accountability mechanisms, we do not take into account the role of the media, important as it may be in its contribution to rendering intelligence agencies more transparent and making them more accountable.

10.5.1 Sufficient Powers and Independence

Most literature on intelligence accountability concentrates on the powers of external oversight committees. Without sufficient powers, oversight and review committees will be less inclined to assume responsibility and the quality of intelligence accountability will diminish.[50] Significant powers comprise, first, full access to agencies' documentation system and archives. This means committee members should ideally be allowed to search themselves for relevant documents instead of depend on the information the agencies provide them with. As such they significantly strengthen their investigatory capability. However, such a privilege is particularly rare and usually only reserved to independent oversight committees. Second, committees should have the right to call for meetings with the agencies and their ministers instead of depending on when the executive deems a meeting necessary. The case of the British Intelligence and Security Committee shows the paralyzing effects of the lack of such a right.[51] Third, a significant criterion of institutional independence is the appointment of committee members without any influence from the executive. Again, the case of the British Intelligence and Security Committee shows how damaging appointments by the executive can be to the committees' independence and power.

Sufficient powers strengthen committees' independence and self-confidence. The main benefit is that it makes them into a more equal partner to intelligence agencies. An equal relationship may encourage intelligence agencies to consider external oversight committees as an asset rather than as a rival or a legal requirement.

[50] See also Sect. 10.5.3 on 'a proactive stance of committee members'.

[51] Phythian 2007, pp. 75–99.

10.5.2 Professional Attitude vis-à-vis Secrecy

Besides specific powers, the effectiveness of external oversight and review committees depends on the professional attitude of its members vis-à-vis secrecy. The relative secret environment in which committee members become involved risks sensationalizing members' stance vis-à-vis intelligence. This sensationalism of secrecy leads to three distinctive patterns of behaviour.[52]

First, it may lead to an overly critical attitude, which usually results from suspicion, irritation, speculation, curiosity and distrust regarding the secrecy that surrounds the agencies. Second, committee members may show a particular attachment to the agency and its need for secrecy. There is a tendency to wonder what can be so horrific, vital or wonderful that specific secrets cannot be revealed. Accordingly, they tend to view the agencies as superior and exceptional. They trust them almost blindly and idealize their efficiency and power. In oversight and review committees such 'loyal' committee members may actively defend the use of secrecy and accept that they, as relative outsiders, have limited knowledge on intelligence issues. A final pattern of behaviour amounts to active defeatism. Such committee members actively and cynically defend the futility of trying to disclose information. According to them, 'that's just the way things are'.

None of these three patterns of behaviour leads to a constructive debating sphere that allows committee members to effectively monitor intelligence agencies. Secrecy creates a rift between those who know—the agencies and their ministers—and those who know less—the committee members. Other research has shown that the most constructive debating sphere on intelligence amounts to a mixture of both distrust and trust (the first and second patterns of behaviour) in combination with agencies' initiatives to provide openness.[53] We suggest that this mixture equals a professional attitude towards secrecy.

10.5.3 A Proactive Stance of Committee Members

External oversight benefits from a structurally proactive stance of committee members instead of a primarily passive one. Even if this may sound self-evident, committee members have a strong tendency to mostly listen and put themselves on the receiving end of what the agencies are saying. A passive stance is a particularly common problem in parliamentary oversight committees, which consist of politicians. Politicians need publicity as oxygen. For them, worse than responsibility with power is power without responsibility. Thus, two problems arise: there is a strong lack of willingness to invest in something that does not pay off politically, and parliamentary committee members have a strong incentive to remain ignorant

---

[52] Braat 2016b, pp. 534–538.

[53] Idem.

on important issues if they cannot act upon them. As Senator Leverett Saltonstall, leading member of the American Armed Services Committee of the Senate between 1945 and 1967, responded to the fact that his committee met so rarely:

> It is not a question of reluctance on the part of CIA officials to speak to us. It is a question of our reluctance, if you will, to seek information and knowledge on subjects which I personally, as a member of Congress and as a citizen, would rather not have.[54]

As such, parliamentary committees may perform a 'ritual dance' rather than actively monitor the agencies.[55] Consequently, the isolated environment of such committees tends to make their members less active than they would be in the open environment of parliament. This tendency may be countered with two possible solutions: first, the threshold to refer intelligence issues to the closed environment of parliamentary oversight committees should be high; agencies and their ministers would preferably be accountable, as much as possible, to the open environment of parliament. Second, parliamentary committee members are often high-level politicians with busy agendas and little time to prepare themselves for the meetings. Even if this provides parliamentary committees with more status and political support, it could be more beneficial to prioritize party members with a specialisation in intelligence. They would have more time to invest in the committee, and face less risk of political damage. Committees would be less politicized and inspire more trust with the agencies.

We did not discuss the possibility of a court review of agencies' activities. Courts may perform a useful role in exercising *ex ante* oversight: before agencies embark on a certain course of action a court decision on its legality is sought. But such an arrangement has a better chance of regulating agencies' activities on the domestic scene than it has of regulating international cooperation. And even there, *ex ante* oversight does not preclude deliberate violations. As most national courts can claim only limited jurisdiction, services tend to resort to outsourcing collection efforts in order to evade domestic regulations. We do not believe that a multinational or international court will be given the possibility to review agencies' actions, let alone sanction them as this implies disclosure of collection capabilities and policy priorities to a third party. Cooperation between national oversight bodies looks far more promising even though they too are bound by national regulations not to exchange information. It is for this reason that we feel that a compound instrument may help ensure a satisfactory level of accountability. As said, historical research may fill the void, although this comes at a price, as the review will always be long after the event. Nonetheless, the certainty that such a review will take place might mitigate agencies' actions.

---

[54] Quoted in Ott 2003, p. 74.

[55] Hijzen 2014, pp. 227–238; Hijzen 2016.

10.6 Conclusions

We have developed an instrument to systematically assess the effectiveness of intelligence accountability mechanisms, moving beyond our dependence on impressionistic and incidental assessments of accountability deficits or overloads. It innovatively places the burden for providing intelligence accountability with both the executive and external actors, and it proposes to consider historical research an important complement to the traditional judicial oversight. Not only does historical research extend the time period that ensures accountability, it also broadens the methodological perspective of accountability.

Our intelligence accountability instrument can be used in both a qualitative and quantitative manner. Each criterion in this model can be rated with a grade, resulting in an average grade, applied to several national accountability mechanisms. In this way, we can arrive at a balanced overall appreciation of the degree of intelligence accountability in a national environment. Our instrument thus allows for transnational comparisons of intelligence accountability mechanisms and, as such, may facilitate to overcome some difficulties regarding international intelligence cooperation and its public accountability.

The model may need additional refinement in that some criteria may be difficult to assess and would require considerable research. One such criterion is 'professional attitude toward secrecy' that, however, is a vital element in many external oversight mechanisms. Further research could include incidental oversight and review instruments, notably the press. It paved the way for the initial wave of legislation and also disclosed unsavoury practices such as the rendition programme. But at the same time it is incident-driven and dependent on sales figures.[56] Its precise relation—complementary or preliminary—to historical research for one deserves additional inquiry.

References

Aldrich R (2010) GCHQ. The Uncensored Story of Britain's Most Secret Intelligence Agency. Harper Press, London

Aldrich R (2011) International intelligence cooperation in practice. In: Born H, Leigh I, Wills A (eds) International Intelligence Cooperation and Accountability. Routledge, New York, pp. 18–41

Andrew C (2009) The Defence of the Realm. The Authorized History of MI5. Random House, New York

Aucoin P, Heintzman R (2000) The Dialectics of Accountability for Performance in Public Management Reform. In: Peters G, Savoie DJ (eds) Governance in the Twenty-first Century. Revitalizing the Public Service. McGill-Queen's University Press, Montreal and Kingston

Baudet FH (2011) The ideological equivalent of the atomic bomb. Journal of Transatlantic Studies 9(4):269–281

[56] For a discussion, see Hillebrand 2012.

Baudet FH (2013) Some thoughts on the utility of the past to the military. Air and Space Power Journal – Africa and Francophonie 4(4):4–14
Baudet FH (2016) A statement against the totalitarian countries of Europe. Cold War History 16 (2):125–140
Blanton Th (2002) The world's right to know. Foreign Policy 131 (July-August 2002):50–58
Blanton Th (2003) National security and open government in the United States: beyond the balancing test. In: Campbell Public Affairs Institute, National security and open government: Striking the right balance. Campbell Public Affairs Institute, Syracuse, New York, pp. 33–73
Blanton Th (2009) The world's right to know. Foreign Policy 11 (November 2009), pp. 50–58
Blaxland J (2015) The Protest Years. The Official History of ASIO, 1963–1975. Allen & Unwin, New York
Blaxland J, Crawley R (2016) The Secret Cold War. The Official History of ASIO, 1975–1989. Allen & Unwin, New York
Blom JCH (2013) De geheimhoudingsreflex van inlichtingen- en veiligheidsdiensten. In: Boink G, Kersten AW, Scheffers AAJ, Van Velden R (eds) Een kapitaal aan kennis: liber amicorum Sierk Plantinga. Clinkaert, Voorburg, pp. 94–98
Born H, Leigh I (2007) Democratic Accountability of Intelligence Services. Geneva Centre for the Democratic Control of Armed Forces (DCAF) Policy Paper 19
Bovens M (2010) Two Concepts of Accountability: Accountability as a Virtue and as a Mechanism. West European Politics, 33(5):946–967
Bovens M, Schillemans Th, 't Hart P (2008) Does public accountability work? An assessment tool. Public Administration, 86(1):225–242
Braat EC (2012) Van Oude Jongens, de Dingen die Voorbij Gaan… Een Sociale Geschiedenis van de Binnenlandse Veiligheidsdienst. AIVD, Zoetermeer
Braat EC (2016a) Für die politische Normalisierung von Geheimdienstarbeit. In: Pahl M, Pieken G, Rogg M (eds) Achtung Spione! Geheimdienste in Deutschland von 1945 bis 1956. Sandstein Verlag, Dresden, pp. 389–407
Braat EC (2016b) Recurring tensions between secrecy and democracy. Arguments on the Dutch Security Service, 1975–1995. Intelligence and National Security 31(4):534-538
Cameron I (2005) Beyond the Nation State: The Influence of the European Court of Human Rights on Intelligence Accountability. In: Born H, Johnson LK, Leigh I (eds) Who's Watching the Spies? Establishing Intelligence Service Accountability. Potomac Publishers, Dulles, VA, pp. 34–56
Committee on Legal Affairs and Human Rights of the Parliamentary Assembly of the Council of Europe (2006) Alleged secret detentions in Council of Europe member states. Information Memorandum II, AS/Jur (2006) 03 rev http://assembly.coe.int/committeedocs/2006/20060124_jdoc032006_e.pdf Accessed 8 February 2016
De Baets A (2009) Responsible History. Berghahn, New York
De Jong B (2015) Official Intelligence Histories: Is There a Problem? Leidschrift 30(3):83–97
Eckel J (2014) Die Ambivalenz des Guten. Menschenrechte in der internationalen Politik seit den 1940ern. Vandenhoeck & Ruprecht, Göttingen
Engelen D (1995) Geschiedenis van de Binnenlandse Veiligheidsdienst. Sdu Uitgevers, The Hague
Engelen D (2007) Frontdienst. Boom, Amsterdam
Eskens S, Van Daalen O, Van Eijk N (2015) Ten standards for oversight and transparency of national intelligence services. Institute for Information Law, University of Amsterdam, Amsterdam
Fung A, Graham M, Weil D (2007) Full disclosure. The perils and promise of transparency. Cambridge University Press, Cambridge
Gill P (2003) Democratic and parliamentary accountability of intelligence services after September 11th. DCAF Working Paper 103, Geneva
Giménez-Salinas A (2002) The Spanish Intelligence Services. In: Brodeur J-P et al (eds) Democracy, Law and Security: Internal Security Services in Contemporary Europe. Ashgate, Aldershot

Hijzen C (2014) More than a Ritual Dance. The Dutch Practice of Parliamentary Oversight and Control of the Intelligence Community. Security and Human Rights, 24(3–4):227-238

Hijzen C (2016) Vijandbeelden. De Veiligheidsdiensten en de Democratie, 1912–1992. Boom, Amsterdam

Hillebrand C (2012) The Role of News Media in Intelligence Oversight. Intelligence and National Security 27(5):689–706

Horner D (2014) The Spy Catchers: The Official History of ASIO 1949–1963, volume I. Allen & Unwin, Sydney

Jaeger PT, Bertot JC (2010) Transparency and Technological Change: Ensuring Equal and Sustained Public Access to Government Information, Government Information Quarterly, 27 (4):371–376

Jeffery K (2010) MI6. The History of the Secret Intelligence Service, 1909–1949. Bloomsbury, London

Lander S (2004) International Intelligence cooperation: an inside perspective. Cambridge Review of International Affairs 17(3):481–493

Long NE (1949) Power and administration. Public Administration Review, 9(4):257–264

Malone C, Fiske ST (2013) The Human Brand. How We Relate to People, Products, and Companies. Jossey-Bass, San Francisco

Ott MC (2003) Partisanship and the Decline of Intelligence Oversight. International Journal of Intelligence and Counterintelligence 16(1):69–94

Phythian M (2007) The British Experience with Intelligence Accountability. Intelligence and National Security, 22(1):75–99

Raad van State (2016) Advies W04.16.0097/I, Kamerstukken II 2016/2017, 34 588, nr. 4, 21 September 2016

Rzeplinski A (2002) Security Services in Poland and their Oversight. In: Brodeur J-P et al (eds) Democracy, Law and security: Internal Security Services In Contemporary Europe. Ashgate, Aldershot

Simmel G (1906) The Sociology of Secrecy and Secret Societies. American Journal of Sociology, 11(4):441–498

Stan L (2009) (ed) Transitional Justice in Eastern Europe and the Former Soviet Union. Routledge, London

Terwel BW, Harinck F, Ellemers N, Daamen DDL (2011) Going beyond the Properties of CO2 Capture and Storage (CCS) Technology: How Trust in Stakeholders Affects Public Acceptance of CCS. International Journal of Greenhouse Gas Control 5(2):181–188

Weber M (2013) Economy and Society, volume 2. University of California Press, Berkeley CA

Author Biographies

Eleni Braat is assistant professor in International History at Utrecht University, The Netherlands. Previously, she served as the official historian of the Dutch General Intelligence and Security Service (AIVD) and lectured at the Institute for History at Leiden University. Her research interests focus on secret government activities, such as intelligence and international diplomacy, and the political tensions they led to in Europe during the 20th century. She obtained her Ph.D. from the European University Institute in Florence, Italy, with a thesis on the disarmament negotiations in the 1920s. She holds an MA with honours in Modern Greek literature from the University of Amsterdam, and a *Diplôme d'études approfondies* (DEA) with the highest distinction in history from the *École des hautes études en sciences sociales* in Paris.

Floribert Baudet obtained his Ph.D. from Utrecht University in 2001. He has written extensively on the history of Dutch foreign and defence policy in its broadest sense and on the former Yugoslavia. He has published in *Cold War History*, and in *Air and Space Power Journal—Africa and Francophonie*. Research topics include human rights, strategic communication, covert action, and the use and abuse of the past by (military) establishments. Since 2006 he has been working as an associate professor with the Faculty of Military Sciences of the Netherlands Defence Academy. He has been a member of the Netherlands Intelligence Studies Association since 2014.